The Whiskey Au Go Go Massacre

Murder, Arson And The Crime Of The Century

Geoff Plunkett

16pt

Copyright Page from the Original Book

Copyright © Geoff Plunkett

First published 2018

Copyright remains the property of the authors and apart from any fair dealing for the purposes of private study, research, criticism or review, as permitted under the Copyright Act, no part may be reproduced by any process without written permission.

All inquiries should be made to the publishers.

Big Sky Publishing Pty Ltd
PO Box 303, Newport, NSW 2106, Australia
Phone: 1300 364 611
Fax: (61 2) 9918 2396
Email: info@bigskypublishing.com.au
Web: www.bigskypublishing.com.au

Cover design and typesetting: Think Productions
Printed in China by Asia Pacific Offset Ltd

 A catalogue record for this book is available from the National Library of Australia

For Cataloguing-in-Publication entry see National Library of Australia.

Creator: Geoff Plunket

Title: The Whiskey Au Go Go Massacre: Murder, Arson and the Crime of the Century

TABLE OF CONTENTS

Dedication	i
Preface	ii
Roll Call (Age)	iv
Quotes	v
1: Jenny	1
2: Origins and Design	4
3: Inspections	8
4: Front Tables	10
5: Middle Tables	19
6: Rear Tables	22
7: Patrols	26
8: Mass Murder	29
9: Balmoral House	31
10: Deathtrap: Front Tables	33
11: Deathtrap: Middle Tables	43
12: Deathtrap: Rear Tables	46
13: Merciless Hellfire	56
14: Morgue	65
15: Australia's Toughest Crim	69
16: Knifing	75
17: 1960s	82
18: Fame	89
19: Rape and Attempted Murder	103
20: Intractable	116
21: 1972	133
22: Standover	155
23: Stuart Returns	162
24: Stuart's Warning	174
25: January 1973	181

26: Bolton's Warning	188
27: You Will Be Bombed	194
28: Stuart's Frenzy (2 to 6 March 1973)	211
29: Disaster Eve (7 March 1973)	223
30: 8 March 1973	289
31: 9 to 10 March 1973	314
32: 11 March 1973	341
33: King of the Cockroaches	347
34: Confession of Sins	354
35: 12 March 1973	374
36: The Trial	386
37: Protests	401
38: Outrageous Claims	406
39: Questions Marks	412
40: Anomalies	423
41: Who bombed the Whiskey and why?	453
42: Finances	462
43: Guilty	494
44: Serial Killer?	502
45: The Interrogators	513
46: Stuart	517
47: Finch	527
48: The Best Fit	531
49: Murphy	542
50: The Victims	545
51: Future	550
Principal Primary Source	553
Acknowledgements	554
Endnotes	555
Back Cover Material	672

Dedication

To All Those Involved

Preface

Renowned true-crime author Matthew Condon describes Brisbane's Whiskey Au Go Go nightclub massacre as the 'horrific epicentre of all the crime and filth, the corruption and deaths that came before and followed that tragic night in March 1973, when 15 innocent people lost their lives'.[1]

Despite the quick arrests and subsequent convictions of both John Stuart and his sidekick James Finch, Condon rightly points out that the arson has never stopped smouldering. Rumours have swirled around that horror-filled night for decades. Were Stuart and Finch framed? Were others involved? Were further atrocities committed to hide the real truth behind the outrage?[2]

It had never been possible to determine the veracity of the hearsay. That changed in 2012 when the author had the privilege of being the first person to view the files created by the original lead detectives. They reveal what occurred prior to, during and after the conflagration. They reveal unsettling facts. They reveal that the story of the Whiskey is unfinished.

This is a work of non-fiction. The quoted conversations are taken verbatim from police eyewitness statements, court transcripts, coroners' reports and other archival material. Unless otherwise stated, the following narrative is based on the original police murder investigative files.

Roll Call (Age)

Jennifer Denise Davie 17
Darcy Thomas Day 19
David John Westren 19
Fay Ellen Will 19
Leslie Gordon Palethorpe 20
William David Nolan 21
Colin William Folster 22
Petrius (Peter) Franciscus Morcus 23
Wendy Leanne Drew 24
Carol Ann Green 26
Paul Ferdinand Zoller 26
Desma Selma Carroll 29
Desmond John Peters 31
Brian William Watson 32
Ernest John Peters 50

Quotes

John Stuart

I can get pretty bloody wild in the head, you know, you've got no idea, after Grafton and things like that, how vicious I can be if I, because if I ever let go Basil, I am going to be a fucking, you've got no idea, I'm cold in the head.

All I am ... is a shit pot thief, that's all. I haven't even got away—I've been pinched for more things than I've ever done, than I've got away with.

They'll, they've worked all this out, that I'm working this out and I've worked out that they're working out that I'm working it out.

I said I went up to Darwin, we don't give a fuck of them cunts he said they're nothing, you know they're going on like the attitude the others said yeahhh, you know as if to say don't try to sort of threaten us with names like that you know, I'm not threaten [sic], but er it was just about all of them are and fucking of you know they're all sort of, they're attitude is the same whether or not each one saids the word, the next time I'll take you.

Detective Basil Hicks

If you haven't heard from them again, how do you know they are going to do anything? You don't know them, you haven't heard from them again, yet you're running round the clubs telling them something might happen.

No. You haven't been lagging anyone. It's been just the opposite. You've always had half a story. You go right round things and tell me nothing. Everything you've said about the clubs has always been so vague. You've had so many different stories I don't know what to believe.

I wouldn't know what they think either. You're the one whose [sic] supposed to have all the answers. You're the one who's had all the information. If these people exist why can't you just come out and name them. I can't see why you have to go into all this business about having a message decoded and then have them named through [Brian] Bolton.

How do you know it's true, that it's a conspiracy unless your part of it?

1

Jenny

It would be exhilarating and scary all in one, moving to Brisbane by herself as a teenager. But Jennifer (Jenny) Davie had already broken the shackles, having left home and gone flatting with her best friend, the budding fashion designer Vicki Lucas.[1] She had done so in her hometown of Melbourne, where she worked at the local South British Insurance office.

The two roomies talked endlessly of their dreams and careers ahead, their adolescence being a thrilling time of life, a time for first experiences and lasting memories.[2] Now the vibrant Davie had ventured north to the Sunshine State, having left Melbourne on 22 December 1972. She had inspired Lucas, who soon followed, joining Davie in a comfortable apartment in New Farm.

To further her aspirations, Davie waitressed at the Whiskey Au Go Go nightclub in Fortitude Valley. The youngster had been working there since arriving in Queensland's capital and was rostered on three nights a week, supplementing her income by working in a restaurant during the day.[3] The location was convenient; it was only one suburb away from her new residence.

On 7 March 1973, Jenny prepared for her late-night shift, donning a two-tone half-tank top, platform shoes and flared casual trousers. Her long, lustrous hair, which almost reached her waist, bounced as she excitedly greeted her boyfriend. He and Lucas dropped her off at the Whiskey at the corner of Amelia Street and St Pauls Terrace at 8pm and said their goodbyes.

The enclave of Fortitude Valley had nothing in common with West Coburg, Davie's childhood suburb; in fact, they were polar opposites. In the 1970s, the suburb of Fortitude Valley (known locally as 'the Valley') was a tangled web of cops on the take and illegal bookies, brothels and casinos, sprinkled with sleazy hotels and clubs, all a magnet for the criminal element, where wannabe gangsters congregated like the Pavlov's dogs they were, drooling over their next crime.

A corrupt government, led by the infamous Joh 'I see nothing here' Bjelke-Petersen, aided and abetted this morass. The premier wilfully ignored the malfeasance and allowed it to penetrate—like the veins in a mouldy blue cheese—into both the political elite and the police force. He actively undermined his own anti-corruption crusading Commissioner of Police, Ray Whitrod, replacing the honourable public servant with a known crooked cop, one who would ultimately be frogmarched to gaol for corruption and forgery.

It was into this reeking cesspool that Davie had innocently walked. This moral decay and badness, which hung heavily over the district like a fire blanket and had, in particular, enveloped the Whiskey for months, would snuff out Davie's hopes, and 17-year-old life, in a few short hours.

2

Origins and Design

One of the many nightclubs plying their trade in the decayed Valley of entertainment was the Celebrity Cabaret, which had opened in April 1971. Unsuccessful, it had closed five months later.[1]

John Hannay saw an opportunity; he was good at that.[2] Smooth and networked, he was a good organiser. Hannay had cut his teeth in the entertainment industry as the long-term business manager of The Planets, a band so successful they had opened their own venue in Brisbane called Birdland.[3]

Hannay, aware of the Celebrity's collapse, approached 30-year-old professional company director Brian Little for funding. The New Zealand-born Little had been booking entertainers through Hannay's business, Prestige Artists, since December 1971. Hannay told Little that the ready-made club was a low rental bargain with two bars, a stage, kitchen and dressing rooms, already appointed. With a weekly rental payment, minimal leased equipment and a little spruiking, it would provide an immediate return.[4]

In March 1972, the liquor license was transferred to Brian Little in the name of Littles Enterprises Pty Ltd, a company that included Brian's father and brother Kenneth (Ken). The Littles took a three-year lease, with an option for two more three-year leases, naming it after the world famous Whiskey Au Go Go in West Hollywood, where The Doors and later Guns N' Roses would play.[5] The Littles advertised 'Girls, Girls, Girls', and go-go girls gyrated endlessly, flaunting their wares at the hotspot.[6] Hannay ensured that he would be the manager, with the right to book the artists.[7]

At the Amelia Street entrance, Jenny was greeted by two freestanding placards emblazoned with *Whiskey Au Go Go, Now Open Monday to Saturday, fully licensed 7pm – 3am*. The cabaret consisted of the entire first floor of a nondescript multipurpose brick and concrete building. An eclectic mix of retail and service shops occupied the ground floor: Modern Tiles (with showroom), a ladies hairdresser, Pfaff sewing machines and Lucky's Hamburger Bar.[8]

Jenny entered the spartan, uninspiring foyer and turned right onto the front stairway, which led to the first floor. Aside from the placards, there was nothing to announce the presence of a 3300-square-foot nightclub.

At the top of the stairs, just past the partition that separated the club from the stairwell, Jenny stood at the reception desk. To her left was the northern bar. Its three-tiered shelves filled with an array of bottles dominated the club's interior.[9] Two keg ends advertised McWilliams Wines and bar stools lined the counter.

To her right, the western side of the cabaret comprised, from front to back, a liquor storeroom, office, kitchen, male and female toilets, the rear stairs (which served as the rear fire escape), the back bar and the male and female artists' changing rooms. Black wallpaper, decorated with a circular silver motif, covered the western wall.[10]

The southern end housed the dance floor and stage. Windows draped with thick black curtains lined the Amelia Street (north) and St Pauls Terrace (east) sides of the building. Small windows in the changing rooms, kitchen and toilets provided light. In front of Jenny, the densely packed square tables, arranged in four rows and licensed to seat 400, left little room for quick movement in the case of an emergency. Shrouded in black and dimly lit, the club had adequate décor for the budget reveller.

Despite denials by management, the criminal element frequented the club. There had been at least one visit by Lennie 'Mr Big' McPherson, a notorious standover man from Sydney, and some of the staff had criminal records. As a result, there was often violence.[11]

Just prior to the Whiskey fire, a lady had barely avoided a kick to the head during a fight between two visitors and one of the staff.[12] Soon after, in another incident, a Whiskey doorman blacked out after an irate customer slammed him into the bar.[13]

The club was an instant hit with its clientele, and after paying rent of just $250, the Littles were netting $1,500 per week.[14] In June 1972, another club, the Sound Machine Discothèque at 74 Elizabeth St, folded. Following the instant success of the Whiskey, the Littles, with Hannay's encouragement, took over the failed nightclub. Renaming it Chequers Nightclub, they aimed for the high-end market, looking to create the most sumptuous nightclub in Brisbane.

The renovations required a serious cash injection of $90,000,[15] but the club opened in mid-August to great fanfare, with the lavish opening attended by Brisbane's VIP set.[16] Hannay managed both clubs at first, until John Bell, originally a bouncer and later sub-manager, replaced Hannay as the Whiskey manager when Hannay departed in November.[17]

3

Inspections

To be licensed, the Whiskey needed to pass several fire inspections. One was conducted just prior to the Littles' takeover, wherein the Metropolitan Fire Brigade Board concluded that the 'means of escape from these premises which were designed for cabaret purposes are satisfactory.'[1] A further inspection occurred in mid-1972, and the Board was perturbed by the Littles' illegal modifications, including the erection of the reception area at the first floor entrance, although they allowed it to remain.

The premises were inspected again in September 1972, and more violations were found. The Licensing Commission demanded that modifications be completed by mid-November.[2] Crucially, the Commission ordered the Littles to seal the windows in a twofold process, firstly by removing the winding mechanisms, and then by riveting the frames to the housing. The Commission had received numerous noise complaints, and so because ventilation could be provided through the airconditioning system, the easy fix was to seal the windows.

Another requirement was to place an illuminated sign above the rear fire escape and remove all boxes, cartons and other debris that cluttered the landing. The Littles failed to comply with these demands, and the Commission decreed that they should appear on 2 March 1973.[3] Unless they provided sufficient explanation, their licence would be forfeited. At this meeting, the Littles announced that they had removed all the window handles and cleared the junk away from the fire stairs. The sign above the rear exit door still hadn't been installed, but the Littles promised that this would be completed in two weeks' time. Their assurances would be moot.

When Jenny strolled into the club, there was no security detail on the ground floor. Anyone could walk unchallenged through the front door and up to the club's reception area above. There had been a security guard, John Ryan, until three weeks earlier,[4] but it would now be up to the massively built John Bell, an ex-boxer, to deal with any undesirables as he roamed through the club.[5]

4

Front Tables

It was a time to celebrate. Telephonist Lola Roy met up with Sandra Thomas and Bernadette Allen after work.[1] The trio walked from the telephone exchange to the Whiskey's sister club, Chequers, where they had a meal and a couple of drinks.

Sandra's wedding was three days away, and what better way to celebrate than to have drinks at some of the Fortitude Valley nightclubs. After visiting Chequers, they made their way to the Jet Club in Brunswick Street. They then moved on to the Whiskey, arriving in the first few minutes of 8 March 1973.[2]

It was no coincidence that the party had chosen the Whiskey as the last club to visit. Wedding girl Sandra had been an employee there, having departed only a fortnight earlier. Before she left Brisbane following her nuptials, she wanted to say her goodbyes.

The joyous visitors moved about the club, making a conscious effort to meet all the staff, with Sandra spending time in the kitchen catching up with chef Jim Chalmers and kitchen-hand Geoffrey Kopittke.[3] The women then made their way to the table closest to the front entrance, next to the reception counter. It was now 1.30am.

At this time, the main act, a nostalgically popular 1950s 'surf-sound' band called The Delltones, came off stage, having completed their one-hour gig. They had a lucrative $1,500 per week contract with Brian and Ken Little to play nightly at both Chequers and the Whiskey.[4] After their last number, Francis Longhurst, the Whiskey doorman, performed his last task for the shift, taking an empty carton down the rear fire escape and placing it in a large industrial bin located in a laneway at the side of the nightclub. Thirty-eight minutes before the calamity, all was in order.[5]

Having deposited the box, Longhurst retraced his steps. As it was a quiet night, he took a break at 1.45am. The Delltones were exiting the club when Longhurst joined the wedding party at their table. The band was in a hurry to leave, as their wives and girlfriends were waiting for them back at their hotel.[6]

Facing the rear cocktail bar, Longhurst could see his friend and work colleague Petrius (Peter) Morcus, who had been working at the club for the last four weeks. In several weeks' time, Morcus was due to leave the Whiskey to set up his own restaurant.[7] Longhurst sat with

Chalmers, who had been the first to join the trio of girls, being keen to catch up some more with Sandra. Chalmers sat facing the front bar.

When they'd finished their drinks, Longhurst decided to shout a celebratory round or two.[8] He approached Bell at the reception desk and asked him what the cost price for champagne would be, explaining the impending wedding and knowing that it could be replaced in stock. Bell responded, 'I'll let you have it for $1.50.' Deciding that the price was right, Longhurst said, 'I'll have half a dozen bottles.'

Longhurst handed Bell the cash and walked past the toilets and rear fire exit to the back bar, where Desma Carroll greeted him. The previous September, Carroll and family had taken their first holiday in a decade, staying at Mermaid Beach on the Gold Coast. It had been so much fun Mrs Carroll had decided to find a job to fund the next holiday, buy a caravan and ultimately purchase her own home.[9]

To kick-start her dream, she had started at the Whiskey as a cashier in October. Her husband had had his concerns, and had tried to talk her out of it. Mr Carroll was worried by the night work, but his wife had argued that the money was good and it allowed her to see the children, Sonya, Kim and Todd, aged six to nine, in the afternoons and evenings before she went to work. Desma had prepared the family dinner as usual, said goodbye to the children, and left for work.

Another concern for Mr Carroll was an incident on 22 February when his wife had run into the kitchen and alerted Chalmers that a maniac was waving a gun around.[10] Chalmers had emerged to see a short, stocky man, later identified as goon Charles 'Chicka' Reeves, pointing a gun at Morcus and saying, 'You shut your mouth.' Morcus had replied, 'Oh Jesus, don't shoot.'[11] This incident had provided an extra incentive for Morcus to set up his own business, as it had left him badly shaken.

'Just give us two bottles of Bodega; John [Bell] will fix you up for them later,' Longhurst said to Carroll. His work colleague handed him two bottles of the popular McWilliams sparkling champagne and Longhurst returned to the front of the club, sat down, popped the plastic stopper and poured a round.

Longhurst also sent a glass of champagne down to his mate Morcus at the cocktail bar, and most of those seated at the table downed two glasses each, quickly finishing the two bottles of champagne.[12]

Then Chalmers invited Bell to the wedding party table.[13] To complete the complement, painter Clarence (Ted) Bingham arrived at the club.[14] Entering just before 2am, Bingham instantly recognised Bell and accepted a seat next to Longhurst. At 2am, Bell briefly left the table to read the till and close the cash register, the nightly routine.[15]

Throughout the night, Bell had been mingling with the guests and keeping an eye on proceedings. With the reception desk now closed, he looked around the club and made a rough head count. There were approximately 50 patrons, down from a peak of 80 earlier in the night, which was okay for an early morning midweek crowd.[16] Scanning the room, he could see that most of the patrons were seated around the dance floor in front of the stage, with a few dancing to the live music. A sprinkling of patrons populated the front bar. With an hour until closing time, Bell rejoined the festive front table.

Donna Porter, a 22-year-old mum, had been working the register earlier in the night.[17] Just before 10pm, Brian Little had approached Porter and asked her to take over the front desk from Jeannette Zidich, Little's partner. Zidich was working there to help finance a visit home to New Zealand at Easter.

This was a double surprise for Porter. She had worked at the Whiskey for various periods since July 1972, usually as a waitress, but never as the receptionist/cashier. What was most puzzling was that the request had come directly from one the club's owners; they generally avoided the floor staff, remaining aloof.

Brian Little, Zidich and Bell then left for the grand opening of Blinkers Nightclub. They returned at 11.45pm, with Zidich resuming her reception duties.[18] At 1.00am, Little approached Porter for a second time and said, 'Donna, come and relieve Jeannette on the door.' Little then walked over to Zidich and said, 'I'm taking you home.' Bell overheard the conversation, and was concerned. 'Has she got a headache, or is she sick? Why are you taking her home?' he asked Little. Zidich looked up in surprise and told Little she would carry on, but he said it was a quiet night, so she agreed to go. She would later say that she had been tired.

Zidich picked up her bag and Little took her home. Meanwhile, Porter wondered whether the departure was related to the mysterious call she had received while Brian Little had been absent at Blinkers. A man with a terse tone had asked to speak to Brian. In her best business voice, Porter had said, 'Mr Little is not here at the moment. Whom shall I say is calling?' The caller had abruptly hung up. When Porter had passed the message on to Little, he had seemed agitated.

After dropping Zidich off, Brian Little briefly returned to the Whiskey, but then left for good when The Delltones left.[19] The staff noticed this, because he usually stayed until closing time at 3am, the Devil's hour,[20] and then retired to the Little-owned Kangaroo Motel. This unusual departure time would lead Porter and other staff members to wonder if Brian Little had some foreknowledge of the horror show that was about to unfold.

Michael Dee, a truck driver from Haulmark Trailers, had known Ernest Peters, the licensee of the Royal Hotel at Goovigen, and his son Desmond Peters, on a casual basis for the past eighteen months.[21] They had breakfasted at the ANZAC club, cruised to the Albion Park Races and then had dinner at the renowned Breakfast Creek Hotel. Late in the evening, they had made their way to the Whiskey.[22] They now sat in the north-east corner at the front of the club, directly opposite the wedding party, separated from them by a single table.

Shortly before midnight, Detective Sergeant Patrick Mahony, from the Criminal Investigation Branch (CIB), in company with Detective Senior Constable Ken Scanlan and Detective Bob Cassidy, ambled into the club.[23] Scanlan, who was with the Consorting Squad, had received a call from Bell, who had had an encounter with a known criminal just after he arrived at the Blinkers club opening.[24] Bell, who had known this troublemaker for many years, thought the interaction was worth reporting to the police. Detective Mahony met Ernest Peters, his close friend of 15 years, who invited him to join the Peters' table. Detectives Scanlan and Cassidy departed.

Ernest Peters was loving life. He told Mahony he had bought a racehorse at the Exhibition Ground Yearling Sales the day before, paying $550 for a yearling colt by French Charm.[25] What's more, Ernest and his son Desmond had won a considerable sum of money at the Albion Park races. Like those at the table opposite, they also had a good reason to celebrate. An unidentified gentleman joined them at 1am.

The conversation at the Peters' table became nostalgic, with the latest arrival and Desmond Peters recalling the good old times, the fond memories they had of attending St Brendan's Convent school at Yeppoon. At 2am, there was a general discussion about the table departing. The unidentified gentleman left first, saying he needed to fly out at 8am.

Dee preceded the others down the front stairs. Bell had been observing several patrons all night, but his attention was focused on this party, in particular the scotch drinker Dee. When Dee and the Peters had entered the club, Bell had judged them to be already boozed, and they had not stopped drinking until Dee's departure at around 2.07am.

Bell could see that 'Dee was very much intoxicated and more or less was a nuisance in that he went out of the club towards the exit a number of times and on one occasion fell down the stairs. He would return shortly after and consume more alcohol ... he left his party and I saw him staggering towards the entrance.'[26] His departure probably saved his life, for escaping the ensuing inferno in his state would have been no mean feat. Mahony made his way to the men's room as Dee stumbled down the front stairs and out of the premises.

5

Middle Tables

Christine Corney worked with Wendy Drew, who had come to Queensland to join the police force.[1] She picked Drew up and they drove to the Colmslie Hotel. They had been bummed out when they found that the night's entertainment had been cancelled. They returned to Corney's residence, and after thumbing through the paper, decided to go to the Whiskey, which would have a live band until the small hours; The Delltones no less.

Arriving two hours after the club opened, the duo parked outside the PMG building next door to the cabaret.[2] On entering, they paid Zidich the two-dollar cover charge and sat at a table directly across from the ladies toilet in the middle of the club. Later in the night, pool servicer Leonard (Lennie) Salmon came over and stood next to their table. 'Do you mind if I sit down?' he asked.[3] Corney did mind, and gestured around the club. 'There are plenty of tables,' she replied. Lennie failed to read the glacial welcome, and pulled out a chair and sat down opposite Corney. The awkward trio had a drink—she a soft drink, Lennie liquor and

Drew a Bacardi and Coke. Corney had a dance with Lennie, and then danced with another stranger.

The Manager of the Toowong Swimming Pool, Jack Carew, arrived at midnight with Allan Littler and Paul Zoller, a Swiss chef from the National Hotel who had booked his passage back to Canada.[4] Upon entering the club, they were ushered to a table near the back bar, on the western side.

Just prior to The Delltones taking the stage, Littler recognised interloper Lennie at a nearby table, so the three friends shifted to Corney's table in the middle of the club.[5] An hour later, a male and female entered the cabaret.[6] They were introduced to Corney as Carol Green and Brian Watson.[7]

An only daughter, Green had gone to see The Delltones at the National Hotel but having missed them there, had followed the band to the Whiskey. Green was thrilled that her mother was starting a job for the first time in 31 years, and had told her that morning, 'Mum, I'm proud of you.' By way of celebration, she had risen early to cut her mum's lunch, and during her lunch break, had bought her a pair of shoes. As Carol left home, she said, 'Don't worry Mum, I'll be all right. I'll be back at half-past ten.'[8]

As The Delltones played their last song, Corney had a dance with Littler and then resumed her seat.

6

Rear Tables

Mid-evening, Hunter Nicol, a Constable in the Queensland Police Force stationed at Windsor Station, met some Military Police friends at the Military Police Mess at Indooroopilly.[1] They included Corporal William (Bill) Nolan and another soldier, Leslie Palethorpe. Palethorpe was 20 years old, recently married and had a 10-month-old son. His wife was pregnant with their second child. He had shifted from Townsville's Lavarack Barracks to Enoggera for training and had only arrived in Brisbane the previous day.

Coincidentally, his mother was in Brisbane to see the monster musical hit *Hair*. While in town, Mrs Palethorpe had heard a voice calling her name and had turned around to receive a delightful surprise. Leslie and his two colleagues were waving to her. Leslie gave his mum a cuddle and a kiss, and told her he would visit her and his siblings on the weekend.

At 10.30pm, the trio left the Indooroopilly Mess and drove to the Lands Office Hotel, but could not enter the floor show as they did not have ties. Nicol intended to show Palethorpe around Brisbane, Palethorpe being an out-of-towner. As they drove through the Valley, Nolan suggested they go to the Whiskey. It would be a new experience for all of them.

They selected a table near the dance floor and sat down. After a short time, Palethorpe recognised another man who was sitting nearby. The man, named Allan, was also a soldier.[2]

Palethorpe went over for a chat, and he and his colleagues were invited to join Allan's group. Allan was sitting with his girlfriend Kathy,[3] while Fay Will and her brother Daniel also sat at their table enjoying the night's entertainment.[4] Fay worked at the Queensland Railways refreshment rooms in Roma Street, and the girls from the rooms traditionally attended the Whiskey on a Wednesday night.[5]

Flora Simpson, a freelance photographer, was working the tables.[6] She struggled to generate interest, but did snap a photo of Fay Will and her brother on her Polaroid 180 instant camera. She later shot one of Zidich. Palethorpe took a girl from the Will party onto the dance floor and returned a few minutes later. Daniel Will then left the club.[7]

There was a second band, Trinity, playing that night at the Whiskey. They served as both a second live band and a backing group for both The Delltones and a popular singer, Julie Amiet, who also made an appearance during the evening.[8] The band members were Darcy Day, Colin Folster, David Neden, Bevan Childs, Graham Rennex and Raymond Roberts. A third of the band would perish on this fateful morning. They had been rehearsing for the last three weeks, and had started playing at the Whiskey on the Monday; this was only their third night.[9]

The group met in the men's dressing room ready for an 8.30pm start, some making an unconscious note of the high window. They took breaks every 20 minutes, reclining at tables next to the stage that were reserved for the band. From half an hour after midnight, Trinity backed The Delltones for an hour, and then took a break until 1.55am. After the break, they played a three-song bracket, stopping at 2.06am.[10]

During the break, Rennex walked across the dance floor to a long table immediately in front of the stage where Neden was resting.[11] A friend of Neden's, Colin Walker, and Leslie Foyle were also seated at the table. Walker had gone to the club to discuss the sale of a musical instrument and the proposed appearance of Trinity at a function the following Sunday.[12] Childs and Day, the Trinity saxophonists sat at a table reserved for the band, four paces from the dressing room.[13] Drummer Folster and Trinity guitarist Roberts stood nearby.

At 2.07am, the wedding and Dee parties dominated the front of the club, the Corney table occupied the middle, the military group were in front of the dance floor, and the Trinity members were either seated in front of or standing around the stage. Fifteen of the attendees, divided by fate, had minutes to live.

7

Patrols

Police Constables David McSherry and Kaye Suhr, both attached to the Brisbane Mobile Patrol Section, patrolled the Valley in Car 525 on the graveyard shift, from 10pm to 6am.[1] After an uneventful first few hours, they took a meal break at 1.30am.

At precisely 1.58am, they recommenced their patrol in Brookes Street outside the Fortitude Valley Police Station, and two minutes later drove past the Whiskey entrance on Amelia Street, turning right into St Pauls Terrace. While passing the Whiskey, something caught McSherry's eye. Looking more closely, he saw a man, about 5 feet 10 inches tall and of slim build, standing beside the driver's door of an iridescent light-blue Holden HK Premier sedan. McSherry saw the man fumbling with his keys. As he appeared to be under the influence, McSherry decided to circle the block and then have a word to the man.

The driver was Gregory Clark.[2] He had just exited the Whiskey, and upon noticing the cruising police car, stopped fishing for his keys. Clark stepped back from his vehicle, mistaken in the belief that he had not been seen. As soon as McSherry disappeared from view, Clark quickly found his keys, unlocked his car and drove off.

In Alfred Street, McSherry saw another potential problem. A white HR Holden sedan had a South Australian registration sticker,[3] but there were no registration plates. McSherry and Suhr stopped to investigate. They then made their way back to the Whiskey. It was now 2.07am.

McSherry and Suhr were not the only police officers patrolling near the nightclub that night. Sergeant Vincent Murphy, who was also based at the Fortitude Valley Police Station, drove past the Whiskey in car 523 at 2am. During his drive-by, he saw a woman who appeared to be about 30 years of age entering the club. It looked to be a quiet, uneventful night, with nothing to be concerned about, so Murphy continued on to Brunswick Street.[4]

Approximately seven minutes after McSherry and Suhr had passed the nightclub, the heavily intoxicated Dee made his way down the Whiskey's front stairs.[5] There was no one visible, either on the staircase or near the Amelia Street entrance. Although he was only metres from the upstairs toilet, Dee could not hold on, and decided to relieve himself around the side of building while waiting for the rest of his table to exit the club. Dee careened a few steps to the left, targeting the western side of the building. Drunk as a skunk, he passed a Whiskey welcoming placard and then stumbled over a foot-high chain link fence that bordered a small garden bed.

8

Mass Murder

Seconds after Dee tripped over the fence, as he lay sprawled in the garden bed, the eerie silence was suddenly shattered. Someone tossed two drums, both without bung lids and at least three-quarters full of super-grade AMOCO petrol, into the club's foyer.[1] A four-gallon BP petrol drum rolled to the right, under the staircase, while a five-gallon SC Johnson & Son container that had once held floor polish hit the rear wall of the foyer.[2]

In less than 30 seconds, both drums were virtually empty and the petrol had spread across the foyer carpet,[3] each carpet thread acted like a wick, soaking up the fuel via capillary action. The club entrance exploded in flames when a lit match hit the carpet.

In his inebriated state at the side of the building, Dee had neither heard nor seen anyone throw the drums of fuel into the club. As he got to his feet, he saw flames engulfing the entrance.

James Stewart, a cleaner for the Brisbane City Council, swept the footpath outside the A. & C.F. McDonald Pastrycooks shop on St Pauls

Terrace, directly opposite the Whiskey, and then proceeded to the bus shed next to the nightclub.[4] Trinity were finishing their set directly above him. It was 2.05am. Stewart searched for a mate of his, but was out of luck. Two minutes later, he headed north, swishing his broom. Turning into Amelia Street, he was only metres from the club's entrance when he first saw a peculiar 'purple glow' in the foyer, next to the steps. There was also a noise like leaking gas, but he could not determine its source. The light grew stronger, and then there was a flash.

9

Balmoral House

Balmoral House, a small residential hotel with 23 rooms, was located close to the club's entrance on Amelia Street.[1] It was after 2.00am, but the music was still blaring from the Whiskey. Despite the permanently shut windows, noise remained an issue, and Trinity had woken Mavis Kann, the owner of Balmoral House, from her troubled sleep.[2] She arose and, with head pounding, stumbled through the darkness to the kitchen.

After retrieving a headache powder and a glass of water, she made her way back to the bedroom. Kann pulled the curtain aside and looked out the window in the direction of the Whiskey. She heard a 'whoosh', and then saw coloured flashes from the nightclub's lobby illuminating the street. The flashes seemed to emerge from the club's entrance.

A horrified Kann thought there had been an explosion. The lights were still on in the cabaret, and now the sense of dread dawned. Now fully awake, Kann realised the club was still open. She screamed to wake her sleeping husband and then ran out the front of the hotel. Mr Kann grabbed a torch and followed his hysterical wife. The couple heard screams of sheer terror emanating from the club.

Arthur Parkinson, a slaughterman, was lodging at Balmoral House. Brisbane remained in the grip of a ferocious heatwave, and he had both veranda doors open in an attempt to gain some relief from the stifling summer air.[3] He slept lightly at the best of times, but was having trouble sleeping at all in the heat. Lying in bed, he thought he could make out footsteps, a car door slamming and then someone yelling, 'Let's go, let's get out of here' before the car started up and sped off. He felt drowsy; maybe it was just a dream. However, Parkinson knew he wasn't dreaming when he heard hysterical shrieking coming from the Whiskey Au Go Go premises; that was real.

10

Deathtrap: Front Tables

The wedding party at the front table was chatting, kicking back and telling jokes. They had drunk two bottles of champagne, and needed more out of the remaining four. Longhurst, his mind on the extra bottles, saw a glow, a 'ripply light effect', reflected on the ceiling.[1] At first, he thought he'd had too much to drink, but later realized that 'I hadn't had much to drink at all, only the two glasses of champagne.'

Chalmers, who had the best view of the entrance to the staircase, saw what appeared to be light-brown smoke coming from the stairway near the front entrance. To no one in particular, he called out, 'Where's all the smoke coming from?' and then hurried to the entrance next to the reception counter.[2]

Looking around the partition, he saw smoke coming up the stairway. Retreating, he yelled, 'There's a fire!', and turning to Bell, said, 'John, the place is on fire.' Knowing that the fire extinguisher was in the kitchen, Chalmers sprinted past the champagne-drinking party. Longhurst darted from the table and held the kitchen door open while Chalmers retrieved the appliance.[3] Chalmers rushed back to the entrance and activated the foam extinguisher. Meanwhile, the situation had changed dramatically. In 20 seconds, the light-brown smoke had turned black and thickened.

The burning petrol produced copious quantities of black smoke and soot, as did the synthetic carpet and underlay in the foyer, both of which were consumed in the conflagration.[4]

The tinder-dry wall next to the five-gallon drum was subject to intense heat. Wood does not burn—this is an extraordinary and little understood fact. As the flames heated the wooden wall, a process called pyrolysis (decomposition) was initiated. The heat began to break down the surface layer, forming a blackened char. In addition, flammable gases were released, and it was these that ignited, forming the flames we recognise as fire. A similar process applied to the petrol; it was the volatile vapour that was burning, not the liquid itself.

Bell had also noticed a glow at the front entrance. He had not heard any explosion, but had detected a very strong smell of what seemed to be burning diesel.[5] As he joined Chalmers, the smoke surged up the stairway and floated across the top of the front bar at a frightening speed, almost knocking them over. Bell and company were astonished by the firestorm's rapid progress, unaware that the developing blaze sat at the bottom of a perfect chimney.

Twelve airconditioners operated upstairs, with the three on the St Pauls Terrace side expelling stale air outside the club.[6] Fresh oxygen, a critical element for a sustainable fire, was being sucked through the open foyer door, into the club and out through these airconditioners. Despite the permanently sealed windows, an invisible river of air swept over Bell and his co-workers. The result would prove to be catastrophic.

Realising the urgency of the situation, Bingham said to Bell, 'Forget about the extinguisher. Have you got a fire escape?'[7] 'Yes, it's this way,' replied Bell, pointing towards the rear cocktail bar. Bingham was one of the first to react. He dashed past the kitchen, but with the club dimly lit and quickly filling with smoke, he could not find the door on the western wall that Bell had indicated. In the developing chaos, he followed some patrons who had moved into a gap in the wall, thereby stumbling across the rear fire escape.

Bingham scurried down the empty stairs, turned right onto the landing and proceeded down the second flight of stairs. With much relief, he stepped through the open exit door at the bottom.

Longhurst was one of the few who knew exactly where to go; he had been at the rear door moments before. He also bolted through the fire exit's sliding door and down the escape stairs to the lower exit.

However, something had changed since Bingham had escaped. The exit door to the alleyway was now closed. The door needed a key to open it from the outside, while from the inside, it could only be opened if the locking button remained undepressed. In addition, it was necessary to turn the Abloy lock-wheel 45 degrees clockwise—a complicated procedure.

Fortunately, Longhurst knew the mechanism well. He opened the door and remained briefly at the foot of stairs to guide those exiting the building. With a locked door, the Whiskey was a death trap. The door should have had a panic bar, that is, it should have been a push-bar door. These doors cannot be locked from the inside. They operate in minimal visibility, and simply require a light push to open them.

Bell told Sandra Thomas, 'You better go down near the fire escape.' He then ran into the main part of the club telling other patrons to do the same.[8] Wedding girl Sandra and her companion Allen stayed together, holding on to each other as they made their way to the only escape route. By the time they reached the stairwell, it was pitch black and visibility was zero.

In less than 60 seconds, no one could see the exit. Even without the smoke, it was hard to see because there was no lighted exit sign, as the Littles had ignored the compliance order. In addition, the door and surrounding walls were black, impossible to see in the descending murk.

In the mad scramble to escape, someone wrenched Allen's bag off her shoulder. It lay on the fire escape stairs, where a fireman found it during the clean-up afterwards.[9] In the laneway, Sandra could hear the people still trapped inside begging for assistance and could see some of those who had managed to escape covered in black soot—they looked like performers from a minstrel show. Bell was one of these.

Constable McSherry missed the firebombing by seconds. On returning to the Whiskey, he noticed the glow of a fire in the foyer. It had not yet spread to the first floor. Still driving, he snatched up the handset and contacted the PVKR (police call sign): 'From Car 525 to VKR. The Whiskey Au Go Go is on fire. I want the ambulance and fire brigade advised.' It was precisely 2.08am.[10]

He parked the police car in Amelia Street and together with Constable Suhr rushed to the club's entrance, but entering the premises proved impossible; there was already an impenetrable wall of dancing flame and cinders.

From the side of the club, an apparition appeared; the stunned, staggering and obviously inebriated Dee approached McSherry and said, 'Do something quickly as there are a number of people upstairs in the nightclub.'[11] Amongst them were his friends, who were now fleeing for their lives. Stewart, who was standing nearby, heard a woman wailing plaintively, 'Try and get us out. We can't get out.'[12]

Bell made his way to the front of the club and told McSherry that there were still people inside.[13] McSherry returned to his patrol car and made a further call for assistance. 'The position is serious; get more fire brigades, more ambulances and more assistance.'[14] Bell could see two drums lying on their sides in the foyer with flames billowing from them. He returned to the rear exit.[15]

Constable Suhr heard the sound of women and men yelling in the alleyway down the side of the club.[16] She immediately ran into the laneway, where she saw a number of men clambering over a six-foot high iron gate, which was kept locked to prevent patrons sneaking up the rear stairs. She also saw three distraught young ladies on the other side of the gate. Suhr assisted the trio over the gate and attempted to calm them. Traumatised, they related how they had escaped. She recorded their names as Sandra Thomas, Lola Roy and Bernadette Allen.

The fire brigade received a call at 2.04am from the auto fire alarm at the Bio-Chemistry building at the University. Five minutes later, the central watch room received an alert from the police line that the Whiskey was ablaze. McSherry's call had been relayed quickly.[17]

David MacIntosh, an experienced Station Officer, left the Kemp Place Fire Station within seconds in charge of salvage engine No.85. Engine 15, led by Second Officer Edward Kropp, followed close behind.[18] The time was 2.09am.

The billowing black smoke that engulfed the top of the front stairs forced Chalmers to retreat after his heroics with the extinguisher. Leaving the extinguisher still discharging in the direction from which he thought the fire was coming, Chalmers fled. As he made for the fire escape, he felt along the wall with his hands.[19] Nearing the exit, he could see heavy smoke near the band section at the back of the club. Maybe there were two separate fires, one at each end of the club; it was impossible to tell in the dark and the pandemonium.

Finding the escape, Chalmers assisted some people down the stairs, but could not linger, as the fumes were threatening to overcome him;

he was choking and gasping for air. In any case, he was pushed through the bottom door by the crush of other people trying to flee the blaze. Some of the bodies were later found to have sustained trample wounds.

As Detective Sergeant Mahony sauntered to the toilet, 'a flash occurred somewhere near the front entrance.'[20] He had never been to the building prior to that night, and was unsure how to get out. The fire was raging at the front of the building, so he looked for an exit at the back—his only way of escaping, it seemed. He did not hear Bell's exit directions, despite being only metres away.

Mahony called out to the Peters and then navigated his way through the maze of tables to get to the rear of the building. Overcome by smoke, he thought he would soon lapse into unconsciousness. Breathing remained difficult, and his lungs were seared. To provide temporary relief, Mahony covered his nose and mouth with a handkerchief. It was not just the smoke; there was also the smell, something toxic, nothing like burning wood.

He called to his friends, and sensed Ernest Peters' presence, but could not be certain in the melee. The detective tried a couple of doors, but they were the toilets. By chance, he found a sliding door, which proved to be the fire escape. Someone had slid the top door shut, perhaps to prevent the smoke entering the fire escape stairs. Like the locked door below it, it was a deadly choice for a fire exit; it, too, should have been a fire-rated push door.

He went down the stairs, but then returned to the sliding door and tried to assist two men down the stairway. Mahony believed that one was Ernie Peters, but he felt faint, and could not be certain.

The most insidious by-product of any fire is carbon monoxide: odourless, tasteless and colourless, it is the biggest killer in most building fires. When a fire burns in an enclosed space, carbon monoxide is created. The haemoglobin in the body's red blood cells is responsible for transporting oxygen around the body. However, carbon monoxide binds to haemoglobin 240 times tighter than oxygen, and the victim suffocates when the toxin invades their lungs.

Mahony's symptoms of dizziness and weakness were typical of carbon monoxide poisoning, which can quickly lead to death, and did so for all the victims on this terror-filled morning.

Mahony was correct; Ernie Peters had been behind him all the way to the top of the stairs, but overcome by the fumes, had sat down with his head on the railing and succumbed. In the turmoil, Desmond Peters moved past the exit to a space between the stage and the dressing rooms. Unable to find a way out, he sank to the floor and expired.

Detective Mahony descended the stairs and kicked at a door, but it would not open. He tried another way, managing to open a door leading to the courtyard at the rear of the premises. The bottom door had been closed again.

Someone who chose a different route was painter Axel Lueck, who had been sitting at the front bar.[21] He had arrived from Germany four months previously and was visiting the club with some German friends. He heard a 'plop' and then saw some grey-black smoke. He could also smell oil.

Lueck did not follow the seething human tide to the back exit; rather, he put his Bacardi rum down, moved to the windows near where Dee and company had been sitting, smashed one of them and jumped onto the St Pauls Terrace awning.

Deathtrap: Middle Tables

Seated at a table in the middle of the club, Corney heard a commotion and saw Longhurst and Bell rush into the kitchen.[1] As Longhurst headed for the fire escape, he ran past Corney yelling, 'Everybody out!' A female staff member reinforced his directive and gestured towards the exit.

Carew, who was sitting near Corney, immediately said to his friends, 'This place is about to go up, we'd better get out of here.'[2] Zoller replied, 'You worry too much, Irish.' Carew and Littler followed the Whiskey waitress to the fire escape. When Zoller belatedly responded, he moved to the St Pauls Terrace side and collapsed face-down in the corner, next to the bandstand.

Corney grabbed her friend Drew's hand and they weaved their way towards the back of the club, avoiding upturned chairs and tables that had been sent flying in the stampede.[3] On reaching the exit landing, Corney tripped over a keg trolley that was positioned in a recess behind the sliding door. In addition to the trolley, there were six cardboard boxes in two stacks of three containing Kirks Colonial Club Cordials and Kaiser Stuhl Cold Duck wine from the Barossa Valley. There was also a wooden crate of Coke bottles.[4] These exit hazards, although removed for the recent fire inspection, had been returned by the Little brothers once the survey was completed.

Regaining her balance, Corney continued downwards, but with the stairs full of smoke, had to grope her way down. With no visibility, her hands were her eyes. At the bottom of the stairs, she lost her balance and fell to the ground. It was here she thought she lost her grip on Drew, but she was mistaken. Corney had been separated from Drew near the fire escape entrance. Drew had then made her way to the back of the club and collapsed near Desmond Peters.

After Corney regained her footing, she heard someone say, 'Keep walking. Go to your right.' She hit a wall, turned back and, by chance, found an open doorway out of the building. The light remained dim, like a solar eclipse, until she reached the laneway, as the smoke exiting the fire escape obscured the outside light.[5]

Lennie Salmon grabbed the hand of a girl and made for the side door where people were running, but he lost his grip. The smoke overcame him, and he collapsed onto the floor.

Littler, who had gone past the sliding door, turned around and yelled out, 'Is anyone left up here?' This revived Salmon, who weakly replied, 'I'm here.' Littler, at great personal risk, selflessly re-entered the cabaret, put Salmon's arm around his neck and dragged Salmon to safety, thereby saving his life.

One of the first out of the rear exit had been Bingham. Others, those with agility, had climbed over the high laneway gate. Bingham saw a large amount of a 'greasy substance' on the concrete just outside the exit door. Many people were slipping upon exiting the club.

Bingham told Bell he was going back inside. Hearing sounds near the fire escape, he re-entered the building and called out, 'Calm down and listen to my voice and I'll show you the way out!' Two girls emerged from the smoke and he assisted them to safety. One of them may have been Corney. Bingham ascended six steps before he had to retreat after the toxic smoke caught him full in the face. When he went back to the door, it was locked.

12

Deathtrap: Rear Tables

Bass player David Neden, who was sitting with Rennex and Colin Walker, noticed Longhurst walk into the kitchen and push the door open.[1] Clouds of roiling smoke seemed to billow from the kitchen, and it looked like a fire had started in the cooking area. In the initial stages of the fire, confusion and bewilderment reigned, and then terror and panic tore across the club like a contagion.

Neden said to Rennex, 'Shit, pick up your guitar and run.' Neden then called out to the other members of the band that the club was on fire, went to the stage, unplugged his guitar and rushed into the men's dressing room. Having prepared in there, he knew there was a window and a possible way out. No one at the rear of the club heard Bell or any other staff member point out the exit; they were too far away.

George Power, who travelled with The Delltones, noticed everyone looking towards the top end of the club, where there was smoke. Someone said it looked to be coming from the kitchen.[2] He thought he heard a 'dull swoosh', but thinking it had come from the Trinity sound system, he initially ignored it. Belatedly realizing the danger and jolted into action, Power followed Neden into the band's dressing room. Having been in there talking with The Delltones, he also knew there was a possible escape route.

Just as Power was about to smash the window, he heard some girls pleading for help in the main part of the club. Retreating from the window, he opened the dressing room door, but the impenetrable cloud of smoke nearly choked him. There was nothing he could do, so he slammed the door shut. Next to him, Neden placed his guitar into its case, but with the room filling with smoke, it was time to flee.

Power and Neden punched out a window, and Neden dropped his guitar through the opening and crawled through after it. Power then dived through, cutting both of his hands on shards of glass. He stepped onto the roof of an adjoining building and stopped to suck in the oxygen. Looking towards the street, Power could see orange flames and thick smoke cloaking the front of the club. After assisting several girls through the window, Neden lingered briefly and after scrambling to ground level, then ran around to the front of the club. Walker followed Neden out through the window.

Rennex, like many others, thought the fire had started in the kitchen. He watched the smoke surge across the ceiling towards the stage, and the lights appeared to go out, row by row.[3] This is a common misunderstanding in fires, but this effect is a result of the lights being smothered by the tsunami wave of smoke, not the electricity failing.

Following Neden's instruction, Rennex immediately ran to the stage, picked up his guitar and entered the female dressing room. Bevan Childs was ahead of him.[4] Childs had been sitting with the other Trinity sax player, Darcy Day. Day, who was facing the entrance, had seen the trouble first and stood bolt upright, proclaiming, 'Fire!' He pointed to the club's entrance. Childs followed his outstretched arm and saw the glow.

Childs focused on an escape route and shut out the mayhem around him; he was vaguely aware that there were people moving about and some general noise, but he could not distinguish what was being said. He moved from the table to the open female dressing room door only three paces from his seat. As he scrambled towards the door, Childs turned back to see where Day was and saw him moving towards the stage.

Childs assumed that Day was retrieving his saxophone, which he no doubt was. Day made it to the St Pauls Terrace side of the stage, but was overcome with carbon monoxide poisoning and collapsed.[5]

Childs smashed the closed dressing room window by kicking it out. A young lady followed him out through the opening. Once outside, he stood on an airconditioner, and then jumped a few feet onto the roof of the neighbouring building. This easy access was a saviour for a number of the survivors. After descending to ground level, Childs then sprinted to the front of the building.

On exiting the building, Rennex ran down the footpath in Brunswick Street looking for a telephone or a fire alarm, but as he ran past the Jet Club, he stopped and decided to return to the Whiskey, where he watched in stunned disbelief as the tragedy unfolded.

While most people escaped through a dressing room window or the rear exit, Trinity band member Ray Roberts, an employee of the Australian Academy of Music, was one of the few to take a different route.[6] When one of his group pointed out a commotion near the kitchen door, he thought it was a fight. He also heard his colleague Neden yell, 'Get your guitar!' so he went to the stage and picked up his guitar.

Instead of returning to the exit on the western wall, he ran the few paces to the St Pauls Terrace side. Moving the cumbersome drapes aside, he stood there aghast; the window grip was missing. With considerable effort, Roberts shattered the pane with his left hand, pushed the remaining glass out, strapped his guitar to his back, climbed onto an awning and then jumped onto a fence that ran alongside the building. Fleeing patrons broke three windows on this side of the building.[7]

Roberts' girlfriend, Donna O'Brien, drove Roberts' car to the Whiskey to pick him up. As she turned into Amelia Street, she glanced at her watch, and could see that it was 2.10am.[8] By this time, the fire was raging out of control. It was bedlam, with people running onto the road and others screaming and wailing.

In total shock, O'Brien slammed on the car brakes and came to a screeching halt in the middle of the street. She sat there trying to comprehend the scene. Recovering, she parked the car in the Caltex garage opposite the Whiskey. She exited the car and went to the St Pauls Terrace side of the nightclub. O'Brien found Roberts next to the bus shed, his guitar still strapped over his shoulder and bleeding from a wound to the back of his head. She tried to staunch the flow of blood, but Roberts shrugged her off and disappeared, saying he had to look for the other members of his band.

Constable Hunter Nicol was relaxing at a table where there would be few survivors from the carnage.[9] He initially felt heat coming from near the front of the nightclub and heard a man call out, 'Fire!' Looking around for the exit, he only found the fire hose on the wall, which he recalled seeing on entering the club. There were only two fire safety measures in the cabaret; the fire reel and the kitchen extinguisher.

A person attempted to leave via a door through which a cloud of black smoke was pouring. Nicol yelled out to other patrons, 'Don't leave that way, come with me through this door.' He had seen people leaving by another exit nearby. The smoke-filled doorway was in fact the door at the top of the fire stairs, which had become a smoke screen within a minute.

Nicol moved blindly towards what he thought was the exit, and looked around to see if his friends were following; they were not, so he repeated his call to them. As Nicol headed towards his target, someone opened the door and smoke poured out of this one as well. Nowhere in the club was free from the suffocating effects of the noxious gas.

Located in the centre of the dance floor and with the smoke acute and pungent, Nicol took a handkerchief out of his pocket and put it over his face. He then lowered his head towards the floor, where there were less fumes. Despite this, he could not see anything in the club. He took hold of a girl who was in front of him and heading towards the same door.

Zombie-like, she repeatedly screamed, 'I don't want to die. Will we all die?' Nicol kept shoving her forward. He then heard a sound similar to rushing water, and thinking that the sprinkler system had been activated, was encouraged. Having passed through the door, he heard the sound of breaking glass and felt cool air. He was not sure whether he was outside or whether he had felt the airconditioning still in operation. Looking up, Nicol saw the sky.

Disorientated, Nicol saw people climbing through an opening in the inky blackness and realised that it must have been a window. He stood there for a few minutes getting his breath as the life-saving fresh air flooded into the room. The handbasin in the female dressing room had crashed to the floor under the weight of those exiting through the window,[10] so he helped five people who were having difficulty with the step up, and then struggled through the opening, dropped to the adjacent roof and escaped the sweltering heat.

Others at the table were not so fortunate. Fay Will made it to the corner of the bandstand and collapsed on top of another female. Recently married soldier Palethorpe reached the south-east corner, next to the stage, and crawled under a table, where he lost consciousness. Nolan collapsed close to the main exit.

Longhurst went to the front of the building and attempted to enter the Whiskey foyer, but a wall of flame blocked his path. Like Bell, he could see two drums in the foyer with flames billowing from them. The temperature had soared, and the wall next to the larger drum had burned through.[11] The majority of the roughcast ceiling disintegrated and the aluminium window frames buckled.[12] It was now a furnace.

As Longhurst stood there, the two plate-glass windows at the front of the foyer exploded.[13] Debris from the ceiling, shattered glass and charred carpet and underlay now littered the entrance. The partition at the top of the stairs disintegrated and the flames surged into the club, igniting the curtains behind the front bar. His heart racing, Longhurst returned to the side alley and climbed over the gate.

Bell had moved Donna Porter from the front desk to waitressing when he closed the reception desk.[14] At the start of the fire, she was at the back servery bar, talking with another female employee about their hours of work while being served an orange drink by colleague Carroll. She then started moving towards the front of the club when the fireball erupted. She saw Peter Morcus begin to run towards the back bar. As he ran, the blaze that had engulfed the front bar curtains swept around to the St Pauls Terrace curtains and towards the back, devouring all in its path. It was as though a madman had swept a flamethrower from the front of the club towards the rear.

Porter watched Morcus's hair and the clothes on his back catch fire. A human torch, he ran to the end of the back bar, where Porter saw him bend down. Porter imagined that he was retrieving the money from the till, but he then collapsed and died.

It was a vista of unimaginable horror. Porter's eyes stared fixedly on the grotesque figure of her workmate. After rousing her from her trance-like state, two men assisted her towards the rear door. She scrambled down the steps, out the back door and then over the security gate. Her red clutch purse remained forgotten in the kitchen.[15]

Carroll, the conscientious Whiskey employee, had paused for a few moments to retrieve the cash from the rear bar till: the takings were later found in her handbag.[16] She was only able to move a few paces from the bar where, incapacitated from the smoke, she perished.

Meanwhile, Murphy had heard Constable McSherry broadcast the message over the police radio that the nightclub was on fire and required assistance.[17] He sped to the building, parked in the entrance of the service station and spotted McSherry with Dee. Murphy saw that the fire had moved up the stairs, with the flames and smoke now visible through the unbroken glass windows on the first floor of the building. The front curtains had been consumed. It was 2.12am.

13

Merciless Hellfire

The first policeman on the scene, McSherry, moved to the corner of Amelia Street and St Pauls Terrace to view the awning and windows at the side of the club. Inside, the conditions at the front of the cabaret were developing into a spectacular phenomenon unique to enclosed areas, the flashover.

Hot gases rose from the searing flames. The plume contained a lethal cocktail of carbon monoxide and other toxic materials, including cyanide from the vinyl-covered chairs. Being hotter than the surrounding air, the gases rose to the ceiling and fanned across to the walls.

The temperature at the top of the room was now much hotter than that at the bottom, and as more of the room burned, this superheated layer, rich with fuel, grew larger and extended downwards towards the floor.

The temperature at the front of the nightspot climbed to 600°C (1112°F), the temperature at which most objects will self-ignite. The firestorm caused all exposed surfaces to flame spontaneously. The surface of everything flammable caught fire in an instant and the room erupted, with all the windows along Amelia Street and the front four on St Pauls Terrace shattering. The bottles of alcohol exploded on the shelves, with the conflagration melting the top portions of the aluminium window frames along the entire length of the northern side.[1] It was now a merciless hellfire. It had taken only four minutes for the flashover to occur.

Murphy, Carew and Littler watched as lethal chunks of glass from the front windows rained down onto the pavement. Orange tongues of flames licked upwards into the night sky. A bystander snapped a photo at this moment, when the fire was at its peak.[2] Murphy then moved to the side gate.

Longhurst was assisting numerous patrons over the back gate, one of whom was Corney. Longhurst gave her a push up from inside the gate, and Murphy pulled her over.

Murphy located some trestles and boards and used them to build a crude structure to help people over the barricade. He could see Detective Sergeant Mahony returning to the club's rear door. Mahony had fallen on the ubiquitous grease and was nursing a broken wrist.

Nicol used the trestles to escape over the high gate. He saw a taxicab, ran over to it and thumped on the roof. The driver wound his window down and Nicol frantically requested that he call for help, telling him there was a fire in the club and people were still trapped. The driver picked up the two-way radio and commenced to speak.[3] Nicol then returned to the Whiskey and noticed people still on the roof. While pointing to his escape route he screamed out to them, 'You can get out this way!'

Murphy could hear the fire brigade arriving. Engines 15 and 85 arrived just prior to 2.13am, with the turntable appliance arriving soon after.[4] McSherry told MacIntosh that people were still trapped inside the building. Thick black smoke billowed from the shattered front windows as the building was now engulfed.

In an attempt to suppress the fire, the brigade issued lines of 2.5inch hose. One worked the foyer entrance, another operated from the top of the bus shed in St Pauls Terrace and the third from a ladder placed on the St Pauls Terrace awning at the rear of the club.[5] A message was relayed back to brigade headquarters that 'the building was going well; going into action, case 2.' In layman's language, the building was burning from end to end and 2.5-inch hoses were being used.[6]

The club was now an inferno, impossible to enter. The firemen worked frantically to quell the voracious flames eating through the club so that they could attempt a rescue. Meanwhile, the super-heated air banked down over the 15 prostrate figures scattered around the rear stage and near the exit door. The blistering radiant heat scorched their exposed flesh and melted the skins on Folster's drum set.

In desperation, Bell and Longhurst tried to enter the closed rear door. A hammer was used but it had no impact.[7] Bell cursed; he had left his keys in the club during the rapid evacuation. Carew and Allan were also there, having returned over the gate looking for Zoller. They hollered, 'Paul', but there was no reply.[8]

Chalmers joined the growing horde. No one could hear any movement or noise coming from the escape stairway or any other part of the building, save the sound of crackling flames. The agonized screams and pleas from those trapped inside had fallen silent.

The high laneway barrier remained a bottleneck, impeding possible rescue. Kropp moved the water line from the club entrance to the laneway on the western side, where he saw the high padlocked gate. He called for a pair of bolt cutters, and when they arrived he cut off the lock.

The firemen then took the hose towards the rear door. Kropp found difficulty in keeping his balance on the slippery surface. On nearing the fire escape door, Kropp spied the throng of staff and revellers around the locked exit and told has colleague Allingham to get a sledgehammer and bash the door down. A short time later, Allingham returned with the sledgehammer and smashed a hole two feet in diameter in the bottom of the fire escape door. It was 2.15. By this time, a fourth engine, No.11, had arrived.[9]

Allingham crawled through the jagged hole and opened the fire escape door. The firemen hauled the hose up the stairs, the beams from their strong hand torches partially piercing the fog. Water cascaded down the stairs from the fire hoses on the opposite side of the club. Halfway up the stairs, the firemen located the body of Ernest Peters. Kropp felt for his pulse at the wrist, but detected nothing.

Longhurst walked to the top of the fire escape in company with Bell, but the intense heat and thick smoke forced them to retreat.[10] Bell and the firemen carried Peters' large frame outside the club and a young Fire Brigade Officer attempted CPR, to no avail.[11] Kropp continued up the stairs, and on seeing that the water line was no longer required, choked off the flow and placed the hose on the ground.

As Allingham was smashing his way into the building, Ken Little arrived with barman Darryl Schlecht. The usual practice was to close Chequers at 2am and then drive to the Whiskey.

When he reached the intersection of St Pauls Terrace and Brunswick Street, Little saw the fire appliances in attendance and smoke pouring from all of the windows on the St Pauls Terrace side of the premises.[12]

Little asked a number of police officers what had occurred, but they were at a loss; they did not know how the nightmare had started. Little went to the entrance and 'noticed a number of persons calling out and screaming near the front door. A number of females were hysterical so I tried to comfort them ... there was complete turmoil ... there was an air of hysteria around the place.'[13] Tears streaked the faces of the bewildered onlookers who were unable to help. They were joined by the morbidly curious.

Once the flames were quelled, MacIntosh looked for a way into the building and targeted the rear of the club. He climbed the ladder against the awning and with the aid of an axe smashed two of the rear windows. One hole was for ventilation, the other for entry. Roberts had broken the third rear window when he escaped.[14]

MacIntosh entered in line with the stage and immediately found Nolan's body in a crouched position near the window.[15] He shook the inert figure and felt for a pulse at the carotid artery, but there was nothing. Close by was another body, again with no pulse. A portion of flesh came off in his hands as he ascertained whether there was life in the casualties.

As Kropp entered the nightclub through the escape door, the hellish vision of three male bodies next to the exit confronted him.[16] He moved to the rear of the club between the dressing rooms and the stage, where another ghastly sight confronted him; like Hiroshima, it was sickening in the extreme. Amongst the ashes, there was a patchwork of burnt corpses wherever he looked.[17]

Firefighter Dennis Kurth came upon the heart-rending sight of a young woman who seemed to be sleeping. The black film lining the corner of her mouth and nostrils was the only sign that something was amiss. The ring on her right ring finger shone among the blackened remnants of the club. The sight of Jenny Davie's body would come to haunt him for a long time afterwards. The carnage was etched into the memories of all those involved with the recovery of the bodies.

Kropp went across to the other side of the club, where he met MacIntosh. MacIntosh told Kropp that he intended to lower the two bodies he had found via the awning and ladder. Kropp then conducted an exhaustive search behind and under bars, under tables, some of which were upturned, and in the various rooms of the club. The final count was a staggering 15 bodies; 10 men and five women.

It was too late. Unknown to the firefighters; seven minutes into the fire, everyone in the main room had been long dead. A flashover is unsurvivable, even for a fully kitted firefighter. Although everyone had moved from the front half of the club where the flashover had been concentrated to the rear, the level of carbon monoxide had risen exponentially, initially rendering them unconscious, and soon killing them.

The coroner would conclude that the victims had died less than three minutes after the fire started, based on the amount of dark sooty material in the air passages and the high levels of carbon monoxide found in the blood. They were dead before the fire engines even arrived.

The men used two Stokes and Neil Robinson stretchers, with ropes attached, to retrieve the two bodies found by McIntosh.[18] These were placed in ambulances. While damping-down operations continued, two firemen who were fitted with gas masks started the sombre task of removing the other thirteen bodies from the club. The removed bodies left outlines on the floor like ghostly imprints on a canvas. The concrete parking area next to the nightclub (off Amelia Street) became a temporary morgue.

At 2.21am, thirteen minutes after the start of the fire, it was declared under control.[19]

14

Morgue

When he arrived, the Government Undertaker handed a quantity of labelling tags to Constable McSherry.[1] With the assistance of the exhausted police, onlookers and numbed survivors, an attempt was made to identify the victims.

A dazed Ken Little stepped forward. After recognising four of the deceased, he could not remember 'exactly what I did or where I went.'[2] Little's driver, barman Schlecht, became inconsolable when he learnt that his friend Morcus was dead.[3] The macabre spectacle of the temporary morgue was too much for many onlookers.

Carew instantly recognised the lifeless figure of Zoller, the Swiss chef, by his maroon-coloured shirt, which was pulled part-way up over his stomach, and his brown boots. Carew attempted mouth-to-mouth resuscitation for a long time, but without success, eventually realising that Zoller was beyond saving. He saw Zoller's wallet tucked into the belt of his trousers, and removed it for safekeeping. Later, Carew handed it in at the City Police Station.

After identifying Zoller to a policeman, Carew moved over to Littler and asked him, 'Where are the girls?' Littler replied that one of their table mates, Corney, had escaped, but the other one must have been trapped in the club with Zoller. The other girl was Carol Green.[4] In her frantic last moments, Green had lost her navy-blue bag, which was found outside the toilets. It contained the minutiae of life—her personal effects, perfume spray, a bag of toiletries and a cheque for 60 cents—a life now gone.[5] Carew found Green's body in the parking lot, but could not recognise her face as he 'didn't take much notice of her in the nightclub.'

A distraught Nicol approached the police and asked if he could view the bodies, as some of his friends were missing.[6] He found Nolan's body, but his mind went blank, and he could not tell the police his friend's name. The pain was unbearable; all Nicol could tell them was that he was a military policeman.

Corney, after seeing the body of Wendy Drew, identified Wendy to a plainclothes policeman and then left the scene and drove home, traumatised. Her brother then took her to the hospital to receive treatment for shock.[7]

The Assistant Government Medical Officer examined the bodies and pronounced them 'life extinct'.[8] After being placed in four ambulances and the undertaker's vehicle, the bodies made their melancholy journey to the city morgue. Here, the fifteen bodies were placed on trolleys in the cold room and each was given a number from one to 15, chalked onto a small board. The youngest, Davie, was now No.15.

Here, they suffered further indignity in death, their personal grooming effaced by the anarchy of the fire and the subsequent corpse recovery. Now, a lifeless, half-naked victim lay sprawled on a gurney exposing her charcoaled areolae.

Photographs and fingerprints were taken and the victims' clothing was examined.[9] The police removed their driver's licences and any other forms of identification.

The blistered and charred bodies, now affected by rigor mortis, were prepared for viewing by the next of kin, who had the harrowing task of identifying their loved ones. Thomas Day, a fireman with the Brisbane Fire Brigade, identified his son Darcy. Constable Suhr was able to identify Fay Will (No.14) at the morgue, as they had come from the same town.[10]

Alfred Green, a truck driver and the father of Carol, left for work just before 5am. He worked from a business in St Pauls Terrace, coincidentally almost opposite the Whiskey.[11] He could see his daughter's car parked at the service station, and on seeing the burnt-out shell of the club expected the worst. This was confirmed at the morgue when he recognised the blackened face of body No.7.

The damage was $47,385 (close to half a million dollars in todays figures).[12] The furniture and equipment was replaceable, but the innocent lives were not. Most of them were young, four teenagers and another eight in their twenties, their lives snuffed out by an act of madness. The mortal dread they had experienced while drawing their last breaths in the Whiskey was beyond imagination. Attention now turned to who was responsible for this unspeakable atrocity.

15

Australia's Toughest Crim

Like all high-profile crimes, many people wanted to be involved, either through a genuine desire to assist or for other, less altruistic, reasons. The usual suspects made their anonymous calls to the police; the pranksters, the crackpots and the overly helpful (one tipster said a check of the drums would reveal that the chemical 88, which was a special chemical used in millinery for the stiffening of hats and extremely flammable, had been used).[1] Others wrote touching poems.[2]

There were also the deranged, including the founder and only member of the Christian Home Defence Party. An anti-Jewish resident of mental institutions, his claims that it was all a Jewish conspiracy were dismissed.[3]

Newspapers printed on 9 March splashed large photos of criminal Linus O'Driscoll, a member of the toecutters gang, on the cover. The reports said he was a person of interest in the arson. However, it was a furphy; the police already 'knew' who was responsible. There was only one real target for the authorities, and O'Driscoll had been associating with him. He was

'Australia's toughest crim', and the police had already interrogated him.[4] However, there was one problem; he had an ironclad alibi.

John Andrew Joshua Stuart (hereafter Stuart, or John if mentioned in conjunction with other family members), was born on 15 September 1940 in Brisbane to David James (Jim) Cochrane Stuart and his wife Edna Ruby Rita Stuart (née Morgan).[5]

John found his naming unfortunate, and was especially sensitive about his third name Joshua (one he shared with brother Daniel), revealing it in strict secrecy to a friend in 1968: 'The kids a[t] school used to tease me about it ... What a laugh. Joshua! They don't even use it in court.'[6]

The marriage produced three sons, Jim, Daniel and John, and a daughter, June. John attended Southport and Surfers Paradise State Schools.[7] He was a superb swimmer, and as an eight-year-old powered through three-mile training swims with the Surfers Paradise lifesavers.

His mother encouraged the swimming as an antidote to tuberculosis (TB), a family curse. John suffered from pneumonia 'every year', and Mrs Stuart was always concerned that this would develop into TB. She told John, 'Living with your father, who had it [TB], made things worse. However, I took great pains to find out how to keep building my family's constitution up, for you know Dan and Jim [his brothers] had pneumonia too.'[8] The doctor warned Mrs Stuart never to kiss her husband or let him kiss their children. Having no friends and no support, all she could do was feed her children and pray, with God her only strength.

She kept away from her husband for another good reason. Until his death, he bashed Edna and the boys with unchained fury. Soon after their marriage, Mr Stuart became an invalid with a 'collapsed spine' and the aforementioned consumption (TB), and Edna suffered twenty years of beatings and cruelty. On two occasions, she defended herself with a knife, cutting her husband's hands in the process.[9]

It was so extreme that the terrified Edna suffered blackouts, and often could not get to sleep until three in the morning. But for her firm religious beliefs, she wrote, she could have easily become a drunk or gone insane. It had been touch and go a number of times.[10] Like many in this situation, she thought of escaping, but there was nowhere to run.

In the many letters exchanged between John and his mother, she seldom mentioned his vicious father. When she did, it was graphic and heart-wrenching. 'I had to keep away from him. But although I fed you all well, I was not so well fed, sometimes not at all. I lived and slept with Jim, I did all his washing, including [his] badly bloodstained hankies, my only protection was prayer.'[11]

John told police that his 'upbringing and environment' was fair, that his father was an alcoholic and therefore his 'upbringing suffered to some extent'.[12] He clearly understated the situation.

Her husband made it plain to Edna that he had no time for the children; they were an unwanted burden. Edna elaborated, 'He used to beat the hell out of me and the kids. See, he was a gambler ... he didn't want the kids, he just wanted me.'[13]

As her husband did not work, Edna was forced to bring in an income, including sorting peanuts and making spreads at Surfers Paradise.[14] Her absence gave Mr Stuart another opportunity; not content with the merciless physical abuse, he was adept at psychological torture.

When brother Daniel returned home from school, he would sometimes be locked in the cupboard under the stairs, which was pitch black and infested with cockroaches. Daniel's screams and pleas for release would cause his sister June to flee to the neighbour's house. However, she could still hear his piercing cries, and was only able to tell her mother many years later. Her lunatic father had threatened June, saying, 'If you tell your mother about this, I'll kill you.'[15]

With Edna away, Mr Stuart would also take John, then aged four or five, on trips to Surfers Paradise to steal from parked cars. When Daniel and John were little, the only confidant Mrs Watts had was their elder brother Jim. She later told John, 'I do miss Jim so much, he is my son too, and once was the only confidant I had when you and Dan were small.'[16]

Unsurprisingly, Edna herself had been the product of an abusive family. Her brutal stepfather had attempted to rape her. Her mother had bizarrely said, 'You might as well have a baby to your young man [David Stuart] as to your stepfather.'

Edna concluded that her mother brought about the marriage from hell, her torment only ending when the TB finally, and mercifully, killed her alcoholic gambler husband in 1956. She would later marry John Clyde Watts, Stuart's stepfather, who received social security benefits. At the time of the fire, Mrs Watts was an invalid pensioner.[17]

John and his brother Daniel grew up with a criminal, arguably psychotic father who bashed their mother and brutalised them. They would become classic products of a violent family environment, emerging as clones of their role model. They would both brutally pummel their partners, and John would add rape and underage sex to his repertoire of assaults on females.

John left school at 13 and a half years of age after having attained scholarship standard. A lack of education would come to be regretted by both boys: 'I wish so much you and I had had the chance of an education as neither of us would be as we are today,' Daniel Stuart wrote to his brother John years later.

Just after he became a teenager, John Stuart made his first acquaintance with the law.[18] On 6 November 1953, at the Bundaberg Local Court, he faced two charges of stealing.[19] He was warned on both counts, discharged, and ordered to pay restitution.

A year later, he appeared before the Roma Court on a stealing charge[20] and was again let off with a warning. At the end of 1955, the young offender would be back at Roma for the unlawful use of a motor vehicle and ordered to pay 67/5/0.[21] When he reached 15 years of age, the seriousness of his crimes escalated dramatically. The legend of Australia's mythical supercrim was born on 5 February 1956.

16

Knifing

Stuart, who at the time described himself as an apprentice baker, stabbed Kenneth Steen, a seaman, at the Valley. Steen had caught a taxi to a hamburger shop, and while waiting to be served, had copped a tirade from Stuart. Steen had told Stuart that he would get into trouble for his young punk cheek. Stuart boasted, 'Wait till you get outside.'

The hot-headed teenager had a different take on the encounter, arguing that 'This bodgie type started to throw his weight around. I used the knife to hit him on the hand, but it hit him in the stomach.' Police found the weapon, a three-bladed pocketknife, hidden in Stuart's flat.[1] He had boasted to authorities, 'Out west a man is not dressed unless he has a hat and his knife', and when out of gaol would always tote a knife. John would later intimate that he protected his brother Daniel from involvement in this crime.[2]

He barely escaped a murder charge—emergency surgery saved Steen's life. Stuart was charged with 'attempt unlawfully to kill' and found guilty of grievous bodily harm.[3] On hearing the verdict, Mrs Stuart wept hysterically and then collapsed in the chamber. Despite the serious nature of the assault, he earned a reprieve and release under Section 24 of the 1911 Queensland State Children Act. The court ordered Mrs Watts to guarantee her son's good behaviour until he reached adulthood (18 years of age). This was the last warning for his delinquency; if there were any slip-ups, he would be committed to the Westbrook Farm Home for Boys.

Released on good behaviour, Stuart was watched by the consorting squad, who questioned the teenage Stuart in April 1956 when he claimed to be working at Hardie Tiles under the assumed name Harry King.[4] Aliases would become a feature of his adult life, and included the names Watt, Watta, Harold King, John Henry Trauts, John Phillip Andrews, John Trauts, John Trouts, John Andrew Harris, Arthur Mason, Robert Neil and John Phillip Harris. Within a month he was charged with disorderly behaviour,[5] but failed to appear in court.[6] Soon after, Stuart crossed the tipping point, and would remain in custody for much of what remained of his relatively short life.

In May 1956, the adolescent Stuart faced four charges in the Brisbane Children's Court for the unlicensed use of a motor vehicle, wilful destruction of property and possession of (presumed) stolen property.

As the family tells it, Stuart played the Good Samaritan, 'borrowing' a stranger's car when his friend's wife went into premature labour. Driving the stolen car, Stuart whizzed the mother-to-be to either the hospital or her home, depending on who tells the story. He then returned the vehicle, but the welcoming police party were unimpressed with his thrilling yarn of a good deed done.[7]

It was a chivalrous tale; myths collect around legends, be they sporting heroes or 'supercrims', and this is one of them. He had stolen a car the year before and in the following years, would become a recidivist car thief, this being a favoured way of escaping custody. There is no mention of labouring women in any of these subsequent adventures.

Regardless, his fate was sealed; he was committed to the notorious Westbrook Farm Home for Boys near Toowoomba until he turned 18. Several years after he left Westbrook, an inquiry revealed systemic physical, psychological and sexual abuse at this establishment.[8] Autobiographical accounts by the survivors reveal the same thing.[9] That Stuart suffered some sort of abuse there is a given; he left as an 'angry young man'.[10] During his incarceration, his cowardly father died, and Stuart was given day release for the funeral.

Stuart had accused Kenneth Steen of being a bodgie, but he was one too, a crazed and notorious example, in fact. Released from the Boys Home before his eighteenth birthday, he was soon spotted by police with a 'redheaded widgie'.[11]

Each generation has a youth grouping where hysteria abounds. In the 1950s, it was the bodgies (male) and widgies (female), labels synonymous with juvenile delinquents. Identified by their 'outrageous' clothing, special jargon and anti-social behaviour, these depraved 'sex-crazed' louts scandalised decent society. Stuart knocked around with fellow bodgies William 'Billy' Phillips and Raymond Patrick 'Ducky' O'Connor, both of whom would reappear in Stuart's future criminal escapades.

Dance halls were a popular youth meeting point, and Stuart became an infamous attendee at many of the most popular ones. According to John Bell, future manager of the Whiskey Au Go Go, his lifelong involvement with Rock 'n' Roll started with Stuart's association with the Cloudland Dance Hall.

Bell said the out-of-control rabble-rouser would frequent the Cloudland, 'bashing up all and sundry ... everyone was terrified of him.'[12] Bell, an intimidating hulk of a man and former boxer, was contacted by the Cloudland management to rein in the nutcase bodgie. Bell knew Stuart well. As boys, they had hung around together at Teneriffe,[13] and had both ended up at Westbrook.[14] Bell had used his pugilistic skills to tame Stuart and the other undesirables, and found a career option in the process: that of bouncer.

The music management industry is a tight circle; John Hannay, another future manager of the Whiskey, managed The Planets, who were the resident band at Cloudland at that time. Following the formation of The Planets, Bell became associated with the band and their shows.

Stuart also frequented the Railway Institute dances, having done so since early in 1956.[15] According to one-time Whiskey manager Hannay, one night he saw Stuart spear a policeman into an open fan. Hannay believed that the unfortunate copper received 'in excess of one hundred stitches'.[16] Stuart also caused trouble at the City Hall dances on Tuesday nights.[17] Wherever he went, trouble stuck to the intimidating bully like Velcro.

Another favourite hang-out for Stuart was The Hub, a hamburger joint opposite the old Dawn Theatre at Chermside.[18] Stuart was a legend amongst the local youth for the stabbing, the stint in reform school and his tough-guy demeanour. The string of offences he committed during the period from 1958 to 1960, which included the unlawful use of a motor vehicle (again), dangerous driving, unlawful assault, obscene language and stealing, amongst others, only enhanced his reputation.[19] He briefly visited Townsville, where he stole rum, brandy, schnapps, wine and whiskey. Stuart moved seamlessly from one crime to the next.

With his growing reputation, he became the leader of the local gang.[20] His mother would say he was like Peter Pan; kids followed him wherever he went, and some knew him as 'Jungle John'. Later, this charisma would fascinate fellow prisoners as well. One, who said he would be dead but for Stuart (who had protected him in prison), wrote, 'I've never really been ashamed to say I love you because you mean everything to me that's fair dinkum ... we['ve] been so close, I used to depend on you so much ... I know no cunt gives a fuck about me now—you was the last person so don't go feeling sorry for me because I am not worth it ... I've tried to do everything like you do and I even try to walk like you and on top of that—I love you, not like a cat or a girl you know, [but] just like a brother...' The writer also admired how his mentor kept clean and had a bath each day.[21]

Stuart indicates that around this period, his uncle Michael Lockyer, a travelling entertainer, sometimes employed him.[22] At age twenty, he listed his occupation as showman.[23]

17

1960s

The rebellious Stuart crossed the border into New South Wales in October 1960. This was the start of a pattern that was to be repeated over the next few years, when he frequently criss-crossed the Queensland/New South Wales border.[1] He made his way to Wagga Wagga, where his exploits made the local newspaper, *The Advertiser*.[2] Someone spotted Stuart acting suspiciously in Edward Street. A detective approached him and hauled him in to the police station to have a talk. The police wanted to question the 20-year-old regarding the 'serious assault of a female' and shoplifting incidents in the sleepy nearby town of Leeton.

Stuart punched Constable Ron Taylor while being moved between rooms and escaped. Taylor recaptured him 100 yards from the station, but Stuart thumped him 'savagely', knocking him to the footpath, and absconded again.

Police then set up roadblocks. A man answering his description stole a bike in Tarcutta Street and was seen travelling in the general direction of the Stuart Highway, and was later spotted near the female ward of the Wagga Wagga Hospital.

Surrounded, Stuart struggled and attempted to resist arrest, but his recapture was inevitable. He was searched, and the authorities found a brass knuckleduster with pennies welded into it.

There were 17 charges laid as a result. He pleaded guilty to 14 stealing offences and one of assaulting a police constable and being armed with an offensive weapon with the intent of committing bodily harm, and was sentenced to six months hard labour for these transgressions.

Stuart had journeyed to the hospital for a reason; he had been trying to visit his sweetheart Lorrie, who later wrote him a letter while he languished in prison.[3]

Dear Johnny

Just finished dinner (soup again!) and wishing like mad I could get my teeth into something and chew!!! Every time I think of a steak I get real sulky and bad-tempered. It's driving me mad, and it's worse now than it ever was.

The dentist has two plastic plates in my mouth, wired together so I can't open my teeth. So I have to have everything through a straw.

I came back to bed last night after he had put the plates in, and they had shifted my bed to the verandah, and it's freezing cold. I asked about four nurses for extra blankets, and finally, two hours later, I get one more blanket.

Then they didn't have any glass straws, and I was starving, and after all the crying I did at the dentist's (he had to push my jaw up into place) (and then screw these pins in my face tighter) (gee, it hurt a lot) and then coming back and being cold and hungry, I just completely broke down. I cried and sobbed for hours, I couldn't stop, so they gave me a needle to put me to sleep.

Then I couldn't have any breakfast, because they still didn't have any straws. Finally, at about 10 o'clock they brought in two glass straws, and I drank something. So for the next two weeks I will be living on egg-flips, orange juice, borox [sodium borate], and soup.

It's still icy cold on the verandah, and it's making my jaw very sore where the pins are pushed in. Each pin is about as thick as a knitting needle, and they are about an inch apart, right along my bottom jaw.

As soon as Mum and Dad arrive I will try to get out of hospital. They said I can leave at the end of the week, but I might be able to leave earlier, then I'll be able to sew and wash and iron, to take my mind off things.

...My poor hands are just about freezing as I write this, gee it's cold down here.

Sometimes I have to stop writing for a while because I get a bit dizzy. Probably not having any solid foods, and I'm getting real weak. I wish you were here to take care of me.

A lot of times, I've felt a sudden need to think about you, or talk to you, or start writing to you, and when I get those feelings, I like to think that maybe, just at that moment, you are thinking of me too. I hope it's right!

Johnny, baby. I'll have to close now, my jaw is really starting to hurt, and I'll have to go to sleep for a while if I can, but I'll write again soon, baby.

Yours, forever,

Lorrie XXXXXXXXX

I love you

Stuart replied on the back of the same letter (a practice he would come to repeat frequently):[4] He said he had received her letter a few hours ago and had 'been bawling like a kid ever since.' What could he say that would 'make you feel just like I do at the moment.'

Stating that it was the first correspondence he had received since his imprisonment, he anticipated that Lorrie would write and tell him she did not love him, but 'underneath I had a funny feeling that told me you did.'

As a result of her communion, he had never been so happy. After all the things he had done to her, Stuart reasoned, 'You still love me so it must really be love.' In return, he still loved her, but revealed something he had never told anybody before—there was something the matter with him. The pugilist had made the discovery, but could not tell her what it was.

He said he had been charged 'over your jaw, and if I beat the charge, I've only got fifteen weeks left.' The wayward son told the authorities he had 'slipped on a banana skin when we were fooling around and [you] hit it on the Jaguar' and unless the police had a written statement, they must take Lorrie's word for it. He noted that somebody was definitely stopping his mail, and remained 'sorry your jaw is painfull [sic] baby. There's nothing else I can say and Christ I feel rotten when I mention it....'

Stuart had watched his mother's bashings and had always professed his love for her, yet the cycle of female violence was on sickening display in pastoral Wagga Wagga. Lorrie would not be the last victim.

As Stuart indicated in his letter, the assault charges were dropped, most likely because Lorrie did not provide a written statement.[5]

In Stuart's cajoling response, we see how men who batter their partners keep them coming back. There is the partial apology (repentance), the effusive affection (nine crosses; it must be real love as after me having inflicted more damage than a professional boxer you still love me) and a (non)-justification for why it had happened (although he could not tell her this). Having 'identified' the undisclosed reason for the assault, he holds out hope to her that he can change.

He never forgot her, and 12 years later sent a postcard, 'It's over 12 years ago Lorrie, and to me it was only yesterday.'[6] There is no evidence of a reply, with his victim, older and no doubt wiser, now recognising him for the vicious assailant he was.

Stuart does not elaborate on what the 'something the matter with me' was, although he knew he had been clinically diagnosed with a serious mental disorder. On 22 November 1960, Drs M & D [names withheld] at Long Bay Gaol (or the State Penitentiary as it was then known) had certified that Stuart was suffering from 'extreme personality disorder'.[7]

By 1960, the scars of battle were evident, not only on his many victims, but also on him: four missing front upper teeth (resulting in a partial upper plate), scars on the upper lip and chin, three knife scars (on the left forearm, abdomen and left hip), a broken knuckle on the right ring finger, a broken nose and needle scars near the left wrist.[8]

Now diagnosed as mentally ill, he was transferred from Long Bay to Callan Park Mental Hospital in Sydney. However, the beautiful, verdant grounds sweeping down to the sea exerted no hold on the runaway. He absconded in January 1961 and skipped to Queensland.[9] Four days later, he was arrested and placed in the Ipswich Mental Hospital.[10]

In July 1961, he earned three months parole. Restless, he could not find work, listing his address as his mother's at 19 Julia Street, Nundah (bordering the Valley), where he racked up yet more offences.[11] These included stealing with 'actual violence' and unlawful assault.[12] His erratic behaviour and peripatetic existence continued. Returning to New South Wales, he was again incarcerated at Callan Park before decamping in January 1962.[13]

18

Fame

On 28 January 1962, Stuart received his first mention in the Brisbane tabloid *Sunday Truth*, a paper that thrived on true-crime stories. The article, titled 'City Search for Maniac,' said the vicious police-hating and drug-addicted mental patient was being sought in Brisbane's murky underworld haunts.[1] The chronicle stated that his former belle had been bashed and that she had given evidence against someone who had received stolen radios and a television set from Stuart. His exploits were numerous; he had jumped through first-floor windows, stolen safes, jumped over a courtroom dock and torn the prosecutor's brief in two—a veritable action-man hero.[2]

Brian 'The Eagle' Bolton, one of the paper's most prolific reporters, had discovered the 'maniac' and would turn the Chermside suburban legend into a national one; a cause célèbre.

Bolton has been depicted by an ex-colleague, Frank Robson, as 'a rotund little crime reporter with Murdoch's since-closed *Sunday Sun*. In the late seventies, when I worked there, Bolton wore appalling safari suits and drank pretty much all through the day. Named for his tattoo, The Eagle was a good-hearted bloke and a clever sleuth, but sometimes trod a fine line between keeping his police sources happy and serving as a mouthpiece for their dodgy agendas.'[3]

The lives of Stuart and Bolton would intertwine until the Whiskey conflagration, which arguably killed them both.

The Eagle would go on to have an eventful career, which included a punch-up with police and subsequent arrest while attempting to smuggle a bag full of cutlery through a departure checkpoint to test electronic security arrangements at Brisbane Airport. Bolton claimed that he was beaten up on numerous occasions during his investigative missions into the sordid Brisbane underworld.

Stuart's ex-bodgie associate, Billy Phillips, had drawn the tattoo. With Phillips down on his luck after his wife had sustained horrendous injuries from a parcel bomb, Bolton had bought the family a carton of groceries. Phillips repayment was the blue and red raptor.[4]

Inevitably, the fearless one returned to Queensland, with Stuart writing an apologetic letter to his medical supervisor at Callan Park.[5] He apologised for the adverse publicity and worry he had caused by absconding from male ward 2 on the 25th of January and affirmed that at no time was he suffering from any mental aberration. To the contrary, every symptom of paranoia he showed before being certified at Long Bay was 'deliberate on my behalf in taking advantage of psychiatrys [sic] uncertainties to get out of prison.'[6] He did this because he had been charged with a crime that he was 'entirely innocent of but there was no way I could prove it.' He would not have run away if he had foreseen all the fuss it would cause.

In the letter, Stuart revealed more of his personality disorder, that of paranoia. Now referred to as Paranoid Personality Disorder, the bible of disorders (The Diagnostic and Statistical Manual of Mental Disorders 5) describes it as a 'pervasive distrust and suspiciousness of others such that their motives are interpreted as malevolent, beginning by early adulthood.' He would repeatedly bear grudges and suspect others of plotting against him, and could attack at any time, both hallmarks of the disorder.

Stuart told the supervisor that he was serving a term of two years for previous crimes in Queensland and still had to appear in court several more times. He would be obliged if the good doctor could send his port (suitcase) full of clothes that he had left in the storeroom in Ward 2, as they would be needed in court.

There was also a signet ring and 5 in cash that he was keen to retrieve.

Gaolbird Stuart had an interest in understanding mental aberrations, quite possibly in an attempt to understand his own behavioural predilections. He asked Marge X (the name she used) to find information on psychoses.[7] She looked up the Scientific Encyclopaedia and wrote to him that it was 'a mental illness characterized by profound changes in the personality, mental deterioration. There are many types of psychoses. The chief ones are (1) the major psychoses, schizophrenia, maniac-depressive psychoses, and involutional melancholia....' The long letter detailed those associated with organic disease, drug use and so on. Stuart also listed the five types of schizophrenia on a scrap of paper.[8]

In 1963, Stuart made a rare and startling admission to the police. He confessed that he had been addicted to stimulant drugs at various times.[9] The claim that he had a drug problem was raised at a later trial and mentioned in Bolton's articles. He did not specify the drug type, but did have an interest in methamphetamines. He asked a friend to look it up and was told that the 'full name you wanted is N-methylamphetamine'.[10] The crystalline form (ice) is the most well-known today, but in the 1960s intravenous injection was a popular method of administering the dangerous narcotic. Medical examinations showed that he carried needle scars.

By June 1962, Stuart had returned to the Ipswich Mental Hospital. From the psychiatric facility, he was transferred to the General Hospital's Mental Ward 16 from where, being a habitual escapologist, he soon vanished.[11]

Bolton broke the story two days later, on 1 July, and made Stuart front-page news.[12] A bare-chested, muscular young man pierced the reader with a defiant stare. The headline blazed, 'The Man Who Tries to be Mad—He Got Out to See a Woman'. Bolton described Stuart as 'the police-hating, powerfully built convict', and related how he had faked madness to orchestrate a transfer to the Brisbane Hospital's psychiatric ward. Stuart then used a table knife to saw his way to freedom and fled the hospital using two vehicles, a car owned by Albert Hanke followed by a utility belonging to a Mr Hovey, shedding his hospital attire in favour of a sports coat.[13]

As the awed Bolton tells it, on the day after his escape (and after a massive manhunt), Stuart, cornered in the Regent Theatre while watching a 'cops and robbers' film and eating ice-cream, attempted to hide by slouching down in his seat.

Captured and under escort, he lashed out at a detective and hightailed it towards the foyer. The detective shot two rounds into the floor to warn the other detectives that Stuart was on the loose. Three more shots were fired into the ceiling as a warning to Stuart.

Cornered, he was handcuffed around his wrists and ankles. The police removed him through a curious crowd of onlookers who had been attracted by the ruckus.

The scene was well captured in a photo snapped as Stuart was about to be placed in a police car.[14] Resigned and apprehensive, Stuart stares into the distance as two detectives restrain his arms. The captive boldly told the arresting detectives that he knew more about 'headshrinkers' than they knew about him. He had cunningly thrown the police off his trail by making fake phone calls.

The *Sunday Sun* readers learned that he had fled the general hospital for two reasons; firstly, to get even with a lady whose tip had led to his previous capture at gunpoint in the Brisbane suburb of Caboolture (the woman had been terrified that he was on the loose). Secondly, he had heard of his forthcoming extradition to Sydney to face safecracking charges.

In the following week's article, Mrs Watts had a different take. She told Bolton that the real reason they had transferred her boy to Ward 16 was because he had gone on a three-day hunger strike after he had been wrongly accused of starting a fire. The gaol authorities had had her son committed to the Ipswich Mental Hospital because 'they can't hold him at Boggo Road.'[15]

She affirmed that 'one of the gaol authorities told me that they didn't want Johnnie back there because the warders were frightened he would kill them. That's not true, Johnnie's not vicious. He's been very foolish in the past by pretending to be suffering from mental illness so that he could get out of Long Bay Gaol and into Callan Park Mental. But he's cried wolf once too often and now he's been certified and put away at Ipswich. Somehow he's got to prove he's sane. He escaped from Ward 16 because he wanted to get his story out to the newspapers so that he would have a chance.' Mrs Watts added that she had taken a part-time job to raise the money to have her son examined by a private psychiatrist to prove his sanity. Her son was no monster.

Stuart, fearing that his stay at the maximum security Ipswich Mental Hospital could extend for years, with no hope of parole, sent a 'dramatic' note to Bolton claiming he was not insane as certified.

To whom it may concern—Mr. Smith, Kerr, Williams, Dr. Hayes, Youngman, Lamb and police—I have not escaped without a reason. Of course, I want my liberty the same as any man, but I have other reasons as well.

Eventually I will surrender myself, but before I do I intend to write letters to the papers as to why I was brought here to Ward 16 to let the public be the judge as to whether I am in my rights to rebel like I have against everything.

The damage that was done [by the fire] in the prison tailor shop WAS NOT DONE BY ME and some way I will prove it, even if I have to beat the truth out of every possible suspect. I am not crazy.

I have told each of you people that I was only taking advantage of all the uncertainties concerned with psychiatry to escape—via a mental home—a wrongful arrest, but you do not believe me. I don't blame you for that. You would be fools to just take for granted everything I said, especially after you know my history, but you have not given me a chance.

Saying he would bash the truth out of the 'suspects' was an unwise ploy, one he would come to repeat in later frolics.

In the same edition of the newspaper, juxtaposed with a photo of a reclining Stuart, a brief obituary revealed that the lead singer of

The Delltones, Noel Widerberg, had perished in a car crash. Stuart's and The Delltones' paths would intersect fatefully again 11 years later, on the night of the Whiskey fire.

Charged with two counts of unlawfully using a motor vehicle and one of escape from lawful custody, Stuart appeared in court heavily handcuffed, wearing a dark-green check reefer jacket, dark sports shirt and black pointed shoes.[16] Due to his growing reputation, his guard included seven detectives and several uniformed police, but he offered no resistance. The only words he spoke were 'Yes, sir' after he was asked if he understood the charges. He was returned to the Sandy Gallop maximum security mental institution.

Revelling in the limelight, Stuart fed Bolton sensational articles as quickly as he could scribe them. A week later, on 15 July 1962, the *Sunday Truth* announced that Stuart was writing a book on his life adventures thus far. Believing his exploits would captivate the Australian public, he had, under a Sandy Gallop hospital tree, penned a semi-fictionalised autobiography. Having written 12,000 words, he was a quarter of the way to completing the weighty tome.[17]

Some, although not his mother, were concerned that he was attracting the wrong type of notoriety with the constant press coverage.

Towards the end of 1962, Stuart received some sage advice (via a letter to his gaol cell) from Con. 'Tell me the truth John, have you tried to adjust yourself from getting in trouble? I knew a chap once who said if he made enough noise everyone would know him and remember him. He was right for exactly one week, and thereafter nobody talked about him or remembered him....'

Stuart replied, 'And as for that guy who talked about making a big noise; I don't know who you mean. If you meant me you are wrong, and I can't see how I left you with that impression of it is me you mean.'[18] Stuart was soon back in the press making an even bigger noise, with his favourite mouthpiece, that dogged 'finder of the truth', Brian Bolton.

At the beginning of 1963, Bolton's true-crime readership scored another treat. Bolton revealed that a plot to blow up a section of Boggo Road Gaol had been discovered by police 'in a coded letter to dangerous Queensland criminal' John Stuart.

By cracking the code, the police had smashed the 'most daring escape bid ever planned in Australia' by the 'Houdini escapologist' (he had gone AWOL five times thus far).[19] The planned Boggo Road Gaol explosion would coincide with

Stuart's transfer back there from the Sandy Gallop institution.

Dynamiting a corner of the Brisbane gaol would distract warders while Stuart made a breathtaking escape over the wall and vamoosed to a golf course where a cache of money would await him. Luckily, staff discovered the coded plan both in a letter and on cigarette paper smuggled to Stuart by a relative.[20] Cigarette papers, etched in miniature cursive, were a favourite means for Stuart to send a secret message; it would become a signature exploit.

It was hard to believe that the feats of the human headline, John Andrew Stuart, could get more fantastic, but they did in the middle of the year. Stuart now gave Bolton an explosive story saying that mutineering prisoners at the Sandy Gallop 'nut house' were planning a violent mass escape.[21] With the institution housing 113 criminally insane inmates and more than 20 murderers, this was, rightfully, an important public safety issue.

Hacksaw blades had been used to sever the bars and cameras would be smuggled into the institution to capture the asylum's layout. What's more, a master key would be fashioned from a scale drawing and the staff attacked. All this was conveyed in a note to Bolton from legendary fugitive Stuart written on three cigarette papers.

Stuart, the 'daring criminal and pin-up hero of Brisbane widgies', did not want to be blamed for organising the escape, so had done the right thing and dobbed.

The story continued in the following Sunday's edition on 18 August 1963. Headed 'Scheme To Get Key Uncovered', the *Sunday Truth* declared that Bolton was 'right on the button' with his disclosure of the planned mass escape of insane criminals from the Ipswich asylum and that the tag-team combo of Stuart and Bolton had saved the day.[22]

After the first article had been published, the startled asylum director had ordered a search, and lo and behold, a tiny plastic package bound by a rubber band had been unearthed in rubbish from ward 2, the criminally insane section. The package contained scale plans of the master key. In addition, a key cut from tin and found in the toilet section was 'an almost exact copy of the ward and dormitories master key'.

With the heat on, a prisoner must have panicked and thrown the package out. As the authorities had now confirmed the story, the most dangerous prisoners would be shifted back to Boggo Road Gaol. Stuart furthered his good deed by writing a personal letter to the Queensland Mental Hospitals Director alerting him to the planned escape. Writing letters to gaol and hospital staff was a Stuart pastime. This astounding 'true-life' story had dominated the August *Sunday Sun* newspapers. It was bedazzling stuff.

Although due for discharge in March 1964, Stuart had a date with the New South Wales judiciary on break, enter and steal charges. Sentenced to two years hard labour, it was off to Long Bay Gaol again.[23] None too happy, the lawbreaker protested by slashing his leg while in custody at the central cells.[24] A strip search revealed a piece of razor in his clothing.

Like car theft, female assault and writing secret codes on cigarette paper, self-mutilation was a lifetime pursuit. Later in the year, the Chief Probation Officer handwrote Stuart a five-page letter extolling the virtues of education as 'a debt we owe to ourselves.' He said it bore a cost in terms of blood, sweat and tears, but was worth it.[25]

The following year, Stuart wrote to his mother on 17 April 1965 excitedly declaring that he only had 19 weeks left in prison: 'I give you a solemn promise that I will not lose one day of my remission.'[26] It was a promise he was unable to keep. He would be out early, and on his release, his life would spiral permanently out of control until his premature death.

As Stuart strode out of Long Bay, there were two pathways ahead. He was 24 years old, by which time some degree of maturity was expected, his turbulent teenage years now well behind him. Tragically, the cycle would continue; after a prison sentence, Stuart would be free for a brief time, and then re-offend and be back in the dock. Like a moth to a flame (link to the Whiskey intended), he immediately gravitated to his former associates, and that could only mean trouble.[27] Within six weeks of release, he would be a prime suspect in two violent crimes.

19

Rape and Attempted Murder

At 8pm on Friday 26 November 1965, an infamous mobster named Robert Lawrence (Jack) Steele left his home in the leafy Sydney suburb of Woollahra.[1] While walking towards the Kelson Hotel, a car occupied by four men pulled up alongside him and a 'fusillade of shots' shattered the silence. A shotgun blast struck Steele in the stomach, causing extensive injuries and knocking him to the ground. This was fortunate, as a second shotgun burst just cleared Steele's head.

Steele picked himself up and hobbled down the street. A further barrage of shots from a .22 calibre weapon hit the crook in the backside and under the shoulder. Steele managed to get to the entrance of the building containing his top-floor flat. One of the men pursued Steele up the stairs. Steele picked up a house brick and tossed it at the pursuer, who then vanished.

Steele arrived at the hospital in a critical condition, with a collapsed lung and perforated bowel, but owing to 'the brilliance of Dr Bridger', he survived. Peppered with at least 30 shotgun pellets and .22 rifle bullets, Steel was dubbed the 'Iron Man' by hospital staff. In an interview after the attempted murder, the 'quiet, friendly gambler' was at a 'complete loss' as to why the men had shot him. He thought it might have been a case of mistaken identity. The notorious hooligan, who had dozens of enemies, said with a wry sense of humour, 'I know of no one who would wish to kill me.'[2]

Stuart was a prime suspect for the Steele shooting, and tried a preemptive strike.

On 1 December 1965, Stuart approached Detective Sergeant Noel Morey saying that he had 'information' about the Steele case. Like many Stuart interviews, although he had come of his own free will to exonerate himself, it revealed little, and bordered on the bizarre.[3]

Stuart had read in the papers that a 'Mr Moffitt' (one of whose guns had been found at the Steele shooting, for which he would later be gaoled for six months) had guns for his own protection, as he feared being attacked by the same people who had been involved in a punch up a month previously. Stuart told Morey he had been at the affray that Moffitt had discussed and had tried to break it up, constraining several brawlers, but he would not tell Morey who was there and why he had attended. Stuart said he just happened to be at the fracas, for no particular reason. Morey summarised, 'So in the early hours of the morning, you were in an alley near the Hampden Court Hotel, doing nothing.' Stuart replied, 'That's right. Perhaps I was talking to people, friends.' Stuart had missed the sarcasm.[4]

Stuart also told Morey that at the time of the Steele shooting, 'I was in the presence of over 100 witnesses of good character at a club in King's Cross. I wish to state here I know nothing about the shooting of Steele and I have nothing to say about it either now or later and I do not know who could possibly have done it....'

The police also received an anonymous two-page typewritten letter proclaiming that Stuart had been framed. Stuart almost certainly wrote it himself.[5] It stated that in the interests of justice, the man named John Stuart, who had been charged with the attempted murder of Steele, was 'completely innocent and at no time could he possibley [sic] know anything before or after in regards to the shooting.' The writer revealed that 'We being the participant[s] in the shooting are the only ones who could possibly know the details we are now going to revail [sic]....'

The letter gave elaborate details about the stolen car used in the assault. The author said *he* fired one shot from a 12-gauge Browning shotgun and then fired seven shots from a long-barrelled .22 automatic pistol. The guns were later tossed off a bridge near Tempe.

Stuart moved to Mascot in Sydney, where he partnered with his exbodgie mate and now career criminal 'Duckie' O'Connor. O'Connor and Stuart soon concocted a way of getting free sex.

It was 4 December 1965, and at 3.15am, the morning was balmy.[6] On Elizabeth Bay Road, near Kings Cross, they approached a woman using the name 'Phillipa' on the street. O'Connor asked if she was 'working', to which she did not reply. O'Connor then said, 'There is a tenner in it from each of us if you are interested,' and he flashed notes from his back trouser pocket. Accepting the proposition, she led them into the building where she and a colleague were doing their business.

O'Connor asked her how old she was. She said she was 21. He said he did not believe her, and she confessed she was 19. O'Connor told her he was Detective Sergeant 'Whitten', working undercover.[7] He then introduced Stuart as a fellow detective.

Stuart said to O'Connor, using plenty of foul language, 'Why don't we lock her up and be done with it?' O'Connor swung to Phillipa and said, 'What do you say, let's go.' She replied, 'I suppose I have no alternative.' They went to the room where her colleague 'Kelly' was entertaining a client. The intimidating ex-bodgies repeated the story to Kelly that they were coppers, and ordered Kelly and her customer out of the building.

O'Connor accompanied them outside, interrogated Kelly on how much she had made, and then extorted the sum of £40, saying the money would ensure that Kelly would escape arrest for soliciting or for an offence under the Vagrancy Act.

In the meantime, Stuart demanded £35 from Phillipa and told her to get undressed and take a bath, which she did. After bathing, she returned to the room and was ordered to get dressed again. As Phillipa started to dress, Stuart changed his mind, and demanded that she disrobe again. Her fear exhilarated him. He had an erection, and intended to use it. Stuart then viciously raped her on the bed. During the rape, O'Connor entered the room and simultaneously 'committed an act of indecency' on the teenager. After Stuart dismounted, O'Connor took over and savagely raped the teenager anally.

At the time of this depravity, O'Connor was married with two small boys. Not only did they get free sex, they made some money; a good day's work. They left sated, while the two women were left traumatised, Phillipa extremely so.

The behaviour was inexplicable, unless you were John Andrew Joshua Stuart. Somewhere deep in Stuart's irrational mind, it all made sense. Just released after a long stint in prison, he impersonates a police officer and participates in an abhorrent gang rape. The mental debate that would have been present in most people's psyche—is this a smart thing to do?—did not occur for Bolton's favourite crim. Although he worshipped his mother, his female companions were objects to be used and abused. 'Molls', a word he used often, aka prostitutes, were beneath contempt. He would not have recognised it as rape; she had it coming. Ironically, Stuart put molls and thieves together in the same lowest category. Stuart would later pimp a girlfriend, organising her rape by five Italian miners at $20 a pop. The bloke who provided the room received a 'free one'. Stuart stood outside the door, weapon in hand, to make sure the clients paid their dues.[8]

At the end of the month, a detective spoke to Stuart in relation to the Steele shooting and the rape,[9] and an arrest resulted. About a week before this interview, the police had found a sawn-off shotgun and nine shotgun cartridges in a calico bag in Stuart's car. According to the police, Stuart admitted that this shotgun was the one used in the Steele shooting.

In June 1966, Stuart faced trial for rape. Evidence was presented indicating that Phillipa had been told, 'Do you realise that if you give evidence you will be killed? This is no joke, you really will be killed.' In fear of her life, she had fled to South Australia to become a go-go girl, having been given money and a one-way plane ticket. Heeding the threat, the terror-stricken victim had twice failed to appear at the trial.

A note intercepted from Stuart read, 'Do something about stopping the girl from coming to court.' Stuart later admitted to Detective Basil Hicks, his future police contact, that he had been involved in the victim's non-appearance as a witness.[10] He pleaded guilty to the 'lesser' offence of illicit intercourse while falsely pretending to be a police officer and was sentenced to 12 months gaol with hard labour on 28 June 1966.[11]

Stuart and O'Connor were lucky they had only raped a prostitute and not someone more reputable, as stated by the judge in his summation: "...in this case the acts of each of you were perpetrated upon a harlot whose way of life cannot call forth any respect in the community and which she herself must eventually forsake and regret ... I am entitled, according to law, to take into account that the woman concerned here is a common prostitute, and that fact alone saves you from what otherwise would have been a severe penalty.'[12]

It was almost straight from one trial to the next. Before his appearance at the Central Criminal Court on 22 August for the malicious wounding charge, and in one last desperate attempt to stave off the charges, Stuart sent a beseeching letter dated 7 August 1966 to Robert 'Jack' Steele via a man named Herb.[13] Again, an 'explanatory letter' was a common tactic that Stuart employed. Stating that he did not know Herb personally, only through a mutual friend, Stuart said he was friends with just about all of Steele's associates and 'just can't possibly see how he [Steele] thinks I shot him.' He swore he had not done it. Not one to 'big note myself or wrap myself', he said he had done 10 years can out of the last 11, and being as solid as any crim, asked rhetorically, 'Do you think for a second I'd be mixed up with McPherson and his dogs?' Stuart then went on the offensive: 'McPherson and Smith are no-good dog bastards. And you can quote me saying so.' He was a 'patsy' for the 'blue' (shooting), and even if he had shot Steele, no one was entitled to send him down the drain. McPherson was responsible for the shooting, even if he did not physically do the actual shooting. What's more, the dog must be working with the police.

The cops had to load Stuart with 'the shotgun, the shells and the verbal', so they must know he could not be responsible. The cops 'fuckin hate me and that can only mean one thing. I don't help them.' He implored, 'Jack—I didn't shoot you Jack. WHY should I have? Just even ask yourself. I can only suppose it's because you think I was mixed up with McPherson.' He had only spoken to Steele five times in his life, and three of those times he had only said 'Hello'.

Barely two months out of gaol for the Duckie O'Connor tag-team rape, how could 'they' let him join their criminal enterprises so early? When that moll Phillipa was missing in the rape case, 'it wasn't being done for me, if it's true what the police say. I can tell you.' It was done for O'Connor, and Stuart just happened to be a co-defendant. Saying he was broke, cold as a maggot and having spent forty per cent of his life in the can, he reckoned, 'I'm ready to die for it. Jack, you have to give me a chance.'

Just to prove he was fair dinkum, he wrote up something that could be duplicated and pinned up wherever they liked: 'McPherson & Smith and anyone who gets in with them ARE DOGS ...—Signed, John Andrew Stuart.'

'Dog' was the ultimate insult for hardened criminals who had spent time behind maximum-security bars. Laggers and child molesters lurked at the bottom of the felon food chain; according to Stuart and his gaol brethren, both categories deserved to die. He asked Steele to 'Give me some sort of help or hope' by sending a card signed 'Harold'. Unsurprisingly, he never heard back.

According to Stuart, in the prison cells below Darlinghurst courthouse, his legal team, Queens Counsel Tony 'Bull Ant' Bellanto, barrister Desmond Anderson (Bellanto's junior for 20 years) and barrister David Baker persuaded him to accept a guilty plea to a lesser charge. The night before, at Long Bay, he had written a statement releasing Bellanto from any further involvement in the case because he had decided to plead not guilty and defend himself.[14] As Stuart tells it, Bellanto, the ferocious cross-examiner, spoke to him for two hours, 'almost refusing to withdraw, consoling me, pointing out the dangers of a trial and the consequences if found guilty (a certain life sentence and no release) and in general taking my emotions and ideals from me in the name of logic and practicality.'

Stuart observed that he knew what Bellanto had said was right, but a voice deep within said 'NO'. Stuart could not figure it out for years, but he later concluded that a part of him was speaking, a 'voiceless something'. Stuart penned his thoughts: 'That day I went before more than just a judge upstairs, Sir, without knowing it then I went before a Greater judge, deep, deep down—no, not God, a God, or any kind of material or mystic idol, but I went before man. Me. Myself. I faced my own self.' Before that morning he had been a blood-and-bone biped. After the epiphany, he said his 'blood and bones and physical actuality' meant nothing. He had found a meaning, or a soul, 'if you want to call it that.'

He claimed that a cop had bashed him with an iron bar on the day of his arrest and sported a black eye in court.[15] The police said he had injured six ribs in a car accident. Stuart was likely telling the truth. One paper reported that Stuart made history at the Central Court of Petty Sessions in Liverpool Street, a court where there had been many violent scenes. Stuart, now dubbed the 'Tornado', a moniker that did not stick, had eclipsed them all. His violence was so extreme that the police prosecutor asked the magistrate to hear the charge against him outside his locked cell door, the first time this had ever occurred.[16]

When Stuart was sentenced to five years gaol, the maximum term permissible, for the Steele shooting, he hollered, 'If it takes me the rest of my life, some way I am going to prove I have had nothing to do with the shooting of Steele; that the Sydney Consorting Squad perjured themselves in the lower court and I pleaded guilty to this charge because the only other alternative was to go to trial on a matter I could have been sentenced to life imprisonment for. That is all I have to say, sir.'[17]

The supercrim would always maintain that Lennie McPherson (Mr Big) had framed him, and that may have been true,[18] as Steele and McPherson were bitter rivals. Later, Stuart would tell anyone who would listen almost the same story; that he had been extorting either clubs or hotels in Sydney and McPherson's ire had been raised when Stuart had 'inadvertently' muscled in on two of McPherson's 'protected' clubs.[19]

Stuart, hearing through the criminal grapevine that these two clubs were McPherson's interests, had approached McPherson directly. McPherson supposedly replied that he had no interest in the clubs in question. Soon after McPherson's approval, Stuart was charged over the Steele shooting. That was no coincidence—he 'knew' McPherson had set him up. The conviction for this crime would eat away at him and be regurgitated endlessly.[20]

Two days after Ronald Ryan's hanging in Melbourne on 5 February 1967, the last legal execution in Australia, Stuart earned an additional three-year sentence for king-hitting Detective Karl Arkins at Long Bay and breaking his jaw while still on remand for the Steele shooting.[21] Arkins was there to investigate a complaint Stuart had laid against the arresting detectives.[22]

20

Intractable

Soon after, Stuart made the newspapers again.[1] The *Daily Mirror* announced that the 'Tornado', with his imminent transfer to Grafton Gaol, 'where most wild criminals are trained', may be reduced to 'a bit of a breeze'.[2] The report revealed that after only a month in Long Bay, Stuart had attacked another prisoner and been stabbed himself (in the back and arm with a 14-inch butcher's knife in the shower). In addition, a guard found him in a wing of the prison that was barred to him—he had no excuse, but was 'no doubt looking for Steele'.

Stuart's assailant was William Harrison, who received an additional sentence for the knife attack.[3] Stuart told his mother, 'There will be no after-effects, I've asked the doctor, and nothing was injured. I was barely even cut. Things are exactly the same here as they are in any other gaol, no harder. I don't work hard at all. I sit down all day. When a judge says 'hard labour', it is merely a formality. Lastly, no one is my enemy here....'[4]

Grafton Gaol was a brutal establishment, and would have a profound effect on the hardened criminal. It was the end of the line for the 'intractables', the hard-core prisoners who could not be contained in a standard prison setting. Stuart was one of them, and this was where he could be subdued.

A Royal Commission confirmed the savage treatment of the inmates.[5] It said that the intractables 'were deliberately and calculatedly marked out as victims of the regime of terror at Grafton.' On admission to the gaol, the 'intractable prisoners were the subject of a "reception biff", which consisted of a physical beating of the prisoner about the back, buttocks, shoulders, legs and arms by two or three officers using rubber batons.' The bashings continued for any further 'indiscretions'. Survivors of this regime have detailed their tribulations in their memoirs.

From Grafton, Stuart wrote a series of letters. Two weeks after saying there were no after-effects from the stabbing, he sent his mother a page of secret 'invisible' writing with a much different message: I'M GETTING SICK. MAY BE SENT BACK TO LONG BAY HOSPT SOON. I GOT TO GET OUT OF THIS GAOL SOON ... GETTING VERY SICK.[6] This was soon followed by another note: '...I EXPECT TO BE BACK AT [LONG] BAY ANY TIME NOW. MAY BE TWO WEEKS OUT SIDE. I'LL WRITE SOON AS I ARRIVE. BEEN VOMITING. OFTEN

BAD NERVES. TELL DES ALSO [?] LOST WEIGHT....'[7]

He would later sign letters with the acronym IBBAGG, which stood for Investigate Bashings and Brutality At Grafton Gaol.[8]

His mother visited him at Grafton in August.[9] He had wanted to give her a heartfelt message, but was unable to because of her distressed mental state; she couldn't stop crying. After her visit, he wrote, 'After all the years I have been a source of misery to you with my lawlessness, and after all the promises I have made you and then broken ... I am sorry mum and I love you. I will now ask God that you live long enough for me to show you.'[10] He saw her as old and tired, and feared that she would be dead before he got out.

In gaol, Stuart had plenty of time to write, and always used his letter allocation, mostly to his mother.[11] Supposedly, he clandestinely exchanged some 'straw' letters (rolled paper) with his beloved mother when kissing in the visitors section.[12] He also penned letters to hospital and prison staff, and, of course, to reporter Brian Bolton. Stuart said he was obsessed with writing.[13] Through the letters, we glean a sense of his personality, beliefs, hopes, obsessions and afflictions.

The letters to his mother were warm with pleasantries. In one letter, he wishes her a happy birthday, saying he had seen a ditty scratched on a cell wall:[14]

It's the only thing I can think of as a present. But how about this;
    M. is for the Million things she gave me
    O. is Only that she's growing old
    T. is for the Tears she shed to save me
    H. is for the Heart of purest gold
    E. is for Everything she did to help me
    R. is Right, and right she'll always be
Put them together, they spell mother. A word that means the whole world to me.

During the mid-1960s, with seven to eight years of gaol time remaining, Stuart remained anxious that his mother might not see him free again. She appeared ill. Every time he looked at her photo, he worried 'like hell', as she looked 'real beat'. He begged her to keep fighting and never give in, because people like her 'never fade away, they go—click!', and that would happen once she gave up.[15] She lived 51 years beyond her son's age.[16]

After the Steele conviction, Stuart knew there would be no early release. With the Liberals becoming stronger in New South Wales, his chance of parole had receded. He wrote, 'On my own merits I am not parole material; my record is too bad, my antecedents stink.' He came from another state, had no profession, no money, nothing.[17]

Despite this, he still had dreams, plans on his release. All he thought about was the 38-foot yawl that he would get. He even knew how to stay alive indefinitely in an open boat with no supplies, as two pounds of raw fish had three to seven ounces of fresh water in its flesh.[18] Because he had studied celestial navigation, he presaged that he would have sailed around the world by the time they got to the moon. When he found the best places, his mother and stepfather Clyde could come and join him.

Stuart spent many hours writing poetry, and had some of it published.[19] Not without talent, he wrote hundreds of lines of poetry on any paper available, even torn scraps and the back of his mother's letters.[20]

Inside the cell the soft voice woke me but I knew

On conscious thought that such could not be true

Fragments of 'sense impression' left behind

Within the deep recesses of the mind

Had recreated springs of memory from my memories frozen dew

In her letters, Mrs Watts often introduced the topic of religion. She was an Assembly of

God devotee who had a literal interpretation of the Bible, it being the authoritative, infallible rulebook of her faith. She despaired that her family did not share her fervour. 'You know, I often wonder, what I'll feel when I'm dying, and I look around at my children and realize that I've not led one of them to accept Christ as their own personal Saviour.' 'What was the benefit of religion?' she asked John rhetorically, and then provided the answer; it had saved her from prostitution. She had always worked honestly for the money she needed to feed her dependants.[21] In another letter to John, she exhorted, 'There is someone who is greater. Though you cannot see it plainly yet. Go to him my son, He'll give you some peace ... Our times are in His hands. But He is also very merciful....'[22]

Her son's replies were diplomatic, saying that he did not want to hear her explaining about religion because of the position he was in, being in prison, but even so, he still had the 'basic God-shaped-blank in my heart, that will eventually, one day, assert itself.'

No, he would never go to church, or get on his knees, or pick up a bible, or ever feel that Sunday was any different to Wednesday, but still had in his outlook 'that thing you seem to think I haven't got.' Hoping that would be some consolation to his mother, he asked her not to write back with her definitions of what his beliefs amounted to.

She tried desperately to instil her deep religious beliefs in her boys, but failed.[23] Mrs Watts said bluntly to her criminal son, 'I've never saved your life [religiously], but I think I wasted a lot of love on you.'[24] John admitted that 'If I picked up a bible at this stage, or prayed, I would be a hippocrite [sic]....'[25]

Stuart did occasionally visit the gaol's church, but also dabbled in other forms of spirituality. He had books on Zen Buddhism sent to him, and explored this spiritual avenue.[26] Although Mrs Watts' letters were consistently supportive, one was unusually damning; religion was the one subject that could arc her up. 'My dear boy, you are as much a real Buddist [sic] as my hat is. Buddists meditate and concentrate on higher, nobler things than petty thieving.' Buddhists hurt no one and nothing, so where did her son come in with his 'negative and useless religion that cannot keep you an honest man...'? Although they loved each other deeply, she lectured him: 'Love is a doing, not saying, word.'[27]

Stuart's missives reveal his extreme mood swings. At times, he soared: 'This is just another few short lines to let you know that everything is still going fine. Extra fine in fact.' It must have been spring, as he was as healthy as anything and jumping all over the place. He had wasted 12 years in gaol since he was 15, but did not suppose it could have happened any other way.[28]

At other times, he hit rock bottom, and the melancholy was visceral. He wrote to Jeff of 'the utter desperation and aloneness of my position ... the injustice of being described as a maniac' and knowing that at any second his life could be torn from him by police bullets. He believed 'they' were hunting him like a wild, slavering jungle animal. Stuart also said the tension had built up so much that he had actually beaten his head into a cell wall to give his 'pain a point.'[29]

He despaired at how gaol life crushed the soul, how little wrongs could grow into an enormous wrong, where gradually a man would become cornered, not only in the gaol itself, but in a corner of his own already tiny corner. If he could be given the voice to speak up against the authorities of Boggo Road Gaol and the underhanded way they operated, it would be a simple matter 'even for a real '"maniac" to make graphic the crushing sterility and despair of that prison's existence' and the way it forced the already pent-up longing for life and freedom to fasten itself almost fantastically on whatever tiny indulgence was granted. 'The utter destruction of individual indignity that the prison cages caused, and the relentless way they reduced a human soul to a numbered, voiceless, automaton, is as great a crime as any for which the men are put into gaol....'[30]

He could distinguish between right and wrong—or at least he said so. But he had an insensitivity that distressed others. One woman wrote, 'I must admit I am very upset about you writing to me C/O Miss S—I have two children now, and I think you could use a little piece of discretion, don't you agree on this point? The point remains, you have practised this routine on each occasion you have written to me—I really can't understand your rudeness at all. I have been nice to you John and thoughtful too—and you repay me with ignorance and a great deal of disrespect on your part—after all, I did name one of my children after you—so please consider this, and when you answer my letter have a little consideration.'[31] It is a recurrent theme, an inability to read others' emotions.

One who did not initially correspond was his brother Daniel, and this stung John.

In 1967, from Grafton Gaol, he wrote to his mother, '...Dan, I'm always hoping he'll write as I'm thinking of our childhood together.'[32] In February 1970, Daniel resumed more regular contact.[33] In a typed letter, which was unusual, as all the following letters were handwritten, Daniel noted that he could not remember the last time he had written to his brother. He said he had turned up at Maitland Gaol (aware that John did not like face-to-face visits), but as John had been transferred to Long Bay Gaol the day before, he had just missed him.

Daniel wrote, 'I'm still brother Dan, and one day I hope you and I can get together again as when we were kids and young men.' Daniel also vowed he was there to offer any help he needed, to get John established again, not morally or socially, but to get a job and some money. He wanted his brother to make it next time and live square.[34]

In her compact running writing, his mother confirmed the sentiment in a letter to her son. She said, 'Dan is so sad about you ... when you come home, he is going to keep you under his wing.' His nice big brother would give him work, or if he could not, he would let John stay with him. She prayed that God would guard and guide her son and make him understand His love.[35]

When the two dysfunctional brothers did eventually reunite, Daniel would not be the nice big brother that John might have hoped for. John did work briefly for Daniel, but would later accuse his sibling of being Judas taking the 30 silver coins, the one who would ensure that he went to prison for life. This was after Daniel had written, 'Have you forgotten we are of the same blood. STUART. All of us.'[36]

Predictably, the letters between John and Daniel were generally of the brotherly-jokey type. Daniel would jest that John had it made in prison with all his free meals, clothes etc. Daniel also told his younger brother that after all his bequests to public institutions, orphanages and retired police, his previous year's tax deductions had amounted to $7,906,423,081,623,104,579,421,642,001.03 and he was now a multi-millionaire.[37]

At times, the brothers delved deeper, exploring their motivations.

Daniel wrote to John, 'I guess you know Del[erie] is divorcing me. Boy have I wrecked my life.' In response, John mentions the family trait of erraticism, and that humbling himself was not for his brother, that it was a phase he would pass through. He knew that because he was the same. They would always be what they were, not what they should be. They'd had no early training bred into them, a feeling for right and wrong. Yes, they had knowledge of it, but no true inhibition that stayed John's hand or Daniel's emotion when the true tests of the socially accepted patterns of life came. He finished by saying that Daniel had been swept along by the cyclone of his momentary desire.[38]

This fatalism, that they were predestined to behave the way they did, that they had no control over their lives (and their criminal tendencies) was further stated by John when he quoted a passage from a Spanish novel. It read, 'Life is a hurricane—If you're in it, you're not a man, you're a leaf, a dead leaf blown by the wind.'[39] He said to someone else, 'What you really are will never change.'[40]

John, like a piece of driftwood following the vagaries of the ocean currents, corresponded with Daniel about Daniel's children and the parallels with their own upbringing, how if he drifted between jobs and girls, the more insecure his kids would become. Because of this inherent insecurity, when they grew old enough to be able to grab, they would grab. It worked that way, he knew, as he was living proof of it. Daniel needed to get stable.[41]

In addition, psychiatrists and other professionals had told John time and again that his own troubles were caused by the instability of his home life in childhood. The material side of things was more important to a child than love. Kids did not even like being kissed—children's and adults' logic differed.

Daniel Stuart would reveal that people bored him, and that his IQ was 139. John's was supposedly high too, although no evidence has been found to substantiate the claim. Daniel also told John how he, his older brother, was a 'well-adjusted nut' who was 'strung up most of the time', and that he had had two nervous breakdowns as well as shock therapy for his mental afflictions. During one of these episodes, he was sedated for five days in the Lowson Psychiatric Ward at Brisbane General Hospital.[42] In 1971, Daniel announced that he had terminal kidney disease, and had only six years to live.[43] John offered to donate his kidney to his brother, and sometimes signed his letters 'Your other kidney'.

'Strung up' was a gross understatement. Daniel did not mention to John the real reason why his first wife, Delerie, had left him, although John well knew Daniel's volcanic temper and violence.[44]

John, Daniel and their father shared an ignominious trait; they shamelessly brutalised women. Daniel's son, Danny, summarised his father as 'a weak, sly, woman-bashing, child-bashing prick.'[45] According to Danny, the abominations Daniel afflicted on his two wives and brood were boundless.

One night, brandishing a rifle, Daniel blasted a hole in their bedroom wall, inches from Delerie's head.[46] Soon after this gutless act of violence, Daniel had a six-week fling with another woman. When Delerie refused to take him back, he beat her so badly she ended up in hospital. Daniel then fled to far north Queensland with his two children and new girlfriend.

The same fate would meet his second wife Rosealie (Rose). Again, Danny watched his father pummelling his stepmother, 'ripping her hair out, smashing her face, blood, broken bones.' Another family member attested to this brutality.[47]

Danny was also subject to bashings and being forced to watch the serial slaying of their pet dogs (once with an axe). Life for him, and for his younger sister Jennifer, 'with their sadistic, gun-obsessed, petty criminal father was a matter of day-to-day survival.' It was so extreme that when he and Jennifer were aged about ten and nine, respectively, they attempted suicide. Holding on to each other and after wetting the floor, Danny removed the light bulb from the refrigerator and stuck his finger in the socket. Thankfully, it only knocked him out.[48]

Oddly, Mrs Watts would blame the divorces on the Stuart sons' strong emotional attachment to her. Two days after Daniel fled to Cairns, Mrs Watts took Delerie's luggage to Delerie's mother's house. Mrs Watts was a bashing victim like Delerie, and would rationalise that it was all the woman's fault.[49] She would say that Delerie blamed her for their troubles and break-up. She could not understand why, as she only saw Daniel's family on Saturday afternoons. Mrs Watts concluded, 'No it's the same as with Jim, their women do not like affection, they showed for their mother, so they altered that, in their own nasty woman way and the weak Stuarts fell.'

In 1970, Stuart was incarcerated in Maitland Gaol, still festering over the injustice of the Steele conviction. He vented to his lawyer, Tony Bellanto, declaring his innocence: 'So many times you must hear the phrase "I'm not guilty" that to you it must have become as phony-sounding as a detective's witness-box bible-oath to tell the truth or a prostitute's tears!'[50]

Having now spent the greater part of his 29 years in custody and been subjected to the wrong of being sentenced to five years for a crime 'he did not commit', he said, 'I did not shoot Jacky Steele and it will not leave my mind. It is causing the time to pass agonaly [sic] slowly ... Mr Bellanto, I can't say "Will you help me now" because I am already in debt to you ... for my life, but I can say to you again, "I am innocent" ... I am appealing to your conscience, because I know it is there—as a man—any man—who is innocent in prison.'

Stuart had been out of the news for some time, but he knew how to rectify it; there was one easy way to make the headlines. In 1971, Stuart 'smuggled' a sensational titbit to Bolton, who grabbed it with both hands.[51] The headline said, 'Letter from Gaoled Killer Predicts Gangland Bloodbath.' Bolton knew how to stroke Stuart's ego by describing him as 'a big time member of the Australian underworld' and 'one of the underworld's most feared men.'

Stuart predicted a gangland bloodbath on his release. He would sort out the injustice of his Steele sentence in an 'unprecedented' way, and if this became an underworld bloodbath, a 'deadly finality', then so be it. Stuart told Bolton he had been shot twice and knifed twice since Bolton had last contacted him and (ironically) stressed that he was not a 'publicity seeker'. In fact, the opposite applied; he was a histrionic attention-seeker of the highest order, with a front-page article a cherished prize.

Mistakenly proud that her son had been telling *his* story and doing it *his* way, Mrs Watts hand-wrote the whole article in a letter to him. How she believed it was helpful for her son to smash his way through the dark underbelly like the Hulk is unfathomable. Mrs Watts also passed on her son's secret coded letters to Bolton for publishing.[52] She was unwilling or unable to rein in his childish outbursts and acknowledge that her son was mentally askew. There is a naivety in her responses to her beloved son's actions. The lioness zealously defended her cub until his death.

Early in 1972, Stuart wrote to the superintendent of Parramatta Gaol offering his wise counsel that any two prisoners who had any enmity could agree to settle their differences with a 'supervised boxing match, with gloves.' He noted that it had been a way of settling 'scores' in the boys' institutions he had been in, and it had not led to further violence. Once again, he did not hear back.[53]

21

1972

On 4 June 1972, one month prior to his release, Stuart returned to the papers. 'Plot to Bomb the Opera House—Criminal Plans Kamikaze Dive', the caption cried, and Bolton was back.[1] This marked a milestone: a ten-year tabloid partnership between the supercrim and the alcoholic reporter.

Stuart threatened to blow up the Opera House with gelignite bombs dropped from a chartered light aircraft, which he then intended to crash into a crowded beach or sports oval in a kamikaze mission. He would only stop if the New South Wales Police Commissioner would meet him on his release from Parramatta Gaol to review the Steele case.

With his release imminent, this was at best a suboptimal sortie, at worst an idiotic red flag to a police force that had no time for someone who bashed their own. Stuart would repeat the story with ludicrous variations, telling his future police contact that after leaving gaol he would spend months learning to fly, fill a plane with explosives, fly it over the Opera House and then demand by radio that the government reopen the Jacky Steele case and give him another trial. If they refused his demand, or attempted to 'bring him down', he would crash the plane into the famed architectural masterpiece in a suicide mission.[2] Although it would have been less time-consuming to truck in the explosives, that approach lacked the necessary melodrama.

Stuart sent an enquiry to the judge asking for a meeting on his release. The blunt reply, dated 30 June 1972, read, 'The Judge has read your letter. He is not prepared to grant you an interview on the information contained in your letter....'[3]

Just prior to his release, the Sydney police sent a message to their Brisbane colleagues.[4] It warned that 'The above named is to be released from prison in Sydney during the coming week and is believed to be going to Brisbane immediately. Has stated he proposes to hold press conference in Brisbane, the object of which is unclear at this stage. You will be advised of exact date of release.' The Queensland police sent out a Crime Circular on 14 June 1972 for Special Attention, describing Stuart as a 'very active criminal who is considered to be violent and dangerous, and one who should be treated with extreme caution ... he is an associate of the worst type of criminals....' If he came under notice, there should be discrete surveillance.[5]

During his incarceration for the Steele conviction, he had made promises to his mother that he would make the most of his freedom: 'Well Mum, all my love to you. It will all work out someday. You must realise I could not possibly leave gaol this next time in the same frame of mind as I went in with. Something will have changed and I couldn't have got worse—all my love—Your Son, John.'[6] The day finally came on 25 July 1972, and when he was freed, he was sporting a beard, which was most unusual for him.

At Mascot Airport, the police 'dogs' (Observation Squad) telephoto lens captured Stuart on film.[7] The photo spies concluded that 'The beard appears to be real, not false.' Stuart had flagged that he would hold a press conference as well as blowing up the Opera House, potentially killing innocents, and so the police saw the need to monitor his initial movements.

After his mother had paid for his ticket, he departed on a 9.30am flight.[8] When Stuart landed 'home' in Brisbane Detective Sergeant Daly met him at the airport, but Stuart refused to talk.[9] He left the airport followed by the Shadow Squad, who noted the make, colour and registration number of the car he was driving (later checks would show that it was registered to his mother). In the car were Mrs Watts and Stuart's stepfather Clyde. The police lost their target at Boondall, and forwarded a message to Caloundra and Bundaberg to keep a lookout. The trio drove to John's brother Daniel's house, where a welcoming party joined the celebration. John stayed there for the first two nights of his freedom.[10]

After arriving in Brisbane, Stuart would doss down at his relatives' houses, principally with sister June (and her then husband Lyall Beckman) at her residence in Zillmere, but on occasion he stayed with his mother and stepfather at Burrum Heads, near Maryborough.[11] After June separated from her husband, he slept at her new dwelling at Kangaroo Point. He would later stay with other criminal acquaintances and girlfriends for short periods.[12] The pattern of no fixed address would be maintained until the Whiskey massacre.

Stuart's paranoia, first diagnosed in 1960, was immediately evident. He lived in a 'state of fear', repeatedly telling his sister June and brother-in-law Lyall that the underworld would attempt to annihilate him, especially Mr Big (Lennie McPherson) in Sydney, as Stuart had muscled in on his rackets.[13] Stuart may have finally realised the folly of sending a personal message to McPherson stating that he was a 'dog bastard'.

Until early September, Stuart did not leave June's house without her accompanying him. He would not open any of the doors in the house when a light shone behind him, and obsessively locked all the external doors.[14] In addition, he drove June and her children to work and school, respectively, as he was afraid for *them*. When he gained enough confidence to go out alone at night, Stuart would phone June multiple times (sometimes as early (or late) as the ungodly hour of 4am), and would ring her each time he changed locality. His paranoia was fuelled by his mother, who wrote to him soon after his emancipation: 'Don't carry your money about with you son. The D's [detectives] might frisk you and have you go each payday and make themselves a steady income....'[15]

On 28 July, three days after arriving in Brisbane, Stuart phoned Detective Sergeant First Class Basil Hicks, who he referred to as 'Baz', at the Crime Intelligence Unit (CIU) office, telling him he was back in Brisbane, having served a long gaol sentence in Sydney.[16] Just prior to his release, a file had been opened on Stuart in the CIU.[17] Based on the information the Sydney police had sent them just prior to his release and Stuart's extreme threats, the head of the unit, Inspector Don Becker, instructed Hicks to record all his contacts with Stuart in the portfolio.[18]

Hicks had known Stuart as a teenager and juvenile offender from 1954 to 1958, after which Hicks had been transferred to Nambour, and had escorted him from Westbrook for his father's funeral.[19] Hicks had monitored Stuart in 1956, noting his movements around the city and recording them in police notes.[20] As Hicks had some rapport with Stuart, he was the logical monitor.

Hicks had a reputation for being an honest cop, a lonely existence in the Queensland Police Force in the 1970s. His boss, Queensland Commissioner of Police Ray Whitrod, would later describe him as a very brave soul, one of the few not tainted by corruption.[21] The CIU investigated police graft, and Tony Murphy, a member of the 'rat pack', had approached Hicks, soliciting his recruitment into a corrupt clique of senior police. Hicks had refused, and later in his career would suffer the consequences.[22]

Hicks recorded the following note after Stuart's first phone call: 'He speaks that fast and with such hate that it is not possible to remember just what he has said.' Stuart revealed his true thoughts on his time at Grafton. He said the gaol was a living hell, that they had tried to break his spirit but he fought them every inch of the way. At least six times he told Hicks that 'he was lying in his own blood and piss and shit at Grafton', and the only thing that kept him going was the hate he felt for everybody. Hicks concluded that Stuart had become a very bitter and dangerous person.

The detective told Stuart that he would be prepared to meet him in person, with Stuart replying that although he did not have anything against Hicks personally, Hicks remained his enemy because he was a copper. Hicks asked why he had rung, and Stuart said he just wanted to know what his position was in Brisbane, asking if the police would hound him. Hicks replied that it was up to him; if he kept out of trouble, the police would leave him alone. Even though Stuart had said he would not see Hicks in person, Hicks felt he would get in touch again. The detective ended his diary note with, 'He would probably be much better off now if everyone just left him alone to see what he is going to do.'

On the morning of Wednesday 2 August 1972, an inspector at the Fortitude Valley Area Office of the CIB phoned Bolton in response to the journalist's message asking that he return his call.[23] The inspector noted that Bolton was 'agitated, very edgy', and expecting a phone call from Stuart. The senior cop told Bolton that he was not interested in any of his ramblings about Stuart, but if he had intelligence regarding any criminal activity, he should inform a police officer. Bolton called back to say he had made phone contact with Stuart and the inspector wrote that the reporter 'rambled on and on about death lists and guns.' The detective then met Bolton in person.

Bolton declared that he understood the police wanted to get rid of Stuart, and he could organise his assassination with a 'Christmas present' in the form of a gun. The detective's brusque reply was that Bolton was 'not to make such absurd suggestions, and further that the police were not wanting to get rid of Stuart or anyone else, and further that [he] did not appreciate his suggestions in any way.' Bolton said that he might be on Stuart's death list, and was terrified of him. He was advised to avoid a 'violent criminal of doubtful stability', and urged not to keep his 9pm appointment with the supercrim, 'as by that time, in my opinion, he would not be fit to interview anyone', being too drunk. It was true—Bolton vacuumed liquor.

Nonetheless, Bolton met Stuart that night at the Hacienda Hotel in Brunswick Street. Downstairs was a gay bar, while upstairs was a lounge and cabaret.[24] Stuart announced that he hoped to buy a house and settle down.[25]

Stuart: Do you know a copper named Hicks?

Bolton: Basil Hicks, who used to be at Nambour, now working with the CIU in Brisbane?

Stuart: Yes.

Bolton: ... he never gave me any help.

Stuart: I am pleased to hear that. I am doing business with him, and it helps to know he is not likely to talk to the newspapers. I have got to have one copper on side, and he is the only one I can trust.

Bolton: How do you know you can trust him?

Stuart: One thing is that he prosecutes other coppers.

Bolton told the inspector (or so he alleged, despite the fact that Stuart had been excellent copy) that he did not desire to have any further dealings with Stuart. The CIB supervisor, so underwhelmed by his face-to-face with Bolton, remained sceptical of Bolton's future disclosures, and was not even convinced that he had, in fact, met Stuart:

Little or no reliance can be placed on what he says, and further, alcohol plays a major part in his ramblings about the doings of Stuart. He is obviously an astute news reporter in a number of ways, and will say and allege anything to suit himself and quote and misquote anything to glorify his own ends. This report is furnished in an effort to show the quality, calibre, and thoughts of this newspaper reporter, and in my opinion little credence can be placed in his information regarding Stuart.

Bolton's 'intelligence' from Stuart from this point on would be regarded with acute scepticism. Like Detective Hicks, the inspector recorded that there was 'no reason to interfere with Stuart'.

One month after his release, Stuart told his mother that he intended to travel back to Sydney, presumably to clear his name of the Steele odium. She was aghast. 'Son, my legs went weak when I read you were going south again. Is that wise? I'm terrified.'[26]

Things were looking up in early September. Stuart found work as a wardsman at the Royal Brisbane Hospital, and his mother was overjoyed. She swelled with pride at the thought that his 'mad acts' had fooled the top mental health doctors: 'You say you must be living in a middle ground mentally. I don't think so.' By anticipating his every move to make it look as though he was 'a shingle short in company' and fooling a board of psychiatrists, he had shown his guile. His mum told him that having battled his way through a long prison sentence, and the tension caused by his enemies, he could confidently resume a free life; the hospital job was proof of this.[27]

Hicks's prediction that Stuart would contact him again proved correct. On 15 September 1972, six weeks after their first communication, Stuart resumed contact, and they met under a tree in Gilchrest Avenue, Herston,[28] where they talked for three hours. The traffic passed them by, mums on their way to the shops and others visiting friends. However, Stuart saw otherwise: a 'very, very cautious' Stuart kept looking at every car that slowed down or any person who walked past them, looking for a gun. His paranoia was overt.

He informed Hicks that he resided with his sister under the assumed name of John Trauts (Stuart spelt backwards), and that he would keep away from all his previous haunts and criminal friends. This was untrue; he had latched on to Billy McCulkin soon after his return. McCulkin was a small-fry, wife-bashing criminal thug who Stuart had known as a youth.[29] One of

McCulkin's claims to fame was a mouse tattooed on his penis, which presumably grew into a rat upon excitement. At first, Stuart spoke about his early life in Brisbane; how he, Billy McCulkin and other young 'fellows' had got into trouble.

Stuart stated that criminals and the police were like soldiers at war, that they were deadly enemies, and if they could put anything over each other, they would. Then he repeated his hatred of Grafton Gaol, lying in 'shit, piss and blood', where he had developed a great hatred of everyone and everything.

He relived the Steele iniquity and how McPherson had framed him, and because of it, either the police or another criminal would shoot him. Hicks could not understand the logic, but had 'no doubt however that he believes that someone will try to shoot him or murder him in some way. He can't give me any particular reason why this is so, but it is certainly fixed in his mind....'

Stuart talked of learning to fly a plane, filling it with explosives and demanding over the plane's radio that the Jack Steele case be reopened. If the authorities refused or if there was an intervention, he would suicide into the Opera House.

Hicks further reflected that 'he has a very deep hatred of the police, other criminals and society generally ... He says himself that all he could think of was ways he could square up for everything that was happening to him. He is a very bitter person and from the way he speaks about his criminal career he blames everyone else but himself for his troubles. I would agree that he could be a very dangerous person if he was really put out.'

One of the reasons Stuart liaised with Hicks was to glean inside information on whether the police would victimise him based on his reputation, while another was for insurance purposes, the significance of which we will soon discover. Stuart did not tell Hicks he had run into his nemesis, Detective Sergeant Tony Murphy, at Stradbroke Island on Saturday the ninth (he would do so during their next meeting).[30]

Murphy had tried to shake hands and talk, but Stuart had pushed past him. Stuart had developed a pathological hatred of Murphy after he had charged his mother with receiving in August 1961.[31] The charge had failed, although another, against Stuart for shop-breaking, had stuck.

Detective Murphy was building a house at Amity Point, a small fishing village. The former high-flying cop had just landed on the jetty when the confrontation ensued.[32] Stuart, knowing that Murphy was under an integrity cloud, having been charged with perjury by the CIU in February, yelled, 'You're nothing now, I'll be telling Hicks about you now.' John was doing manual work for Daniel (as Daniel had promised years previously) on the island. This involved a week of labouring and laying pipes.[33]

On 22 September, Stuart met Hicks in the parking lot of the Royal Brisbane Hospital, where he worked, and gave Hicks a numbered code.[34] The method used numbers in pairs. The first number selected a horizontal line, the second a vertical line. The grid intersection of the two lines showed the letter (a letter could be represented by multiple double numbers e.g., 11=J, 12=O, etc.). Noughts were sometimes used to separate words and sometimes used alone with dots to confuse continuity.

	1	2	3	4	5	6	7	8	9
1	J	O	S	H	U	A	B	C	D
	11	12	13	14	15	16	17	18	19
2	E	F	G	I	K	L	M	N	P
	21	22	23	24	25	26	27	28	29

Stuart explained that the cipher would 'protect his information.' As a child, he had created codes with brother Daniel. This one he had developed in prison, and had revealed it to Daniel when he returned to Brisbane in mid-1972.[35]

He also told Hicks that he always made sure he had an alibi; if he wanted to be seen and remembered, he did something unusual.[36] In a café or nightclub, he might tip salt into the sugar basin and then call over a waitress or the owner. Stuart emphasised the importance of having an alibi all of the time, just in case someone might try to incriminate him. With his siege mentality, he would often repeat the line, 'You never know when you might be grabbed by police.'[37] During this meeting, Stuart also revealed that he would use the code name 'Emu' if he wanted to contact Hicks secretly. He now admitted to Hicks that he had hooked up with his old pal McCulkin, although they were 'going straight'.

In late September 1972, according to then Whiskey manager John Hannay, although the line of reasoning appears feeble, Brian Little approached him and said that John Bell had to be sacked because of his theft, in the sense that he was giving away drinks over the bar and letting people in for free (John Ryan believed that the Littles regarded Bell as too thuggish).[38] Hannay immediately discharged Bell from his employment.

Bell railed at Brian Little about his dismissal, and was reinstated. Hannay then employed Jack Farr as the manager of the Whiskey Au Go Go. After Bell's reinstatement, Bell told Hannay that

Zbigniew ('Spiggy') Staniszewski was coming out of gaol, and that Bell intended to employ him as a bar attendant.[39] Hannay said no, and became concerned when he saw Spiggy working at the cabaret. Nevertheless, Spiggy stayed on.

Working for a living held no interest for Stuart, so he and Billy McCulkin schemed. Stuart called at the pay section of the Royal Brisbane Hospital on 6 October 1972 to claim compensation for a chest injury he maintained had been caused by a floor polisher in the EEG department two days earlier.[40] The extension cord had become entangled, and in straightening it out, the polishing machine had swung around and hit him in the chest, causing paralysis to a muscle.

Stuart later admitted that it was a con job. McCulkin had whacked Stuart to create a visible injury, and Stuart collected compensation until the Whiskey fire. McCulkin himself would go on compensation for a back injury at the start of 1973.[41]

Out of work and looking for things to do, Stuart suggested to brother-in-law Lyall Beckman that he be a front man for the disposal of stolen property. It was not his plan, Stuart said, but the idea of his criminal friends. They needed a respectable businessman to open up a legitimate refrigeration or electrical shop. Stuart would bring in the stolen items (passed to him by associates) through the back door, erase the serial numbers and then resell them.[42]

Stuart spent a lot of time with McCulkin, and they visited Pinocchio's nightclub at least twice together.[43] Gerry Bellino, one of the owners, had been a school acquaintance of Stuart's. On his first visit, Gerry blocked Stuart's entry because of his footwear; he was wearing thongs.

On 9 October 1972, Stuart invited Detective Hicks to McCulkin's place at 6 Dorchester Street, Highgate Hill.[44] Stuart said he was just out of work, and thinking of selling prawns with McCulkin, who could buy the prawns through the fish board and make enough profit for him and Stuart to live on. This was an interesting career choice for two crooks who had done very little honest work in their entire lives and had fraudulently received workers compo payments.

They both spoke about their early life together in Brisbane. Stuart also revealed that he had hooked up with a woman named Sue, and she had a bit of money. Hicks got the impression that Stuart would be 'sponging off her', and observed that McCulkin 'appears to be doing very little legitimate work and if the two of them continue to associate together there is nothing surer than they will commit offences.' It proved to be a prescient observation.

Stuart targeted troubled females, and Sue was one.[45] She had just had her children taken from her by the State, and would voluntarily admit herself to a mental health hospital after she separated from her new flame. She had met Stuart when he and McCulkin were standing in the foyer of the Lands Office Hotel.[46] He told her his name was John Trauts, and that he was a fifth-year medical student at the Royal Brisbane Hospital.

A month later, she discovered his real identity. While reporting a road accident to the City Police, she recognised Stuart's photograph and particulars on the wall of the station. Sue spent her days 'knocking about' with Stuart, Billy McCulkin and the 'Lands Office mob'; the hotel was a magnet for the criminal element.

On 10 and 12 October, Hicks again visited the McCulkin household.[47] During the second visit, he was surprised that Stuart was there again. Hicks had intended to talk to McCulkin alone. The bemused detective concluded that 'It looks like both meet at McCulkin's place every morning.' They were inseparable during this period. On the 10th, Stuart said he had heard that Lennie McPherson was trying to get in touch with him, and he would let Hicks know what he wanted. On the 12th, he acknowledged that McPherson had not made contact.

The problems at the Whiskey were not only caused by internal politicking and rivalries; Stuart was also proving a handful. During October 1972, the ruffian threatened both Jack Farr and door attendant Trevor Coulter.[48]

Farr and a couple of waiters had previously ejected Stuart from the club after an altercation. Stuart had threatened to return with a knife, and did so. Ken Little initially confronted him. 'You can't come in because you are not dressed properly.' Stuart countered, 'I am John Andrew Stuart, and I can do what I like and I am looking for John Farr.'

Coulter herded Stuart towards the door. Stuart had walked down about six steps when he suddenly spun around and flew up the stairs with a flick-knife in his hand (he often used this type of weapon).[49] Stuart charged towards Coulter and Ken Little threw a stool to Coulter, which he used to fend off the attacker. At this stage, three customers entered the club. Stuart saw them and left, stabbing at the light fittings in the foyer, which he broke. He then raced from the premises.

Stuart later appeared at the Whiskey for another purpose. He attempted to stand over Hannay for $2000, believing that Hannay owed this amount to entertainer Doug Parkinson (who sang at the seedy Lands Office Hotel, Stuart's watering hole).[50] Stuart's reward would be half of the total. Hannay told Brian Little, 'John Andrew Stuart has come up from Sydney to shoot me.'[51]

Brian Little, knowing that Stuart believed that Hannay had a financial interest in the Whiskey and Chequers clubs, went to the Lands Office and made it known that he did not.[52] This was a guaranteed way of getting the message through.

Hannay walked into Chequers one Friday afternoon in early October and saw Parkinson and Stuart sitting in the office.[53]

Stuart: You know who I am, John Andrew Stuart.

Hannay: Yeah, I have known you for a long time. What's your problem?

Stuart: This young fellow here tells me you owe him two grand.

Hannay: I don't, and I have got proof that I don't...

Stuart: [as he is leaving] You have got twenty-four hours to pay up.

As Hannay stood outside Chequers that night, Stuart, accompanied by McCulkin, walked past and deliberately brushed against the club manager. Stuart then sat on the front of Hannay's car. The heavying continued. Stuart and McCulkin drove by Hannay's residence and shadowed him to work.[54] Hannay told the police that messages were continually left with Brian Little and Bell saying that Hannay had 'only got four days to live' and he would get 'seven bullets in the heart'.[55]

Billy McCulkin rang Hannay.[56]

McCulkin: You should go and talk to John Stuart.

Hannay: What does he want?

McCulkin: All we want is a meeting.

Hannay: I am not going to meet anybody.

The tormenting moved back to the Whiskey. Bell saw the troublemaker cut a four-by six-inch piece of black leather armrest from around the cocktail bar.[57] Two round holes also appeared in the windows on a Sunday (when the club was closed), one on the St Pauls Terrace side and the other near the reception desk on Amelia Street. Ken Little said Stuart admitted he had fired two bullets as a warning to Hannay, but no evidence was produced that they were, in fact, ammunition holes.[58] The Littles taped them over.

22

Standover

Four days after their previous communication, Stuart rang Hicks at home and recounted that he had received a message from Lennie McPherson that he would like to see him; that Mr Big had made his way to the iconic Iluka apartments at Surfers Paradise and would 'probably' have some proposition to put to him.[1] Stuart indicated that McPherson had probably looked over the nightclubs and would want him to 'do something with them', that he was probably going to take some over. It was more than curious; someone who he had called a dog bastard and who had supposedly put him in prison now wanted to partner with him.

Stuart and McCulkin arranged to meet McPherson the following day, and Hicks agreed to follow them. Hicks first met Stuart at McCulkin's home, en route to the Grand Hotel in Southport, where he rendezvoused with the two villains at midday.[2] Hicks then arranged to see Stuart outside the dressing sheds at Surfers Paradise Beach: Stuart arrived an hour late, saying he had copped a flat tyre.

Stuart beckoned Hicks into the sheds and informed his handler that McPherson had booked out of Iluka the day before; that he had been staying there with hit man Stan Smith, but they had returned to Sydney. Stan Smith, a known gunman, enforcer and criminal heavyweight, worked with McPherson at the time. Hicks well knew that Smith's name was synonymous with protection rackets.

To lower tensions, Hicks organised a meeting at the CIU office between Hannay and Stuart. The encounter did not augur well. Stuart started proceedings by turning to Hannay and barking, 'You're nothing but a dog, a dobber and a fucking cunt. I wouldn't speak to you to save your life.'[3] Stuart added that the place was 'all bugged', and would say no more.

Stuart rang Hicks on 18 October 1972. He had to go to Darwin because Hannay was on his back and the police would give him trouble.[4] Hicks asked him about his job at the hospital, and Stuart contended that he would get it back on his return. He was taking his new lady, Sue. To her, he gave a different reason for the trip; to pick up an illegal Chinese immigrant and convey him to Brisbane for a fee of $500.[5]

Sue received the same treatment as Stuart's former girlfriend, Lorrie, that is, he smashed her. The first attack occurred after Stuart took Sue to meet his brother Daniel and wife Rose. They only stayed there for an hour. When they got home, Stuart accused her of making eyes at his brother. In her statement, she said:

> When we got into the bedroom he pushed me over when I was sitting on the bed and he tied my hands and ankles together behind my back with the wire of a coat hanger. He also gagged me by stuffing my mouth with a handkerchief, and he left me there for about ten minutes. I still had bruises on my ankles a week later from where the wire had cut into them.[6]

In later correspondence with Hicks, Stuart scribbled of Sue, 'I got the girl under control. All she needed really was a sure knowledge of a smack in the ear for misbehaviour.'[7]

They left for Darwin, and had numerous adventures.[8] The first destination was his mother's home at Burrum Heads. Initially travelling in two vehicles, they left one there and continued on in Sue's car.

Arriving in Rockhampton, they picked up a .243 rifle (with a telescopic sight) from some 'hippie types'. They then left for Biloela, where Stuart stole $20 from the proprietor of the petrol station, telling him he was from the Maritime Services Board, giving a telephone number to verify the loan. He repeated the confidence trick at other stations, and siphoned petrol from other people's cars. Stuart seldom paid for petrol, and had two drums in the back of his car for this purpose (he told the police the drums were for long-distance travel).[9]

Stuart sent an informative postcard to Hicks from Daly Waters, 'All going well, more or less—I saw some genuine, primitive blacks as we passed through Camooweal & Tennant and its [sic] sickening—I'll keep you informed as we progress.'[10]

The day after this postcard was sent, there was more turmoil at the Whiskey, which culminated in Hannay being savagely assaulted and sacked.[11] There were differing accounts of what happened (as there always were when the Littles and Hannay squared off).

The end game had been building for some time. According to Hannay, on 30 October, 1972, he and John Farr were standing in the foyer of Chequers when Brian Little came in raving that Bell had to be sacked. Hannay berated Little. 'I told you last time, Brian, after you reinstated him, never to ask me to ever put him off, or tell him what to do.'[12]

Little demanded that Farr sack Bell, and he did so that night. Bell went to see Brian Little, who denied any knowledge, saying it must have been Hannay's doing.

During the next two weeks, John Bell contacted Hannay several times, wanting to find out what was happening about his job. Hannay palmed him off, saying it was not his decision, and to see Brian Little. Brian Little said he should see Hannay. It went around in a circle. Although not employed, Bell still received a wage from the Littles.

Meanwhile, Stuart and Sue arrived in Darwin, where they stayed in a camping area near the beach. Stuart robbed some rooms in an 'accommodation place' and broke into a shopping arcade, while Sue traded in her car.[13]

After they left Darwin, Hicks received a radio message on 6 November, sent from the Richmond police, signed EMU: 'AM LEAVING CLONCURRY NOW 08.30 HRS 4.11.72. ON WAY BACK VIA CENTRAL WEST CHARLEVILLE DARLING DOWNS ETC. EVERYTHING AS BEFORE.'[14] The detective had previously received three postcards.[15] In one, Stuart wrote, 'Hope you got my other cards and messages okay ... I sent you those especially for a reason which I will explain to you. (Unbreakable far-off alibis for those particular days & time!).'

They drove to Pentland, where Stuart stole four suitcases from a hotel that contained Queensland Railways paraphernalia and a wallet with about $180 in it. He sent one white suitcase (containing clothes and several items of men's toiletries in leather zip-up cases) to his brother Daniel, who was not as 'straight' as he made out. At Charters Towers, Stuart raided a small safe in a hotel. They drove to Townsville, and then headed south.[16]

Sue would later tell police that Stuart lit multiple bushfires on the trip. One large fire was set between Tennant Creek and Darwin, and some between Ayr and Bowen, where he torched a cane farm. She stated that 'I actually saw him light a bundle of dry grass or thrash and set the fire along the edge of the cane. He drove down the road and stopped and watched the fire for a while, but not for sufficient time to draw any suspicion to himself. When we were driving away, he kept saying, "Look at it; look at it fucking go."' Sue said she pleaded with him not to light the fire, saying, 'Look, you've lit four already, that will be five, please don't light any more.' His alleged reply was, 'Before I finish I'll light ninety-five; I've dreamt about this for years, when I've been locked away.'

This was an intriguing admission, and the allegation of incendiarism proved useful for the Whiskey prosecution. Although he had been accused of starting fires before, for instance at Boggo Road Gaol in 1962, it seemed to be a rare occurrence, and he could not have lit the Whiskey fire. Other people made no mention of any obsession with arson. The bashings, thefts (including safebreaking) and petrol stealing are consistent with Stuart's MO, but the constant fire-lighting sounds exaggerated. When Stuart returned to Brisbane, he hooked back up with his favourite cop.

23

Stuart Returns

Stuart rang Hicks on 9 November to say he had returned to Maryborough.[1] The next day, he arrived in Brisbane, and immediately found trouble.[2] At 11.15pm, while a police car performed a City Night Wireless Patrol in Alice Street, one of the policemen saw someone crouching behind a car.[3] They did a U-turn and spotted a man carrying a drum and a length of hose. The suspicious male moved to a green 1972 Ford Fairlane sedan with Northern Territory numberplates.

They stopped and asked him his name. 'Arthur Mason', came the response. The police were interested in the drum. He replied, 'The airconditioner on the car got hot and I went to the corner to see if there was a tap there.' They told him they believed he was John Stuart. Stuart fessed up, 'Yes, I'm John Andrew Stuart, but would you go around telling people who you were if you were me?' They searched for a firearm, but found none. He told them the car belonged to a lady called Sue. They escorted Stuart to Sue's place to check out his story. She verified that she had purchased it in Darwin and that Stuart lived with her. The police left without charging him.

At the end of the week, Detective Hicks met Stuart again in Gilchrest Avenue.[4] Stuart showed him Sue's new car and talked of his northern escapades. He inquired if his postcards had arrived, talked of police harassment, Duckie O'Connor and McPherson collecting money from clubs. Hicks wrote, 'He never had anything new to say ... he can't give me any real instance at all where he has been hounded since he came back to Brisbane.'[5]

Hicks visited Sue's place in Banyo on the 15th.[6] Since he had been back, Stuart had heard that Lennie McPherson and murderer John Regan (who were in town) had been looking over the nightclubs in Brisbane and might be trying to obtain an interest in them.

Stuart said he had been to some of the nightclubs himself, talking to them, hoping they might suggest that he protect them from standover men. He wanted Hicks to know this just in case anyone suggested that he was trying to pressure them.

Nope, he had not asked them for money or suggested that they pay him any, but if they were prepared to offer him some cash, he would take it. The detective warned him that he could get into 'a lot of trouble' if he started suggesting that he was offering them any form of protection.

It was all talk; there is no evidence that he had in fact visited any clubs in this capacity. The only one he would ever intimidate directly, the Whiskey, was not approached until the following year.[7]

Stuart maintained his fear that the police in Brisbane would try to 'load him up' with some offence. He now mentioned his police-car encounter to Hicks. He said he was just minding his own business when he saw a patrol car approaching and ducked down behind a car so they would not see him. The patrol car drove some distance past him and then backed up quickly as he stood up. When the detectives spoke to him, he told them a 'bodgie' name, that he was a cattle buyer from the Northern Territory and that he knew Hicks. They were 'pretty sour' on him for trying to put it over them but when he kept saying he wanted to get in touch with his police contact they backed off. Hicks castigated Stuart; if he found out that he was using their friendship to get out of trouble, he would not tolerate it. Stuart added that he would have some information in the near future, and that Billy McCulkin was tied up with three men who had stolen some cameras and wanted to sell them.

When Stuart and Sue returned from Darwin, Hannay's dispute with Stuart was resolved. Hannay received a telephone call at the Whiskey from Stuart. He and Brian Little retrieved a note written on a little piece of brown paper and placed on Hannay's car, a light-blue Ford Mustang. Hannay said the message read, 'If you want any protection I can arrange the best. Contact me.' According to Brian Little, it read, 'with words to the effect that he [Stuart] would do anything for Hannay, and that he only had to contact him.'[8] Little concluded that things were patched up.

Shortly before 14 November, Rees and Rees liquidators informed the Whiskey building owner Thomas Leighton of a proposed meeting of creditors of Littles Enterprises Pty Ltd and associated companies.[9] The companies were in deep financial crisis; the Littles had known this for at least two months, since September.[10] They owed Leighton $2000 in rent, and there were other substantial debts.

On 20 November, two weeks after Bell was put off, Brian Little entered Hannay's office in Brunswick Street and screamed 'at the top of his voice' about an amount of money that Hannay had taken out of the week-end's banking.[11] This totalled $792 worth of air tickets for his sister, Beverley, and brother, Ken, to travel to and from New Zealand. It had been debited to the account of Prestige Artists (Hannay's company) with King's Travel Agency.

Little rebuked Hannay that he should become a creditor like everybody else. Hannay replied, 'This was done, Brian, as a personal favour and I'm not going to have our air travel stopped and bugger up the who[le] of our business.' After abusing Hannay further, Little terminated Hannay's employment.

Hannay's version of what happened next is as follows.

Little stormed out of the office. Later that night, at 10.30pm, while resting at home, John Hannay received a call. Brian Little wanted to apologise for what he had said earlier in the day and pleaded for Hannay's return. Hannay agreed to go to Whiskey, where they had a further discussion, a repeat of the earlier telephone conversation.

Hannay then said his goodbyes. Little asked if he would check over Chequers on the way home, which Hannay agreed to do. Leaving for his car and accompanied by Brian Little, Hannay noticed Ken Little crouching and talking on the telephone. Hannay did not take much notice, but had the feeling he was talking to Bell. When Hannay went to get into his car, Ken Little came to the window and sang out, 'Brian, you are wanted on the phone.' Brian Little retreated while Hannay drove to Chequers.

Hannay parked at the Chequer's entrance and went inside. He chatted to the receptionist Lin and checked on the bars and the overall running of the place. Hannay then left.

As he went to get in his car, he heard a familiar voice say, 'How are you?' With that, he spun around and saw Bell standing in front of the arcade beside Chequers. A menacing Bell pressed, 'What's happening about my job?' Hannay quipped, 'I can't tell you any more than I've told you. One day you'll find out the truth.' Bell replied, 'Ralph's in the car, let's go and sit in the car and talk about it.'[12]

As Hannay moved to the car, which was parked in front of the Arcadia Hotel, Bell pushed Hannay into the lane beside the hotel, where Whiskey staff Frank Longhurst and Spiggy were standing. Hannay maintained that Longhurst smashed his head with a piece of timber and the others proceeded to hit and kick him.[13] Hannay bled freely from the scalp and nose and yelled out in anguish.

Luckily, a couple of men staying in the Arcadia Hotel had been watching the scuffle through a window and came running down. Bell, Longhurst and Spiggy scampered off, hopped into their car and sped away. Hannay suffered a fractured jaw, and had twelve stitches inserted in his head in the casualty ward of the Royal Brisbane Hospital. Hannay decided not to press charges 'out of consideration for my elderly mother', but did report it to the police.

The Littles denied that they were involved with the assault, saying 'there would be a thousand people who would do Hannay over, as he has done the wrong thing by everybody.'[14]

Hannay returned to his office the next day, 21 November, at 5.30pm. Brian Little arrived, accompanied by two private investigators. Little then handed him an envelope, the contents of which he decreed be read in front of him. Hannay did so and learnt that he had been sacked for the second time.

On the day Hannay was terminated, Mr Lloyd George Rees of Rees and Rees Accountants was appointed provisional liquidator of both the Whiskey and Chequers clubs.[15] The company took over the administration of the clubs. The Littles' companies were massively in debt. Brian Little believed it was a result of two of Hannay's actions: stealing and mismanagement.

Brian Little said he had first got wind that Hannay was pilfering about two months before the sacking. Jeni from the office had told him she suspected Hannay was stealing large amounts, although the method was unknown. Brian Little conferred with the liquidator, who raised enough doubts for him to go to the Fraud Squad.[16] They suggested the books be audited, but they were later destroyed in a fire in a Hannay-owned shop.[17] The Littles also believed that Hannay had racked up debts by financing the Chequers start-up costs through the wrong company.

The day after his bashing, Hannay phoned Bell at home. 'What did you do that for? I've known you a long time, and I've done you plenty of favours. You are big enough to handle me without getting others to help.'

Bell parried, 'I had to do that to you to get my job back. I've got a busy day today, phone me some other time and I'll talk to you about it.'[18]

Hannay told the police that for seven to ten days after his dismissal, Brian Little 'went around telling people that I had robbed the clubs for amounts varying from $30,000 to $70,000.' A figure of $20,000 was mentioned at the future trial; the Littles said it was up to $30,000. Hannay argued that it was his ideas and promotional capacity that had made the two clubs the initial success they were. He said the Littles' own bad management and the lack of capital in setting up Chequers was their downfall.

With Hannay sacked, Farr became general manager of both the Whiskey and Chequers. He based himself at Chequers, and Bell acted as the hands-on manager at the Whiskey.[19]

On 23 November, two days after Hannay's sacking, Hicks visited Stuart at Sue's house at 28 Westcliffe Street, Banyo, and had morning tea with the couple.[20] Transient Stuart had been living there since his return.[21] Stuart repeated his claim that he had been going around the nightclubs hoping they may offer him some sort of a deal 'protecting' them. He did not want to try to stand over them, but would be prepared to accept anything they offered. He said that he had never made any approaches to any clubs to pay him anything.

Stuart insisted that other criminals were coming up from Sydney to shoot him over the Jacky Steele affair. Hicks wrote, 'I think that he really believes that someone will try to kill him over that business.' Hicks asked if he had heard any more about McPherson and Regan looking over the clubs. Stuart had not; his priority was to travel to Sydney and get someone to re-examine the Steele travesty. Hicks noted that 'There is no information to date to suggest that Stuart is standing over any of the clubs or offering any protection, but it's obvious that he has something in mind. It's possible that he's going to offer himself as a general bouncer come trouble shooter for them.' Stuart left on the same day, sending a note to Hicks, 'Gone. Not coastal route', signed EMU.[22]

Stuart and Sue drove to Sydney, arriving there late on the Saturday night.[23] Sue described what happened next. 'We were broke when we got to Sydney and we drove to a back alley where there are lots of billiards rooms not far from the El Alamein Fountain [in Kings Cross]. He pulled the car up outside the back of a place and said, "Wait here, keep the engine running with the lights off." I remained at the wheel of the car with the motor running and the lights off until he returned to the car about 10 minutes later and pushed me aside, got behind the wheel, and drove off. We then drove to an eating place, where he started counting out money, and it amounted to $240. I said, "How did you get that?" He said, "I went inside cleaning my nails with my flick-knife." I should have got a little monkey (meaning $250). This isn't the pay-off; just enough money to keep me going.'

They then drove to Richmond and to Sue's sister's leased house at Freeman's Reach in north-west Sydney. She was not there, so they broke in to sleep. Stuart stole a large quantity of clothing including an Army Captain's uniform, an Army ceremonial sword and a TV set.[24] On the same day, Stuart sent a postcard to Hicks. 'Hi Bas, On our way back now. Plenty to talk about. Sent you a coded note from Armidale, and have one on me now (re Maloney's murder) in case I am picked up ... Sue and John.'[25] Hicks also received a special gift—Stuart enclosed a partially nude image, presumably of Sue.[26] Although no doubt temporarily bug-eyed, what Hicks made of this he did not say, but nothing could surprise him anymore; he believed, correctly, that Stuart had a mental illness. One senses that Hicks viewed Stuart as a tragicomic figure.

A circular released on the day of the break and enter reported that Stuart was wanted.[27] The couple then drove to Taree, where the law caught up with them on 30 November.

In front of a mystified Detective Sergeant, Stuart opened a tobacco packet and took out a piece of paper filled with numbers.[28] Stuart had been holding on to it just in case he was nabbed. He asked the policeman to send it to Detective Hicks and said, 'I will no doubt be a suspect for the Maloney murder and that message will clear me ... it will get me off the hook for the Maloney murder....'[29] The message read:
WE ARRAVED SYDNEY ABOUT MIDNITE SAT AND BOOKED INTO

HOTEL THEN—MALONEY SHOT BETWEEN ELEVEN AND TWELVE—AM AFRAID OF 'LOEDUP' BY COPS. IF THEY SEE ME OR FIND OUT WHERE I AM. BUT A CANT LEAVE BECAUSE SUE HAS RUN OFF ON MENTAL TANGENT AND I CANT FIND HER. ONE CRIM SAW ME SAT NITE SO COPS HERRE MUST KNOW I AM HERE—WHA[T]V DO I DO—WILL PHONE CIU AT EIGHT TONITE AND DO ALL YOU SAY BUT ALL STRICT CONFIDENCE UNTIL AFTER CALL—ELU [SIC].[30]

Sue's parents bailed her out and she only saw Stuart once more, when he came to her parent's house just before Christmas and retrieved the Capri transistor radio from the Pentland heist.

24

Stuart's Warning

On 20 December, Stuart left Parramatta Prison.[1] Early in the evening, Lebanese kitchenhand Norman Koazeaha bailed him for $300.[2] Crook Graham 'Lou or Louie' 'Mad Dog' Miller sent Koazeaha in after he had picked him up at the Lebanese Club in Redfern.

Miller had known Stuart for eight years, having first met him in Long Bay Gaol. After their release, they had met in the Surrey Hills/Darlinghurst area, as Miller knew many of Stuart's friends, aka dubious associates.[3] Miller said that David Baker, who had acted as legal counsel for Stuart (and Miller) previously, organised the bailing.

Stuart asked the Principal Prison Officer to book a plane, which he did: Trans Australia Airlines flight 408. He said he had a job waiting at Brisbane Hospital and carried $48.16 in his pocket. The Officer asked Stuart to ring from the airport once he arrived safely. Stuart requested the prison staff to check the streets before he left so he was not 'knocked'. With bail formalities complete, the officers released Stuart from custody.

He jumped into Miller's purple Falcon GT and slid into the back seat. Miller drove, with Koazeaha sitting in the front. At 8.50pm, Stuart rang the officer as requested. 'I made it, there has been a hold up because of refuelling difficulties.' Stuart appeared to be in a happy mood; he would be home for Christmas, the first for a very long time.[4] His bail conditions required him to report at the Brisbane CIB on Tuesdays and Fridays.[5]

On arrival in Queensland, Stuart rang his sister-in-law Rose, irritated that his brother Daniel was not there to meet him. Daniel finally picked him up at midnight.[6] John insisted that Dan drive to Sue's place at Banyo, as he wanted to get the car. They could not locate it, so Daniel dumped his brother at his sister's house.[7]

On 22 December, two days after his arrival back in Brisbane, Stuart rang Hicks and asked to see him in the Valley at the side of the Shamrock Hotel.[8] Stuart took the detective to his sister June's new flat at 96 Thorn Street in Kangaroo Point.[9] He again said that an attempt would be made to stand over the nightclubs in Brisbane for protection money, and revealed that he had been bailed out in Sydney by career thug Louis Miller, who had met him outside the gaol and driven him to the airport.

On the way, Miller had asked him if there was any money in the nightclubs in Brisbane. He told Miller that he did not know. Miller then suggested that he let himself be seen at the nightclubs, as if he was about to start standing over them.[10] Then Miller would come to Brisbane to offer them security. Stuart did not agree or disagree, so Miller would expect him to do what he asked—out of appreciation for bailing him out. No, he did not intend to help Miller in any way, but Miller would come to Brisbane in the near future and make contact.

Stuart also indicated that hoods Lennie McPherson, John Regan and Louie Miller had a big interest in the new nightclub Blinkers (which Bell and Little would attend on the night of its grand opening, 7 March 1973).[11] However, there was no evidence they ever did. Hicks mused, 'To date there is no other information coming in to suggest that anyone is standing over the clubs. We will be checking this further.'[12]

Soon after, Stuart saw Brian Bolton (on either 30 December 1972 or 6 January 1973).[13] Bolton received a telephone call and recognised Stuart's anxious voice. Bolton went across to the Hacienda Hotel and they had one drink. Stuart was excited 'in a jittery sort of way' and chain-smoked.

Stuart: I'm over at the Hacienda. Can you slip across and see me? I've got something urgent to tell you. The biggest thing ever to happen in Australia is going to happen here and the Gold Coast.

It's an extortion racket on all the nightclubs and restaurants. I was asked by some people to do some fronting for them, which I've done, but I've now found out it's much bigger than I was told.

Brian, they're going to blow up a joint that's empty as a warning and then if no one takes any notice of the warning they're going to bomb a joint that's full. They don't care how many people are killed—40 or 50 even.

I was bailed out of gaol by a well-known bondsman in Sydney and on the way to the airport and at the airport I met a couple of young crims I know. I was asked to do a favour and have a look at the nightclub businesses in Brisbane and the coast. I felt a bit obliged, and I agreed, and they told me to make myself seen and heard at all the places without getting into trouble, but just to let the nightclub people worry that something might becoming.

But for Christ's sake, I didn't know it was going to be this bloody way. I've been around some of the clubs and made myself seen and heard and I'm going to be [the] number one suspect with my record if any of them go up.

Bolton: Have you been in touch with these people since, and have they picked out any clubs as targets?

Stuart: Yes, I got a call from one of them since I've been home and doing this job for them and I've told them what the set-up is here particularly.

Bolton: Which club do you reckon they would bomb full of people?

Stuart: The Whiskey Au Go Go.

Bolton: Jesus Christ, John, you can't be serious.

Stuart: Believe me, fuck you Brian. It's on, and I'm trying to find a way out to let the coppers know without ratting on anyone. I've never done that in my life.

Bolton: Who are these people, John?

Stuart: You know fucking well better than to ask me questions like that. What's the matter with you? Are you fucking well drunk? I'm not saying any more about it until I see Hicks.

He had not mentioned to Hicks which club would be targeted, but did so to Bolton. What's more, he had said it would be 'blown up'.

Bolton returned to his office and rang Police Commissioner Ray Whitrod and Inspector Don Becker, Chief of the CIU, at their homes. He knew Becker's number by heart, and had called him many times on a Saturday using his CIU silent number. Whitrod had also given Bolton his silent number. Those were the days when privileged columnists had a 'bat phone' connection straight to the top.

They were not answering, but he did get Becker a couple of days later. 'Don, this man is telling the truth about this.' Bolton opined that Stuart may be involved and alibiing himself. Becker said in reply, 'Yes, Hicks has mentioned it to me too. You can't put anything past Stuart, but I can't see any nightclub extortion in Brisbane or the Gold Coast. There just isn't the money there.'

When Bolton stressed that he was certain Stuart knew what he was talking about, Becker said, 'Well, Hicks is handling him.' Bolton asked him if he wanted to be informed of anything Stuart might tell him, and Becker responded, 'For your own sake don't get in too deep with Stuart. He's a violent and dangerous man. But anything you do hear, I'd appreciate knowing.'

Not long after he spoke to Becker, Bolton caught Commissioner Whitrod on his home telephone. Bolton asked, 'Is Stuart causing you any concern?' and was surprised when Whitrod said, 'No, why should he?' Bolton thought that by then he would have known of the threats made against the Whiskey and taken steps to prevent a possible calamity.

Bolton continued, 'Well, I've told Don Becker of a talk I've had with Stuart in which he says an extortion racket is going to start on nightclubs in Brisbane and the Gold Coast and could culminate in the bombing of a full nightclub.' Whitrod pondered for a moment. 'That's interesting. I must make some inquiries.' Bolton got off the phone thinking he may have been responsible for getting Becker 'carpeted' for not reporting it to his boss.

25

January 1973

On 2 January, Hicks met Stuart near the Egg Board in Gilchrest Avenue in Herston, a regular meeting place, at 7.30pm.[1] He rambled on about his usual fixations; the Steele case and how he may be murdered by either Regan or Stan Smith.

He had a variation to the Miller airport story. When Miller had conveyed him to Sydney Airport, the car had stopped without warning. There were four men beside the road; two got into the car and spoke to him, while the other two were silent. They told him to visit the nightclubs in Brisbane and 'show himself'; they would then follow up and extort them. If the clubs failed to comply, the men would put a bomb in one of the clubs to cause just enough damage to make the other clubs 'want' to pay up. Stuart listened to what they proposed but remained silent—so they took it for granted that he would comply. Hicks asked him for details, but Stuart signalled that it was all 'pretty vague', that he did not pay that much attention to them because he thought they were just big-noting themselves.

Hicks probed about Louie Miller, with Stuart saying that Miller did not talk, but as he was there, he must be the one behind it all. Hicks typed, 'This is different to what he told me before. When he first came back, he said that Louie Miller had put up the proposition to him about the nightclubs. I tried to find out who the four men were, but he claims that he doesn't know them.'

In between times, Stuart threw his weight around.[2] One night he attempted to enter the Jet Club with McCulkin. When told, 'You haven't paid your cover charge,' Stuart replied, 'Get fucked'. In February, he was again refused entry. Stuart grunted, 'I am going to cause a scene.'

On Monday 12 January, Stuart rang Hicks.[3] He was agitated, and said he had to leave town, it was 'too hot for him' and 'they' would blast him if he stayed here. Hicks again asked Stuart who the shooters were, but he could not say, just that 'some cunts' were trying to set him up (Stuart was big on cunts). He had heard that Lennie McPherson and Stan Smith were in town and that it could be McPherson who wanted to see him. He was going down to Broadbeach with Bobby 'Bodgie Bob' Glover, and would let Hicks know of any developments.

Glover, a criminal who described himself as a foreman stevedore, sought out Stuart after he found out that Stuart had been trying to contact him.[4] He knew where to find him, and drove to the Land's Office Hotel, where he saw Stuart drinking in the company of McCulkin.

Glover wanted to go to the Gold Coast, and Stuart invited himself along so he could 'meet a fellow and a sheila down there at the Broadbeach Hotel ... She is a moll and a sure thing ... we can both bung her [have sex] and she goes off well. She will be a walk up start.' Glover told Stuart he was not into threesomes.

On the way to the coast, Stuart talked of his hatred for other people and authority. He talked about ringbarking the entire Brisbane Domain and about killing all of the koala bears in the Brisbane Sanctuary.

They went to the Broadbeach Hotel and had a few drinks in the Racing Club bar. Stuart went looking for the 'moll' who he was going to 'fuck'. They then moved to the Surf bar. There, Stuart made a move on two married women who were on holidays from Melbourne.

Glover related, 'Stuart told them that he was in the French Foreign Legion and pulled up his shirt and showed them his scars. He told them that I was a racing car driver. We finished up in the women's room at the Broadbeach Hotel. I bought a round of drinks and Stuart bought a round of drinks. He was rambling on and talking to them and told them both about shooting a donkey on his way up to Darwin. He said that the donkey had been hit by a semi-trailer and had its guts hanging out and he went into all the details of its guts hanging out.'

Glover could see that Stuart's anecdotes were causing the women's sexual interest to wane, so he suggested to Stuart that they leave, which they did. Stuart would maintain that the purpose of the trip was to meet McPherson; Glover knew nothing of this.

The following day, 13 January, Stuart was again in touch with Bolton and asked him to meet him at the Hacienda Hotel.[5]

Stuart: This nightclub thing is still on. I've got the shits because I know I'm going to be [the] number one suspect if one of them does go. These young crims that intend pulling it off are inexperienced and junkies [crossed out in handwriting and replaced with hopheads] as well.

Bolton: How many are there?

Stuart: Two at least. A couple of brothers could be involved. I've talked to Hicks and he doesn't like me talking to you about this. He warned me not to tell you anything, but I said that I had decided to let someone else know as well so that if anything happened at least no one could say I didn't do all in my power to stop it.

I think I can tell you a bit more now. The person who put up my bail for me in Sydney is a bondsman named Miller, and at first I thought he might have arranged for these young crims to meet me at the airport to get me to have a look at the set-up in the nightclubs in Brisbane and the Coast.

But I'm sure now that he is not part of the deal. Nothing is likely to happen for five weeks or so [end of Feb/beginning March which is when the Torino fire happened, see further], but by then if the club bosses aren't on the verge of getting ready to pay up, one of their places will go up.

They'll probably pick an empty place first. I'm going to try to get Col Bennett [anti-corruption campaigner who had a long career in the State government] to go around with me, and I'd like you to be present too, to warn the proprietors of these clubs personally. Christ, I can't do more than that. You can believe me, Brian, I'm doing all I can to stop anything like this happening and putting my neck out and putting the safety of my family in jeopardy as well.

Stuart called Hicks at 2.10am the next morning, Sunday the 14th.[6] He was 'in a frenzy'. He rang from a phone box outside the Jet Club (from which he was now barred), and stated that there was a 'big red-headed cunt', a bushy-haired fellow in a green Fairmont parked outside the Jet Club.[7]

The 'big red-headed cunt' had a shotgun in the car and would shoot him. Stuart gave the license plate number (PWN 506) and added that Bobby Glover had tried to set him up to be shot and that James 'Paddles' Anderson (another bandit) was in town.[8] Stuart considered this a multi-pronged pincer attack on his being.

Hicks tried to get Stuart to stay in the phone box while he sent a patrol car down, but Stuart said he had to get out of Brisbane ASAP. Hicks inquired how he knew that the thug in the car had a gun and was going to shoot him. Stuart answered that he 'just knew', and would not tell him anything more.

A patrol car arrived at the phone box outside the Jet Club, but neither Stuart nor the car were there. The vehicle was checked (a Hillman Hunter), and its owner was unrelated to any criminal activity. The 'big red-headed cunt' who owned the car was in fact a reputable senior lecturer in surgery.[9] Stuart had the police running around in circles again.

26

Bolton's Warning

Bolton wasted no time after his meeting with Stuart; he went back to the office and punched out the following on his typewriter, for release in the Sunday newspaper on 14 January: 'Death Threat to Club Bosses'.[1]

Bolton wrote that armed guards were now at the Whiskey and Chequers, as well as the home of Jack Farr, the manager of Chequers. Farr had received threatening phone calls to get out of the cabaret business, and therefore needed an escort home.[2] The day before, the acting manager of the Whiskey, William (Bill) McAlary (who had been employed by the liquidators and temporarily replaced Bell), resigned and left town after his Holden sedan was firebombed at 9.50pm on Thursday the 11th.[3] He had only been employed for three weeks.[4]

Some paper was thrown onto the front onto the front passenger seat of McAlary's car and torched. It had been parked in Amelia St, two doors down from the Whiskey, and was unlocked due a locking fault on the driver's side door.[5] John Ryan named Whiskey employees Frank

Longhurst and Spiggy as the culprits, the same tag team that had allegedly crunched Hannay.[6]

Ken and Brian Little talked to Bolton, saying they had been threatened with death multiple times; once a man had held a loaded gun two inches from their heads while menacing them. Strangely, they never mentioned these incidents in their police statements following the Whiskey fire tragedy.

Bolton reported that on the 12th, a staff member took a loaded automatic shotgun into the Whiskey and kept it behind the counter for two hours. This was true. A rattled Alary did keep a shotgun handy.[7] It was all getting rather tense. In addition, the Fraud Squad was investigating the disappearance of $50,000, which was expected to reach the courtroom.[8]

Around this time, Jack Farr's wife received threats.[9] Farr, concluding that it must have been Stuart, based on the skirmish the previous year, confronted him. Stuart denied it, but told Farr, 'You'd be better off out of the clubs anyway as things are going to get really heavy in the next few weeks in the clubs around Brisbane and it won't be child's play like threatening calls.' Stuart also said the Bellino brothers, owners of Pinocchio's nightclub, had been threatened and were trying to sell at any price. The brothers denied that this was the case.

Two small fires were lit at Chequers.[10] They only caused minor damage, although the second one damaged the dance floor. Some of the Littles' clothing was also damaged at their motel by persons unknown.[11] The Littles deemed these incidents not important enough to mention to the police.[12]

Six days after the car bombing, there was another fire. Alice's Food Bar went up in flames at 2.59am in the Turrisi family-owned building.[13] Alice's was run and owned by Poolside Holdings Pty Ltd, the directors of which were John Hannay and James Constantine.[14] The upper floor combined a coffee lounge and food bar, but had not been open to the public for several weeks.

The fire brigade did not establish the origin of the blaze, but the most severe damage occurred at the rear of the premises, and the buckled roller door pointed to an explosion. There was no evidence of a break-in. The official report on the fire, generated by a senior constable from the CIB, who conducted his investigation six days later (and did not state his expertise—or lack of it—in this area), said that no accelerant was detected.[15] Hannay ascribed it to a faulty toaster, which was not mentioned in the police dispatch and could not have led to an 'explosion'.[16]

On the 20th, Bolton rang both CIU head Becker and Commissioner Whitrod.[17] He told Becker of Stuart's latest information and the firebombing of McAlary's car. Becker replied, 'I just can't have this extortion business; The Whiskey Au Go Go and Chequers, they'd be two of the biggest in town, are in liquidation for a start, so where is the money going to come from?' Bolton said, 'Well, I don't know, Dynes (he often called him that, it being his real name), but Stuart is so definite.' Becker commented, 'Yes, he's starting to become a regular sight in our office these days. Hicks is handling him.' Bolton said, 'OK, Don, I'll keep you in touch.' Bolton rang Whitrod and told him the same story. Whitrod observed, 'I'm sure Inspector Becker is looking after everything in his normal capable way.'

On the 23rd and 24th, Stuart rang Hicks.[18] He was going to Sydney for his Richmond stealing case. He had been in hiding because some cunts were going to shoot him. Stuart revealed that he had a new 'bird' named Jo, a 'squarie', 18 years old, who came with no convictions. He was taking her to Sydney, stopping at Gosford for the night. He was lying; she was 15, a vulnerable, underage adolescent girl—it was statutory rape.

Here was another troubled female, ripe for Stuart's picking. She had left home as a young girl after her mother had had a breakdown and argued with her (the mother's) boyfriend.[19] She had met Stuart at Willy's Bazaar when he was in the company of tattooist Billy Phillips (who she knew).[20]

She had met Stuart again a week later at 'The Great American Disaster' in Adelaide Street in the city, Brisbane's first pop-art Yankee diner, where she gave him a wave. The same day, she went to Phillips residence to get a tattoo, and while being inked, Stuart arrived. Stuart asked her to go with him to Zillmere, where he said he owned a house (which he did not). She remained at his ex-brother-in-law's residence for a week, and during that period did not leave the house. Stuart came and went at all hours of the day and night.

They next took up residence at tattooist Billy Phillips' house in Vulture St (coincidentally backing onto the McCulkin residence) for a week. Then the couple travelled to Roseberry in Sydney and stayed with a Mexican family. The day they set off back to Brisbane, the Mexican father handed Stuart about $300 in banknotes.

On the northern side of Port Macquarie, they picked up a girlfriend of Jo's who accompanied them to Brisbane. When they reached Brisbane, they stopped at a road construction site, where Stuart introduced his brother Daniel. They then travelled to his mother's place in Burrum Heads.

That night, the two girls slept on Clyde Watts's boat, which was moored nearby. While Stuart slept in his vehicle, Mrs Watts had a têteà-tête with Jo. John's mother told the underage girl that her wayward son had 'raped two girls, robbed banks, broken into different shops and houses and had been in gaol and had just been released before she met him.'

'She told me that it would be best if I got out of his company,' Jo said.

Although not a great reference, it was likely the wisest counsel Mrs Watts ever gave in relation to her errant offspring. Jo decided to leave during the hours of darkness. While Stuart slept in his car, the two girls slipped away. They hitchhiked to Brisbane and Jo never saw him again. Stuart described Jo to his sister-in-law Rose as 'dumb as they come and only good for the cot.'[21]

27

You Will Be Bombed

On 25 January 1973, Rees and Rees liquidators disclosed to a creditors meeting that a small profit was being made.[1] The Littles were reinstated as managers, and although Brian Little spent most nights at the Whiskey, Bell liaised with the staff and organised the routine (by this time Farr had had enough and left). Two weeks later, a further creditors meeting was told that business had picked up and there were 'improved profits'.[2]

The exact date of Stuart's first direct approach to the Whiskey management is uncertain, but it seems to have been a contact with Bell in the last week of January or the first week of February.[3] Stuart saw Bell at the club and told him the same story about Sydney gangsters. 'They have bailed me out of gaol in Sydney. There are two brothers named the Butler brothers and another man [Miller] bailed me out of gaol in Sydney, and they took me to the airport and put the proposition to me that I was to collect the money for them and to set up the situation before they arrive in Brisbane, as I was pretty well known in Brisbane.' Stuart agreed to go along with these men, but did not really intend to. Stuart also proclaimed, 'There are young Sydney criminals involved in this extortion racket.' He repeated this advice a number of times. Bell said to him, 'Is it McPherson or any of those older criminals?' Stuart replied, 'No, they have gone too soft. It is the younger criminals, and they don't care if people are killed. They'll even drive a lighted car into the entrance of the nightclub to set it alight.'

The first standover-related encounter with the owners of the Whiskey, the Littles, is more certain, being between 5 and 7 February.[4] At 9pm on one of these dates, Stuart spoke to Brian Little in the presence of Bell.

Stuart: I want to give you some advice. There are some criminals coming from Sydney, and they are going to take over all the Brisbane clubs.

Brian Little: What do you mean taking over all the clubs?

Stuart: They are going to ask for protection money, and they are going to use me to front the clubs and collect the money. To set an example they are going to blow one club up. I am telling you as I don't want to be any part of it and I will not collect any money for the criminals.

Seeing Little's disinterest, Stuart turned to Bell.

Stuart: You don't fucking well believe me. Johnny, he doesn't fucking well believe me.

Bell: They are new to this sort of thing. Anything that happens, it goes through me. I'll talk to them.

After a tirade of obscenities and trying to intimidate Brian Little, Stuart closed the discussion. 'What I have told you is true, I am serious and I am telling you the truth.' John Bell later told Brian Little that Stuart was 'mad' and generally carried on in an incoherent manner.

Brian Little affirmed that 'As a result of this conversation with Bell, although I was concerned about Stuart's behaviour, my fears were somewhat allayed by what Bell had told me.' Brian Little did not take the information from Stuart seriously until weeks later when another nightclub, the Torino, was burnt down. He then brought Stuart's information to the notice of his solicitor, John McGrath, and phoned the consorting squad.

In mid-February, Stuart rang Hicks to tell him that he was out of action with the flu and an infected hand.[5]

Bolton, resumed work after a 'nervous collapse' on 20 February.[6] Stuart had been trying to contact him a number of times during the two weeks he had spent recuperating. On this day, Bolton rang Police Minister Hodges on his direct office line and asked for a statement about the dangers of girls hitchhiking and leaving themselves open to rape and molestation. There had been numerous cases over recent weeks. The following conversation ensued.

Bolton: I suppose you've been told of the bombing threat on the Whiskey Au Go Go?

Hodges: No, what's that all about?

Bolton: I've told Mr Whitrod and Inspector Becker of several yarns I've had with John Andrew Stuart, you know of him?

Hodges: Yes.

Bolton: And he says that an extortion racket is soon to blow up in the nightclubs in Brisbane and the Gold Coast. He says the men behind it are going to blow up an empty club first as a warning and if none of the owners takes any notice they're going to blow up the Whiskey Au Go Go because it's the easiest one to get at, while it's full of people.

Hodges: No, I haven't heard anything about it. Next time I'm talking to Ray [Whitrod] I must ask him what he knows.

On either 20 or 21 February, Stuart again harassed the Littles. Despite their animosity, Hannay drove Brian Little to Chequers. Hannay said that he did not want to go in while Stuart was there; he could see him on the steps. Brian Little got out of the car, entered the club and passed his brother Ken, who was now sitting with the troublemaker (Ken had told Stuart they could not enter the club because contractors were working). Stuart had been making threats to Ken Little, saying, 'You probably know what's going on,' to which Ken Little had replied, 'What do you mean by that?' Stuart responded, 'You know what's going on with the rackets and so forth in the south ... There are clubs already paying protection money and that these criminals are going to use me to put pressure on the Whiskey and Chequers. I have been asked by certain people in Sydney to get protection money out of the clubs in Brisbane. McPherson was one. I have also been asked by certain southern criminals to shoot Brian and you, which I don't want to do. The only way out of it is for you to say to me, "Here's a thousand dollars, go ahead and shoot them in Sydney." The persons in Sydney such as McPherson and other criminals have told me if the clubs don't pay up to bomb [the] Whiskey, if they don't pay up and [sic] there will be innocent people killed.'[7]

Two days later, Bolton rang Commissioner Whitrod at home for a statement on a story he was publishing on the Hare Krishna sect in Brisbane.[8] Bolton said, 'I've been away for a couple of weeks. What's been doing on the Whiskey Au Go Go business?' Whitrod replied, 'Nothing new to report.' Bolton added, 'It's getting close to the time when Stuart says something is soon to happen.' Whitrod retorted, 'I don't think anything is likely to happen.' Bolton took that to mean that the police had taken corrective action. Bolton had not heard from Stuart that week, and thought he had disappeared off the local scene for a while.

Following the Alice's fire, the empty Torino nightclub and restaurant at 671 Ann Street, Fortitude Valley, which was owned by two brothers named Frank and Anthony Ponticello went up in flames on 25 February.[9] The fire, which started at 9.20pm, obliterated the establishment.[10] There was evidence of an explosion, with entry forcibly gained through the side entrance.

There were two four-gallon orange plastic drums recovered from behind the bar, and both had evidence of having contained petrol. Investigations revealed that when the explosion occurred, three men were seen moving out of the laneway situated near the premises and scuttling along Ann Street.

On Monday morning 26 February, Bolton picked up The Courier-Mail and saw that the Torino nightclub had been bombed.[11] He felt physically sick, because he now felt sure that Stuart's story was coming true in its entirety.

He knew the Valley and City detectives under Brisbane CIB Chief Superintendent Don Buchanan were investigating the Torino bombing. That afternoon, while Bolton visited the Valley on personal business, he telephoned Buchanan. 'Superintendent, I think I know a great deal about this nightclub bombing, and apart from that, I have information that it won't end with the Torino. Have you heard anything from the Commissioner, or particularly the CIU, on what I have been telling them as well as what John Andrew Stuart has been telling them?' Buchanan said, 'No, but I better get a couple of my men to see you. Where are you now?'

Bolton told him he was in the Valley, but would be home by 6pm. Buchanan said, 'I will get Sergeant [Howard] Kay and someone else out to your home to see you.' Bolton was pleased. 'Super, please keep my conversation as confidential as possible. I particularly like Don Becker, and if this whole thing rebounds on him, I would prefer he didn't know that I'm going to tell your blokes all that I've already told him. The information I have and that you apparently don't is that the Whiskey Au Go Go is going to be next, and it will go up when it's full of people. I can't sit by and say nothing if that's going to happen, and it doesn't seem to me that anything has been done to stop these things from the CIU end.' Buchanan attempted to soothe Bolton. 'Don't worry, son, I'll have these two blokes out at 6 o'clock.'

The conversation with Detective Sergeants Howard Kay and Ted White lasted for about an hour. Bolton told them exactly what he had told Becker, Whitrod, Hodges and Buchanan. Kay, paraphrasing Bolton, recorded the following note of the conversation.

> It will almost certainly be the Au Go Go. It will be easy for them to get at [it] because they can throw in the torch bomb underneath, and they don't give a stuff for the people upstairs. They reckon that will

be enough to frighten the shit out of the rest of the proprietors between Brisbane and the coast, and it won't be long before they are paying out big.

Brian [Bolton], I want you to know that I won't have any part of this deal because I've got other things in mind and I don't want to do life. They're a pair of bloody inexperienced mugs; no decent experienced crim would do anything as silly as this. These fellows don't give a fuck.

They are both young and inexperienced and they're both hot [replaced in hand writing with Hop]-heads. They wouldn't think twice about how many people they burnt to death ... then if those bastards go ahead and do what they say they are going to do, I'll shoot both cunts through the fucking head, because they are going to bring on nothing but trouble for me....[12]

Kay was sceptical. 'Stuart is probably up to his ears in it.' Bolton hesitated before replying, 'I don't know. I really don't know. His story sounds convincing, but that's incidental as far as I'm concerned. Can't checks be made in Sydney to see if it might be right? Anyhow, I'm only talking to you blokes because I'm sure now that there is going to be an attempt to blow up the Whiskey. I don't care whether you think Stuart is implicated or not. What I'm worried about is that he is so certain that this is going to happen.' Bolton asked them to keep the conversation confidential for Becker's sake.[13]

After Kay and his companion had left, Detective Sergeant William 'Bill' Humphris from the Commonwealth Police (Brisbane office) arrived at Bolton's home at 9.30pm.[14]

Coincidentally, Bolton had met Humphris in the Saloon Bar of the Empire Hotel just before he left for home. Humphris had indicated that the Commonwealth Police were investigating the Torino. A surprised Bolton wondered why it had become a Commonwealth inquiry. Humphris explained, 'Because it's frequented by a lot of migrants. Do you know anything about it?' Bolton hesitated, as he thought he had told 'just about everyone', but since he had known Humphris since boyhood (they had grown up in the same neighbourhood in Toowoomba) and he could be completely trusted, he said he could tell him more.

He told Humphris everything he had told Kay and his companion. Humphris took notes and later read them back to Bolton, including the mention of the Butler Brothers and the fact that they could make $5000 per week in protection money. Stuart told Bolton that Hannay's café fire was an insurance job. Humphris reported to the Commonwealth police in Canberra that the Whiskey Au Go Go could be the next target for bombing in Brisbane, a fortnight before it happened.

The following morning, 27 February, Commonwealth Superintendent D Morrison instructed Humphris to reveal his discussion with Bolton to the State Police CIU, preferably Becker or his next in charge.[15] Humphris saw Detective Senior Sergeant Voigt, as Becker was not available. Voigt made these notes:

We believe the recent fires have been for insurance purposes. We believe Len McPherson or Lou Miller to be Mr Big in Sydney[16], however we are more inclined to think Lou Miller, and he is the one who bailed Stuart out of gaol in Sydney last year. We know that Stuart has been standing over club owners in Brisbane. However, we of the Crime Intelligence Unit are of the opinion that threats by Stuart and recent publicity is only a front for owners of various places to burn them down for insurance reasons, and we are almost certain that was the case with the burning of Hannay's nightclub.

In recent months, clubs have been having a very lean trot and in many cases have had to put off a lot of staff. However as it is still possible that there is a protection racket in operation. We, the CIU, are not interfering with the investigations being carried out on recent bombings by other sections of this Force.

It is Stuart's MO to be locked up while a job he is connected with is being carried out, but we believe he was at large at the time of the Torino fire and was not locked up until the Monday. We suspect him of the Sunnybank Hotel security robbery of last weekend. I appreciate the information you have given me, and your contact would be best maintained, as from what we already know, his information is pretty accurate and could in fact all be correct.

Humphris did not name his source. Voigt had erred in one respect; Stuart could not have torched the Torino, as he had been arrested over a firearm charge, and was in the lockup.

On Monday the 26th, the day after the Torino fire, John went to Daniel's house and said that the police had beaten him up.[17] He showed him some marks on his body. The following day, Stuart appeared in the Brisbane Magistrates Court on a charge of possessing a concealable firearm and was granted self-bail of $500.[18] He was to report to the CIB city headquarters between 6 and 8pm each Tuesday night and remanded to appear on 27 April. He said the same people who had bailed him in Sydney had bailed him out here.[19] That night, he rang Hicks.[20]

Stuart slept at his brother Daniel's house on the night of the 27th. The following morning he left the house in his Valiant station sedan and later returned with a man named 'Doug'. John told his brother, 'You will call him "Doug" and don't tell anybody he is here....' They sat down, had dinner and Doug talked about his home country, England, from where he had just arrived.

Later that night, Daniel's wife Rose saw a passport in the lounge. She picked it up, flicked through the pages and said to Doug, 'Oh, you are two years younger than I am.' Her birthday was due on 5 March. Stuart said he and Doug were going to his mother's place at Burrum Heads for a few days. Rose hoped they would be back for her birthday.

Hicks saw Stuart at his sister's flat at Kangaroo Point on 28 February.[21] There was no mention of Doug. After the meeting, Hicks wrote, 'I don't believe his story about the people from Sydney. He has changed his story so many times. It is possible that he is just making the whole thing up to get more publicity from Brian Bolton. He is still trying to convince me that he has had some approaches to stand over the clubs but doesn't want to be in it. Also [he] wants to make it known that if anything happens he's not responsible.' Stuart told Hicks that some cop cunts had loaded him with a gun (also called a throw down) and he was in the lockup when the Torino flared.[22]

It had all started when the coppers had picked up some friends of tattooist Billy Phillips. Stuart had gone to the Woolloongabba police station, as he wanted to find out what was happening to them. On a pretext, he told the police someone had stolen his wallet, even though it was not true. The police thought, correctly, that Stuart had arrived with an ulterior motive and searched his car, where they allegedly found a gun. For his efforts, Stuart said a 'big copper cunt' belted the 'shitter' out of him at the watch-house. At least the overnight internment had alibied him from lighting the Torino fire.

Hicks recorded the following discussion in his official records on all say that the only one who ever mentions anything about it, blowing up clubs or paying protection, is you. Even [Brian] Bolton gets it from you. the 28th.[23]

Hicks: This is the part that I can't understand. I have been around, as you know, and asked everyone about this, but you are the only one who knows anything about it. They all say that the only one who ever mentions anything about it, blowing up clubs or paying protection, is you. Even [Brian] Bolton gets it from you.

Stuart: Don't you turn on me too.

Hicks: I'm not turning on you. It's just that you've got so many different stories. First you told me that you had been going round the clubs yourself. Then you told me that Louie Miller wanted you to go round them and put a frightener into them and you thought that he was trying to take them over. Do you remember that?

Stuart: Yes but that was just shit. Louie Miller's got nothing to do with it.

Hicks: What about Blinkers? You told me that Miller had an interest there and Regan. You told me that Miller wanted you to go into Blinkers looking after the place.

Do you remember saying that?
Stuart: I remember something about it.

Hicks: Now you've come up with this story about four fellows from Sydney you don't know, asking you to make contacts around the clubs, so they can come up and bomb one and collect money from the others.

Stuart: You don't understand. It's real. Your [sic] not taking it serious enough.

Hicks: Have you heard from them again since you came back from Sydney?

Stuart: No. But I know they will be expecting me to do my part. I don't want to do it but I know if I don't they will want to kill me.

Hicks: If you haven't heard from them again, how do you know they are going to do anything? You don't know them, you haven't heard from them again, yet your [sic] running round the clubs telling them something might happen.

Stuart: You don't understand. They told me what they were going to do, their part, and they'll expect me to do my part. I want someone to [go] round the clubs with me while I tell them I won't have any part in it.

Hicks: You've already told everyone in Brisbane. It couldn't get any more publicity than what it's got.

Stuart: Look Basil, will you just remember what I've told you about this club business? If anything happens I don't want you to turn on me.

Hicks: I'm going to record what you have told me today. Will you let me know if you hear any more about these fellows from Sydney?

Stuart: If I hear anything I will let you know straightaway. Help me, won't you? Don't let me down, will you please [crying at this point].

Hicks: Never mind about letting you down. Don't you let me down. Don't you try to use me. Do you understand?

Stuart: Yes.

28

Stuart's Frenzy (2 to 6 March 1973)

Stuart took his new friend Doug to his mother's place at Burrum Heads on 2 March and they stayed until the 5th, when they returned to Brisbane.[1] Clyde and Edna Watts had first met Doug on 28 February, the day after he arrived in the country.[2] Mrs Watts knew the mysterious interloper, as he had been a pen pal of hers for many years, and knew that 'Doug' was a pseudonym.

Four days before the Whiskey fire, Bolton anonymously (calling himself a staff reporter) put out another thrilling article. On Sunday 4 March, the chilling title ran 'Bomb Blast Heralds the Big Squeeze'.[3]

The Torino club fire was the first shot in a massive shakedown threat by Sydney criminals. For the first time, Bolton revealed to a general audience that the bombing of an empty club was the start of something bigger. If nightclub operators did not heed the threat, there would be a follow-up bombing, with no warning.

Although he knew the target, he did not name the Whiskey Au Go Go.

The faithful Sun readers learnt that one Sydney crime lord and another ranking crime boss were plotting to milk the clubs for $10,000 per week. One notorious criminal had told a crime reporter (i.e., Bolton), 'Publish that story and you will wind up in concrete boots at the bottom of the river.' This was pure Stuart; Queensland was poised on the brink of its worst crime crisis—a bloody gangland war to gain control of the nightclubs.

Mr Big (McPherson), the undisputed crime boss in Sydney, had sent his top gunman, 'one of the most feared in the underworld', to Brisbane. Before he broadcast the exposé, Bolton had rung Commissioner Whitrod at his home and read him the unsubbed copy of the article. Whitrod answered, 'That's the usual Stuart guff. I don't want to particularly comment on it.' Bolton replied, 'Well, we're running it and I've been asked to call you in case you wanted to say anything.' Whitrod distractedly said, 'I'm in a hurry to get to the St Lucia post office before it closes to mail away a parcel ... as far as I'm concerned Stuart is the main suspect for the Torino fire.'

The following day, the start of the second week in March, the Kostellars, the joint owners of a block of flats situated at 67 Heussler Terrace, Milton, received a visitor in response to an advertisement in a newspaper.[4] The man said his name was Mr Trauts. After inspecting Flat 1, Trauts accepted the asking rental, saying, 'I like the flat. I will take it. I am a Christian; sometimes we will have friends to read the Bible at night. I don't drink. You won't have trouble from me.' Mr Trauts then paid the owners $18 and was issued with a receipt for one week's rent.

A lady living in a house backing onto the property watched Mr Trauts carry square suitcases and boxes up the rear steps. Later, another man lay under the clothes hoist. He stared at her fixedly, making her nervous. The next day, he did the same thing.[5] She thought his behaviour was very odd. He was Stuart's new companion, Doug, and the luggage was his.

Stuart had wanted Doug to stay at his brother's house, but his wife Rose had refused and told him to get a flatette so that they could cook and look after themselves. Daniel loaned his brother John $20 to pay for accommodation.

Chalmers was at the Chequers club when the telephone rang at 10 45am.[6]
Stuart: Who is speaking?

Chalmers: Jimmy from [the] Whiskey.

Stuart: Is Ken or Brian in?

Chalmers: No.

Stuart: What time will they be back or where are they?

Chalmers: I don't know where Brian is, but Ken has gone to the doctors. If you'd like to leave a message I'll give it to either of them when they get back.

Stuart: Well just tell them that John Andrew rang.

Chalmers: OK, Mr Andrew.

Stuart: No. That's not my last name. That's my second.

Chalmers: OK then.

Stuart: I'll ring back later.

Stuart slammed the phone down. When Ken Little returned, Chalmers mentioned the call from Mr John Andrew, but Little made no comment.

An hour and a half later, Stuart phoned again. This time Longhurst answered the phone at the Whiskey.[7] Soon after, Longhurst looked out the window and saw Hannay talking to Stuart.[8] According to Longhurst's sworn statement, Stuart arrived in Hannay's car.[9]

Stuart entered the club and told Longhurst that he wanted to speak to either Ken or Brian Little. Longhurst revealed that they were not in. Stuart said he would call the Littles' motel, even though Longhurst had advised him they were not there.

Half an hour later, at 12.30pm, Longhurst was shifting some band equipment when George Freeleagus entered the club. He was an employee of Hannay's and drove artists for him.[10]

Freeleagus: Did you have a visit from Stuart?

Longhurst: I don't know. I don't know him.

Freeleagus: Don't let this go between me and you. This Stuart is supposed to be mad, with a gun or something.

Longhurst: I've heard a bit about him. He's supposed to be a bad character.

Freeleagus: I'm dropping out with Hannay. He's done the dirty on me in a few ways and I'm looking for a job and wondering if there are any jobs vacant.

Longhurst: I don't know. See John Bell.

Freeleagus then left. According to Freeleagus, he was getting into Hannay's car (at the Caltex service station opposite the Whiskey, thereby confirming that Hannay was there) to go and do some banking when Stuart approached him and asked, 'Where can I get in touch with Brian or Ken Little? I want to see them. Where is their address?'[11] If Longhurst's report is accurate, Freeleagus's assertion is not consistent with his conversation with Longhurst (which was a follow-up to Stuart's entry into the club).

Stuart called Longhurst at least three times that day asking for Ken or Brian Little, and hung up when asked if he wanted to leave a message.[12] Later in the day, Stuart rang Hicks.[13] He was also scheduled to make a court appearance, but failed to appear—his mind was on more important matters.[14]

Meanwhile, Hannay had been hanging round the cabaret. On 2 March 1973, Brian Little saw Hannay by chance in the service station opposite the Whiskey.[15] Hannay asked if there was a possibility of Little hiring acts through him. Little replied, 'No.' His next question was, 'How is Mr. Rees (the liquidator) these days?' Little asked Hannay what he was doing, and he said he was going to Rockhampton the next morning. Little thought this was a deception, as he later learned that Hannay was at the Night Owl nightclub in Surfers Paradise that night. Little's intelligence proved correct; Hannay did not leave for Rockhampton until the seventh.

Stuart's frantic efforts to contact the Littles resumed early the next day, Tuesday the sixth. Mervyn Little, the Littles' other brother, was at the family's motel, the Kangaroo at Kangaroo Point, when he received a telephone call from a public phone box.[16] A male voice said, 'Johnny Stuart here. Is Brian Little there?' Mervyn said, 'He is not here at the moment.' Stuart replied, 'It's imperative that I speak to him or Ken today.'

'Have you got a phone number that I can get Ken or Brian to ring you on?' Mervyn said. Stuart said that he had an unlisted number and could not give it out. Mervyn then had a conversation with his brother Brian on another line. He asked Brian if he would take a telephone call, but he refused.

At 9.15am, Stuart rang Bolton on his Daily Mirror line, but Bolton was tied up on a phone call and told him to ring back.[17] Stuart left a message saying he would ring again at 3pm. Bolton had to meet two people in the city at 12.30pm. He went across to the Crest Hotel on the off chance that some of the Channel 9 TV personnel might be there.

He met Don Seccombe and later Renton Winders, the Channel 9 News Editor. Occasionally, he had a drink with them on a working friendship basis.[18] Before Winders arrived, while Seccombe and Bolton were having their second beer, Stuart moseyed into the Goldfish bar.

Smartly dressed in a charcoal suit and dark tie, he sported a goatee beard.[19] For a moment, Bolton thought he must have been following him, but he was, in fact, looking for McCulkin.

Bolton excused himself from Seccombe and walked over to Stuart.[20]

Bolton: Good-day John, I got your message. Do you still intend ringing at 3?

Stuart: I'm carrying 20 cents in my hand.

Bolton: What do you mean? Are you broke?

Stuart: Don't you know what that means?

Bolton: No, it's a newie on me.

Stuart: It's the latest for meaning I'm not armed.

He then opened his hand to show Bolton a 20-cent coin and said, 'Why I rang is I've got to see you soon and urgently. Those crims are in town to do that job.' Bolton gasped, 'Christ, already?' Stuart responded, 'Yes, I saw them last night at a nightclub. I haven't got time to talk now but when can you see me?'

They arranged a meeting at 10.30am the next day at the Hacienda Hotel. Bolton never did get to find out why Stuart was trying to make a point of not being armed (he asked numerous policemen if they had heard the '20 cents in the hand' expression, but they had not). Bolton told the TV crew about the nightclub extortion story, and they expressed an interest in having Stuart tell his story on Seccombe's talk show.

Stuart rang Hicks in the afternoon at the CIU and arranged to meet the next day.[21] He then had a medical examination for his compo payout.[22] He also turned up at the flat he had rented and asked the owners if they had a spare key, saying he had lost the original.[23] Stuart said he would get two keys cut the next day. The owners handed 'Mr Trauts' the spare key, but did not see him again. They were not able to re-enter the flat, because Stuart had kept the duplicate.

The busy Stuart visited brother-in-law Lyall Beckman and introduced a friend of his named 'Terry'. They had a Chinese meal.[24] Terry was otherwise known as Doug.

At 10pm, Stuart arrived at the reception area of the Whiskey Au Go Go and spoke to John Bell.[25]

> I have been trying to contact Ken or Brian Little, but have not been able to get in touch with them and it was imperative that I see them tonight. I have been to see you before and you have taken no notice.
>
> I will be in tomorrow night with Mr Col Bennett, a member of the CIB [sic CIU] and a reporter from the Sun newspaper. There is a gang of young Sydney criminals who intend to throw hand grenades into [the] Whiskey Au Go Go and then use it as an example to get protection money from the other clubs.
>
> They don't want a weekly payment. They want a lump sum, and have asked me to collect it. I don't want to be any part of this and will bring these men along with me while I give you this statement so as I can keep my name clear.
>
> I am in a bad situation. I have to do one of three things. Leave the country, inform on these people, which I won't do, or kill them. If I kill them, I will be doing it for your clubs and if I did it, will you help me with finance to help me legally or with finance to leave the country?

Bell had heard it all before, and said that the two Little clubs had no money, were in the hands of a provisional liquidator and there was no chance of him getting any money. Bell then went to see Brian Little and told him that Stuart was 'raving on like before'.[26]

Reluctantly, Brian Little went downstairs to talk to Stuart. 'Who are you?' he demanded. 'I have met you before,' Stuart offered and they shook hands. Stuart continued, 'There are criminals from Sydney who are going to come to the club and want a large amount of money. They won't be claiming protection money, they want one large sum. If they don't get it they will blow the place up and kill people. They will kill you and they have already taken photos of you with a telescopic lens and stood beside you and they followed you home. I've only got two alternatives, one is to kill them first or go back to gaol. If I kill them and deliver you the bodies, will you help me to get out of the country? I'm doing this for you. I'm out on bail now, I will go back to gaol; the police loaded me up with a revolver and the case comes up on the 27th of April.'[27]

He then went on to say, 'I want to bring Col Bennett, a Sunday Sun reporter [Bolton] and Detective Hicks to the club to tell you the same story in front of them, so that if anything happens I will be in the clear.' Stuart then left, making his way down Amelia Street.

After this encounter, Stuart went to tattooist Billy Phillip's residence at 10.30pm for reasons unknown.[28]

29

Disaster Eve (7 March 1973)

Hannay left Brisbane in the morning and drove to Rockhampton, arriving at 5pm.[1]

Bolton rose early to take a friend to the airport for an early flight to Sydney.[2] He met Stuart as arranged later in the morning. Bolton sipped a stubby of Diet Ale and Stuart an orange drink.

Stuart was wired. 'Now this is really urgent. I saw those two crims on Monday night [5th] at the Flamingo nightclub. I thought they hadn't seen me but one of them gave me the wink. I walked out then before they could talk to me but I reckon they're up here to do the big job within the next two or three weeks. I've been around to some of the clubs trying to get the message across that there's big danger about and by doing this I'm sticking my head out a mile. I'm endangering myself but I'm not anywhere as worried about that as I am if they get to my family. And another thing, if the Au Go Go gets bombed, who do you think the bloody coppers are going to blame? Me of course, so I want you to come round with me tonight while I warn the nightclub operators, and that should make it look official. You can write the story on Sunday of how I went around and gave them this warning in your presence.'

A concerned Bolton said, 'Are you sure they're up here to bomb the Au Go Go, or could they be here for some other reason?' Stuart wavered. 'No I don't know for sure. But everything is fitting into place the way I was told it would happen and I want to try to stop it if that's what they've got in mind.' Bolton then asked, 'Have you told Hicks yet?' Stuart responded, 'No.' Bolton then provided some advice. 'The best thing you can do is beat it up to see him fast, tell him what you've told me, and meet me back here at 3.30 this afternoon.'[3]

Stuart saw Hicks in the main office at 12.15pm.[4] The recorded interview took place in police room 123. Stuart told Hicks about the possible appearance on TV. Hicks told him not to go on TV, as they were going to use him. This extended transcript provides a cogent insight into the minds of the two protagonists.

Stuart: Yes, they're going to use me. I'm going to protect my life and protect my freedom as much as I can at the expense of my solid beliefs and even like, what I was saying the other day, like this and it is a toss-up in my mind now.

Last night [Tuesday, he told Bolton the Monday] I went to the Whiskey and I saw one of the Littles and went to the Flamingo and had a few drinks and that, because I told them what I'm going to say now, that I've been propositioned by these people.

I've either, I've either got to kill them as I told you or go to gaol or piss off out of the country. Run away, you see, now I'm saying to myself which is the weakest, to run away or be a dog or what do I do, just put my life on the line by killing people for the defence of people.

I don't even know, such as the Whiskey, the Littles and them and all that. I'll just start, when I was picked up from Parramatta Gaol and driven to the airport by Louie Miller, Graham James Miller, ah, some wog bloke [Koazeaha, Lebanese] was the bloke who actually handed the money over to get me out, then on the way to the airport the car stopped and he was let out.

Hicks: Who, the wog?

Stuart: The wog. I've got his name and that, I've got it, this thing, it's a [sic]. On a piece of paper. I tore the bit off somewhere at home,

I've got it amongst my junk and that like what his name was and that.

Hicks: Don't you know his name?

Stuart: Oh yeh, some wog, some dago name, you know, I've got it at home. He's nothin, you know, just a front man, you know. Money and that. At [sic] bit further along the road we stopped and two guys got in the car. See this is the hard bit, Basil. Two guys were standing beside the car and two got in. The two who were standing beside the car give me the nod, hello John and were all friendly and that, you know, I know their heads, I saw them last night.

    Two were in the car, the other two did the talking and I think that they are the ones who aren't going to actually, ah, see there's more than two, there's about half a dozen of them get to know about it and half a dozen of them, they would have told their best friends and their girlfriends so there's a heap would know.

    That's why it's got me beat that it doesn't come undone. Either people, either people think it's too big, you know, too much and they won't believe it or, or that they're all solid. I don't know, either that or the police do know about it and they're [sic]. I'm just going to be the fall guy or something, you see, but anyway, as I told you what was said to me, that I was so pleased to get out, you can imagine, can you, how I felt and anyway, I found a way out of actually spewing on them by telling you somebody else who knows, who's seen, fucking Jesus Basil.

Hicks: Tell me what? By telling me something else.

Stuart: I can tell you something else that will make you like, like. The words won't pass my lips, you see, but it doesn't really matter, you know, it's only a matter of degree from that point on, isn't it? Like when I tell ya.

Hicks: You lost me just in that second.

Stuart: Like like, I've found a way out of not actually telling you their names by telling you somebody else who knows, you know, like who knows what they look like and everything.

Hicks: Oh is that what you mean?

Stuart: Yeh, then you can sorta take it from there, can you?

Hicks: Is that what you meant?

Stuart: Yeh.

Hicks: Tell you something else, tell you somebody else, of somebody else.

Stuart: Yeh, yeh, ah I don't know how long these guys have been in Brisbane, but they come up to Brisbane, that Alf [Quick] the bouncer at the Flamingo. We saw them last night, one of them gave me half a wink. These are the two guys who walked [a]round and didn't get in the car. You see.

Hicks: Yeh.

Stuart: Understand?

Hicks: Yeh.

Stuart: You know, and they weren't quite sure it was me because when I got out at Parramatta, I suppose that's being in gaol for those years, I didn't quite look the same, or anything; you know, with me beard and hair long and all that, you know. One wasn't quite sure, you know, he gave me half a wink to see how I reacted, you know, but I didn't, you know but, they kept on going. Then Alf said to me, he said watch out, he said, they come from Sydney, then I got up then.

Hicks: Alf?

Stuart: You know, Alf the bouncer, the big guy, you see.

Hicks: Yeh.

Stuart: He'll be able to help you from that point on. Well where does it end, that's all you need to know, isn't it? ... I can get pretty bloody wild in the head, you know, you've got no idea, after Grafton and things like that, how vicious I can be if I, because if I ever let go Basil, I am going to be a fucking, you've got no idea, I'm cold in the head ... I'm getting emotional about this matter, you see, and it's getting to a point, you know, after these people coming here last night you know, after I'd given them a wink, you know, and me not sort of recognising them, I going like [sic], that sort of touches things off, it's becoming real, it's no longer sort of just supposition or what may happen, if it's gonna happen in the future, it's now, it's starting to show... My danger is from these criminals because when I drop, I've dropped out of this.

I've supposed to have made contacts here, there and everywhere and I haven't, therefore they'll say to themselves, what's wrong with this cunt, you know, and then these two blokes that come up here, they're sorta, they're sorta, casing the joint, you know, I suppose for the blokes that are gonna plant the bombs and things.

Anyhow when a fucking nightclub full of people goes up and splatters guts everywhere. It's not gonna, it's not gonna, they're too young to know, that you don't do this. It's like, a criminal always knows never to touch a newspaperman, copper or just an innocent bystander.

Hicks: Ohhhhhhh.

Stuart: Or a member of the public, they're pretty young Basil, don't keep on puttin' me to pinpoint things because it's gonna make me feel bad.

Hicks: Well, you, you've got to feel bad. What are you going to tell me, half of a story or part of the story?

Stuart: I've already told you enough.

Hicks: No you haven't.

Stuart: Yes I have, I've told you about this Alf, to see him now you take it from there, now you go and get a detective.

Hicks: What can Alf tell me?

Stuart: He can tell you, he can describe him, whatever he wants to tell you, the name or whatever he wants to do then.

Hicks: Does he know the names?

Stuart: I don't know, but, but, he knows where they come from, he knows a bit about it too. See, I can't pimp, I can't pimp on 'em because it's gonna make me feel fucking like a cunt.

Hicks: Oh look.

Stuart: OK what've I got, in me life, like you know, if I haven't got, you know, a little something a little bit of something left, understand.

Hicks: Who are you loyal to?

Stuart: I'm loyal to principle [sic], not to any particular person.

Hicks: Where do your principles start, where?

Stuart: Well principles start to me as something.

Hicks: When did it ever start that bloody criminals had principles?

Stuart: Well, it started, because I suffered because of fucking squealers and when those things happen you hate them so much you've got such fucking disrespect for them, you hate them so much that you know that you'd do it yourself, you become one of them yourself, you're gonna be hated...

Hicks: Do you know anything that's happening on the eighth? Is the eighth important to you? The eighth is tomorrow.

Stuart: What is the date today?

Hicks: Seventh is today. The eighth is tomorrow.

Stuart: No.

Hicks: Did you ever suggest that there was anything important going to happen on the eighth to anyone?

Stuart: The eighth to anyone?

Hicks: Well suggest to anyone, meaning, did you talk to anyone or tell anyone that anything was going to happen on the eighth?

Stuart: No never, no never, never have I ever. No dates mean nothing to me. As you know I don't even know what day I've even got to go to court. You know it was the fifth. I knew I went to court on the fifth [March], but I didn't even know Monday was the fifth, all I just kept in my head was it was next Tuesday and I go to court and I thought it was you see but there's twenty-eight days. What I've been thinking to myself this was when I first rang the solicitor, there's only, there must be only twenty-eight days in February this year, you see...'

Stuart: Yes, now what's going to happen, wait a minute, what's going to happen to me?

Hicks: When?

Stuart: If something goes off.

Hicks: When?

Stuart: If a fucking club full of people goes off, look I must get pinched mustn't I?

Hicks: Listen, I'll tell you something about the clubs here, you know the clubs here are that broke that they [sic].

Stuart: Well I don't care a fuck if they're broke or not.

Hicks: I'm just telling you.

Stuart: Yeh.

Hicks: They haven't got a bean.

Stuart: Yeh.

Hicks: So whoever thinks that they can get something?

Stuart: Yeh, I can believe that.

Hicks: So whoever thinks that they can get money out of these clubs, they haven't planned very well at all.

Stuart: Yes, that's what I mean, they're young, these guys I'm talking about, they're not so much interested in that.

Hicks: Yes, so I see Alf and Alf doesn't tell me that, he doesn't know who these fellows are and...

Stuart: Basil as far as I know Alf is a fucking, is a dog [informant].

Hicks: Alf?

Stuart: Will you get somebody to see him, and say there are a couple of blokes up here, one bloke there.

Hicks: I can get someone to see him, but say Alf.

Stuart: Wait a minute because if you do it's just going to end up. Look, he's got a blue T-shirt on this guy and he's got a moustache.

Hicks: Who has? Alf or one of those fellows?

Stuart: One of these blokes.

Hicks: Give us a bit of paper over [to write the details on], I'll forget it. This was last night?

Stuart: Last night. If you get someone to talk to him.

Hicks: Blue T-shirt?

Stuart: Yeah, blue T-shirt.

Hicks: Moustache.

Stuart: Late twenties, a little bit plump.

Hicks: What about er, whats-his-name himself? Louie, did he come up?

Stuart: Who's Louie?

Hicks: Miller.

Stuart: Louie Miller. No. I don't think he's really in this to any depth, he just sort of knows the coordinating points.

Hicks: Blue T-shirt?

Stuart: And the other guy and the other guy, medium to long medium hair this guy.

Hicks: This guy?

Stuart: Yeah medium hair.

Hicks: This is Alf at the?

Stuart: Alf's at the Flamingo.

Hicks: Flamingo.

Stuart: Let me suggest this if you go down there say, now it happened when I was standing out there in front talking to Abe [Abraham Yasse] the owner and Alf. Alf said to me I saw these two guys, they kept on coming between me and the other bloke, I was leaning on a white Jag that had just pulled up, see.

Hicks: Alf said this?

Stuart: Now wait a minute. I'll tell you. A white Jag pulled up and I'm leaning on it talking to Alf and Abe and these two guys come along, you see, one came around the car and one came from behind me, understand, get this into your head Basil.

While I am standing there talking to Abe and Alf these guys are sort of half like try to catch my eye [sic]. They weren't fucking sure it was me, you see, and I'm trying to look a bit different and all you know, because I didn't want them to. As soon as I seen them my fucking heart went cold you see and Alf then said to me, do you know those two guys, they both come from Sydney, and I said, I don't give a fuck, I don't know anything about them, so anyway somehow or other they can put it across themselves. Can you tell them to go at it from that angle.

Hicks: What time was this?

Stuart: Oh. I don't know what time it was, it was night time and...

Hicks: Well what time would you have gone there to the Flamingo?

Stuart: At the Flamingo. I don't know. Midnight before midnight, 11 o'clock or something.

Hicks: Night?

Stuart: I don't know what time it was, let me try any work it out will you? Oh fuck it, oh between 11 and 12, between 11 and 12.

Hicks: Tuesday?

Stuart: Between eleven and twelve, about that, at that hour of the night.

Hicks: Have you heard anything about Hannay being in circulation now?

Stuart: No he's up in a place called, up the North Coast, he's a postmaster at a place called Kin Kin and I haven't heard anything about him coming back, no. He's up at a place called Kin Kin.

Hicks: Umm.

Stuart: He's up at a place called Kin Kin.

Hicks: Kin Kin?

Stuart: ... See I don't know nothing about these things, Basil, like what's going to happen to me now if something does go off. How am I going to protect meself [sic]? Hey? I told you I've worked this out in great detail, I've either got to leave the country somehow, go to gaol tomorrow or today you know, I just can't say within a couple of weeks anyway before I, they get themselves into action up here, I either go to gaol, or leave the country, give them up or kill them. Now you, now, now, just fancy that, now you try just working out just what to do, what can I do? Will you?

Hicks: Give them up.

Stuart: Yeah, that's because you're a copper, you got to say that.

Hicks: Well what did you expect me to say?

Stuart: Yeh.

Hicks: What would you bloody well expect me to say?

Stuart: Okay then, okay then, then I say to you, right then, what then, how can I? Listen, whether I do or I don't they're going to think I have.

Hicks: Well they do that anyway, because they do it all the time, they think everyone else has.

Stuart: Look, these guys, we're all seeing each other like in the can and that ... I've been trying to give them the hint of who these people are, I've been going to the Whiskey last night and talking to Bell and Little and today I'm coming around or the next day or within a week.

Hicks: Are they back there again Bell and his mob?

Stuart: Yeah, I, I've been going to come around with me fucking solicitor and Bolton and someone from the police force you know and say well I had nothing to do with it, you see.

Hicks: So all right, you've told me you've had nothing to do with it.

Stuart: Hey?

Hicks: So you've reported you've had nothing to do with it.

Stuart: ... what's going to happen, what's their game, what say I'm just home and asleep in bed and this happens or something, not tipping salt in the fucking sugar canisters and things [providing an alibi]. What's going to happen to me?

I don't know about it till the next morning that they're gonna, well I'll go to bed or something after TV, wake up at bloody half past seven, I would be probably hear [sic] the news or reading the paper where forty people are dead and that but, they're gonna to fall on my door at 4 o'clock in the morning, say ten minutes after it happened or something, you see and it's too late for me, well what am I doing to do, see? What am I going to do, come on, I'm just saying that as an expression, what am I going to do?

Hicks: Cause it's a whole hypothetical if they fall on you at 4 o'clock.

Stuart: Look, I've got no one but you.

Hicks: I'll report it now today, that you've been in here that you told me that you are not involved with any clubs.

Stuart: But look, what good are you going to be Basil against six or eight detectives saying that we questioned Stuart and he said?

Hicks: They've got to get other evidence, now they've got to get other evidence. It's different.

Stuart: Okay, other evidence, what about they're going to come out with little sticks of gelignite and be saying we found this gelignite poking under his lino and er here's a bit of fuse we found out the backyard and er here's all this, see, there's the other bits of evidence.

Well if they try to get me right for something I didn't do, like they knew I didn't do for Jacky Stewart [sic Steele]. They loaded me up with a shotgun, shotgun shells, they got me verbal, they've got all this [sic] little bits of fucking thing see? They would have tried and they would have got me life and I didn't do it. Okay what are we going to do about this when there's a heap of citizens blown to the ceiling? Hey? You think they're not going to fall on me because they know that I've been going around there talking about they're, they're at least going to load me up with a bust and try to suck it out of my brain all I know. Aren't they? Course they are.

Hicks: But?

Stuart: Hey? Why don't you think so?

Hicks: I don't think it will happen.

Stuart: Why?

Hicks: I don't think they will do anything like that.

Stuart: I hope you're right, mate. I hope you're right.

Hicks: Your biggest worry is not so much the clubs, your biggest worry is just yourself personally.

Stuart: Why? About what?

Hicks: Well er, you put the police in.

Stuart: Yeah, no it's, Basil let me tell you now, what just flashed through my head. I'm being level with you all the time, you see you're sort of saying that you're [I'm] trying to lead you on a bit, a bit more.

Hicks: Lead you on to what?

Stuart: When you, I don't think anything is going to happen.

Hicks: Lead you on to what?

Stuart: To say that, oh yeh, this is going to happen and so on blah, blah, blah.

Hicks: As you say, you just said, told me what, what you know.

Stuart: Now when I seen these two guys last night they tried to sort of go, they weren't friendly like the first time I ever saw them standing beside the car. When the other two guys got in they were friendly, 'hello John, how are you mate' and all that. I'd seen them in gaol years and years ago and that, and then that, and then last night when they saw me, see, they were sort of not sure. I could tell they weren't sure and me not recognising, them like, I didn't sort of keep my eyes on them once too many times or anything like that, I just sort of let them go you know and that and er and er and er [sic] get someone to see Alf, get someone to go and see him.

Hicks: Your biggest worry at the moment is you're charged you're charge, you're charged with [sic].

Stuart: You think so? Yeah. Basil if there is something you don't know, give me something.

Hicks: Well I just told you what I think.

Stuart: Well if there's something you know that I don't know ... Yeah so what, so how long is this going to go on? All my life I suppose. My mother as soon as she reads it, they're [sic She'll] broke down when I told her about it. They're the things that get me, not so much going to gaol because I've done enough can to fucking know, you know not to worry too much about it, but when I've got to go up there and tell her and show her the bruises and all that and then tell her I've got to, leave the country you know and she sort of takes that over dramatic, oh oh that the police are trying to force her son out of the country and I'll be dead before he ever comes back and all this you know.

I've told her these things, you see, you see, they're the little things that get you. I know I'm not a mummy's boy or anything like that but she's stuck with me for so fucking long you see and every time I leave, my mother, it's like a[n] emotional bloody volcano because I'm either the emotional upheaval of me just being home and then a few weeks later you're up a a a [sic] emotional upheaval of my being pinched again, and a few weeks later the emotional upheaval of me being in gaol.

The whole, my whole life, the whole reaction, the attitude between me and my mother is one of intense bloody love or hatred or emotional what's going on you know, you see. I've tried to explain this to her now, let's just settle down and be calm and then and then I've got to go back up there and fucking tell her I'm pinched again Mum, like they've loaded me up with a gun and Danny and the kids were in the car for 20 minutes before this you see and now, and now what chance have I got of ever beating it [Torino fire night]. The only thing I can do is call the police liars and there's going to be six or eight police there all say they heard me verbal and not only that they're going to get dirty on me, they're going to get shitty on me and load me up or be ready to load me up.

Hicks: They don't love you now, do they?

Stuart: No, no but they're going to get dirty on me even more so because I'm telling the truth, see.

Hicks: That's what you're entitled to do.

Stuart: Hey?

Hicks: That's what you're entitled to do.

Stuart: Yeah I know that's what I am entitled to do, but what good is it going to do like, I'm not a dill completely, and look here's another thing, I can't go now I should be at Burrum Heads [mother's house] now but I can't because of these fucking, you know I got to go and see these compo people, but I went and saw that Dr B last night again, I got another copy of the one they didn't get, I got the doctor's certificate, he's rung up and then I went and saw that Tonaki and he rang up Dr P, so I got to ring Dr P's secretary and make a fucking arrangement for 12 o'clock tomorrow and then it will be tomorrow or Thursday and then it will be Friday or something before I see him and then what's the good of me going up there on Saturday, to come back on Monday, you see, and here I am now stuck in Brisbane again, see? What am I going to do? Tell me what to do will you?

Hicks: I can't tell you what to do, you've got to do those things, you've got to stay here. You've got to go to the doctor, you've got to see them. You've got to make the appointment.

Stuart: Yeah, and then again, what say something happens in the meantime. Can I, what what, I'm getting into such a frame of mind that I've had the radio going beside my bed all fucking night, you know and things like that, now I've sort of got to half way sort of hear it and just listen to the bloody news flashes I set, you know what I've started to do, set me alarm clock every hour when the news came on, you know, on the Macquarie news you know, set every hour.

The alarm would go off at five to, I'd half-awake until I've hea[r]d the news and set the alarm again an hour ahead and it's waking fucking Lyle [Lyall Beckman] up, see and I can't get any sleep because I'm desperately afraid that's somethings going to happen and they're going to get at me before I can get any sort of bloody defence for myself, like get a solicitor or something. Once they get me by myself, they'll verbal me, what then? What chance have I got? I tell you, the only chance I've got is either to go to gaol, leave the country, or kill the people involved because this is what they've always got it worked out.

Hicks: Wait on, you're talking about the people in what? In nightclubs. Well how does that solve the problem?

Stuart: No the people who are going to, no you are, Basil, as I said, you are not taking it, you're not taking it strong enough. I've already...

Hicks: Just a moment, you're talking about killing the people, people involved in the nightclub business?

Stuart: No the blokes that are going to blow the nightclub up.

Hicks: Right and how does [sic] that going to solve your problem. You've still got the police.

Stuart: Okay, this solves the problem this way, for one thing they're not going to kill ordinary people, they're not going to get me.

Hicks: Your personal problem is, according to you, is the police.

Stuart: Yeh, police too, yeah, okay.

Hicks: What they're doing? [sic]

Stuart: Okay, if I did, just say I did and, and I arranged a situation or something, so it was over self-defence or something, they have guns, they've always got guns and Christ only knows what, they go at me and I'd have to shoot them both down first. All right now just what say that happens and then I go along, ring you up, then get a solicitor who'll go straight along and report the matter myself and give myself up easily and say these men have just attached [sic] me and I was defending myself, I got at least a chance for doing a brick for manslaughter or something.

Hicks: You already told me that you're going to do it.

Stuart: Well?

Hicks: How can you ring me up and tell me you're going to knock them off?

Stuart: Yeh, yes, that's what I am saying you've got to do, you see. If, if, if it comes to that, because look when I don't go and do my part. It simply is that they have asked me to do something like, I haven't said yes, yes I will, that I will, I will agree to collect the money, but I haven't said no either, you know.

Okay now when they come to interview me and it is my turn to front up and say look where's the money, you know the clubs and I don't do that, they're going to say this cunt's fucking weakened, you know, and not only that, not only that he knows that, we've done this damage so he's a potential danger, so therefore they'll want to kill me, right.

Because if they're going to go ahead and blow people up they're not going to worry about me, one man, because any man in this country could shoot me down now and it wouldn't get past the Coroners Court with the fucking reputation that I've got, you see.

What cop would pinch me, pinch someone over shooting me? Okay it's right what I'm saying and then okay when it comes that if I don't go along and collect anything they'll say they worked all this out, what I'm working out now. They'll say well this cunt knows we're going to hit him, therefore he's got to kill us. First to stop this and all this sort of thing. They'll, they've worked all this out, that I'm working this out and I've worked out that they're working out that I'm working it out. It's sort of an endless bloody, anyway, this is the end Basil, I become a dog for you. I told you to go and see Alf and he'll describe these people and if you've got enough photos, they're crims, they've done time in gaol so if they've got any mug shots and er and you'll be able to er just, you know, check it out. That's enough isn't it? Well see I'm a dog aren't I?

Hicks: Ummm.

Stuart: I'm a dog. I'm a squealer aren't I?

Hicks: Because you use the expression, I don't use it at all.

Stuart: Yeh.

Hicks: I don't use the expression.

Stuart: In other words you're not saying no either. You think?

Hicks: I'm just saying, I'm not saying dog at all. I don't use the bloody expression. You think your way and I think my way. I'll talk to anyone about anything at any time, anyone it suits me to talk to. Even you. I've never asked you for anything, never asked you to tell me anything. Who, who was it that was giving us a roast amongst those [Woolloon]Gabba [police] fellows?

Stuart: Oh Jesus fucking Christ, just about all of them. You know.

Hicks: They were giving you a roast for being associated with me.

Stuart: No, no, I mentioned the CIU I, I, I, I said look you don't have to worry about chasing them, I said there's a bloke in the CI Unit I said that knows where I am at all times.

I said I went up to Darwin, we don't give a fuck of them cunts he said they're nothing, you know they're going on like the attitude the others said yeahhh, you know as if to say don't try to sort of threaten us with names like that you know, I'm not threaten [sic], but er it was just about all of them are and fucking of you know they're all sort of, they're [their] attitude is the same whether or not each one saids [sic] the word, the next time I'll take you. I wasn't worried of taking notice of them because others have done it too you know, they sort of mentioned the thing, well that, well that's what sort of puts me on your side, the moment anybody cooks a copper, like Bolton, he said to me this morning, he said, oh you don't want to take any, put too much faith in fucking Hicks and all that because he, he, he's just a mug ... The moment anyone ever does that to me like, like to the coppers, that's, that's good, you know.

Hicks: But he's friendly with Mr Becker.

Stuart: Yeah, that's, that's what he said, he said Don Becker, that's why I wanted to see him this morning because Don Becker said, you know, shaking his hand that's why I wanted to shake hands with him. You see, because I'm getting desperate. When I first came out of gaol I was still with the gaol blood in me, you know, as a sort of...

Hicks: Right, I'll tell you what we will do.

Stuart: Yeah.

Hicks: I'll take you around to meet him and you can say hello to him.

Stuart: Yeah.

Hicks: I'll report today what you have told us.

Stuart: Yeah.

Hicks: That you're not involved in anything at all.

Stuart: Yeah.

Hicks: And if there's anything involved...

Stuart: Yeah.

Hicks: If anything does happen...

Stuart: I want to tell you this, if even I get picked up by the police, if even I happen to be in bed or got no alibi or something like this.

Hicks: Well then I'll do something about it then, but...

Stuart: Where I can't be where I am. At the time I want to say this that I've got nothing to say except that I'm innocent and I want a solicitor.

Hicks: You can record that with Nolan [Patrick Nolan, Stuart's solicitor].

Stuart: Nolan. Yeah but you can't make a statuary declaration for something that may happen in the future. I've tried that before. I want to go to the police commissioner and say that if ever I am picked up and questioned by the police I want a solicitor present, because that's what McPherson and Smith did down with Alan and the coppers could never pick them up and verbal them because they could subpoena then [sic], the commissioner, to the Court to say what was said to him, you see.

Hicks: You could still say that to Mr. Becker.

Stuart: Yeah. Will that be enough? You know. That's why I want to go on TV Basil to say that over the air loud and clear, that ever I'm nicked up by the police I want...

Hicks: Look, it's your business if you want to go on TV.

Stuart: Yeah but what do you reckon I ought to do?

Hicks: Well...

Stuart: [silence]

Hicks: Well you're notorious now aren't you, you'll be more notorious then.

Stuart: No, but I don't want to, I well, what can, how can I be unnotorious, how can I? You know, as I said, all I can do is...

Hicks: Time.

Stuart: Is go to fucking gaol or leave the country.

Hicks: No it'll be just time. See unfortunately you had to go and poke your bib in the bloody police station and somebody immediately puts two and two together, the notorious John Stuart's here, he must have a reason, he's got to, he wants to establish an alibi, what would it be for, what's happened tonight, a hold up so they picked you up the next day.

Stuart: Bolton was telling me that fucking Whitrod said that we know that Stuart did the robbery some fucking Sunday.

Hicks: Ohh.

Stuart: Yeah I know I didn't believe anything he said, he just sort of I think he just said things to me he thinks I want to hear. He said when.

Hicks: You're good news value for them, you're good news value for them, they like it.

Stuart: You know that shit in the paper on the Elite Cl.

Hicks: Well that's your good news value.

Stuart: That poor reporting, I said, I said to him why didn't you just say John Stuart's lagging people to Basil Hicks. That's what I said to him.

Hicks: That's real good news value, come around and meet him anyway.

Stuart: Yeah, I will. All right, anyway that's it.

After the meeting Hicks took Stuart to see Inspector Becker as agreed.

The Flamingo club doorman, Alf Quick, and owner Abraham Yasse would confirm they had asked Stuart who the two recent regulars from Sydney were, although they were vague when indicating the date, variously saying it happened on the Monday, the Tuesday or the Wednesday on the week of the fire. They were purely making conversation; there was nothing special about the men in question. Hicks did not reveal who his informant was, the person who said Stuart had indicated the eighth as being important.

Stuart met Bolton as arranged at 3.30pm and said, 'I have seen Hicks and have told him everything. I also went in and met Becker. I still want you to come around with me tonight.'[5] Bolton agreed to meet Stuart back at the Hacienda at 9pm. Stuart indicated that they should be no longer than an hour going to two of the Little-owned clubs, Chequers and the Whiskey Au Go Go, and at least one other, the Jet Club (which was a furphy, as he was barred; the last time he'd attempted to enter, the manager had threatened to set the police on him).[6] Bolton intended to listen to what Stuart had to tell the nightclub managers or proprietors and contact Commissioner Whitrod after the visit.

The reporter then met Commonwealth police officer Humphris one hour later. Bolton apprised, 'I have just had a couple of beers with Stuart and he told me that the bombing of the Whiskey is still on and there are two Sydney criminals in town. Humphries inquired, 'Do you know when it is to go off?' Bolton lamented, 'No, I wish I did.'[7]

John took his new companion Doug to Daniel Stuart's at 6pm. John bought fruit and soft drinks for Daniel's children, had dinner and then watched the Mike Willesee-hosted *A Current Affair* on Channel

9.[8] Subsequently, John left for his ex-brother-in-law Lyall Beckman's residence.[9] With John away, Doug talked to Daniel Stuart and told him he was only staying in Australia for six weeks. He told Rose he liked to break windows, which she found unsettling.[10]

Stuart told Lyall Beckman he had a problem with the tail-lights of the Valiant station sedan and he would be on TV the following Tuesday.[11] In a hurry, Stuart had a shower and changed his clothes, then left at 8.30pm for the appointment with Bolton. They had arranged to rendezvous in the Siesta bar.[12] Stuart rang Daniel Stuart at 9.10pm from the Hacienda Hotel and then called Lyall Beckman a short time later to see if Bolton had rung either of them.[13] He was furious: Bolton had stood him up.

Stuart stormed over to Bolton's office and left a note:
B-(10.15P.M.)
I waited from 8.55 until 10.10
Why didn't you appear? I want to know
John A.[14]

Bolton had returned home at 6pm, and later told the police he was feeling tired and said to his wife, 'I'm going to have a doze. Whatever you do, wake me at 8.30pm. I've got an important appointment in town at 9.'[15] She woke him at 10pm, saying he had gone into a deep sleep and could not be woken.

His son would, years later, reveal that he had been tasked with waking him. 'He said it was important, but in our house a sleeping Brian was always better than a drinking Brian, so I let him sleep. It's troubled me for a long time.'[16] Although Bolton had missed the appointment, he was not particularly perturbed, as Stuart had said it would be two or three weeks before anything was likely to happen.

Stuart then went to Chequers and asked Kopittke, 'Is Brian or Ken Little here?' Kopittke replied, 'No.' Stuart discovered that Bell was at Blinkers and obtained directions on how to get there.[17]

Meanwhile, larger than life Bell, and company, had made it to the opening of the new Blinkers nightclub in Albert Street.[18] Someone told Bell there was a guest at the door, and when Bell went to investigate, he found Stuart wearing jeans and a lightcoloured sports shirt. An agitated Stuart said, 'I expected to see you at the Whiskey, and told you that I would be in. Why didn't you wait to see me, as I was bringing the reporter in to see you tonight? The reporter hasn't turned up and I'm disappointed that you weren't there to meet me. What I told you was not a joke, and I expected you to take me seriously.'

When Bell returned to the table, he did not immediately inform Brian Little about what he had discussed with Stuart, but waited until they returned to the Whiskey to do so. Bell then rang Detective Scanlan of the Consorting Squad, who decided to visit the Whiskey with some colleagues. Fortunately, they all managed to escape from the fire.[19]

John returned to his brother Daniel's house to pick up Doug, who had been watching TV and playing with the children.[20] They left at midnight, saying they were going to have a sleep, presumably at their newly rented accommodation in Milton.

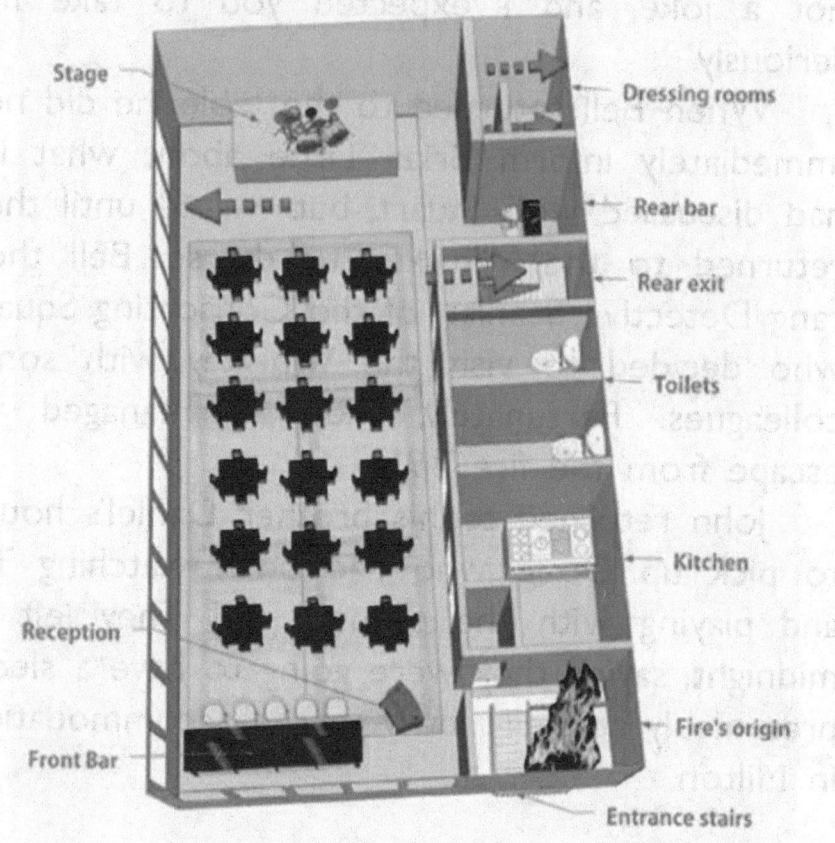

Whiskey layout. The dashed red arrows show successful escape routes

The Whiskey before the fire. Facing the rear stage

The Whiskey's northern bar

North west corner of the Whisky. Finch supposedly waited with the petrol filled drums here (as indicated by the rubbish bin)

The remains of the west side of the cabaret. Looking south to north. The rear bar and only fire extinguisher can be seen

View of the Whiskey from the north showing the Caltex service station

Rear top exit stairs showing the keg trolley Christine Corney tripped over when fleeing

The top front stairs showing the gutted entrance partition.
Escape was impossible via these stairs

The destroyed partition at the entrance to the Whiskey

Arson petrol drum in situ next to the back wall of the Whiskey entrance

Facing the north bar. The Caltex petrol station is visible throught the broken windows

Bottom rear exit steps showing the clutter

St Pauls Terrace side of the Whiskey showing the bus stop

Fire hose snaking through the Whiskey entrance

Front door and spotlights illuminating the club's entrance

Grease stains outside the lower exit rear door

Petrol 'bomb' drum under the entrance stairs to the Whiskey

The complicated Abloy lock on the lower rear exit door

Balmoral House Residential (right) where many witnesses to the fire resided

The Whiskey post fire. Modern Tiles dominates the bottom floor

The locked side gate which impeded those fleeing the blaze

The remains of the west side of the cabaret. Looking north to south. Note the airconditioners

The two drums used to masscare 15 innocents

Top to Bottom: Billy McCulkin. John Stuart's best mate – Graham Miller who John Stuart implicated in the Whiskey bombing – Lennie McPherson. John Stuart suggested he was interested in intimidating Brisbane's clubs – Mugshot of James Finch. He had been hiding in the bush – Killer John Regan offered to assasinate John Stuart.

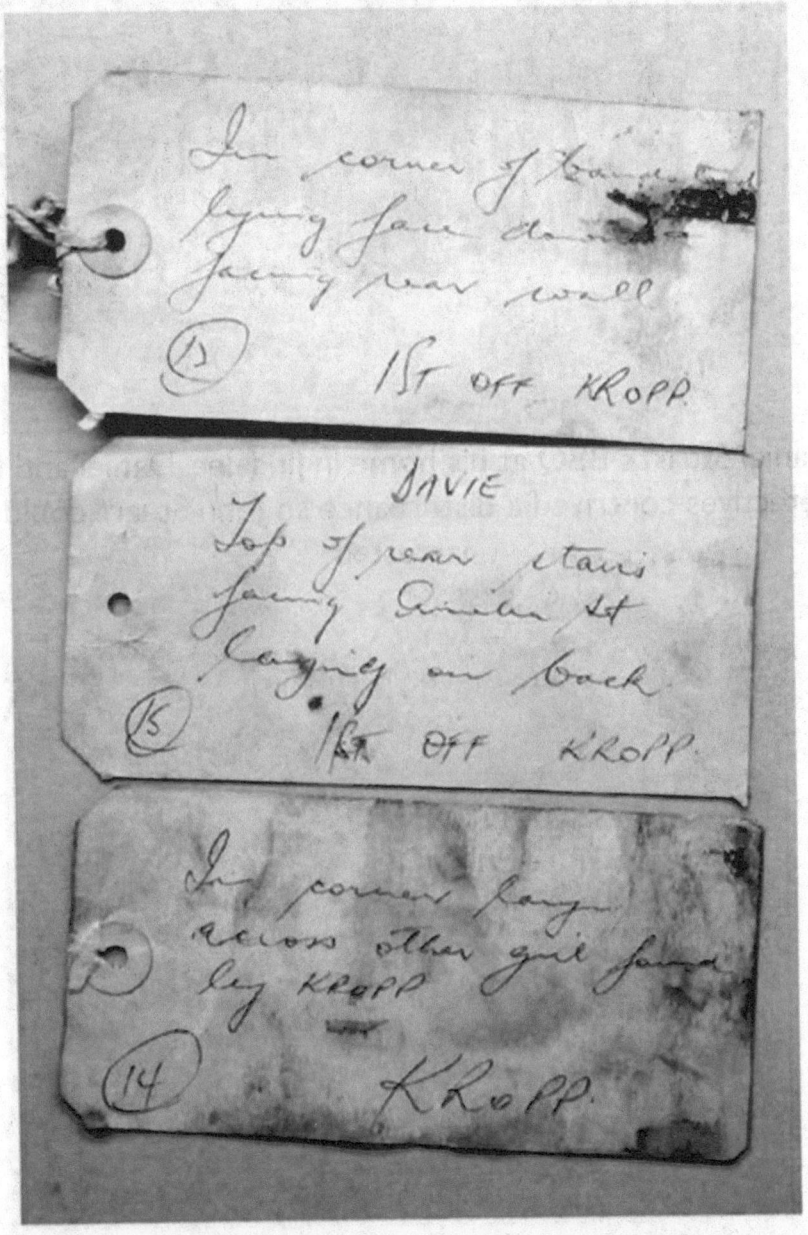

Body tags showing location of the corpse and assigned number. Note the soot stains

Daniel Stuart's BBQ at his home in Jindalee. Daniel and the detectives contrived a disturbance so John Stuart could be arrested

Daniel Stuart's residence at Jindalee where his brother John was arrested

Jindalee Shopping Complex where Finch was found by Detective Atkinson

The watch-house where Finch and Stuart were charged. Finch sat on the bench to the left

The moustached men Stuart said were in Brisbane to bomb the Whiskey

Whiskey admittance card

Birthday card sent by Finch to Stuart

13th. November 1972.

John Andrew STUART.

Stuart rang me at home yesterday and wanted to see me. I met him at Gilcrest Avenue, near the Egg Board end.
Mainly he wanted to talk about his trip to the Northern Territory. He showed me his car, a kelly green Ford Fairlane with Northern Territory plates 86 - 787. He says that   traded in her other car on this one at Darwin.
He asked if I had received his cards. I had. They are on file.
He never had anything new to say. He spoke about his life in Sydney when he first went there, how he got tied up with Ducie Duckie O'Connor how he met Lennie McPherson and how he made the mistake of trying to collect money from some clubs which McPherson was interested in. He says that he didnt find out until to late that McPherson was interested in these places.

Stuart got on to being hounded by the Police again. He claims that every time they see him in a Hotel they wantto speak to him. I told him that no doubt at the time he is with some other criminal and there is no way in the world that any Detective wont be speaking to him again. He cant give me any real instance at all where he has been hounded since he came back to Brisbane.

Detective Basil Hicks's notes of one of his many interviews with John Stuart

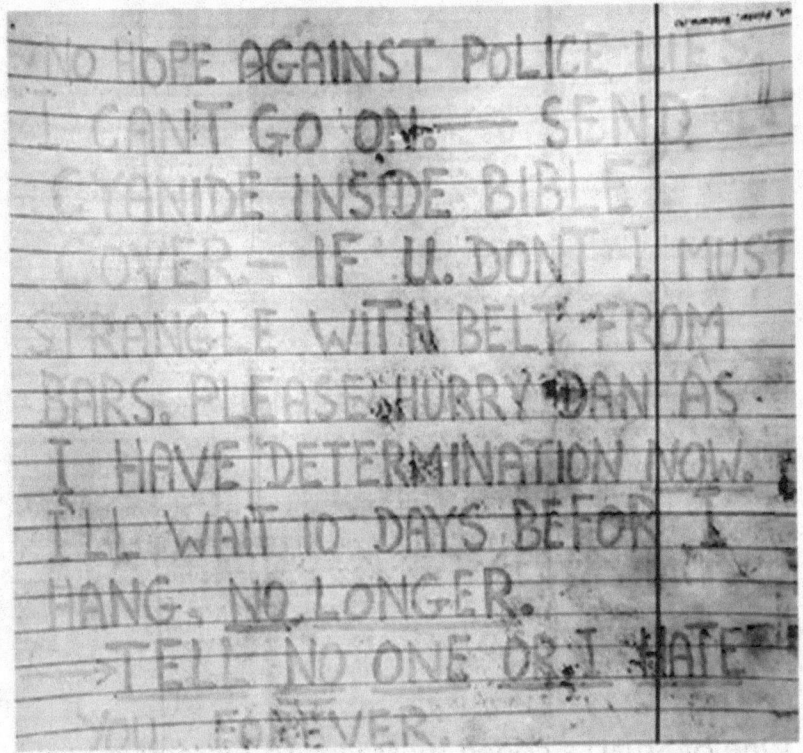
One of John Stuart's secret writings to brother Daniel

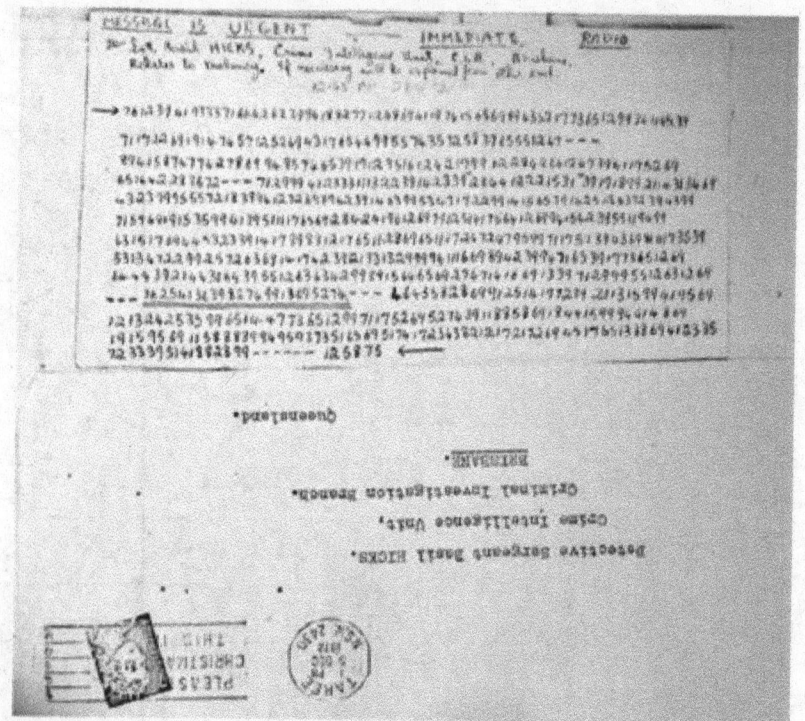

One of Stuart's coded messages to Detective Hicks

Post card from Stuart to Detective Hicks

Stuart wanted poster released hours after the massacre

30

8 March 1973

Stuart entered the Flamingo club alone at around 12.45am, walked down the stairs[1] and went to the bar, where bar attendant Robyn Hall poured him a Galliano by mistake. It cost 80 cents, and Stuart refused to accept it.[2] He said he would stick to beer, as it was cheaper, and purchased a stubbie. Stuart then talked to the doorman, Alf Quick. They discussed the fuse issues in his car, which Quick went to inspect.[3] At 1.30am, they both re-entered the club.

By 1.45am, they were sitting in the office. Quick said, 'Do you want a drink John?' Stuart assented, and Quick bought two stubbies of beer at the bar. When the beers were nearly finished, Stuart asked, 'Can I use the phone? I want to find out the time.' Quick said the phone was not working, as a part of the handset had been removed by Yasse to prevent patrons and staff making long-distance STD calls. Quick then relented, repaired the handset, dialled the number for the time and listened.[4] He later said he 'heard the recorded PMG [Postmaster-General's Department] announcer advise that the time was 2.15am.' Stuart remarked, 'That fellow on the phone is either an Englishman or a Scotchman [sic], and he sounds a bit camp to me.' They both remembered it as a cultured, well-spoken voice.

Stuart promptly stood up and walked out of the office. As he left the club, he asked Yasse for the time. Yasse's watch also showed 'quarter past two'. Stuart said his goodbyes and left.

Stuart departed the Flamingo and went straight to Bolton's office, where he left a second message:[5]

B-2.20–

I've been to 'blinkers' & everywhere looking for you-you've stood me up

J.A.

Soon after, he drove to his sister June's house.[6] He entered the unlocked house, crept to the bedroom door and whispered, 'Sis, are you awake?' June Beckman replied softly, 'Yes, but don't make a noise and wake Ron [her partner]. He has to start early.' Beckman then slipped out of bed and walked into the lounge room, gently closing the bedroom door behind her. Despite the early hour, she noted that Stuart was neat and tidy in appearance and his clothing was clean. 'What's the matter love?' she asked. 'They have done the Whiskey Au Go Go,' her sibling responded. She asked him if he was there, and he replied, 'No. But I'm worried.' 'Tell me true, love,' she implored. Saying he had never lied to her, he said, 'Somebody is sure to think I had something to do with it, but I was nowhere near the bloody place. I was at the Flamingo [Club] until quarter past two and I went down to the *Truth* office and left a note for Brian [Bolton].

'I was supposed to meet Brian [Bolton] at nine o'clock at the Hacienda in the Valley and I waited there until the pub closed at quarter past ten. Then when Brian did not turn up I went out to Danny's and stayed there until the telly finished. Then I come back into town and I wondered [sic] around looking to see if I could see Brian Bolton and ended up at the Flamingo. At about quarter past two I wandered around to the *Truth* Office to leave a note for Brian. When I came down, some bloke said to me, "Somethings happened at that club up on St Pauls Terrace." I could see smoke all over the Valley and then I come over here.'

Beckman could see his anxiety and fatigue. 'You're worried, John, arn't [sic] you?' He replied in the negative, 'Not worried but apprehensive. I will have go and see them [police] in the morning. I'll get a solicitor and go in and see them in the morning, because I have nothing to do with it.'

He declined an invitation to stay and then left; it was 3am. She did not hear of the deaths until a radio broadcast later in the morning.

At this time, Detective Senior Sergeant Robert 'Brian' Hayes (who was in charge of the Homicide Squad and this investigation), Detective Sergeant Ronald Redmond, Superintendent Don Buchanan and Detective Sergeant Thomas 'Syd' Atkinson (all CIB) arrived at the Whiskey and walked around the smouldering ruins.[7] Their shoes crunched on the debris and caused the still-warm ashes to waft in their wake. Early eyewitness reports said that grease had been smeared all over the escape route; it looked like the fiends had not only torched the joint, but also deliberately hindered egress.

At 4am, a reporter from the *Sunday Sun* arrived at Bolton's home.[8] He called out, 'The Whiskey has gone up; 15 dead and 40 injured ... come to the office with me to cover it for *The Daily Mirror* in Sydney.' When Bolton reached his desk, he saw the two notes and recognised Stuart's handwriting, but put them aside until he had completed a story for *The Daily Mirror*—it would be a multi-page scoop. Bolton then informed Superintendent Buchanan that he had the correspondence from Stuart. Buchanan instructed Howard Kay and Ted White, who had interviewed Bolton previously, to go to Bolton's office and retrieve the two notes.[9] When they arrived, Bolton repeated the sequence of Stuart's movements over the last few days. They waited in Bolton's office in case Stuart called Bolton, and men were posted at Bolton's house in case Stuart tried to contact him there.

Soon after, a special circular was released by the Office of the Commissioner of Police with a photo and description of Stuart saying he was 'urgently required in relation to the destruction by fire of the Whiskey Au Go Go Nightclub....' Commissioner Whitrod had signed the notice.[10]

At 8.30am, Commonwealth Police Superintendent Morrison told colleague Bill Humphris that in view of the morning's 'bombing' of the Whiskey, he had better get in touch with his contact and tell him that he should reveal his identity to the Queensland Police.[11] Soon after, Humphris called Bolton and said, 'Brian that was an awful thing this morning.[12] Your information was correct.' Bolton responded, 'I know it was, and I could end up with concrete shoes. Stuart wanted me to go with him last night around various clubs to inform them that he would be no part of any bombings. Like a fool, I did not keep the appointment, and look what happened. Stuart has left me a note here at my desk signed about 10 minutes after the fire started abusing me for not keeping our appointment.' Humphris told him he would have to reveal his identity to the state police. Bolton replied that they already knew about him.

Humphris revisited the CIU (he had previously been there on 27 February) to reveal the mole's identity and disclose that Stuart had left two notes at Bolton's office. He and Constable J Holloway saw Voigt, who confirmed that Bolton had already given them information via Becker. Voigt still felt that it was an insurance job.[13]

A neighbour saw Mr Trauts and Doug at the Milton flat at 9am.[14] They removed their gear and left a key at the premises, not intending to return. Their tenancy had lasted four days.

Stuart then telephoned his sister-in-law Rose. 'Have you heard the news?, she asked.[15] Stuart seemed surprised, 'What?' he replied. She mentioned the Whiskey Au Go Go and said 15 people had been killed. He was taken aback, '15 fucking killed?' he exclaimed in disbelief. Rose urged him to go to the police and see a solicitor. He said he would and told her he had nothing to do with it.

Rose was taken aback with the language, as Stuart was careful not to swear around her. After pretending to be astounded, he hung up.

At 10.15am, Stuart called Hicks, 'Have you heard the news? The fucking Whiskey went up last night. What am I going to do?'[16] When Hicks asked Stuart when he had heard about the blaze Stuart spoke quickly and excidedly, 'Just now. I just heard it. I'm coming in to see you. I got an alibi Basil. I'm lucky. I'm coming in and get it put down just what I did last night. I don't want those cunts getting at my witnesses, getting them to change their story.' Hicks assured Stuart he would await for his arrival.

The inevitable call to Bolton came through to the newspaper office at 10.30am.[17]
Stuart: What the hell has happened at the Au Go Go?

Bolton: Come on John, for Christ's sake, I didn't come down in the last shower. You know bloody well what has happened at the Au Go Go.

Stuart: I wouldn't be fucking well asking you if I did know.

Bolton: There's supposed to be 46 injured and 15 dead.

Stuart: Now you bloody well know why you should have bloody well come with me last night. What time did it happen anyhow?

Bolton: At 2.08a.m.

Stuart: Well, I've got an alibi for that time. Surely to Christ the police don't think I had anything to do with this. Now you can see what sort of a situation you've put me in by not turning up last night. Well, will you come out with me and my solicitor and go around the nightclubs so that I can tell the proprietors I had nothing to do with this.

Bolton: If you poke your head in any nightclub, you're likely to get it shot off by a trigger-happy guard. Why don't you give yourself up to the police. If you'd like to come in here—as a matter of fact there are two policemen here now—I'll make sure you're taken into their hands safely.

Stuart: Not without my solicitor. I'm not going to be verballed again. I will ring him back and ring you back and make arrangements to give myself up through the CIU.

Half an hour later, Stuart again telephoned Rose and told her he was at his solicitor's office, and as soon as the solicitor was available, he was going to the police.[18] He phoned her yet again saying he would go to the police station.

The calls kept coming. Straightaway, Stuart told Hicks he was coming in with Bolton. 'I'm not fucking coming in without a witness, Basil.[19] It's not you, it's those other cunts. What chance will I have now? They'll get at my fucking witnesses and twist them.' Hicks said Stuart could talk to Superintendent Norm Gulbransen, which he did. Stuart then said he would come in to the CIU in ten minutes, alone.

Stuart was in a tangle, trying to work out the best way to make himself available to the police. Half an hour later, at 11.30am, there was yet another call.[20]

Hicks: Hello?

Stuart: Basil I'm not coming in without a solicitor. I can't trust the cunts to give me a fair go. I'm at my solicitor's office now. I'm waiting to see him, then I'll come in with him.

Hicks: If that's the way you want it. When you see the solicitor, ask him to ring me and let me know when you're coming in.

Stuart: Right Basil. I have to do it this way to protect myself.

Hicks: Right. Ask him to ring me.

Stuart: Alright.

He also called Bolton saying he would go direct to the CIU in company with his solicitor. He asked Bolton to meet him there and rang off.

Belatedly, Stuart made a decision. Mr Weir, from the legal firm Gilshenan and Luton, and Stuart met Hicks and Detective Lewis in front of the Ansett Building. The police drove them to the CIB.

Stuart: Sorry I have to do it this way, Basil.

Hicks: Look, you are with your solicitor. You had better be guided by him now.

Stuart: Alright.

Hicks dropped them off, and then left.

CIB Detectives Hayes and Atkinson interviewed Stuart, with Detective Redmond typing.[21] The exhausting nine-and-a-half-hour interview, which started at 1.12pm and ended at 10.45pm, soon became testy, with Hayes believing that Weir was interfering with the process.

Hayes: Mr Weir, can I see you privately for a minute, please? Are you prepared to allow us to question Stuart further without interruption by you? I want you to understand that your roll

[sic] here is to advise your client and not answer for him. Up to now, you have obstructed us in our questioning. If you are not prepared to consent to those arrangements, you can leave the office.

Weir: I want to know of any allegations against my client before we continue.

Hayes: The allegations will be outlined in the Record of Interview as we progress.

Weir: I want to know now.

Hayes: You and your client will be told during the Record of Interview. I think that is fair.

Weir: That is no good to me. I want to know now.

Hayes: If you persist in this attitude, you can leave the building now. There's the front door. [He then indicated the front door of the building.]

Weir: I want to get some advice, can I use the telephone?

Weir was in fact fully entitled to ask what the allegations were.[22] As Weir sought legal advice (for 45 minutes), Hayes started questioning Stuart while he was alone.[23]

Hayes: What is your full name?

Stuart: My name is John Andrew Stuart and I wish to add that in the absence of my solicitor many questions and suggestions were put to me to which I said I will reply in full to these and give details of my movements last night [a hand-written addition by Stuart states 'when my solicitor is present.']

When Weir returned, the interview continued.

Hayes: I have been instructed to allow you to return to the interview room to continue the interview with your client. But I request that you not answer for your client. Are you agreeable to this?

Weir: Yes. I found out that I have been exceeding my authority. I didn't want to be in this, but I had to, as Pat Nolan is out of town. Anyhow, I'm sorry for hindering you. Can we continue now?

The interview continued.

Stuart gave an accurate account of the night's events. He said he had driven to his ex-brother-in-law Lyall Beckman's place, where they looked at his tail-lights, and then changed his clothing at 8pm. He then drove to the Hacienda Hotel, expecting to meet Bolton at the Siesta bar.

As Bolton had not arrived by 10pm, he proceeded to the Osborne Hotel and saw his friend Jim.[24] He then went to the *Sunday Sun* office at 10.15pm looking for Bolton. Next, he visited the Whiskey, inquiring of Bell and Bolton. Hearing that Bell was at Blinkers, Stuart parked near Chequers and went in to get directions to Blinkers. He then made his way to Blinkers and talked to Bell, who told him he didn't know where Bolton was.

He next drove to his brother Daniel's place, arriving at 11pm, and then left at midnight, making his way to the Flamingo. Stuart told them about bouncer Quick fixing the phone and dialling to check the time, which was 2.15am.

Subsequently, he went to the *Sunday Sun* office and left another note for Bolton. As he left the building, he asked a man, 'Where's the ambulance going?' The gentleman replied, 'There is a big fire up the road, or something up the road.'

Stuart then said 'casually' to a passing man, 'Where's the fire?' 'In the nightclub near the

Shamrock,' he was told. A nightclub had become an orange beacon of flame. Stuart assumed he meant the Whiskey. He then went to his sister's place. He said he left there at 3.30am, but would not tell his interrogators where he went. 'Where I went after that is private. It concerns another person, a female, who I have great respect and love for, and who I do not wish to implicate.' Thomas Atkinson then interrogated Stuart. Atkinson got straight to the crux of the matter; who was responsible for the fire at the Whiskey Au Go Go.[25]

Atkinson: Do you know the identity of the persons responsible for this crime last night?

Stuart: I am not one hundred per cent certain of the names, their last names, but I know their faces and habitats [sic] etc.

> To begin, I have to set a background that will make my explanation more understandably [sic]. I have spent many years of my life in prison. During that time I have met many criminals of every type. During these years in prison and amongst the underworld I have gained a reputation as what is known as a solid crim. Meaning I am not a squealer.

I have also been charged with assaulting police on different occasions and through that I am looked on by younger criminals as someone to be trusted. About 1965 and 1966 while on remand in Long Bay I met casually, several men who at that time looked up to me. One's name was Les. One Ross and one called Rodger the Dodger.[26] After I was sentenced to my last term of imprisonment our paths separated but we always mentioned each other to other prisoners, sending regards in and out of gaol etc., and things like that.

In November last year, I was charged with [the] break and enter of a house in Richmond in N[ew] S[outh] Wales. I was arrested at Taree and eventually sent to Parramatta Gaol. On the fourteenth [it was actually the 20th] of December 1972 I was granted $300 bail and returned to Parramatta Gaol. When I arrived back there that night someone arrived at the gaol to pay my bail.

I was very very keen to go out on bail as I was anxious to spend Christmas with my mother and family as I had not had one at home for seventeen years. The person who bailed me out was a new Australian [Koazeaha]. I had never seen him before but I do have a copy of his name, and his address. When I was released through the prison gate I met the man who had put up the money for the bail. He was waiting there in his car for me. The man who had actually come into the gaol with the money was only a front man.

Atkinson: What was the name of the man who put up the bail and who you say met you outside the gaol gates?

Stuart: The name [is] Graham James Miller, known as Louie Miller.

Atkinson: Is he also known as 'Mad Dog Miller' in the underworld?

Stuart: He is.

Atkinson: What happened after Graham James Miller met you outside the prison gates upon your release last December?

Stuart: He drove me to Mascot Airport. On the way he discussed with me quite openly if I thought there was any money to be had in the nightclub circuit in Brisbane. By that I mean [for the] purpose of intimidation and standover. I said I did not know, and didn't particularly care, but because I was so pleased to be free and to be able to go home for Christmas I more or less agreed with everything he said and kinder [sic] yes-manned him. You know.

Atkinson: When you say you kind of agreed with everything he said, did he suggest to you that you come up to Brisbane as his agent and commence this protection racket amongst the nightclubs?

Stuart: Yes, but not in so many words.

Atkinson: Did you agree to try it out or assess the position up here when he suggested this in not so many words?

Stuart: No, I did not agree, but I did not disagree either. As I said, the man had just been responsible for my freedom and I was pleased and happy with him. So I could not directly argue with him or turn him down so to speak.

Atkinson: Did you make any contacts subsequently or make any inquiries subsequently with any clubs here in Brisbane regarding the establishment of a protection racket?

Stuart: No I did not.

Atkinson: Did you speak to any employees or to any part owners of the Whiskey Au Go Go at any time after your arrival in Brisbane to suggest to them that a team of young criminals from New South Wales intended throwing hand grenades or other explosive substances into their nightclubs, unless they were paid protection money.

Stuart: Yes, I did tell them that violence was pending and I explained my full position in it as I am doing here to them [sic]. When I arrived at Mascot Airport, the Maltese who actually bailed me out was let out of the car. He walked away. I then entered the terminal, after Louie indicated to me where to go inside the terminal. I went to this spot, where I saw the three men who I previously mentioned in this statement. They said to me, explained in rather wild terms their intention to stand over clubs in Brisbane.

Atkinson: Who were these three men?

Stuart: The men I knew as 'Les', 'Ross' and 'Rodger'.

Atkinson: Can you describe these men?

Stuart: Yes. First of all, I want to say that at the time I did not give full credit to the statements that they made as they were obviously under the influence of a drug and in my years in prison I have heard many similar exaggerated stories of this nature. I wish to mention here also that nearby there was one other man, who was obviously in their company, but standing back about 15 feet just watching. I did not know this 4th man. I have never seen him before.

Hayes: Will you describe these men?

Stuart: Les, at that time, this is last November, December, when I got out. In his late twenties, he has brown hair, normal build, and was dressed rather nattily. His height would have been about a bit shorter than me, 5 feet 9 inches, as far as I can remember, because I did not take particular notice of him at the time.

Ross is a little overweight, he is about 5 feet 10 inches, roundish faced, a bit tubby, his age should be about middle or a bit later than middle twenties.

Rodger who I always called Dodger is [a] happy-go-lucky type, nonchalant in appearance and dress, about 6 feet, and lean, about middle to late twenties. They are all in about middle to late twenties. They all have moustaches, Mexican type, you know.

Hayes: Have you been in contact with these persons since that time?

Stuart: Yes.

Hayes: Will you tell me about it?

Stuart: Rodger phoned me several times after our parting at the airport. Once he told me to go to a bar at the Broadbeach Hotel one Saturday night, as he would have someone there to meet me and speak with me. By this time I began to fear that these men were genuine in their claims of violence here in Brisbane. A detective who I have known for many years, and who has always been friendly to myself and my family, Detective Basil Hicks, I told him of this pending meeting at the Broadbeach Hotel. I also discussed in detail with a man named Bobby Glover, also known as 'Bodgie Bob', that these three men had asked me to be their frontman to collect money for them after they had done damage to nightclubs...

Hayes: You have mentioned here that they wanted you to be their collect man after they had done damage to the nightclubs. In what fashion did they intend to do damage to the nightclubs?

Stuart: They did not tell me any explicit plan, but in general, they indicated to me they intended to blow them up.

Atkinson: If you had been faced with the situation of having to kill them, where did you intend contacting them immediately?

Stuart: I did not know where to contact them. They contacted me, and I could have easily sent word to Sydney on the grapevine that I wanted to see them, as we have mutual friends ... About two nights ago two of the men who were at the airport were standing on the footpath in front of the Flamingo. Alf the doorman, who is a friend of mine, said to me, 'Watch out, these two guys are from Sydney.' About the same time that he said that, I saw them myself and averted my face. It appeared to me they were either drugged or drunk.

Hayes: Which ones were these?

Stuart: The ones I knew as Les and Ross, not Rodger the Dodger. When I saw them actually in Brisbane I shit myself ... Yes, but I had no idea that this would all occur so soon...

Hayes: Did you suggest to Mr Bell that they were going to make an example of the Whiskey Au Go Go to get protection money from other clubs.

Stuart: No, I did not say specifically any club, but when we were talking it was just in general—I said they would probably make an example of the Whiskey or somewhere, because we were at the Whiskey.

Atkinson: Do you know Billy McCulkin, the man about whom I had spoken?

Stuart: Yes, I know Billy well.

Atkinson: Have you ever in his company mentioned this proposed protection racket to any of the nightclub proprietors or employees in Brisbane?

Stuart: Yes, I have.

Atkinson: To which clubs?

Stuart: None specifically if I recall, but just in general. When I left Miller's car and the Maltese guy got out and walked off, I walked into the terminal and saw three of them standing around the corner against the wall. At the time my immediate impression was they had greatly aged since I had last saw [sic] them, as I always remembered them as young boys. It had been seven years since I had seen them personally. My immediate impression was they seem detached and disorientated. Their speech was slurred slightly and I realised it [sic] once, that they were under the influence of a drug ... They immediately went into their plans for this Brisbane protection racket ... They were speaking too loud and everything.

When asked if they were going to charge him, Detective Hayes told solicitor Weir, 'I have my suspicions but I feel at this stage that I haven't sufficient evidence to charge him with anything.'

When the interview concluded, Stuart read it aloud and signed it. After the interrogation, Weir left the office with Stuart shortly after 10.45pm. Detective Constable Patrick Glancy and Detective Lewis shadowed the suspect. It was obvious to them that he thought he was being tailed, as he walked in circles, making an effort to lose them, which he did.[27] Later in the morning, the police released another alert saying Stuart should be kept under constant surveillance.[28]

Stuart immediately rang his ex-brother-in-law Lyall Beckman and told him of his cross-examination, saying he was 'well and truly gruelled [sic]. They are going to pin the nightclub fire on me but I'm innocent.'[29] At 11.32pm, he entered Chequers and asked for John Bell.[30]

He then went to his brother Daniel's house at 1.30am in a taxi.[31] John told Daniel and Rose about the interview. He also told them that when he caught up with Doug at Milton and revealed the aftermath of the fire, that there were 15 dead, 'he got a surprise and although he was eating grapes at the time he took off like a rocket.' He said Doug was frightened of the police and did not want to become involved in the fire.

Early reports suggested the arsonists had deliberately greased the exit route to hinder the patrons' escape. All the people who escaped through the rear exit encountered the oil from the bottom of the rear stairs to the high gate. By the end of the day, the police had an explanation for the lubricant. However, they never made this widely known, and this famous myth surrounding the holocaust has endured to this day.

The explanation was mundane. Chalmers had tasked Kopittke with cleaning out the kitchen at 9.30pm, as it was not a busy night for food orders.[32] Subsequently, at 1am he told Kopittke to take two five-gallon drums (one containing used cooking oil and the other empty) downstairs. The drums had open tops and a handle, similar to a bucket.

Kopittke took the two pails down the fire escape, placed the empty drum in the industrial waste bin outside the building and deposited the full drum of oil inside the fire escape against the wall. There were already two other full drums of oil next to the wall that had been there for at least a week. One or more of these drums had simply been knocked over in the stampede. The oil was then trampled towards and over the back gate.

31

9 to 10 March 1973

Stuart stayed overnight at his brother's house. In the morning, he said to the children, Danny and Jennifer, 'Wasn't that a terrible thing I did, killing those 15 people.' He then laughed, and said, 'Only thing is, it wasn't me.' Rating the comment a minus ten on the amusement scale, Rose said, 'Don't talk like that, John, to the children.'[1]

Rose: Why are you ringing up all these people, that's the *Sunday Sun* and Mr Hicks, and letting them know where you are because your name is in *The Australian* that you informed, and whoever done it will come looking for you and the kids and I will suffer. Look what happened to Billy Phillips's wife [maimed by a parcel bomb]. Why don't you tell the police who it is if you know who they are?

Stuart: I know what I'm doing. I know who they are who had done it, and don't you think I would tell you if you were in danger?

Rose: Why did you go to the police with the story about the bombings if you were not prepared to go through with it?

Stuart: If I didn't tell them about the bombing, I would be charged with murder today.

Rose: That's a terrible thing that's happened, why protect these people?

Stuart: They're well and truly out of the country by now, no one will get them.

Stuart got the papers and read them—there was only one story.

Before he left, Stuart gave Rose a list of phone numbers and said that if Doug made contact, to give Doug the list, but just in case the phone was bugged, she should say they were 'casket [lottery] ticket numbers'. He later gave Rose more numbers to add to the list, asking on each occasion whether Doug had been in touch.

At 8.45am on Friday, the day after the fire, Detective Senior Constable Raward had a conversation with Inspector Bardwell (both from the Scientific Section, Commissioner's Office) and then proceeded to the Little-owned Kangaroo Motel. Ken and Brian Little waited in the switchboard room. Raward went to one of the motel units, where he positioned himself next to a telephone extension. At 9.10am, Raward heard the phone ring and on lifting the receiver heard the voice of Brian Little talking to a male person.[2] Establishing he was talking to Brian Little, Stuart said, 'I suppose you know that I was released last night. I had nothing to do with the deaths of those people. The police after they interviewed me let me off at the corner of Queen and George Streets, where I waited for a cab. As I said, I had nothing to do with it and I have told you that I would never put my hand out for money.' Little directly asked who did it. The response, 'I don't know, but I would say that they are not going to be captured and they would be out of the country by now. Do you think that if I knew I would be alive today? I am not going armed because I have got no chance. If they want me they can get me anyway. After years in gaol I am worried about my family and my only concern is for my family. My family always know where I am going because I am afraid that someone may harm them to find where I am.' Stuart could not reveal the culprits as he was not going to put his life in jeopardy, 'I am not interested in anything but the life of my family. They can kill me, it's only my family I am worried about.' Little confronted him on his foreknowledge of the fire. Stuart countered, 'You know me, I always exaggerate things. I told you I thought there might be violence, but I did not think they would go this far. These events must have been caused by drugheads. From my experience with police, I am always cautious, as the police always load me, but I did not care because I told the truth and they checked my story. I was lucky that night that the police could check my story as I almost did not go to the Flamingo and was going to leave before 2am and drive home in my car, but luckily I stayed at the club at the time of the fire. I don't want to go anywhere where I can't account for my movements these days. I have got to see a bloke from the CIU at 12 o'clock.' Little asked for a meeting yet Stuart deferred and suggested Little was taping the call. All he could add was that two or three people for responsible for the disaster.

Stuart then had a four-hour interview with Bolton at his offices wherein he divulged that he had told the police the names of the three plotters.[3] Stuart further said that before he went to gaol for 'allegedly' shooting Steele in 1965, he had met the three young criminal culprits. They were middle to late twenties, all drugheads and psychopathic killers with Mexican-style moustaches.[4] He would not give

Bolton their names. 'I have never dogged on anyone in my life and I would rather rot in my grave than do that.' As payment for the story, the *Sunday Sun* gave $200 to Stuart's solicitor. Bolton's reward; another exclusive story to publish.[5]

Coroner Birch was quick to swing into action, and commenced an inquest into the deaths. It continued on the 10th and 12th, but was adjourned under Section 42 of The Coroners Act with the arrest of Stuart on the 11th.[6]

The police announced that they were offering a $50,000 reward, the highest ever, for information in relation to 'the country's worst crime'.[7] They were scrambling to defend themselves against accusations that they had been forewarned. In parliament, Police Minister Hodges answered with an emphatic 'No' when asked whether the police had been tipped off prior to the fire.[8] Commissioner Whitrod denied that he had been warned that the Whiskey would be bombed. Accepting Bolton's statement as accurate, they were both lying.

Hicks interviewed Stuart at 12.55pm.[9]
Stuart: Hello Basil.

Stuart: So what am I going to fucking do? Now fair dinkum. What am I going to do?

Hicks: Do you want to come in here?

Stuart: ... I said no, I can't come in without a solicitor. They are my explicit instructions, instructions from my solicitor.

Hicks: Will that include me too?

Stuart: Just let me say what I was gonna say. It doesn't include you. The reason I'm telling you this is 'cause I trust you. The reason, if I go in there without a solicitor, that sort of ah, shows that I do that. They wouldn't hesitate to blow me to pieces. They wouldn't hesitate to load me up and verbal me and Christ knows what, now if I go in there without a solicitor. It shows that I voluntarily do that. Do you understand what I mean?

Hicks: Right.

Stuart: And if I went in there to see you, I couldn't deny that I did. It shows that I do go voluntarily and they could pluck me off the street or anywhere and take me in, and I couldn't say they took me in because they could use as a reference the fact that I do go in there voluntarily.

Hicks: Well you have been in here voluntarily. You put me in the position where it's suggested now that you told me that the Whiskey Au Go Go was going to be blown up and even the night when it was going to be done.

Stuart: Basil. I have mentioned to no one, to nobody, that you said to me, right does the eighth mean anything to you. Like. I have mentioned it to no one. Remember you said to me does the eighth mean anything and I said I don't know. I said I don't even know what date I went to court. It meant nothing to me. Why did you ask me that?

Hicks: Somebody who claimed to know you had said something important was going to happen on the eighth.

Stuart: I never told anyone that. Whoever told you that is a liar.

Hicks: Yes.

Stuart: OK now. So all I'm gonna go along with and what I have tried to get the *Mirror* to go along with. Gees they're gonna give it a shocking cook tomorrow. I've seen some of the stories.

Hicks: Whose [sic] going to get the cook?

Stuart: Not youse. Not youse. Not the CIU. It's Whitrod and Hodges. They're gonna give them a shocking cook. They're out to get them. They wanna bring them undone.

Hicks: Why Whitrod and Hodges?

Stuart: It's political Basil. It's not just Bolton, it's the paper.

Hicks: That's nice.

Stuart: Wait on. Now listen. I have said all along, and I made doubly accurate certain that they did not write me up in the papers. I've read everything that's gone in it and they did not write me up as anybody who would tell the police anything.

Hicks: Well.

Stuart: Listen. Wait a minute Basil. On TV on Wednesday night I'm going to stand up and thump the table when I say I have never spoken to the police about this matter. Never.

Hicks: What matter?

Stuart: About these pending bloody bombings.

Hicks: Well you told me about it.

Stuart: Well I'm gonna tell a lie on TV in front of everybody.

Hicks: Don't tell any lies because I won't be telling any lies.

Stuart: You want me to? Hey Basil. You want me to get up and say, yeah I've been lagging people to the police?

Hicks: No. You haven't been lagging anyone. It's been just the opposite. You've always had half a story. You go right round things and tell me nothing. Everything you've said about the clubs has always been so vague. You've had so many different stories I don't know what to believe.

Stuart: Listen. Wait a minute. If you hadda kept a tape recording of what I said and went back over it you would have found the key to everything. If you could have only got on to what I was saying.

Hicks: The key. All you could ever say was that you didn't want to lag anybody.

Stuart: That's right.

Hicks: Even on Wednesday the best you could say was to go and see Alf at the Flamingo.

Stuart: That'll do me fine. I have never lagged anybody. Right.

Hicks: That's the truth. You could never give me names or anything definite. Do you remember the last time I saw you at Kangaroo Point [Stuart's sister's house]? I showed you the photo of Jimmy Driscoll. You said you'd never seen him before.

Stuart: Oh. I've seen him in gaol and things. He's been in can [gaol] or something. Listen. They don't want Driscoll over the bombing. He's got nothing to do with it. Driscoll is involved in the toe cutters. That's the reason they want him. They think he's tied up with the toe cutters thing. They're using this bomb outrage to get public sympathy so they'll lag him and Regan's up here because he was involved in the toe cutters thing and he knows if Driscoll goes down things'll probably point to him. That's why he's here. To solve the problem.

Hicks: The information is that you're tied up with Driscoll, that you've been associating with him for months.

Stuart: Ha, ha, ha.

Hicks: Well have you?

Stuart: He's been in gaol. I've probably seen him. I haven't been tied up with him or anybody else. The only ones I have anything to do with is Phillips and Billy McCulkin. I haven't seen Billy for months [even though he was looking for him on 6 March when he met Bolton].

Hicks: Yes.

Stuart: Well anyway, I rung you up. I rung you up this morning when you wer'nt [sic] there to tell you that Regan was here. That shows I'm doing the right thing by you.

Hicks: I won't be telling any lies for you or anybody else.

Stuart: Will you tell them that I never ever lagged anyone to you?

Hicks: Well who said you did?

Stuart: No one said I did but I haven't, but Whitrod, they're saying in the paper that Whitrod said I was lagging cunts to the police. Did you read *The Australian* this morning?

Hicks: No.

Stuart: Well they said that I was lagging cunts to the police too. Well they retracted it. They retracted it and said it wasn't Stuart, he had nothing to do with it because I was in custody at the time and the man's name was John Ryan, the private detective. They retracted it. The heading just read John Stuart, then it went on to tell how they made an error in their story.

Hicks: It was a convenient error. The suggestion is still there that you told the police that the Whiskey was going to go up on Wednesday night.

Stuart: That's shit. I didn't tell anyone that. That's Bolton talking. I'll tell you now it was Bolton who had to put the retraction in *The Australian* because I told him, I said—I'll tell you nothing. I'll discuss nothing with you until there's a promise of the retraction of that in the, in tomorrow's paper, which is so. Which happened.

Hicks: Yes.

Stuart: See, anyway I rung you up this morning. You didn't know Regan was here until I told you.

Hicks: Good. That's something definite you told me for a change.

Stuart: Alright. Listen. I'll hang up Basil. This phone box is cooking me to death. I'll ring you again at say three o'clock, four o'clock.

Hicks: Make it four o'clock.

Stuart: Right oh. See you.

Hicks: OK.

When Lyall Beckman arrived home at 3pm, Stuart was there. Stuart left at 5.30pm, but returned a few minutes later to get the typed interview, which he had forgotten.[10] He drew Lyall's attention to the time when he left.

Stuart immediately rang Hicks.[11]

Hicks: Is that you John?

Stuart: Yes. It's me.

Hicks: I couldn't pick your voice, at first.

Stuart: No. But what I do is this. I've been standing by the phone. When I get a certain call, I tell them to ring a certain number of times first, then stop, hang up and then ring again.

Hicks: Well I didn't know that.

Stuart: Have you seen the record of interview?

Hicks: Yes.

Stuart: Yesterday. Or last night actually, I found something in my letter box. Did Bolton mention it to you?

Hicks: I haven't spoken to Bolton. From what you've said his story is just a conspiracy to destroy some police. I've never had anything to do with him.

Stuart: Yes. That's true. It is just a conspiracy. I don't fucking trust him neither. But he's my insurance.

Hicks: How do you know it's true, that it's a conspiracy unless you're part of it?

Stuart: Well, Basil. Ah. That's what they keep saying to me. They're a Labor publication and they keep saying they're after Whitrod and Hodges. They're not after you. They're after fucking Whitrod and Hodges' heads and tomorrow they're gonna get them.

Hicks: Go on.

Stuart: One thing that's happened has put the shits up me. Nobody knows this but I will tell you. I found this note in the letterbox last night. It's in code. I can't crack it. It's a gaol code. I think it was one of the ones we used in Boggo Road. I've got a copy of it but I gave the thing itself to Bolton. Part of the deal I made with them was that they would publish the code and also a statement I made regarding my innocence.

Hicks: What for. What did you give Bolton the letter for?

Stuart: I want any crims who can read the code to come forward and tell me what's it about. Someone must think I know it but I don't.

Hicks: Can you tell me any more than you have about the fire?

Stuart: No I can't.

Hicks: You can't or you won't?

Stuart: I can't Basil. What's going to happen to me? What am I going to do? I'll tell you this, to be quite honest, I didn't do it, as everybody knows. I wasn't there. I didn't see the people do it, so I can't say this or that, can I? How can I be pinned to it? I wasn't there.

Hicks: Everybody is saying that you have been giving all the details, what's going to happen and where.

Stuart: Well they're lying. They just want to squeeze the hell out of me. If I had been giving you anything precise you would have had to arrest them. I didn't know the details. I said to Ron Richards, the manager of the *Sun* this morning—if I can get this code cracked it won't be me who shelves the people. I'll tell Bolton their names and he can shelf them. I'm afraid that once I tell someone it's going to all come out as though I've been talking.

Hicks: If you're so afraid why can't you just come out with their names? If you're genuine as you say and if they exist, why can't you just come out and name them yourself?

Stuart: Basil. I haven't told you anything have I? I knew you were keeping friendly with me to find out.

Hicks: I didn't chase you.

Stuart: No. I was ringing you up and going to you all the time. I think if I can get to the bottom of this code thing I've got it. It'll be in the paper tomorrow.

Hicks: You talk about this code thing. From what you say yourself you know who set the fire. What has this code got to do with it? You either know or you don't. The names you gave in the record of interview, you never mentioned those to me.

Stuart: No.

Hicks: Why?

Stuart: Basil. Tell me this but. The Commissioner, he must know that I wasn't the one who set the bombs?

Hicks: I don't know what he thinks.

Stuart: What about the others? What do they think?

Hicks: I wouldn't know what they think either. You're the one whose [sic] supposed to have all the answers. You're the one whose [sic] had all the information. If these people exist, why can't you just come out and name them. I can't see why you have to go into all this business about having a message decoded and then have them named through Bolton.

Stuart: Because I can't lag people to the police. That's why I wanted it to get back to them that I'm loud mouthed around the town and make them drop off me. Didn't you read that part in the bloody statement?

Hicks: That was before the fire you wanted them to drop off. You've given them three names in the statement. If they're right, how can it make any difference what else you say?

Stuart: I still say I hoped it would get back to them and they'd drop off me. It wouldn't be enough to make them come up here gunnin' for me but it'd be enough to say, oh, Stuart's a bit of a risk.

Hicks: What difference would it make now but if the names you've given them are right? Do you know there's a fifty-thousand-dollar reward already been offered?

Stuart: What, on the Whiskey?

Hicks: Yes.

Stuart: Fifty grand?

Hicks: Yes.

Stuart: Basil. Let me tell you this. They'll never catch me. I'll tell you now.

Hicks: How can they catch you if you were at the Flamingo?

Stuart: They'll never catch the others because if they're smart enough they're gonna stay in hiding for months. If ever anyone pulls them up they're gonna blow them down because they know they're never gonna see daylight again.

Hicks: You were lucky you were at the bloody Flamingo that night. If you'd left twenty minutes earlier you'd have had some explaining to do.

Stuart: Yeah. You can say that again. I nearly left about three times. The only reason I stayed, I'll tell you, the only reason I stayed there Basil is because I didn't want to insult Alf [Quick]. He was telling me all about how he was in New Guinea and all the rest of it you know. He just hung on and I said—Oh yeah, I'll go—and then he bought me a bloody midi, a stubby or whatever you call 'em and I sat there drinking that.

Hicks: Yes. You're lucky alright.

Stuart: Look Basil. I gotta go. I'll only get in touch with you again if something really important comes up.

Hicks: Right.

Stuart: See you Basil.

Hicks: Right oh.

Stuart: All the best.

Hicks: Right oh.

Before lunchtime, Attilio Bianchetti, a partner in a banana plantation, and his wife Nanette, as well as his sister-in-law Rose Stuart and her mother, Mrs Conlon, went to Daniel Stuart's place at 12 Mankinna Street, Jindalee.[12] A barbeque started mid-afternoon.[13] At 6pm, while the children were playing with a tape recorder, a stranger to the Bianchettis turned up.

He was unshaven, with three to four days' worth of facial growth, had dirty clothes, an overnight bag and carried one shoe, which had the heel cut out. The man said he had a sore foot. He had called Daniel just prior to his arrival.[14] An agitated Daniel Stuart introduced him as Doug, telling the extended family that Doug would be leaving in a couple of days. He then led his mystery guest into the house.

An hour later, Doug emerged clean and shaven.[15] Doug handed the children a packet of biscuits and three quarter-pound blocks of chocolate. Sipping a half glass of wine, he sat apart and remained aloof. John Stuart then entered through the front door.[16] Daniel then introduced his brother John to Nanette.

John, dressed in a yellow T-shirt, carried a knife sheath in the hip pocket of his long trousers. John drank a Coke, and then he and Doug went into the sewing room, just past the main bedroom, and shut the door.

When Rose knocked, John said, 'What do you want?' The door was ajar, and she saw Doug sitting on the floor in the corner of the room reading the transcript of Stuart's police interview. She heard John say to Doug, 'So you can see we have got nothing to worry about.' She would later retrieve the interview, left on the floor, and read it herself.[17]

Shortly after, Bianchetti walked outside to the BBQ. Daniel had a conversation with him and they drove off to get some more drinks. On the way, Daniel Stuart told him that he had to place a phone call, 'as he was sure that John and Doug were the two who did the job at the Whiskey nightclub.' He told Bianchetti they were both murderers, and it was a hard thing to give his brother up, but he had to do it.

They went to a nearby shop and bought some Coke. Daniel made a call after checking the police numbers in the telephone book. Bianchetti overheard Daniel Stuart say, 'I know where the two murderers from the Whiskey Au Go Go are.'[18] Daniel had initially attempted to contact the State Premier at 3.30pm and tell him his brother was a killer, but had only been able to converse with his daughter and secretary.[19] This time, he got the message through.

When they returned to the house, John Stuart announced that he and Doug were going to the 'flicks' (pictures). While Mrs Conlon and Nanette were washing up, Daniel Stuart started abusing both his wife Rose and Attilio Bianchetti. By now, Bianchetti had Daniel in a headlock in the kitchen.[20] Mrs Conlon told John, 'Don't touch my Attilio, John.' John replied, 'I'm not going to hurt anybody.' According to Daniel, he yelled to John, 'Get him, John. Grab him.'[21] John tried to pull Daniel and Bianchetti apart. Bianchetti pushed John aside, saying, 'This argument is between Daniel and me, keep out of it.' The women and children, having fled the melee, were screaming in the courtyard.

At this point, Detectives Hayes, Atkinson, Evan Griffiths, Redmond, Glancy, and Colin Sullivan gatecrashed the festivities. One of them heard one of the females yell, 'I am getting out of here, it's going to be a bloodbath.'[22] Atkinson to Glancy: Watch out Pat, He's got a knife.[23] [John Stuart moved from the kitchen to the lounge brandishing a knife]

John Stuart to Glancy: I'll slit your guts open, get out of my way. [The knife was two feet from Glancy's body]

Glancy to Stuart: Drop that knife. Drop it right now—don't come any closer or I'll shoot you. [Glancy produced a revolver and pointed it at John Stuart's head]

John Stuart: All right but he was in my way, I was only trying to get away.

Atkinson: When you pointed that knife at Detective Glancy, what were your intentions?

John Stuart: I'd have cut his guts out if it meant getting away.

The detectives hauled John Stuart away for threatening them with a knife. Daniel Stuart, who was drunk, was still 'raining abuse on everyone'. Meanwhile, Doug had disappeared. Rose later told Lyall Beckman that John Stuart had pulled out the knife to frighten Bianchetti, not to threaten the police.[24]

The party arrest was a complete set-up, a contrived scene orchestrated between Daniel Stuart and the detectives. An entry in Atkinson's police notebook gave this away; for 10 March 1973, he wrote, 'Walk straight in and *Dan Stuart will put on a show to throw suspicion off himself.* Search behind the Bar-B-Q and also search in a children's toy horse in the lounge for something....'[25] Daniel Stuart had set up his brother's arrest and attempted to disguise the fact. For the detectives, it was important to have a reason to hold Stuart in custody, as he had the Flamingo club alibi. The attempted wounding charge was a means to that end.

After being escorted to the watch-house, Stuart attempted to swallow an object retrieved from his shoe, but was foiled.[26]

Stuart: Alright, alright, now you know that I use the name of Arthur Mason and that I've been overcharged ninety-nine cents on a money order I sent to my best mate over in England. There's nothing wrong in that.

Atkinson: That's alright, but why did you try to swallow this envelope and letter addressed to you as Mason?

Stuart: I didn't want anyone to know that I was using the name of Mason, only Lyall Beckman and the close members of the family know.

Atkinson: Who is your mate over in England that you sent the money order to?

Stuart: Doug Jones. He's my best mate. He lives at 11 Castleton House, Pier Street in London.

He's left there now and I don't know where he is.

Atkinson: A man named Doug ran away tonight from your brother's place at Jindalee when we arrived. Is he the Doug Jones who lived over in London and whom you sent the money order to?

Stuart: Nobody ran away from Dan's place tonight. I don't know what you're talking about.

Atkinson: I intend keeping this envelope and letter to make further inquiries.

Stuart: You can do what you like. I've told you that I'm Arthur Mason. Check with Lyall Beckman if you like, but you'll get nothing out of me about Doug Jones.

The envelope was addressed to 'Mr A Mason, 234 Beams Road, Zillmere, Q. 4034', the address of Stuart's ex-brother-in-law.[27]

Doug reappeared at Daniel Stuart's house after the police had left.[28] He came into the kitchen and walked directly into the sewing room. He then opened the door to the backyard and left again. Daniel went looking for him. In turn, Bianchetti walked down the road looking for

Daniel, and found him in a nearby side street. They returned to the house, and Daniel rang the police again, asking them to remove everyone from the house. The family described Daniel as nervous and abusive.

Attilio Bianchetti searched behind the BBQ in the courtyard and found a parcel wrapped in plastic under some pieces of pine. He knew it contained a black rifle. After unloading the .243 weapon, he took it for safekeeping (it was given to Detective Peter Slatter the next day) and with the family in tow, left for Mrs Conlon's residence at Acadia Ridge. John had obtained the gun on his trip to Darwin.

Daniel then walked to the Jindalee golf course, where he said he fell asleep until 3am. It was all too much; he could not get over the terrible thing his brother and Doug had done.[29] On waking, he walked home. On the way, a concerned couple pulled up in their car and asked if he was OK. When he got home, the house was empty—his wife, his kids, the police and the visitors had all gone.

32

11 March 1973

After collecting their paper, imbibing their coffee and sitting back to enjoy breakfast, readers were confronted by a headline that took up most of the *Sunday Sun*'s front page: HEADS MUST ROLL! Bolton blasted, 'Some people in the Queensland Police Force appear very naive, deceitful or just plain stupid.'[1] A furious Bolton said the Minister and Commissioner persisted in saying there had been no warnings. He wrote that the disaster could have been prevented 'but for the arrogance of some of the policemen.' Bolton had warned them personally. It was true; he had told every conceivable senior police officer in both the State and Commonwealth forces and some politicians that he was genuinely concerned that the Whiskey was a target. This included the Commissioner himself.

Doug woke Daniel in his bed. 'Danny, wake up, what's happened?' Daniel replied, 'I am destroyed. My wife and kids have gone, I am ruined as far as living here, I've just had it. I don't care anymore about nothing.'[2]

Doug: Dan, I am soaking wet. Did the police take my clothes?

Daniel: Yes, they took your bag.

Doug: Can I have some clothes?

Daniel: Help yourself.

Doug: Can I lay down on the floor and sleep?

Daniel: Yes there's a bed in there (indicating another room).

Doug: No, the floor will be all right.

Daniel: Yes, do whatever you like. I don't care.

At 9.15am, a group of detectives returned to the Jindalee residence.[3] Doug looked out the window and said, 'The jacks are here. What will I do?' He then darted out through the back door before Daniel could respond.

Detectives Hayes and Morey went to the rear of the house, with Atkinson and Paul Delanus (from Melbourne) covering the front. Within a few minutes, Hayes emerged and shouted that a man dressed in a long-sleeved mauve shirt, white trousers and white shoes had fled from the rear of the home. Hayes and Morey gave ponderous chase.

Daniel Stuart told Detective Delanus where Doug's passport was located.[4] Oddly, although the police had been told where they could find it by Daniel the night before, Atkinson had failed in his search. He said, 'I felt the stuffed horse on the outside, but did not search inside the zipper because it was tightly packed....'[5] Delanus had more success this time. He retrieved the passport and gave it to Atkinson. It was passport number C159691 in the name of James Richard Finch (aka Fred Harris), born 20 December 1944, England.[6] Doug (aka Terry) Jones's real name has been revealed.

John had asked Daniel to hide Finch's passport when he arrived in Brisbane. He said it was imperative that no one knew that Finch was in the country and he did not want his passport on him so he could be identified. Daniel had put it in a wardrobe drawer amongst other papers.[7] On the Wednesday evening, just before the fire, Finch asked Daniel if he had hidden it. Daniel said he had, but John was not happy with the location. Daniel then deposited it in a more secure site, the stuffed horse, sealed with a zipper.

Detective Atkinson phoned Superintendent Buchanan with Finch's description and asked for a general broadcast over the police radio network.[8] He then drove to the Jindalee shopping complex, where he noticed a man dressed in a mauve-coloured long-sleeved shirt, long white slacks, white shoes, no hat and carrying newspapers under one of his arms walking across the shopping mall. It matched Hayes' description of Finch. The suspect disappeared behind the shops, so Atkinson stopped the police car, jumped out and ran through the shopping complex, eventually confronting the suspect.

Atkinson: I am Detective Sergeant Atkinson. I belong to the police. Are you James Richard Finch?

Finch: No. Doug Jones. I only arrived in this country from England ten days ago.

Atkinson: I recognise you from your photograph in your passport, which you left in the home of Daniel Stuart around there in Mankinna Street when you decamped from there this morning when I arrived with other police officers. I know that your name is James Richard Finch. Why did you run away from Dan Stuart's home last night and again this morning when police arrived?

Finch: Wouldn't you if you'd done what I've done? Kill me now, go on kill me. I deserve it.

Atkinson: Come on, calm down, calm down. Sergeant Hayes and other detectives are waiting for me up at Dan Stuart's home, and he wants to ask you some questions about the fire at the Whiskey Au Go Go Nightclub and the deaths of fifteen persons last Thursday morning. Before you start making any further statements, I warn you that you are not obliged to do so or answer any questions, as anything you say will be recorded by me and may be later given in evidence. Do you understand your position?

Finch: Shoot me. Put me out of my misery, I should have run and made you shoot me. Go on, shoot me.

Atkinson: Don't get upset. Come and jump into my car over there and we'll go back to Dan Stuart's home in Mankinna Street where the other police are and then we'll go into the CIB in the city and talk about the matter.

Finch: I saw you get Johnny Stuart last night from his brother's place. Johnny paid my way out from England a fortnight ago and he got me mixed up with that fire and now there are fifteen dead. I nearly died when he told me last Thursday morning. We didn't mean to kill those fifteen. You must believe me. I've been hiding in the bush over there since. [He then indicated the bush area on the eastern side of the Jindalee bypass Highway]. The ants nearly ate me and the kangaroos attacked me and I hurt my heel on a stump getting away from them.

Atkinson: What have you been living on in the bush?

Finch: Tinned stuff, there's still some in my gear at Johnny's brother's place.

Atkinson: Come on and we'll go to Johnny's brother's place.

As they walked towards the police car, Finch could not stop talking.[9]
Finch: God, why did you have to catch me? It would be easier for me to die. Go on, shoot me. Blow my brains out.

Atkinson: Come on, jump into the car. We'll talk about it later.

33

King of the Cockroaches

James Richard Finch was born on 20 December 1944 at Bow, East London, one of five children. There was a sister Joan and brothers John, David and Anthony.[1] John and David worked in the dock area.[2]

His father had been previously married with six children, but had deserted them to be with Finch's mother. The father did not work for the last six years of his life, was an alcoholic and on National Assistance—he bludged an existence. The family were poor, Finch attending one party wearing an overcoat to cover the patches in his clothes and the gumboots on his feet.[3]

Finch senior was extremely violent with an explosive temper. He thrashed his spouse, threatening her with an axe and striking her with a bottle. He also beat up his sons, including Jim. The uncle who lived in his mother's house was also a brutal man who filled James Finch's head with 'horrors and lurid stories'. There are eerie parallels with John Stuart's upbringing.[4]

After his father's death, Finch showed anxieties and proved 'behaviourally difficult', falling asleep at school and in cinemas, where he frequently went—it was here he retreated into a fantasy world.

Finch did not like his mother. John showed Daniel a part of a letter he had received from 'Doug'. It wailed that there was 'a woman in the house as I write, I can hear that stupid mongrel bitch humming a hymn. It makes me sick. I want to go out and strangle her....' James lamented that she never showed him any love, never hugged him.[5]

Although arson was not known to be a big part of Stuart's repertoire, the opposite applied to Finch. Even as a six-year-old, the brown-haired, blue-eyed kid was an addicted firebug. An official report shows Finch's admittance to a child guidance clinic in 1951 for treatment for 'aggressive fantasies with a history of incendiarism'.

The authorities placed James in a special tutorial class, to no avail. On 18 November 1952, his mother, having lost control of the seven-year-old, had her son admitted to Dr Barnardo's at the request of a children's care officer of the London County Council. The home was at Barkingside, Essex, and there were 10 other boys living there. His mother promised she would pick him up in a week, but did not return. The matron in charge terrified him, and he wet his bed as a result.

Selected for migration to Australia, he arrived on 13 October 1954, aged nine, on the ship *Otranto* and was placed in the Barnardo's home at Picton. In Finch's first Picton report, we learn of the 'tough little boy who resents any show of affection or sympathy.' He was, however, a good cricketer and boxer.

His first job, in 1959 when he was in his early teens, as a sports salesman and racquet re-stringer at Mick Simmons Sports in Haymarket, was brief. He constantly changed jobs for 18 months, and then drifted towards crime. He accumulated the paraphernalia of a tough-guy criminal and sported the requisite tattoos—a parrot on a flowering branch on his right bicep, a peacock on a branch on his left bicep and a knife scar on his left forearm. Like many criminals, he started his career with misdemeanours, progressing to those carrying a prison sentence.

In October 1960, he earned a £10 fine for damaging a railway sign with rifle fire. In May 1961, there were three charges of car theft and six of breaking, entering and stealing. He was committed to Mt Penang Training institution for boys. In June 1962, at the Liverpool Central Court, he faced three charges of stealing, including a car valued at £700. It was off to another institution.

Finch was sent to the Institution for Boys, Tamworth, housed in a former gaol. Notorious gangster Neddy Smith states in his autobiography that 'Tamworth boys home was a real concentration camp. They treated the young boys like animals, with daily bashings and starvation ... I've been to the notorious Grafton Gaol twice for a period of more than four years all told: I was systematically bashed daily, flogged into unconsciousness several times but, believe me, that was nothing compared with the treatment I got at Tamworth.'[6] Many inmates from here became notorious criminals. These institutions had no rehabilitatory function; they were there to punish.

From 1962, the convictions accumulated in Queensland and New South Wales; vagrancy, stealing, escape from lawful custody and break and enter.[7]

These were not high-end crimes; however, this changed on 20 December 1965, at Barrack Motors, 25 Paddington Road, Sydney.[8] At 11am, three men stood on the left side of the petrol station. Initially, they talked, but then a scuffle developed, with two of the men 'grabbing each other by the coat'. One man then stepped back and fired a gun.

A bullet struck the shoulder of his rival, who clutched at his wound. The wounded man then ran off, yelling to a colleague, 'Get the gun out of the car!' The man who had fired the shot ran up a laneway, and as he ran, turned and fired another round. This one hit a pump attendant, Mr Cappa, in his right leg, near the groin.

Although criminal Stuart Regan would never testify, Finch was sentenced to 14 years gaol for shooting him.[9] Finch had two trials. The first was aborted when the name of John Andrew Stuart came up, but he was convicted in the second trial. After the shooting, Finch gave Stuart the gun. The police found it in Stuart's possession and initially charged him with the offence.[10]

At the time of the shooting, the pair had been teaming up for break-and-enter engagements, taking assorted items of interest. There was an association between the two for at least seven years before the Whiskey fire.[11] Finch also knocked around with Duckie O'Connor, Stuart's gang-rape mate.[12]

While in prison, Finch maintained contact with Stuart, exchanging postcards. 'Make Love Not War—Hippie Birthday. To John from Jim F' was one of these.[13] They were also next to each other in the cells at Grafton.[14]

Dr Barnardo's Australia manager wrote to Stuart in gaol in 1970 asking if he could 'offer information which could be of assistance to Jimmy Finch whose plea for release under the Queen's

Prerogative of Mercy is still with the Minister of Justice.'[15] Stuart would later say he had been helpful in getting Finch paroled.

Stuart persuaded his mother to regularly write to Finch, as he was an orphan festering in Australian gaols. She told John, 'I must write an impersonal and friendly letter to Jim Finch. He is on my conscious [sic] and his family is far away ... but for my foolish son he would be free.'[16] She was referring to the Regan case.

Stuart described Finch as his other half, and Finch did likewise, although just prior to Stuart's release in 1972, he and Jim briefly fell out.[17] At the Whiskey trial, Finch would say, 'We are as close as two men can get, we have suffered together.'[18] Stuart told some people, including Des Sturgess, Director of Public Prosecutions, that *he*, not Finch, had shot Regan, and there was an obligation on his behalf.[19] Contradicting this, in 1988, Finch admitted that he was responsible for the shooting. However, with both of them being professional liars, it is difficult to know the truth of their assertions.

Finch loved football, and supported Tottenham.[20] At Parramatta, he was the gaol referee, and also played himself when he wasn't refereeing.[21] He earned a release from this gaol in 1972, six years and eight months into his sentence; on 28 September 1972.[22] The authorities deported the troublemaker to the United Kingdom on the same day. On his return to England, he often played soccer with children in Millwall Park, and was 'very popular with young children'.[23]

After Finch returned to England, he corresponded with Stuart. Letters to a 'Mr A Mason' arrived regularly at Stuart's then brother-in-law Lyall Beckman's place. Beckman said that 'He used to refer to this friend as his better half or his other half. I recall that on one occasion John showed me a document, which was a parole or probation paper, which he received from this friend with whom he had served time in gaol in New South Wales. John explained to me that this friend had done time for John in relation to some offence [Regan] and that John had done something to get him paroled [sic, letter to Dr Barnardo's] and that the sending of this paper to John by this friend meant that the debt was then paid in full and that each was not indebted to the other.'[24]

34

Confession of Sins

After Finch's capture, Atkinson conveyed Finch back to Daniel's residence. Sydney detective Morey squeezed his large frame into the back seat next to Finch. Morey inquired, 'Don't you remember me from Sydney a few years ago?' Finch sputtered a confession. 'Johnny was pinched last night, has he told them about us and the fire? I wish that copper had shot me back there.'[1] Morey admitted that he did not bother to tell anyone about this 'confession' until 10 hours later.

They drove to the CIB office in Upper Roma Street. Upon their arrival, Finch was placed in an interview room. He folded his arms onto the table, slumped his head into his arms and commenced crying.[2] Atkinson said to him, 'I'll leave you alone for a while.' Shortly afterwards, the detectives returned to the interview room.[3]

Hayes: Come on Jim, compose yourself, we wish to talk to you.

Finch then sprang to his feet, grabbed the front of Atkinson's shirt and with his right fist clenched, commenced screaming.[4]

Finch: Kill me. Kill me. Why don't you kill me you bastard? I'm not frightened, kill me. Why did you have to catch me?

Atkinson: Calm down, come on calm down, calm yourself, take your hands off me.

Finch: I copped twelve fucking years for Johnny Stuart over shooting that Regan bastard in Sydney. So I'm not copping it again for him this time. Kill me, go on kill me.

    Hayes and Atkinson broke Finch's hold by pushing him back against the table and the wall. After letting go of Atkinson, Finch punched the wall several times. He then kicked the wall and table and stood like a slobbering hyena, eyes staring, teeth bared and saliva cascading from his mouth.

    He kept screaming, 'Why don't you kill me, go on kill me you bastard, kill me.' At this stage, Finch's face was close to Atkinson's, and spittle sprayed the left side of Atkinson's face. Finch instantly composed himself, reached forward with his right hand and wiped his saliva from Atkinson's face. He immediately reverted to his hysteria and recommenced shrieking, 'Kill me, kill me, I deserve it!' At this stage, CIB

Superintendent Buchanan came to the doorway of the interview room and addressed Finch.[5]

Buchanan: Calm yourself, son, do you want a doctor?

Finch: Fuck the doctor and you too. Who are you, you big cunt? Have you come to look at a mass murderer too?

Buchanan: I am Superintendent Buchanan. I'm in charge here. Calm yourself and stop that language. You can be heard out on the street, and there are other people in this building.

Finch: Fuck them too.

Atkinson: Calm yourself, Jim, calm down now and sit down there. Come on, calm down, calm down.

Finch stood staring for a few moments, still with his teeth bared and his eyes glazed, staring into the abyss. He then sat on the seat beside the table, folded his arms in front of him, placed his head onto his arms and recommenced bawling. Hayes then said to Finch, 'Jim, we have to make other inquiries. Take it easy for a while. Settle down and we'll talk to you later on.'

At 5.25pm, Detectives Hayes and Atkinson walked into the homicide room, where they saw Finch standing in the company of Detective Sergeants Griffiths and Morey and Detective Senior Constable Roger Rogerson. The latter two had flown in from Sydney so that the Brisbane detectives could liaise with their New South Wales colleagues and establish the truth of any southern criminal involvement.[6]

Hayes then said to Finch, 'I now intend interviewing you, and in view of what I have been told about what you have told Detective Sergeant Atkinson and Detective Slatter, I must warn you that you are not obliged to make any statements or answer any questions, as anything you say will be recorded on the typewriter in a record of our interview and may be later used in evidence.[7] Do you understand?' Finch replied, 'Yes.' Hayes said, 'Do you feel well enough now to be interviewed?' 'Yes, I'm alright,' came the defeated reply.

Detective Sergeant Redmond gathered his typewriter and seated himself at a table, and Hayes then commenced the interview in the homicide room at the rear of the second floor of the CIB premises at 366 Upper Roma Street.[8] The room was sparsely furnished, with long tables around the walls and a locker and a small table in the centre of the room. Six detectives took part in the interrogation; Atkinson, Griffiths, Morey, Hayes, Rogerson and Redmond.[9] It started at 5.45pm, and would prove to be the most crucial piece of evidence at the forthcoming trial, sealing Finch and Stuart's fate.[10]

Hayes: We have already introduced ourselves. I intend to interview you in the form of a record of interview, when all my questions to you will be recorded on the typewriter in the record of interview in your presence and your replies, if any, will be recorded also in this record of interview. Do you understand?

Finch: Yes, that's OK by me.

Hayes: What is your full name?

Finch: James Richard Finch.

Hayes: What is your place and date of birth?

Finch: I was born in London on the 20th of December, 1944. I cam[e] out to Australia first when I was a boy. I was educated in N[ew] S[outh] Wales.

Hayes: Where do you reside?

Finch: I have no residence here.

Hayes: How long have you been in Brisbane?

Finch: I went back to England last September and John Stuart wrote to me with a proposition and you will see from my passport that I arrived back here on the 27th of February—a couple of weeks ago.

Hayes: Is this your passport? [Hayes shows him Passport No. C159691]

Finch: Yes.

Hayes: You will see the endorsements in it.[Hayes looks at the passport, indicates page 6, and says, 'The Department of Immigration stamp shows that you arrived on the 27th of February, 1973, at Brisbane Airport.']

Finch: Stuart arranged my flight out.

Hayes: Why did Stuart arrange your flight to Brisbane?

Finch: John and I have been friends for years.

Hayes: We are investigating the fire at the Whiskey Au Go Go Cabaret, Fortitude Valley, Brisbane, at about 2.10 am on Thursday, the 8th of this month, when fifteen persons, namely, Colin William Folster, Darcy Thomas Day, William David Nolan, Ernest John Peters, Desmond John Peters and Carol Ann Green ... [at this point he is cut off by Finch].

Finch: Don't name them all, I've been sick ever since it happened. It has worried me. I dry reached [sic] for a day after I heard and then took to the bush until yesterday.

Hayes: Are you admitting that you were involved in the deaths of these people?

Finch: Yes, unfortunately. It was not intended to be this way. It was intended to intimidate them so as Johnny could get what he wanted. Hayes: From what you have told me, you are involved in the arson and deaths of the people I have told you about earlier and named, and in addition Wendy Leone [Leanne] Drew, Brian William Watson, Peter Marcus [Morcus], Fay Ellen Will, Desma Selma Carrol [Carroll], Jennifer Denise Davie, Leslie Gordon Palethorpe, David John Westren and Paul Zoller.

I intend to ask you further questions in connection with these matters but I warn you that you are not obliged to answer any questions or make any statements, as anything you say will be recorded in this record of interview and may be used in evidence. Do you understand that?

Finch: Yes, I know all about that.

Hayes: What do you mean by saying Johnny could get what he wanted?

Finch: Well, I will tell you the story, but before I do, I will tell you it is all Johnny's idea, all I was to do was to start a bit of a fire downstairs with some petrol and frighten them.

Hayes: Are you prepared to tell us the full story in your own words?

Finch: As you know, I went back to England last year and Johnny was writing to me and he told me about this business of trying to stand over the nightclubs in Brisbane to try and get money out of them. He told me he couldn't break into it because the people running it wouldn't play ball and he wanted to know if I would come out. I agreed to because I would do anything for him. We exchanged several letters and frankly, I was glad to get out of the place because things weren't too happy at home.

Hayes: What was the agreement between you and John Andrew Stuart?

Finch: He told me that he would pay my fare out; he wanted me out here real bad to give the clubs a real shake up. When I arrived, Johnny met me at the airport and told me his plans. He told me that he was having trouble breaking into the protection racket with the clubs and it just needed a good scare to bring them to the party. He had ideas of getting a protection racket going and kept telling me how McPherson had it tied up in Sydney and was known as Mr Big and there were big openings here in Brisbane for him.

Hayes: Did he tell you how he hoped to succeed with this plan?

Finch: Yes. He told me he had studied psychology and that he had worked out a plan to fool you coppers and set himself up with a perfect alibi. I was to be kept in smoke and nobody was to know that I was here and all I had to do was start a couple of fires and then he would move in and start collecting and I was to get back out of the country. He told me how he had been setting himself up for months with an alibi by making out to police and some reporter that some toughs from Sydney was [sic] pressuring him to act as their agent but that he had pretended to everyone that he didn't want to become involved in it.

Hayes: Do you know if Johnny Stuart is in any way connected with Leonard Arthur McPherson of Sydney?

Finch: No. He just wanted to be like him and be the Mr Big of Brisbane.

Hayes: What did you expect to get out of John's protection plans?

Finch: It was unlimited, Johnny told me and that he would look after me and I just wanted to see him set up and he was going to take care of me.

Hayes: Are you prepared to tell me of your movements on the night of the 7th of March, 1973, and the early hours of the following morning?

Finch: Johnny and I had discussed a plan and he told me that he would have to have a good alibi because he would be the first one suspected as he had been talking about this around Brisbane to the nightclub people for some time. We were out at Johnny's brother's place early in the night and he told me to stay there and he went off about half past eight to get his alibi going. He was going to see some reported [sic] (Bolton). He had been building up to this all the week. He told me that he would pick me up later.

Hayes: What time did John meet you?

Finch: About 11 o'clock. His brother was helping him fix the lights of his car and we left about midnight.

Hayes: Did John give his brother any explanation as to where he was going at that time?

Finch: He just said we were going to where we were dug in to sleep [Milton].

Hayes: What did you do after leaving Johnny's brother's place?

Finch: We drove in towards town and on the way Johnny pulled up in the bush and picked up two empty drums, he told me he planted them there. Before we got to town, Johnny drove into a side street and there were some cars parked there and we took a drum each and a piece of tubing—Johnny filled his first from a car parked in the street and then I put my drum under the tank and as I was filling mine a dog barked and we decided to give it away. We put the two drums of petrol into the back of Johnny's station wagon.[11]

Hayes: Did you fill both of the drums?

Finch: Johnny's was fairly full, but mine was only about half full when the dogs started barking.

Hayes: What did you do after getting the petrol?

Finch: Johnny dropped me off close to one o'clock with the two drums just past the club—there was no one around, and I put the petrol drums in the dark at the side of the club. Johnny drove off.

Hayes: What did you do then?

Finch: I walked around and had a look at some of the shops.

Hayes: What arrangements were there for the lighting of the fire?

Finch: Well it was like this—Johnny said he had been at the club a few times and there would only be a handful of people there at about 2 o'clock and that they would soon get out the fire escape. Oh God, why didn't those people get out, why did they stay there?

Hayes: What were the time arrangements for the ignition of the fire?

Finch: Johnny said around about 2 o'clock I was to take off the caps of the drums and roll them into the entrance and then light a full packet of folder matches—you know the ones, like you get at the hotel and clubs and all.

Hayes: Where did you get the folder matches from?

Finch: Johnny gave them to me. They were from some club or hotel. I can't remember which.

Hayes: Well what did you actually do?

Finch: I returned to near the Whiskey Nightclub just after 2 o'clock and I waited until there was no one about and I rolled the tins with the caps off into the entrance and I threw the lighted packet of matches on to the petrol and I ran.

Hayes: Where did you go after you ran away from the club?

Finch: Johnny had arranged a place for me to go, I got cab [sic] to the place. I caught it about half a mile away. I'm not going to rell [sic] you where I went, I don't want to involve any person.

Hayes: When did you first learn about the number of persons killed as a result of the fire at the Whiskey Au Go Go nightclub?

Finch: Johnny told me in the morning and I bloody near shit myself and I went through [ran off]. I stayed in the bush for a couple of days and last night I went to Johnny's brother's place. I was sick with worry all the time and it makes me sick to think about it now.

Hayes: Are you prepared to accompany me to the Whiskey Au Go Go premises, Amelia St, Valley, and indicate to me where you placed the drums? You are not obliged to do so unless you wish to do so.

Finch: No. I don't want to go back near the place.

Hayes: Will you look at this photograph. You need not comment as the previous warning still applies. [Hayes shows a photograph of the entrance to and the building of the Whiskey Au Go Go nightclub to Finch].

Finch: [Looking at photograph] That's the place.

Hayes: By the way, what name did you use here?

Finch: Doug Jones.

Hayes: Are you prepared to read this record of interview over aloud and sign it if it is a correct record of our conversations? You are not obliged to sign it unless you wish to do so.

Finch: Gentlemen, I want you to understand my position. I have given you my side of the events, but I have never signed anything. That is always the code that I have followed in the past and that is my desire in this case.[12]

Hayes: By the way do you wish to add anything further?

Finch: No. Only that I am sorry now about the dead people.

Hayes: Do you wisk [sic] to read the record of interview taken from John Andrew Stuart?

Finch: No. I have already read it. I should have known that we had no chance of getting away with it, even though Johnny said he had the perfect alibi.

Hayes: Now, are you prepared to sign this record of interview, the same warning still applies?

Finch: No, I told you before, I don't sign anything.

Redmond removed the statement from his typewriter at 8.15pm—Atkinson, Morey, Redmond, Griffiths, Rogerson and Hayes all initialled it.[13] Hayes then said to Finch, 'I am arresting you on a charge of arson and fifteen charges of murder.'

Finch, who was handcuffed, and the posse of detectives left for the city watch-house in two cars. Five minutes later, Sergeant Leslie McDonnell admitted them.[14] Finch sat on a bench in the watch-house charge room.

Hayes handed the watch-house keeper, Sergeant Colin McDonald, the relevant charge documents. Hayes, Morey and Atkinson then went to Stuart's cell in the company of Constable Samuel Sheehan.[15] They removed Stuart and took him to a watch-house interview room.[16] While doing so, Stuart asked Hayes, 'Is my solicitor here?' Hayes replied, 'No.' They then entered the interview room, where Hayes questioned Stuart.

Hayes: I intend to tell you certain things. I warn you that you are not obliged to make any statements or answer any questions, as anything you say will be recorded by Detective Sergeant Atkinson in his notebook in your presence and may be later given in evidence. Do you understand?

Stuart: Yes.

Hayes: Do you want your solicitor to be present?

Stuart: No, what have you found out?

Hayes: Today, James Richard Finch was located and he admitted that he was imported by you from England about ten days ago for the purpose of terrorising the nightclubs to further your plans of extortion. He has given us a Record of Interview and has admitted that at your instigation, he set fire to the Whiskey Au Go Go on the 8th of this month. Do you want to read it?

At the same time, Hayes gave Stuart a copy of Finch's Record of Interview. Stuart then hit his forehead with his open hand.
Stuart: No, I don't. I told the bastard to go through [disappear] as soon as we knew fifteen were dead. Now he's brought me undone. I went to a lot of trouble to set it up. We didn't mean to kill anyone.

He again slapped his forehead.
Stuart: I didn't light it, he did.

Hayes: Do you wish to sign these notes? You are not obliged to.

Stuart: No, I don't.

Hayes: I'm arresting you on a charge of arson and fifteen charges of murder.

Stuart stood staring blankly for a moment and made no reply. The detectives then moved him to the charge room section, where Finch remained seated on the bench. Stuart said to Finch, 'Did you tell them everything about the fire?' Finch replied, 'Yes.' Simultaneously, Finch, whose handcuffs had been removed, handed Stuart a copy of his statement. Stuart took the record of interview. Finch implored, 'I didn't sign it, fifteen dead, fifteen dead!' Stuart glanced through the pages of Finch's interview.[17] Stuart then announced, 'You were certainly loose mouthed about it. Why didn't you keep quiet?' A deflated Finch looked up at Stuart and did not reply.

Hayes commenced reading the charges to Stuart and Finch.[18] As each charge was read out, Stuart called out, 'I plead Not Guilty to that and you're the same, Jim.' When his charges were read, Finch would add, 'Not guilty too.' Stuart and Finch repeated the reply for each charge of murder. When Hayes had finished, Stuart said to Finch, 'You needn't have told them I gave you the matches, Jim.' Finch agreed. 'Well, Johnny, you did, but we'll have to try to beat these, Johnny.'

Finch and Stuart were led away by the watch-house staff, with Stuart calling out loudly, 'Don't let them print you, Jim,' to which Finch responded, 'No, no one will print me, Johnny.' When placed in padded cell No.5, Finch struggled violently.[19]

35

12 March 1973

On 12 March, a Monday morning, the owner of Mr Trauts' flat saw the key in the door.[1] She entered the room, and was mystified to discover that it had been abandoned. There was one empty Coca-Cola bottle on the table, and a water bottle and a pineapple in the fridge. The tenants had fled without notice.

Meanwhile, Mr Trauts and his companion had a date at No.1 Magistrate's Court.[2] In the corridor leading to the court room, Stuart yelled, 'Don't let them take you to court Jimmy, don't let them take you to court. You won't get me into any court.' With the assistance of six burly detectives, Stuart was pushed and dragged into the court room.[3]

Detective Glancy stood on a dock seat and held Stuart in a headlock, while another detective locked his left arm and two held his right arm.[4] Stuart continued bellowing, 'I've got nothing to do with this. The police told us they had to arrest someone.' As they read the charges, Finch quipped, 'I never done that or any of them.'

The two appeared for twenty minutes, charged with 15 counts of murder and arson.

Stuart faced the additional charge of possessing a knife with intent to wound. During the proceedings, Finch asked the presiding stipendiary magistrate, Mr Haupt, if he could say something, but did not wait for a reply before howling, 'I am not guilty to all these charges. Last night as I was being brought into the watch-house, police put a record of interview in my pocket and said "cop that". I made no admissions. I was beaten up by the police a couple of times yesterday. I am innocent.'[5]

In the summary of facts, Atkinson had written, 'Nothing can be said in this incorrigible criminal's [Stuart] favour.'[6] The evidence was overwhelming, and the accused were ordered to the next step in the judicial process, a committal hearing.

Two days later, John sent two letters to his brother Daniel.[7] On the reverse side, there were secret messages written in invisible ink.

WE ARE INNOCENT. JIM WAS GOING TO COPS WHEN WE CAME BACK. HEARING YOUR ROW, THEY SAY I ATTACK COP WITH KNIFE THERE AND ADMIT TO BOMB AT CIB. YOU MUST HELP NOW OR HANG MYSELF. AM SINKING FAST—YOU ROSE + DANNY [SON] MUST MAKE A STAT DEC TO WEIR NOW THAT JIM SLEPT ALL WED

NITE ON YOUR COUCH + LEFT FOR FLAT AFTER LYAL RANG. AS IS TRUTH EARLIER STATEMENTS BECOS I TELL U TO AVOID INVOLVEMENT BUT IS NOW TOO BIG + CONSCIENCE.

The second message read:

NO HOPE AGAINST POLICE LIES. I CANT GO ON.—SEND CYANIDE INSIDE BIBLE COVER—IF U DONT I MUST STRANGLE WITH BELT FROM BARS. PLEASE HURRY DAN AS I HAVE DETERMINATION NOW. I'LL WAIT 10 DAYS BEFOR I HANG. NO LONGER. TELL NO ONE OR I HATE YOU FOREVER. REMEMBER WE WERE INNOCENT.

Daniel heated the letters over a hotplate to read the concealed writing.[8] John had told Daniel he would hate him forever if he told anyone about this communiqué, but his plea was ignored. Daniel called the detectives and they picked up the letters.[9] Over the next two months, detectives picked up more of John's correspondence to Daniel and also took possession of four of his letters to his sister June.[10]

Elements of his family had turned on him, and he knew it. John wrote to June on 25 March 1973, saying, 'I won't go into the rhapsodies of the depth of my concern, misery, utter dejection and bitterness—to say nothing of my innocence—of my plight, as it would take too many volumes....'

He had recently been visited by his mother, who had told him of the attitudes taken by his own family towards him in his greatest moment of need. 'If I am to be left for dead by you all now, (at a time when I need you all, heart and soul) I am offering you salve for your conscience in the years ahead when you think back on these days....'

He asked June to contact Daniel and see if he had received the letters. John also asked Daniel to come and see him.[11] He never did.

Stuart had not finished his secret epistles. On 30 March, Detective Redmond received a tip from Rose Stuart that there were coded messages in a telephone booth in St Pauls Terrace.[12] Redmond, in plain clothes, approached the nominated booths, but had to wait, first for one booth and then the other to be vacated, before entering.

It took a while to find them, but there they were. Under the ledge of the second booth was a small 'peanut-sized' capsule of six cigarette papers stuffed into a plastic bag tied up with a thread of black cotton and sealed with chewing gum. It would be sensationally decoded by

Stuart's brother Daniel at the forthcoming full trial:

> BEGIN HERE. BOTH JIM AND ME ARE INNOCENT. INNOCENT. YOU KNOW THE ANIMALS AR LYING. WHENN WE LEFT YOR PLACE SAT NITE WE WERE ON WAY TO GET LAWYER AND GIVE COPS STATEMENT OF ALL JIMS MOVEMENTS BUT WE WENT BACK TO YOUR PLACE INVESTIGATING ROW. THAT BUGGERED US. THATS FACT DAN NOT LIES. NOW TO TRY TO AROUSE YOU IN OUR FAVOUR...

The rambling message was completely contradictory. Firstly it said that Finch had slept at the Milton flat on the night of the fire: 'WHEN WE LEFT YOUR PLACE THAT WED NITE EYE TOOK JIM BAK ... JIM WAS AT FLAT IN BED' but it also stated that he stayed at Daniel's: 'YOU ROSY AND DANNY MUST MAKE STATUATORY DECLARATNS TOO WEIR—NOW NOW—THAT JIM DIDNT LEEVE WITH ME WED NITE BUT SLEPT ALL THAT NITE ON YOUR COUCH THEN LEFT FOR FLAT AFTER LYAL PHONEDD HE WAS ON COUCH ASLEEP WHEN YOU GOT UP AT DAWN....'[13] This latter comment matched his secret message sent earlier in March.

The cigarette scroll also avowed that Stuart went to find Bolton and got stuck at the Flamingo (luckily) and that they verballed Jim. In truth, they were getting jobs on an oil rig and slaving their guts out to get their fares. Finch would later maintain he was in Brisbane because he and Stuart were planning to work in the Bass Strait oil fields. Finch had to avoid the police because he was breaching his parole conditions; that is, a return to Australia was disallowed.[14] Reiterating the threat of his previous dispatches, he would commit suicide if Daniel did not help. He signed it, 'Yor [sic] Kidney'.

While Stuart protested via his cryptic and paradoxical messages, Finch remonstrated (according to the *Sun* on 1 April 1973) by going on a hunger strike.[15] He sent a letter to the Boggo Road Gaol superintendent to say he had not eaten since March 20. There was talk of him being force-fed.

Stuart kept up the writing campaign. He had penned desperate letters before other trials, but these were different, directed to his family. One, dated 16 April to sister June, implored, 'I am not guilty of this one June, that's for sure. If my family (Dan included) are not too yellow to get up and tell the truth and give evidence on my behalf I will be found not guilty.' He might have done a lot of things in his life, but that did not include going around burning down buildings full of people. Why would he extort money from a club that he knew was in the hands of a receiver? Her brother was no longer on some 'shit pot bust', but something that concerned his life. Admitting that he had never been more 'down-and-out' in his life, he made a promise to the family: 'If justice is done and I'm found not guilty, I guarantee this; whoever has stuck to me I will never, never forget. Not ever. They will have a backstop ally, mentor and guardian forever. Love John XXXX.'[16]

He wrote to Daniel on the same day, the most fawning letter he would ever write to a family member. 'I don't know what's wrong with you—There are lots of things I could say to you, speaking down, but I refrain', he started the entreaty. He asked to see Dan in person, as his life hung in the balance.

He was not guilty of the charges, and Dan must know that. What if their positions were reversed? Yes, John would help him, always. When free, John always gave Dan what he needed, even his girl once. He had also backed him up over the Steen stabbing.

'Don't just ignore me please. If you do, in the years ahead you will have to question yourself,' John pleaded. The supplication ended thus: 'You are still my brother; my own flesh and blood. If you let me down now when all I am asking for is the facts, then you are in a sad, sad way Danny. I've spent enough of my life in gaol. I've had 13 months' freedom since April 1956. And all I'm asking for now is the truth from you. That's all.' He signed it, 'Your brother John. PS Regardless, that kidney is still there for you.'[17]

On 9 May 1973, Brian Little was approached at Chequers by an intermediary and threatened. The man told him that Billy McCulkin was 'not very happy' about his best mate Stuart being charged over the Whiskey fire and that he had been asked to send him the message that 'they' were going to get square with Little for putting Stuart where he was now. The messenger also said that Johnny Bell, Ken Little, Frank Longhurst and the Littles were responsible for having Stuart charged, even though he was innocent. Little was told that hitman Paddles Anderson would be coming into the club 'to have a chat' and John Bell would be knocked off by toe cutter Linus O'Driscoll, who was in town. On the same night, Billy McCulkin and two others arrived at the club. More intimidation occurred, along with an attempt to extort money, although not directly involving McCulkin.[18]

The starvation method was unsuccessful, so Finch tried another mode. On 28 May 1973, he arrived in casualty at 7.30am with a partial amputation of the little finger on his right hand.[19] Doctors sutured the wound and preserved the severed digit in a jar.[20] The reports varied; he'd either bitten it off or it had been amputated using a foot stabiliser from a mop bucket.[21] He had also swallowed several pieces of antenna. The first X-ray did not reveal anything, but a second showed some metallic objects in his stomach.[22]

It would prove to be a busy day; their committal hearing was due to start within hours. However, Finch's situation resulted in a deferment. A committal is a preliminary hearing in the local court before the charge is heard in a higher court. The magistrate decides whether the prosecution has enough evidence for the case to be committed for trial. When they were put in the cells immediately outside the courtroom after Finch's health-related adjournment, Stuart gloated to Finch, 'Plan one successful.' Finch replied, 'We could stretch it out for two years.'[23]

On 12 June, at Holland Park Magistrates Court, number one courtroom, the committal proceedings finally commenced.[24] A van containing Stuart and Finch passed through a huge steel cage under the courts. A guard slammed the heavy gate shut before the accused were unloaded and handcuffed to police guards.

Finch appeared in the court smartly dressed in a fawn sports coat and mauve trousers, while Stuart wore a dark suit. Counsel asked for the removal of the handcuffs. Magistrate Haupt compromised, allowing one hand to be freed.

Detective Hayes took the stand first. This prompted Stuart to leap to his feet and shout, 'This is where the lying begins!' There was a procession of 80 witnesses; the police, survivors and Brian Bolton. The Stuart family featured for the prosecution. John could feel the family's antipathy like a tidal wave, one that would drown him.

As Daniel entered the room to give evidence, he looked at everyone but his sibling, and was nervous while reading the oath. When he quoted John, 'If I could get $100 a week from each club I'd be right,' the accused could not contain himself. With tears in his eyes, John screeched, 'Dan you're lying. You're lying now for the reward. It mattered when we were kids, didn't it?' An adjournment was called, and in the stunned silence, a shaken Daniel left the witness stand. Again, the evidence was overwhelming; with Finch and Stuart's confessions and the damning testimony from Stuart's brother, the two were ordered to face a Supreme Court trial.[25]

After they were committed to stand trial on 26 June 1973, there were more threats to Brian Little, this time in the form of a letter.[26]

to the three basteds [sic]

you have hurt a lot of people in Brisbane and elsewhere, if you are left to live you will keep on hurting them, you have already helped to convict two of our mates through lies through yourselves and the cops, there has been 15 killeds [sic] before the case comes up again, altogether the toll will rise to 19 because you, little, and your bloody brother and bell and a certain cop will be put to sleep, dead witnesses don't talk, you were warned before the case started, we did the slashings to your clothes at your motel, we did mean to cut you up, also we thought you would take the warning but you didn't, your killings will be a warning to other people conducted [sic] with the case to keep out of it and also to the jury, we are telling you this now so you can run like rats as you are being watched every day, in fact one of us spoke to your brother on frid nite [sic], we know where you all live and maybe we may visit you one by one, we hope your last few weeks will be a memorable one, don't think we are cheap punks, we are not, we mean everything we have said as you will find out very soon.

36

The Trial

On 10 September 1973, the trial commenced at Brisbane's modern Supreme Court building. Described as the 'most sensational murder trial in Australian legal history', 'the crime of the century' and the 'most horrifying crime in Australian history,' it attracted nationwide media coverage. The court indicted the two on a charge of having murdered Jennifer Denise Davie. A twelve-person, all-male jury was sworn in.[1]

Similar to the committal hearing, the start of the trial had been delayed. On 20 August, Stuart told the Government Medical Officer that he had swallowed some pieces of metal.[2] An X-ray revealed that they could never pass naturally. The device consisted of two pieces of wire, each five centimetres long, with the ends sharpened to needlepoints. Stuart had 'ingeniously' placed the metal pieces in parallel and bound the ends with sticky tape, with a rubber band around the middle. His stomach juices would eventually destroy the adhesive coating on the sticky tape, allowing the rubber tensioned wires to spring apart to form a lethal cross.

He had swallowed wire previously, and had multiple scars on his stomach from what the police described as suicide attempts.[3] He would do this on two more occasions during the main trial, requiring a laparotomy each time.

The two accused appeared in court with both hands handcuffed to a heavy leather belt strapped tightly around their midriff. The handcuffs were chained to a heavy iron bar beneath their seat. The judge ordered that a towel be wrapped around the chains to stop them clanking.[4]

Eight policemen were seated around the dock, with two checking who entered into the room and two more doing the same at the entrance to the public gallery.

The Crown Prosecutor, Mr Lloyd Martin, QC, then proceeded to outline the case against the two accused, which took a marathon nine hours. There were three essential elements of Stuart's plan, he said.

The first was for Stuart to intimidate the clubs by telling them that southern criminals were going to blow up a club and extort protection money from them. The second was to liaise with Bolton and Hicks and keep them informed, thereby setting up an alibi. 'How could someone suspect a person who was informing the police?' Martin asked rhetorically. The third was to import someone to Brisbane who the police did not know. 'That, of course, was Finch.'[5]

Legal argument to try the two men separately proved unsuccessful. Stuart sought a separate trial, as he believed that Finch had a strong case, with only the unsigned interview as evidence. This is a common defence tactic. He told this to the future Director of Public Prosecutions, Des Sturgess. Two people charged with an offence arising out of a joint enterprise will usually be put on trial together; if they are not, nearly always, some parts of the evidence will only be admissible against one of them, and therefore ought not to be taken into account when considering the case against the other.

The public gallery, although packed during the first week, had emptied by the third. Finch remained impassive throughout, sipping water from a paper cup.

For the first six days, Stuart attended the trial.[6] On the 17th, Lennie McPherson, who Stuart had constantly mentioned to Hicks, gave evidence while Stuart watched the 'dog bastard' from the dock. He said he had met Stuart seven years previously. McPherson told the jury he lived in Gladesville and did managerial work. No, he was not in Surfers Paradise in October 1972, and had not been there for four years. He had no connection with the Iluka Apartments and had not visited the Whiskey (which was untrue). He had no business dealings with Stuart, including protection rackets.[7] Mr Big was never going to say otherwise.

The next day, Tuesday 18th, Stuart was at it again. Further X-rays showed two more crosses consisting of four pieces of wire. This time he had flattened the ends.[8] Escorted back to the cells, Stuart said to Finch, 'Jim I couldn't tell you before. I have got a belly full of wire.'[9] Finch chortled, 'You're fuckin dead this time.' It would require further surgery, and it would absent him for most of the remainder of the trial.

Normally, a trial must take place in the presence of the accused unless 'he so conducts himself as to render the continuance of the proceedings in his presence impractical, in which case the court may order him to be removed and may direct the case to proceed in his absence',[10] which was exactly what Justice Lucas ruled. This was reported as the first time someone had been tried for murder in their and their representative's absence (Stuart having dismissed his counsel).[11] Witnesses would have to go to the hospital to identify Stuart before they made their court appearance, and the daily court transcripts were sent to the hospital for Stuart to peruse.

After McPherson, there was a procession of top-brass criminals. One commentator said that '...the prosecution produced a motley crew of witnesses including the finest collection of Sydney villains since the police found the Double Bay Mob having a meeting.'[12] They all had chunky police records for every possible offence; collectively they had murdered, raped, bashed, extorted, pimped, defrauded, peddled drugs and stolen. Indeed, this was the finest collection of perjurers to ever hold court: they all lied for a living.

A highlight was Arthur Murdock,[13] who was serving 20 years for rape. His rap sheet ran for eight pages.[14] He said he had known Stuart for 20 years. Murdock said he had supplied the wire Stuart was swallowing.[15] Murdock had met Finch shortly after his arrival at Boggo Road Gaol in March 1973. They became friends and talked about football, racehorses and fighters. Then Finch had talked some more.

Murdock said Finch, in a conversation on 1 August 1973, had confessed, 'I set the place on fire. I burnt them, Arthur ... the owners deserved it. The fucking dogs. They wanted that. They wanted that. There should be more places like that burnt. Them's the fucking dogs. Fucking innocent people. Them's the ones who get you in there. The fucking dogs. They deserved it. I poured the petrol. I poured the petrol ... We didn't mean to kill them. We wanted to scare them.' Murdock would also swear that 'I believe in God. I am telling the truth about what is contained in this statement....'

Known as the 'Black Stallion' and 'Fury', one Boggo Road gaoler described him as a 'rabid tree ape' straight out of *Planet of the Apes*. The gaoler recounted that Murdock had raped a 'white' boy in a cleaning gang and left him bleeding from the anus. When Murdock raped, he behaved like a frenzied shark and bit his victims. This boy was bleeding from teeth marks on his neck, shoulders, back and buttocks.[16] Murdoch also chomped a prisoner in 1964.

Despite the racist overtones, Murdock was indeed a deranged offender. He spent nearly 11 years of his life sentence in a cage in Townsville's Stuart Gaol. Prison officers claimed that this was the only way to protect other prisoners from Murdock's demented sexual attacks.[17] A previous trial judge had called him a 'pathological homosexual rapist'. He could have added 'pathological heterosexual rapist'.

Being a stool pigeon was profitable; Murdock received a $1000 reward. Gaoled in 1960, the sadistic rapist was out in 1977, arrested again within months for the same offence and then gaoled for life in 1978.[18] Murdock maintained that the victims he terrorised were willing participants in his vile crimes. He remained adamant that his victims would say that they lusted after his beautiful black body, and he gave them the best sex they had ever had.

In an affidavit in June 1977, this twisted individual retracted his original testimony against Finch, and then perjured himself again, restating that it was true. A request for a pardon for Finch, based on the affidavit, failed.[19] He had perjured himself at least twice before. In 1963, he had made a 'groundless complaint' against a senior prison officer and repeated the offence three years later against two fellow prisoners.[20]

Stuart had attempted to protect himself from snitchers. On 19 April 1973, he penned a letter (co-signed by Finch) to the prison superintendent requesting that other prisoners be kept away from them. He asked that 'no prisoner be allowed any access to me whatsoever ... so that at a later date, that prisoner could not give perjured testimony to the effect I "admitted" this or "divulged" that to him.'[21]

Krusty the clown would have been a more credible witness. The circus continued, and the clowns kept appearing on centre stage.

One was the hoon 'Mad Dog' Miller. After he and Koazeaha had identified Stuart at the hospital, he made his appearance.[22] Graham

Miller, expensively and immaculately dressed in a suede jacket and grey pinstripe trousers, swaggered on stage.[23] When in the spotlight in the dock, he appeared nervous. For a tough-guy boxer, he was softly spoken. Justice Lucas repeatedly told him to speak up, which he would do for a while before fading again.

He told the court he was a self-employed salesman who 'bought and sold everything, toys (bought from Silknit House), blankets, clothing, things like that.' He did it door-to-door, in hotels and via friends. This was a disingenuous admission from someone who regularly stole, beat people up and possessed lethal weapons (including a grenade) for no good cause. Miller had known the two accused for many years. He had last seen Stuart when he went to Parramatta Gaol to bail him out. Under questioning, Miller concurred that the bailing was for old times' sake.[24] Miller's solicitor David Baker had rung him, and he had gone to Parramatta Gaol. He had sent Koazeaha in to the gaol office, as he (Miller) had a criminal record.

On the trip to the airport, Stuart had lifted his shirt to show Miller his numerous scars. 'Look what they've done to me in gaol.' Stuart also stated that he had been eating metal (bedsprings). When asked why he swallowed the metal, Stuart had replied, 'So they'll think I'm crazy and they'll send me to Morisset (a hospital for the criminally insane) where you get grouse steak and eggs and television.'

In Miller's car, Stuart said he was 'dirty' on McPherson. Stuart asked, 'Do you think there's a little section down here for me?' and stated, 'I will be Mr Big and McPherson will be Mr Little.' Miller advised Stuart to leave him out of any plans. In his statement, Miller said that Stuart was a homosexual who hated McPherson.

Whenever they stopped at a red light, Stuart would hide, saying, 'Try not to pull up behind a car, so as we can drive off quick, because someone's likely to come out and shoot me off the street.' This is entirely consistent with Stuart's deportment, including what he said just before he left the gaol.

The toy seller told the court that he was just an amateur boxer who did not want to be involved in crime. Miller maintained that 'I did not arrange with any other persons to meet Stuart at the airport.

I did not leave my car at the airport. It has come to me through "the grapevine" that Stuart has involved me in this wicked crime, which I believe is the worst in Australia's history.'

Criminals John Regan and Paddles Anderson also made an appearance. Anderson had his fingerprints all over a diverse range of criminal activities, from gambling to prostitution. John Regan rang Detective Glancy on 13 September saying he was concerned he had been associated with this depravity. Regan said he would fly to Brisbane that afternoon. He did so, and offered to perform a public service by blowing Stuart's head off. This was no idle threat; he specialised in killing people and making them vanish—hence his nickname, 'the Magician'.[25] Ironically, the would-be assassin was assassinated himself the following year.

None of the detectives flinched under cross-examination; the record of interview was authentic, the dialogue Finch had had with Atkinson at the shopping centre was accurate and Stuart's admissions just prior to being charged at the watch-house were verbatim.

Stuart's story had more holes than an oversized colander. There was no question that he had bought and paid for Finch's ticket to Brisbane. On 20 February, Stuart had gone to the Qantas ticket sales office and stated, 'I want to pay a fare for a friend to travel from London to Brisbane tomorrow.'[26] He told the lady the friend's name was Mr Finch and his name was Mr Mason.

The booking for flight 728 was made, and a deposit of $260 was paid.[27] The loquacious Stuart told a disinterested cashier, 'My friend is in trouble in London; he has been bashed up over there and I have got to get him home quickly.' The next day, Stuart returned and paid the balance of $159.70 in cash.[28]

There was no good reason why Finch was in Brisbane. To work on an oil rig was underwhelming; to visit Stuart's mum, for old time pen pals' sake, was no better. John told Rose Stuart that it was because his mother was ill, and John and Mrs Watts were the only friends Finch had. If he was innocent, why had Finch gone into hiding after the fire? Why had he hidden his passport? Why was he using a false name? There were no innocent answers. Although he was not meant to return to Australia, he had used his real name when entering, so why did he change his approach after arriving? Finally, he had a solid track record of lighting fires.

Stuart had named three suspects, 'Rodger the Dodger', 'Les', and 'Ross'. He told Bolton that 'Rodger the Dodger' had called him in Brisbane before 6 January (although he told Hicks on 28 January that he had not heard from the Sydney crims).[29] Rodger the Dodger was easily identified by the police as Rodger Brennan,[30] who had known Stuart since 1963, when they were both inmates at the State Penitentiary, so that part of Stuart's narrative held true.

He then met Stuart again at Parramatta Gaol prior to Stuart's release following the Steele shooting. Brennan also knew Finch from there. The problem was, he was continually in gaol from 1970 until *after* the fire. The Dodger was behind the brick walls of Bathurst Gaol on 20 December 1972, the date on which he supposedly bid Stuart au revoir at Mascot Airport. Stuart's assertion was false.

'Les' was identified as Leslie Newcombe, who had spent time in various prisons since 1957. He saw Stuart in 'the circle' while on remand at Parramatta Gaol in December 1972 and knew Finch well. Newcombe had never been to Brisbane, and he was in gaol on 20 December.[31] 'Ross' was Ross Gardner, another who was in gaol on 20 December. Furthermore, Les and Ross, the ones nominated as being present at the Flamingo and identified by Stuart, were incarcerated during the week of the Whiskey fire.[32]

It got worse for Stuart, terminally so. The police tracked down and questioned all the moustachioed men from the Flamingo. A photo was produced showing them partying together at the Hacienda Hotel. There were four men who had been hanging out together; two had departed for Sydney before the fire, while two had stayed on that week. They were Reginald

Hannam, Richard Harris, Peter O'Connor and Jerry.[33] Quick and Yasse recognised them. Harris and O'Connor said they were probably at the Flamingo on Monday and Tuesday, when Quick asked Stuart their names.[34] After extensive interviews, it was determined that none of them could have been involved in the fire (if only 'casing the joint' as Stuart had stated).

His brother Daniel's testimony added to John's misery. According to Daniel, John had said there were Sydney criminals involved in the extortion plan who wanted him to be their front man and ask for money. If the club owners refused, the extortionists would burn their premises down with petrol, throwing it in the front door. Daniel testified that John constantly mentioned one target, the Whiskey.

The adverse evidence from brother Daniel continued. He quoted his younger brother as saying, 'If only I could get a hundred dollars from each nightclub, I would be alright, I wouldn't have to work.' Daniel's advice, he said, was for his brother to not get involved and to live a quiet life. Daniel bluntly told the court that his brother was guilty: '...John had used a great deal of psychology to set this whole thing up and also had a perfect alibi and that as far as the other man [Finch] was concerned he did not exist ... Now that I look over the whole of the circumstances of the last five months or so, I feel in my own mind that this was a perfectly set-up job, Stuart set himself up with an alibi and got Doug, a non-existent man, to do the actual job of setting fire to the Whiskey Au Go Go.'[35] He had parroted the prosecution's opening address.

Towards the end of the trial, it moved to the Royal Brisbane Hospital. A seminar room in Block 8 was set aside for proceedings. The jury and Finch (heavily handcuffed and guarded) were taken in. Justice Lucas asked Stuart, who was lying on a bed trolley with only his head and handcuffs visible, 'John Andrew Stuart, can you hear me?' He told Stuart that the trial was finished and the next move was up to him.

Stuart lifted his head and then lowered it again. 'Can you hear what I'm saying?' Lucas repeated. Stuart did not reply. The Judge outlined the various options he had, but again there was no reply. Finch stood nearby and mocked, 'I thought they only done this in Russia.'[36]

They summoned the doctor. The judge asked the doctor if Stuart could hear. The examiner asked Stuart if he was in pain, and Stuart spoke for the first time: 'It's sticking into me here,' he said, indicating his stomach and his standard non-hospital-approved diet; metal butterflies.

Stuart refused to cooperate so the judge and entourage departed.

37

Protests

In summing up, Justice Lucas said that if the jury accepted the interview, it amounted to a full admission by Finch of every element of the murder offence.[1] With written and oral confessions from both of the accused, the verdict was a given; they were found guilty and convicted on 23 October 1973. The indictment stated that they had murdered Jennifer Denise Davie, for which they received life sentences with hard labour.[2]

There were rumours that Daniel took at least part of the reward. He bought a 25-foot Bertram powerboat and a new Datsun soon after the trial. His son later disclosed that Daniel sold the family home at Jindalee around this time. Although possible, there is no definite evidence he received any financial benefit. Under oath, Daniel said, 'I would like to make it quite clear that I am not interested in any reward for my brother. I love my brother.'[3] In 1992, a police note concluded, 'There has been no result to date from government rewards offered.'[4] The only confirmed payment was $1000 to the barbarous Murdock.

After the trial, Stuart sent yet another coded message, this time to the Public Defender's Office. He planned to commit suicide 'to find freedom ... Even if I were set free I would commit suicide now that I have my answer.' The key to the code would be supplied after his death, in parts, by separate people unknown to each other.[5]

He also sent a suicide note to his mother: 'There is no more freedom for me, ever. Death is the only answer ... I am now completely wholly whole. I now understand life, so have no fear of, and am ready for, death. I can die and want to now, before I lose what I found.' Regarding Daniel, 'He is my brother no longer. I am impatient to begin death. You broke my heart Dan. You were the closest and only link I had with a childhood that did have its happy days, the only ones I ever had.' He had been placed on suicide watch earlier in his prison career, and thoughts of suicide would come to dominate his final years.[6]

Stuart dealt with the conviction in his practised ways; by protest, self-mutilation and blaming others for his predicament.

In late 1973/early 1974, Stuart swallowed more 'pills.' Their design was now so famous that the inmates called them Stuart's patents. It was his fourth admission to hospital since the

Whiskey fire. He had done so as a protest against being forced to shave. He had also emptied his toilet bucket on the guards (something he and Finch were both wont to do).[7] The butterflies were removed on 2 January, but soon after, he did it again.[8]

Even though the guards had padlocked him to a hospital bed, he 'amazingly' had broken off a piece of steel wire from a bedspring, made a pick and unlocked his handcuffs—or so the unlikely narrative went. Discovered by the guards, he again tipped his toilet bucket over their heads. A search revealed that he had two sharpened pieces of wire in the pocket of his pyjamas and another taped to his head (with abdominal dressing adhesive). He was given a buzz cut to prevent this happening again.[9] Nonetheless, 'Mr Houdini' swallowed more wire, this time using rubber bands and cellulose. After five major abdominal surgeries in a year, a surgeon told the *Sunday Sun* that Stuart was close to becoming inoperable, and could die from peritonitis during future operations.

Next, he went on a hunger strike, not taking fluids for three days because 'prison officials had withheld a Christmas parcel.'[10] Now Finch tried to get one up on his other half by tearing off one of his big toenails.

At the beginning of 1974, the wife of Stuart's criminal mate Billy McCulkin disappeared, along with her two daughters. They were last seen in the company of two unctuous low-lifes, Vincent O'Dempsey and Garry Dubois. Previously, O'Dempsey had lived with the McCulkins for an extended period.[11]

Bolton ramped it up in April 1974. He said there was a hero worship cult of prisoners who were plotting a mass wire-swallowing suicide.[12] This, of course, had been discovered in a 40-page coded letter and 'decoded by an underworld associate from thousands of pieces of cigarette paper'. Stuart had a massive collection of butterfly crosses. His sixth wire-eating trick would surely kill him. Sixteen other prisoners were ready to go. Oh, and he was writing another book, 'In case you are interested.' It was an autobiography that had already reached 100,000 words. The one he had been writing in 1962 had never seen the light of day. Bolton continued to milk Stuart's notoriety.

There was an element of truth to this story. Indeed, there was a mass protest by eight to ten prisoners in No.2 yard C wing who were swallowing Stuart's patents. The inmates manufactured the implements with flattened 50 mm metal staples from the bottoms of cardboard boxes (with the ends sharpened by rubbing them on a concrete floor). As usual, a rubber band bound them in a cross. As an innovation, and replacing Sellotape, kneaded lumps of bread encapsulated the trinkets. The men swallowed their medicine with their heads held back, forming a straight line from mouth to stomach. The metal went down the chute, and the stomach acid did the rest.[13]

Stuart was on a roll. In May 1974, he sewed his lips together with paper clips after the police took over the gaol when the warders went on strike.[14] None of this made any difference; the Court of Criminal Appeal dismissed their application in the middle of the year.[15] Seven appeals in all, right up to the Privy Council, would all fail.[16]

Meanwhile, entertainers including Big Daddy and Dan Martin organised a benefit in 1974 to raise money for the victims' families.[17] The fifteen families shared a total of $3700, although for reasons unknown, the Folsters received nothing.

38

Outrageous Claims

In 1974, author and editor William 'Billy' Stokes (aka David Wensley) published a series of sensational articles in the *Port News*, a low-profile, esoteric, bi-monthly publication of the Waterside Workers Federation's Brisbane Branch that had first been published in June 1973.[1] To appeal to a wider male audience, there were promotions for the porn film *Deep Throat* and photos of topless women. Stokes, like a number of the players in the Whiskey saga, had been at the notorious Westbrook Farm Home for Boys.

In April, Stokes turned his attention to the Whiskey with the heading, 'The Whiskey—A Whitewash'. Someone had leaked some of the police correspondence revealing how they had been forewarned. The following year, Stokes became more brazen. The February 1975 *Port News* had a scoop and the editor lifted the: 'Lid on Who Really Burnt the Whiskey.'

Stokes introduced a freak LSD gang, the 'Clockwork Orange' gang, who had emerged in late 1972. They specialised in petty offences; a bit of stealing, some break and enter and car theft. Stokes compared the gang to those portrayed in the film of the same name; a pack of no-hoper thugs (aka droogs, the name used in the film), an apposite comparison.[2]

At first they were described by aliases. There was Clockwork Orange (Thomas Hamilton), The Three (Peter Hall), Shorty (Garry Dubois) and Jimmy (Keith Meredith). The Three's special talent had been to vomit, defecate and urinate simultaneously when drunk. This was a measure of the groups' sophistication and contribution to human advancement. The gang had torched the Torino club for $500 on behalf of Stuart's great mate Mr X (Billy McCulkin) and The Loner (Vince O'Demspey). O'Dempsey and McCulkin had also arranged for the same gang to torch the Whiskey.

The series appeared in three parts, but Stokes continued to add detail in other editions. Hamilton and Hall had approached Stuart, dressed in their most flamboyant 'Clockwork Orange' apparel, playing the role of southern criminals. The two redheads had asked Stuart to be their front man and collect extortion money from club owners. These were the two 'Butler' brothers Stuart had told Bolton and others about.

There was another astounding assertion; that McCulkin's wife and daughters had been murdered by O'Dempsey and Dubois because she knew of her husband and O'Dempsey's involvement in the Whiskey outrage. Stokes believed that Stuart and Finch were innocent patsies to the gang and their overseers, O'Dempsey and McCulkin.

A month prior to Stokes' bombshell inside story, on 10 January 1975, someone abducted none other than Clockwork Orange himself, Thomas Hamilton,[3] who had fought as a welterweight in Queensland under the name of Ian Thomas. Snatched from his girlfriend's residence at gunpoint, Hamilton's body was never found. Police said there was no evidence that his disappearance was related to the throwing of a fight for a gambling syndicate.

Stokes got into trouble himself, and kept his readers up to date through a rolling 'blog' in his magazine. The police, executing a search warrant, found a shoulder holster and a plastic container with four bullets hidden beneath a cannabis plant. Five days later, the police found a .38 Smith and Wesson revolver loaded with six bullets. Stokes said he kept the gun in his flat as protection against O'Dempsey, who he had accused of murder.[4] During the firearm trial, Stokes reiterated the astounding claim that members of the Clockwork Orange gang had torched the Whiskey; this gave the story a wider audience.[5]

Stokes received a six-month sentence for possession of a concealable firearm.[6]

Stokes then reversed his earlier defence of Stuart and Finch, now branding them as executioners in the *Port News*.[7] He declared them guilty, albeit with the assistance of the gang of drug-addled droogs.[8] Stokes based this on a prison chat with Stuart while Stokes was on remand. As a consequence, Stuart confronted Stokes in October 1977 and another prisoner attacked Stokes, who was relocated to Wacol Gaol for his own protection. In a remarkable twist, Stokes was later accused of the Hamilton murder, convicted and gaoled.[9] The Whiskey saga had more twists and turns than a giant slalom.

Meanwhile, the letters from Stuart's mother continued, trying to elevate his flagging morale.[10] Stuart was haggard from his continual operations and his suicidal proclivity. She told him to never to give up, and named those who were really responsible for the fire.

In November 1977, Stuart shimmied up a drainpipe onto the top of A wing at Boggo Road Gaol.[11] There, he went 'berserk'. Grabbing one of the separator bars that held the barbed wire entanglements, he prised off a sheet of iron roofing. He also made a flag from his shirt and a piece of wood. Stuart then formed the words

'INNOCENT—VICTIMS OF POLICE VERBAL—F & S' using loose bricks. Yelling abuse at the prison officers, he hurled bricks and timber at the lights. After smashing two of them, he turned his attention to knocking down the power lines. The media recorded all his moves; he was in the limelight again, and for his psyche, that was always a good thing.

Fellow inmates threw him tennis balls filled with food and water so he could sustain the barrage. With this support, he was able to maintain his protest for 52 hours. It ended while he was resting next to a hole in the roof. Two members of the special squad that dealt with maximum security prison emergencies, were able to rein him in. After this escapade, Stuart said he was thrown in the infamous black hole cell below A wing, where he was stripped naked and left for five days in complete darkness. That may be true.

On the morning of 2 January 1979, Stuart was found dead in his cell.[12] The cause of death was recorded as an acute heart infection, possibly the result of a virus. However, there are many conspiracy theories as to how it really happened. The family believes that prison guards poisoned him, but these claims can be dismissed. Stuart had self-mutilated and abused his body for his entire life. He had slashed himself with razors, been wounded by others and swallowed countless metal objects (followed by the requisite operations to remove them). There is also evidence of drug use. After the fire, he continually talked of suicide, and of how life was not worth living. This combination of physical and mental deterioration led to his death. There is no reason to surmise otherwise.[13]

The McCulkin abduction case developed slowly. Six years after the tragedy, the coroner found that O'Dempsey and Dubois had abducted and murdered the mother and daughter, and recommended that they stand trial.[14] However, the Attorney General withdrew the charges, as there was insufficient evidence to establish a prima facie case of murder.

39
Questions Marks

There had always been a question mark over the difference between the 'elegant' language Finch used in the interview and his utterances elsewhere. A simple comparison showed an educational disparity. For example, at the trial, he said, 'I never done that or any of them', while the interview recorded him as saying, 'Gentlemen, I want you to understand my position.' He was a 28-year-old cockney with limited education.[1]

In 1984, the Reverend Andrew Morton, an international expert on stylometry, the scientific examination of speech patterns, analysed Finch's record of interview and his answers during the trial. Analysing the habitual placement of common words (such as *a, and, to, of,* and *the*) and sentence structures, he came to the startling conclusion that there was only a one in 236,472 chance that the wording was Finch's.

Among seven significant differences between the statement and his court answers was the habitual use of *the* with *and*. The combination was used a 'striking' number of times in the confession, whereas Finch *never* used it in court

(...to stand over the nightclubs in Brisbane to try and get [the] money out of them[2]).[3]

The Reverend concluded that 'It would be totally unsafe to accept the replies of this record of interview as the utterance of Mr J R Finch. The number of habits may not seem large to a layman, but in 10 years of experience, I have not seen as high a proportion of habits to differ.' An appeal to the Governor for a retrial or pardon, based on this evidence, was rejected.[4] The police noted in their records that 'Despite much fanfare from the media about the expertise of Rev Morton, his recent visit to Queensland did not result in any new inquiry being commenced.'[5]

Also flourishing during these years were multiple support groups; Friends of Finch, Citizen Justice Group, National Freedom Council and a community group that had fought for the release of Lindy Chamberlain and had now swung its support behind Finch, The Plea for Justice Committee.[6] These organisations liaised with Finch's legal representation and offered financial support of up to $31,000.

In 1984, reporter Dennis Watt became involved in the case.[7] He had always had an interest in the firebombing of the Whiskey, and coincidentally was assigned to do a story on

Cheryl Cole, who had befriended Finch in Boggo Road Gaol.

Notorious murderers always develop a following, with naive women believing in their innocence. Cole was one of these; a terminally ill, wheelchair-bound groupie. She spent the rest of her life dedicated to the cause of securing Finch's release. Cole wrote letters to the Prime Minister, and although she was on a disability pension, was willing to sell 'everything she had' for a retrial. She sold her furniture and cooking utensils to contribute $1000.[8] The invalid first wrote to Finch in 1983, and visited him every week. She described Finch as a political prisoner and, replicating Finch's protests, went on a hunger strike.[9]

Watt wrote a series of articles on Finch, his background and his legal fights. Convinced of his innocence, Watt corresponded weekly, visited Finch in gaol and helped him write his parole application.[10] On 19 February 1986, 25 friends and relatives attended the wedding of Finch and Cole at the Brisbane Women's Prison Chapel, with Watt presiding as master of ceremonies.[11]

All the work of the support groups, Cole, Watt and the legal team eventually came to fruition. On 1 February 1988, the Minister for Corrective Services said that Finch's release was recommended unanimously by the Queensland

Parole Board and approved by State Cabinet.[12] The Minister for Police said he was willing to extend the terms of reference and re-examine the Whiskey saga, if asked, by the Fitzgerald Inquiry.[13] This Commission of Inquiry was established to investigate the rampant police corruption in Queensland, and would claim the scalp of the Commissioner of Police himself, Terry Lewis. The release was conditional on Finch's deportation to his home country, Britain (although his lawyers considered a court appeal against the deportation order). Finch left Australia on the day of his release, with the newspaper headline greeting him at his destination reading 'Welcome Back Killer'.[14]

With Finch gone, a number of informants came out of the woodwork. On an ABC Four Corners episode, two serving policemen claimed that Detective Atkinson had told them that Finch's confession had been a fabricated verbal.[15] However, the detectives who were present at the interview held firm. Roger Rogerson appeared on Channel 7 and said that 'the interview that was produced in court was the actual interview between him [Finch] and the Queensland police.'[16]

Later in the year Watt, now Chief of Staff at the afternoon *Sun* newspaper, wrote a series of articles.[17] The readership enjoyed another breathtaking development, the three-word headline saying it all: 'I DID IT'. After 15 years of proclaiming his innocence, Finch had confessed to Watt that he *had* torched the Whiskey.

After Finch had been paroled to England, Watt had maintained contact with him. Eventually, after a series of phone calls, Finch had admitted his guilt in relation to the heinous crime. Finch wanted Watt to sell his story to the highest TV bidder, believing it could be worth $100,000. Watt contacted a couple of TV stations, but neither responded.

For the sake of putting the record right, Watt obtained permission to get a professional film crew to film Finch's confession. A copy would be given to the Fitzgerald Inquiry and sold to a commercial TV station to recover the outlays. Watt informed Finch that he could keep any monies remaining after the costs were deducted.[18]

In October 1988, Watt flew to London and spent five days in Finch's company. Watt travelled to the council flat Finch shared with his sister, Joan, in Basildon, Essex. At a nearby park, where Finch trained every day, Watt made an audio tape of Finch's confession. A couple of days later, they recorded the same interview on a video tape. Finch not only confessed to his involvement, but also named names.

He maintained that Stuart had planned the Whiskey Au Go Go fire to set up a protection racket. Stuart had driven Finch to an isolated street and introduced Finch to two other men, Billy McCulkin and Thomas Hamilton. Stuart had then departed for the Valley to 'cook up an alibi'.

McCulkin was the driver, while Hamilton and Finch were in the back seat. They did some practise runs with two drums three-quarters full of petrol with the lids loosened. They drove to the Whiskey dressed in black, like the 1972 Munich Olympic Games terrorists.

After McCulkin pulled up outside the entrance, Finch took the drums inside and Hamilton lit them. Ten to 12 seconds later, they were gone. Finch left his gloves and other clothes in the car and jumped out near his flat in Milton. Finch said that Stuart had received his orders from Vince O'Dempsey, who was in cahoots with police officer Tony Murphy, Stuart's arch enemy.

The *Sun* published the first article on October 31, and follow-up articles ran for over a week. The video tape sold for $40,000.[19] Finch soon learnt of this, and rang Watt at home demanding to know how much he would receive. When Finch heard that the payout only covered costs, he was apoplectic. He told Watt he knew where he lived and that there were 'plenty of mates up the road who knew where I was, meaning threats.'

Jana Wendt interviewed Finch on Channel Nine's *A Current Affair* on 1 November 1988, the day after Watt's story broke. Early in the satellite interview, parts of which were not broadcast, Finch said he stood by his confession, and admitted he had lied for 15 years. He told Channel Nine's London correspondent Michael Holmes that it was time to speak out—the moment of truth.

When Wendt told him that he had only been charged with Davie's murder and could still be charged with 14 more murders and extradited, Finch was stunned, having thought he would be immune from further prosecution. He then started to sputter and stammer like a misfiring lawnmower. The embarrassed chameleon blurted, 'I can't remember saying this, I haven't been very well. I don't know what's going on, I have no idea. I don't know what's happening to me. But I didn't kill anybody. I'm not guilty. I've done 15 years of my life in Australia for a crime I didn't commit. I am innocent of that charge. I never confessed. I haven't been very well, I don't know what's going on....'[20]

Shortly after Finch finished his disastrous interview, he called his wife Cheryl in Brisbane for the first time in more than a month and said,

'Hello Chirpy, I really do love you. Our marriage is not over. I need help, I need you.' Mrs Finch agreed that her husband was confused, sick and did not know what he was doing. Mrs Finch had initially followed her husband to England, but had returned to Brisbane a few months later 'due to the weather'.

Politicians on both sides of the world were outraged. British MPs demanded that Finch be sent back to the ex-penal colony. The Queensland Minister of Justice stated that he would investigate whether Finch could be extradited from England to face perjury charges and 14 more counts of murder.

Watt had a few more contacts with Finch in the form of correspondence. He wrote to Finch once to try to pacify him because of concerns about the safety of Watt's family. Finch sent Watt a postcard saying the world was full of conmen and users, and he was both, and he would be seeing Watt soon. Another time, he sent a photo of himself standing in front of a coffin with the following notice: 'I was going past a church and there was a funeral going on.' The inference was obvious and insidious.[21]

Watt's articles were soon followed by a three-part series written by journalist Bruce Stannard and published in *The Bulletin*.[22] Stannard said he had a confession from one of the unnamed detectives who had signed Finch's interview record. The detective said the interrogation was a complete fabrication, but had been necessary, as Finch had refused to confess after a beating. In addition, the detectives had then perjured evidence at his trial. The fraud was justified, as the detectives were completely convinced of his guilt, but unable to prove it by honest means.

Under public pressure, there was an inquiry instigated by the Acting Commissioner of Police, Ronald Redmond, on 1 November 1988, the day after Watt's first article. Its brief was to examine 'all allegations surrounding the Whiskey Au Go Go nightclub firebombings and other murders between 1973 and 1977.'[23] It became known as 'Operation Graveyard', a nod to the body count involved, including those of the McCulkins, Hamilton and associated cases.

A detective inspector submitted a report arising out of the inquiry on 8 March 1992. It concluded that there was no evidence to connect Stuart or Finch to the members of the Clockwork Orange gang. They had interviewed Daniel Stuart and the detectives involved including Hayes, Atkinson, Griffiths, Murphy, Morey and Redmond and 'all police officers have denied any fabrication of evidence or perjury.' The report acknowledged that due to the long period since the people disappeared, witnesses recollections had faded and 'it is highly unlikely that any of the criminals involved here are likely to confess, and therefore the crimes will most probably remain unsolved.'

A detective superintendent remained concerned that Redmond had unnecessarily initiated the probe in response to the intense media pressure he faced. He believed that there had been no real need for the investigation, despite Redmond having an obvious conflict of interest, being the typist of the original interview.[24] The inquiry, disappointingly, became sidetracked when the lead detective inspector sought and obtained permission to proceed with legal action against a reporter he believed had slandered him. He also sought an apology from another newshound regarding the 'misrepresentation of the truth'. This was an unnecessary distraction from the real issues surrounding the case.

The report also examined the case of informant Robert Griffiths. There are always those who want to inject themselves into the melodrama of a murder case, either for morbid reasons or otherwise. Griffiths claimed that Vincent O'Dempsey had been loitering near the Whiskey prior to the fire, and that Redmond had asked Griffith to meet O'Dempsey and make him confess to the McCulkin murders. His payment would be $50,000. Following extensive investigations, Griffith was convicted of making false representations causing a police investigation, fined $200 and ordered to pay in excess of $5,000 costs.[25]

Operation Graveyard concluded that 'The claim by Finch that he was verballed still remains. However, there is no new evidence to hand which otherwise confirms or proves the contrary.' But is this the case?

In parallel with Stannard's secret mole, there are a number of inconsistencies in the police narrative that provide reasonable grounds to believe that some of their evidence is contradictory and should be rescrutinised by an appropriate legal authority.

The basis for this opinion is as follows.

40

Anomalies

That Finch's record of interview was ridiculously brief was obvious from the start. This was the crime of the century, the most sensational murder trial in Australian legal history, and yet despite being suspected of killing 15 people, Finch's 'interview' extended to only five typed pages. Despite his confession, there should have been multiple interviews; it should have been a lengthy interrogation.

There were so many obvious follow-up questions. The detectives did not inquire about where Stuart's car had stopped 'in the bush' to pick up the empty drums and which side street they parked in to milk the petrol. Had the drums disturbed the ground? Did they drop anything? What was the colour, make and year of the car they were in? What make of cars were they milking? Were their fingerprints on the cars? Did some car owners notice their petrol missing? What matches did they use, as most hotels and clubs at this time had their own 'brand' and logo? They asked no questions as to the route they may have taken; although Finch said he would not go back to the Whiskey, why not offer to drive him along the routes they took? That there were canines nearby was the only clue, although dogs are common on every street: it was a worthless descriptor.

'Corroborative evidence' is a basic tenet of good detection, and yet six experienced senior detectives did not think to ask any of these follow-up questions. Finch was in a 'tell-all' state at this time, and surely he would have obliged the good detectives with answers to any further queries they may have had.

There were other issues. Regarding his refusal to sign his confession, Finch said, 'That is always the code that I have followed in the past and that is my desire in this case.' This was patently false. On seven previous occasions when Finch had confessed to a crime, he had *always* signed his own handwritten confession.[1]

Why had six senior detectives interviewed Finch? This number was highly unusual, as two would have been sufficient. One of Finch's interrogators revealed a motive to *The Bulletin* reporter Stannard in 1988—safety in numbers.

Why was there no independent witness, e.g., a Justice of the Peace, and why did they not use any recording equipment such as a tape recorder, which Hicks used to record Stuart? In the interview, in one instance he said he shot through the next morning after Stuart told him about all the deaths, but elsewhere he said he 'dry reached' [sic] for a day before going bush.

When asked about it at the trial, none of the detectives said they noticed his speech 'impediment', whereby he pronounced 'th' as 'f', e.g., 'months' as 'munfs'.[2] They never asked what clothes he was wearing—there may have been evidence of an accelerant. They never checked whether his arms were singed. Why did he violently refuse to be fingerprinted at the watch-house when he was compliant in all other matters? Why had Atkinson drawn a map of the seating layout for Stuart's interview in his police diary (when a solicitor was present) but not bothered with one for Finch's interrogation?

Outrageously, Atkinson had Detective Slatter prepare Stuart's 16 charge sheets before he was charged and before there was any evidence against him.[3] This was before Stuart's mini-confession at the watch-house. In court, Atkinson was asked, 'And yet you speculated when you spoke to Slatter and told him to prepare 16 charge sheets that in fact you would have a conversation with Stuart, that a solicitor would not be wanted by Stuart and that in fact he would admit to his involvement so that you could in fact charge him with 16 charges?' Atkinson's lame response was, 'It was speculation on my part.' The defence counsel concluded that it was a case of act first, get evidence later.

Why did Finch window-shop for an hour before torching the Whiskey? Some of the shops had lighting, and this exposed him to being seen. In theory, Stuart could have dropped Finch off, but could not have picked him up. Having arrived at the Flamingo earlier, Stuart could account for his time until 2.15am. The police have a taxi picking up Finch, a risky and flaky escape plan. Why had Finch not bothered to work out a more reliable means of escape?

There were few taxis at this hour, and all those operating in the general area of the Whiskey just after 2.08am could have been checked. They did not ask Finch what company the cab belonged to, get a description of the driver, or ask what roads he travelled along or at least the general direction. A check would have verified Finch's confession, and Finch might have left something in the cab, if only fingerprints.

The police did send out an alert to 400 taxi drivers, a general notice 'to any driver who may have picked up a male person, 25 to 30 years, 5' 8", thin build, fair complexion, brown hair of medium length.'[4] They did not disclose what Finch wore, and the amateur boxer was solidly built. Nothing came of it, and evidence exists that it was unlikely to have actually happened.[5]

Independent testimony indicates that the murderers used their own means of conveyance.

The anonymous detective at Finch's 'confession' told Stannard that the detectives were confident that their 'unity ticket' could never be countered by a 'fucking animal' like Finch. Although the informant pointed out that they 'were very careful not to get too specific in the statement, not to give too many details because they might be challenged in court', there was always a danger that witness statements either prior to or after the 'interview' of 11 March could contain evidence contrary to their 'fabrication'. The informant indicated that they were smugly confident in their practised deceit; that they could collectively counter any adverse statement.

The verbal was a widely practiced art. Not only were interviews forged, but the police also concocted evidence in their diaries, and there are questionable entries in Atkinson's journal describing his first encounters with Finch.[6]

By the time they interviewed Finch, they had already interviewed two witnesses whose statements conflicted with Finch's confession in relation to the method of drum delivery.

Finch supposedly said, 'Johnny dropped me off close to one o'clock with the two drums just past the club—there was no one around, and I put the petrol drums in the dark *at the side of the club*. Johnny drove off.'

There is only one position 'Finch' could be referring to. The only realistic drop point was the north-west corner, only metres from the entrance. Hayes admitted that this was where the police assumed he meant.[7] For completeness, it is worth considering the only other possibility, the rear south-east corner of club, on the St Pauls Terrace side, but that was 35 metres away.

That was the least likely position because of the distance to the entrance doors and the fact that Finch said *at the side* of the cabaret. The south-east corner was at the rear of the building. Finch would have had to lug 23 kilograms (assuming the drums were three-quarters full). This would have taken some time, and meant that Finch would most likely have had to carry them separately because of their weight and size. He would have dumped the first drum, and then retrieved the second.

Regardless, this was impossible. The police had already interviewed James Stewart, the cleaner for the Brisbane City Council. He had been sweeping next to the Whiskey, after first checking the bus shed in front of where the drums would have been placed, but there was no one on the St Pauls Terrace side when he moved across the area. What's more, before that, he had been working on the other side of the road, and could not have missed someone lugging two heavy drums (either separately or together) down the length of the building. He had been looking over towards the bus shelter, looking for his mate, at the time, so his attention was on this area.

Stewart then moved down St Pauls Terrace while sweeping. It had taken less than two minutes. As he turned into Amelia Street, he first noticed the 'blue purple glow', as the fire had started only seconds earlier.

Thus, the only possible drop point lay at the north-west corner, *on the western side*, no more than three metres from the entrance. The police had already interviewed Michael Dee, who was in precisely this location, albeit in embarrassing circumstances.

As Dee exited the club, 'I did not notice any other person on the stairs and when I arrived at the front door I did not notice any person about the front of the premises. I decided to go and urinate around by the side of the building while I was waiting for the others. I walked a few steps to where a garden bed is situated and about this time a [sic] heard a noise like glass shattering and I tripped over a small chain at the front of the garden bed. As I was getting up I looked back and saw flames in the ground floor entrance....'[8] He also said the garden housed a prostrate bush, no more than a foot high. A photo of this spot, taken immediately after the fire, shows that Dee's description is precise.

Finch would have had to literally step over Dee to get into the club's ground-floor entrance. However, Finch supposedly added another detail; he did not carry the drums, he rolled them. Finch: I returned to near the Whiskey Nightclub just after 2 o'clock and I waited until there was no one about and I *rolled* the tins with the caps off into the entrance and I threw the lighted packet of matches on to the petrol and I ran.

The drums could not have been *rolled*, as Finch supposedly told the interrogators. Not only was Dee blocking the way, there was also a bush and a low-slung fence, a foot in height.

There is also the exit and entry of the clubbers to consider. Despite the ungodly hour (with closing time just one hour away), there were still partygoers entering and leaving the Whiskey.

Bingham entered just before 2am, and there were several people who left at 2am (Gregory Clark, Jennifer Armstrong, Maree German, Anthony Coates and Betty Kidd).[9] A male and female entered the club at 2.03am and then left at approximately 2.05am.[10] Chalmers said that after 2am, 'about half a dozen other persons left the club.' Finch said that he was loitering near the entrance from 2am, but he was not seen by anyone between 2am and 2.08am, when the fire started, despite the presence of two floodlights. They not only highlighted the welcoming placards and entrance to the cabaret, but also illuminated the anterior part of the western wall. No one could have escaped towards St Pauls Terrace, as sweeper Stewart was standing at the intersection.

Dee stated that the drums were dumped and then torched at the same time he was falling into the garden bed next to the club. This would have put his exit through the front doors at very close to 2.07am. He saw McSherry arrive in his police car at 2.08am.

The people who did the job were amateurs. They were extraordinarily lucky, because their window was small—less than 30 seconds. A few seconds either way and they would have encountered either Stewart rounding the corner, Dee extricating himself from the garden bed, or McSherry returning to the club to check on Clark.

Logistically, the most reasonable mode of drum delivery was by vehicle, *seconds before the fire*. This explains how the offender(s) arrived at and exited the scene so quickly. Balmoral House boarder Parkinson said he heard a car door slam and people yelling, 'Get out of here.' He thought he had dreamt it, but most likely he actually heard it. Finch said that Thomas Hamilton yelled out as they fled.[11]

After producing a woefully inadequate record of interview, including details that other witnesses rendered problematic, the detectives immediately took Finch to the watch-house, where they intended to charge him.

The watch-house charge room was small, and was crowded with detectives and watch-house staff. It was only two metres from the wall to the counter, and the room was approximately six metres wide. The area behind the counter was also tight, no more than two metres deep. At least 11 people occupied this space.

As Finch entered the room in handcuffs, he could see the cigarette vending machine next to the two-person wooden bench he sat on. On the wall near the cigarettes were, with 1970s irony, three cancer fund posters (Help Fight Cancer). There were two typewriters and a drunks register on the counter. A prominent sign stated, 'Prisoners are to be searched by Arresting Officer before Keyman'.

The detectives who escorted Finch from the his confession were consistent in recounting what had occurred. Aside from the arresting detectives, several watch-house personnel gave statements. There were at least four other watch-house staff in this small room; Constables Wayne Jarred and Samuel Sheehan and Sergeants Cornelius McDonnell (in charge) and Bruce Anderson.[12] For the detectives, it was standing room only. Finch was the only one seated; there were no other chairs.

The watch-house personnel also made internal police statements. They, too, were consistent in their account of what occurred, but their eyewitness testimony differed from that of the lead detectives in one key regard; *not what Finch and Stuart did, but what they said.*

After his mini-interrogation and confession, three detectives took Stuart to the watch-house charge room where Finch was seated.[13] The detectives who signed the confession, Morey, Hayes, Rogerson, Redmond, Atkinson, Griffiths and Slatter, recorded the following verbatim exchange between the two.[14]

Stuart: Did you tell them everything about the fire?

Finch: Yes.

Finch: I didn't sign it, fifteen dead, fifteen dead.

Stuart: You were certainly loose mouthed about it, why didn't you keep quiet?

Remarkably, no one else in the room heard this exchange. The entire watch-house team, despite the fact that they were packed in with the detectives, missed it.

After their first encounter, Hayes, reading the bench charge sheets, commenced to charge both defendants at the watch-house counter. He read out all 16 charges (15 of murder, one of attempting to wound) and the following words were repeated by the accused after each charge. The variations recorded by each officer are shown below.

Stuart: I'm not guilty, not guilty [Jarred]

I plead not guilty to that [Morey, Hayes, Griffiths, Rogerson, Atkinson]

Not guilty [McDonnell]

Not guilty, not guilty to that [Redmond, Slatter, Anderson]

Not guilty, not guilty [Sheehan]

Stuart: You're the same Jim [Jarred, McDonnell]

And you are the same Jim [Morey, Rogerson]

And you're the same Jim [Atkinson, Slatter, Hayes, Griffiths, Redmond]
You're not guilty either [Sheehan]
And the same goes for you Jim [Anderson]

Finch: Not guilty [Jarred, McDonnell, Sheehan, Anderson]

Not guilty too [Morey, Hayes, Griffiths, Rogerson, Atkinson, Redmond, Slatter]

Everyone in the room heard this exchange with the expected variations, although the detectives' records were almost identical.

After the charges had been read, Stuart turned to Finch.

Stuart: You needn't have told them I gave you the matches, Jim [Morey, Hayes, Griffiths, Rogerson, Atkinson, Redmond, Slatter]

Finch: Well, Johnny, you did but we'll have to try and beat these, Johnny [Hayes, Griffiths, Atkinson, Redmond]

Well, Johnny, you did but we will have to beat these, Johnny [Rogerson, Morey]

Well, Johnny, you did but we have to try and beat this, Johnny [Slatter]

Again, this was an incriminating exchange, yet no one apart from the lead detectives heard it. In their detailed statements, the other four eyewitness officers made no mention of it.

Just before they were led away, a fourth exchange was recorded.[15]

Stuart: Don't let them print you, Jim [Slatter, Morey, Hayes, Griffiths, Atkinson, Redmond, Rogerson]

Don't let them fingerprint you, Jim [Jarred, McDonnell, Sheehan]

Don't let them take your fingerprints [Anderson]

Finch: No, no one will print me, Johnny [Hayes, Griffiths, Rogerson, Slatter, Atkinson, Redmond]

No one will print me, Johnny [Morey]

I won't Johnny [McDonnell]

I won't let them Johnny [Jarred, Sheehan]

No, I'm not going to let them [Anderson]

For these watch-house exchanges, the detectives' recollections were virtually identical, even regarding 12-word sentences, while the other officers' records showed more variation.[16] At least they heard it.

In total, there had been four sequential exchanges. Two of these, the most incriminating, were not heard by any of the staff except those who had signed Finch's confession (and Slatter). The other staff only heard banal responses. The detectives' memories are virtually identical, and seemingly in conflict with those of the other witnesses.[17] One of the watch-house staff told a TV station that Finch was bricked (verballed), but would not reveal his identity.[18]

Other staff recorded exchanges at other times in the watch-house. Stuart's letter-gobbling episode the day before is a case in point. Watch-house staff Constables Samuel Sheehan and Ian Timms and Sergeants Cornelius McDonnell, Bruce Anderson and Leonard Mellow recorded the interaction between Stuart and Atkinson.

Another remarkable incident happened when Finch and Stuart admitted their guilt in the watch-house. On his charge sheet, the watch-house keeper Constable P Black recorded the following inventory: 'A brown wallet with $36.41, brown belt, 5-page copy of record of interview, black shoes, brown socks, brown trousers, orange shirt and white underpants.' He had noted the five-page typed confession.

Finch, after having admitted to police that he was guilty, firstly to Atkinson at the Jindalee shopping centre, then at the CIB in his interview (less than three hours earlier), and then at the watch-house, seconds after saying to a room of a least 11 police officers that he should not have talked of the matches, etc., had his first opportunity to put his true thoughts down in his own handwriting. He did so on the charge sheet, writing 'This property sheet is signed under protest as I have no knowledge whatsoever of record of interview. This is a police fabrication.'[19] He signed his message J R Finch, and for good measure corrected the description of the colours of his shoes, socks and trousers.

Colin McDonald, the officer in charge of the reception centre, recorded the conversation that occurred when he asked Finch to sign his property sheet.

Finch: I won't sign for the record of interview because no record of interview was made and it is a police fabrication.

McDonald: Are you satisfied that this document is a record of interview?

Finch: Yes.

McDonald: I am not concerned whether or not it is a fabrication. It is a record of interview and a record of interview is recorded on your property sheet.

Mr Aderman, the second-in-charge of the reception area, also heard this. He said to Finch, 'You can sign the sheet under protest if you claim that it is incorrect.' Finch did so.[20]

The following day, Finch and Stuart immediately wrote multiple letters on official prison paper to the detectives from 'neutral ground', again after their multiple full confessions. These were not afterthoughts; they penned them as soon as was practical.

Stuart to Hayes (12 March 1973):[21]

A Wing Boggo Rd 2pm
12/3/73
Det. Hayes

Last night at about 9 PM when you and Dets. Morey & Atkinson took me, against my will, from a cell at the City Watchhouse to a closed room in the same premises and tried to ask me questions. I told you then as I tell you again now, that I have nothing to say to any of you what-so-ever, except that I am not guilty of the terrible crime I am accused of and will say nothing more until my solicitor is present.

I ask you to let Morey & Atkinson read this letter as it is meant for them also, as they were also present when I spoke those few words. I request this of you in the name of justice.

Respectfully
John Stuart

Here, Stuart had said the mini-interview was a fabrication. An hour later, Stuart wrote to Morey:[22]

> I wish to officially deny to you here, in this letter from a neutral zone, that I made any admissions of guilt to you concerning the 'Whiskey Au Go Go' fire. Det Atkinson said to me today that you, and others, intended to attribute statements to me that I did not make, either to you or any other police officers
>
> I ask you to please tell the truth in that I have denied at all times any complicity whatsoever in the crime and have never spoken otherwise.

Stuart also wrote to Atkinson from A Wing Boggo Road on the same day.[23]

Finch to Hayes (12 March):[24]

> TO DETECTIVE SGT HAYES. For the first time I am on neutral ground. I wish to state that I have made no confessions or statements concerning the charges I am on. The record of interview which was put in my pocket outside the watchhouse was a fabrication by the police. I have not and will continue NOT to speak to police.

He then wrote a more detailed letter to Atkinson:[25]

> TO DETECTIVE SGT ATKINSON For the first time today I am on neutral ground. The Police record of interview allegedly made by me is a police fabrication. Whilst I was at the CIB I refused to answer any questions to you or any other police officers and the first I knew there was a record of interview was when I was being dragged into the city watchhouse and a police officer [Redmond] reached over and said 'cop' this record of interview and put it in my pocket. My hands were handcuffed behind my back. When I got into the watchhouse I was shouting and telling other police officers in there that it was a fabrication. I grabbed the fabrication from my pocket with my teeth and spat it on the floor. I have made no statement in the past or shall I do so in the future to police concerning these charges. I am innocent of all these dreadful charges.
>
> J R Finch

The detective who in 1988 told *The Bulletin* of 'the truth' of Finch's Record of Interview confession was identified in the 1992 communiqué, Operation Graveyard, as Roger Rogerson:[26]

It is general knowledge that the person whom has apparently spoken to Stannard has some intimate knowledge of the persons involved, locality and time span.

Rogerson's statement with no date or signature indicates that he was present when both Finch and Stuart were charged at the Brisbane Watch-house on the evening of the 11 March 1975.

It indicates that no improper conduct was witnessed there. Rogerson has been reported on television interstate as purportedly admitting that 'verballing' did take place years ago, though he had not been a party to any indiscretion himself.

An examination of the unsigned record of interview reveals that the initials RCR on each page. These are the initials of then Detective Sergeant Rogerson.

In this event then, if the allegations are true, Rogerson himself is liable to possible criminal prosecution.

The fact remains that this record of interview has been witnessed by five other police officers, tested in every area of appeal, and has remained intact, until spurious allegations have now been made by a totally discredited, ex-police officer, who was recently released from prison himself on appeal of serious crimes, and secondly, making these allegations to a journalist, who has a proven record of lying on oath and also plageurising [sic] another journalist's article. He is considered a person who will go to any lengths to get a story for publication and which will benefit himself.

The 1992 police investigators attempted to contact Rogerson's solicitors, requesting an interview with the suspended detective sergeant, but they refused. It was no big surprise that the 'dog' was Rogerson—he loved talking to the media (even if surreptitiously) and, like Stuart, courted publicity.

Rogerson told *The Bulletin* correspondent Stannard in 1988 about what he observed on the day of Finch's arrest. Although some claimed that Stuart had a genius-level IQ of 160, the cops classed him as 'a fucking psychopath—a real nut case' and 'a fucking pyromaniac'.

As a small-time petty hood, Stuart had landed in Brisbane and started up the extortion rumours, intending to pick up protection payments in hundred-dollar lots from the numerous clubs.

Rogerson rightly pointed out that '15 years ago Brisbane was a pretty small place, not much more sophisticated than a big country town.'

Therefore, the rumours, via Brian Bolton, spread and multiplied.

The southern crim heavy involvement was 'bullshit'. Why would Lenny McPherson and 'Paddles' Anderson bother with small-time clubs in Brisbane when they were so busy in Sydney?

Finch was no supermind, simply a firebug imported just before the fire. Tellingly, Rogerson said, 'Stuart was pinched for having a knife—which meant we could keep him incommunicado, well away from all the press mob.' The problem was, Stuart would not admit to anything, so they concentrated on Finch.

After Syd Atkinson brought him in to Roma Street, 'He was handcuffed to a chair and we knocked the shit out of him. Siddy Atkinson was pretty fit then and he gave him a terrible hiding.' Everyone punched him, yelling, 'You fucking cunt, Finch. You fucking murderer: you killed 15 fucking people, you mongrel.'

Rogerson admired Finch's toughness, in that he took it all and never squeaked. They then hid Finch from Commissioner Whitrod, as the evidence of the pummelling was clearly visible. Atkinson worked Finch over again with no result, 'So, in the end, we said, right, fuck you, smart arse, we'll do it our way. So we left him. We went into another room and that's where we proved that the pen really was mightier than the sword.'

Ronnie Redmond manned the typewriter and all the participants added to the confession. Verbals and fabrication were taken for granted by the police in all states. It was a way of life, and you only did it to those who you knew were guilty. Rogerson elaborated, 'Finch did it. We all knew that for sure. That's why we had no hesitation bricking the bastard. We were very careful not to get too specific in the statement, not to give too many details, because they might be challenged in court.'

With six coppers against a 'convicted fucking criminal', a jury would have no choice, the only concern being Redmond near the end of the trial when the devout Catholic came under strain, conflicted by his religious beliefs and his questionable actions.

Rogerson further justified their actions: 'As far as we were concerned, both Finch and Stuart were fucking animals. They had to be taken off the streets for the public good. They got what was coming to them. They got what they deserved. I've certainly never had a moment's regret about putting the bastards away. Given the same circumstances, I'd do exactly the same thing today and, you know something, people would thank me for it.'[27]

Finch's evidence in the Supreme Court regarding his interactions with the detectives matches Rogerson's admissions. For this reason, they cannot be dismissed outright.

He said that at the Jindalee shopping centre, when Atkinson approached him, he did so with a .38 Smith and Wesson revolver raised and said, 'Stop, you fucking bastard. Put your hands in the air. If you move, Finch, I'll blow your fucking head off, you murdering bastard.' And when Finch had said he was getting a solicitor, he had replied, 'You won't be getting a solicitor. All you'll be getting is a bullet in the brain.'[28] Atkinson later admitted that he had his gun out.

Just before entering the watch-house, Redmond had called out, 'Hold him there. Cop that.' Redmond then stuffed the fake FOI into Finch's top pocket. With his arms handcuffed behind his back, Finch could do little as he was manhandled into the watch-house. While seated on the bench, he managed to pick up the confession with his teeth and spat it onto the floor. It was returned to his pocket and he promptly picked it up between his teeth and spat it out again. 'That will do you no good, just put it in his property,' someone said.

He also said detectives at the watch-house laughed at him, saying to others, 'Come in here. You'll probably never see anyone charged with

15 murders again. You will remember it until your old age.'

They had also, with a dash of black humour, twisted the reality of what happened at his interrogation. Yes, he had told the detectives to kill him, but the wording and intent was different. Buchanan: We are the law here and we do what we like.

Finch: That's evident.

Atkinson: Don't give any cheek to the superintendent.

Finch: I'll say what I like.

Atkinson: I've had you, you cheeky bastard.

Finch: I've fucking had you too.

The burly Atkinson then backhanded Finch and threw him against the wall.
Finch: Go on you fuckin' cunts. You will have to kill me before I answer any of your questions. Kill me, kill me—go on.

Unidentified: For Christ's sake don't cut his face up.

Atkinson: Jimmy, I feel sorry for you son. You're a tough man, all right, but you're going to be charged with the murder of 15 people at the Whiskey Au Go Go.

Finch: You cunt.

Yes, he spat on Atkinson's face—but he did it with contempt. At the committal hearing, when Hayes related Finch's crying in the interview room, Finch could not contain himself and burst out laughing. Yes, his eyes were watering, but with rage. All of Finch's assertions are consistent with Rogerson's secret admission to Stannard. Multiple people heard thumping and shouting in the room when Finch was being interviewed, including Daniel Stuart (who was there for an interview himself), who heard Finch yell, 'Go on, why don't you kill me you bastards, kill me.'[29]

It is not only Finch's confessions that are suspect; so are Stuart's. Stuart had a paranoid obsession about being verballed, and mentioned it many times to Hicks, as seen in the quoted interviews. On 7 March, he predicted that he would be verballed by six to eight detectives. He spent several hours on 8 March organising an interview with the police, insisting that his solicitor be present. He made this point repeatedly in calls to Hicks, Bolton and his sister-in-law Rose.

When he and solicitor Weir appeared on 8 March, and then Weir left briefly to check the limitations of his brief, Hayes tried it on and attempted to interview Stuart in isolation. Stuart protested, both verbally and in writing. At the completion of his police interview, he said to Hayes, 'I want to make clear again that if I am questioned over this or any other matter I want a solicitor present.'[30] At their trial, the defence suggested that Buchanan had said to solicitor Weir, 'In the interests of justice I have decided you [should] not be present whilst your client is being interviewed.' They also argued that Weir was physically prevented from seeing Stuart after he left the interview room. This was denied. As he was being hauled out after supposedly threatening Detective Glancy with a knife at Daniel's house, Stuart yelled, 'Get me a solicitor Dan. Get me a solicitor.'[31] This was admitted by Atkinson.[32]

With a solicitor present, he said little; when his solicitor was absent, like Finch, he could not stop talking, as in his mini-confession in the watch-house interview room with Morey, Atkinson and Hayes (just prior to him being charged, along with Finch). Stuart wrote to the detectives the next day to protest that this brief interview was a fabrication.

When given a chance, Stuart *always* insisted that he would never be interviewed without a solicitor: 'Basil I'm not coming in without a solicitor. I can't trust the cunts to give me a fair go. I'm at a solicitor's office now. I'm waiting to see him then I'll come in with him.' He mentioned numerous times that he would not be interviewed without a solicitor, including the day before the fire.

At 10.14am on 28 May 1973, the day of the start of the committal trial, Hayes recorded the following in the cells at the Holland Park Magistrates Court: 'I intend to show you certain property which will be referred to in evidence by various witnesses. I warn you that you are not obliged...'. Stuart interrupted, 'Yes we both understand it, but we have something to say. It appears at the moment we are defending ourselves. This morning, Finch had a finger amputated ... I feel that he is not in a position to answer that question or make any statement ... and I ask that what you are doing now be withheld until Finch is in a position to speak for himself.[33] He has informed me in the van on the way to this courthouse that he is in pain, he is physically sick and from the words he has spoken to me I believe his mental standard is not normal.'

Detectives Hayes and Atkinson ignored Stuart's plea and ploughed on. The 27 pre-prepared questions they asked related to evidence the police were going to use in court and included a letter John had sent to Daniel Stuart, photographs of the fire aftermath and the notes Stuart had left at Bolton's office immediately after the fire. Finch point blank refused to answer any of the questions, and Hayes wrote either 'No Reply' or 'No Comment' next to all the questions Finch was asked.

To all the questions bar two, Stuart gave the following replies:[34]

No reply. I want a solicitor
No comment. I want a solicitor.
I want a solicitor. No other comment.
I want a solicitor.
No comment.
I want a legal representation.
No comment. I want a legal representation.
No[t] until we have legal representation.

There were only two questions to which he gave a slightly different answer. Regarding the code that Redmond had found in the phone booth, he said, 'Let me see these things. I want a solicitor', and when shown two letters he had sent to Daniel Stuart he said, 'I want to have a look at that.'[35]

Both at the Supreme Court trial and when interviewed by the police during Operation Graveyard, Atkinson agreed that at the end of the interview on 8 March at which Weir was present, Stuart had made it clear that if he was to talk to the police again, he wanted a solicitor present. Yet after this, we have the mini-confession and admissions at the watch-house, made when he was unaccompanied by a solicitor.[36]

They nicknamed Hayes the 'Bishop' because he was so successful at receiving confessions. The honorary cleric had an amazing strike rate.[37]

41

Who bombed the Whiskey and why?

Stuart, the only source of the Whiskey firebombing story, said was it a southern takeover protection racket. Good liars are consistent, and Stuart was an abysmal one. In the early interviews with Stuart, Hicks wrote summaries and dated them. He taped the later ones and had them transcribed. The variations in the narrative were irreconcilable and nonsensical.

In chronological order Stuart said:

1. McPherson may be looking over the nightclubs (16 October and 15 November). Someone described as a 'dog bastard' would never have worked with Stuart.
2. Stuart himself was going around the nightclubs offering a protection deal (23 November).
3. On the way to the airport, Miller had asked him if there was any money in the nightclubs in Brisbane (22 December).
4. While Miller was driving to the Sydney Airport, the car stopped and there were

four men beside the road. Two men (whom he did not know) got into the car and spoke to him about the nightclub scene in Brisbane, while the other two were silent (2 January).[1]
5. McPherson and Smith were in town (12 January).[2]
6. The young crims were at the airport (13 January, to Bolton).
7. The two men who stood next to the car as Stuart made his way to the airport (who either did or did not speak, his recollection was inconsistent) turned up at the Flamingo club just prior to the Whiskey fire (7 March).
8. Les, Ross and Rodger were at the airport and one other person was standing nearby (8 March, when interviewed with Weir present).

There were other variations. For months, he said he did not know their names—after the fire, he said he did. However, the suspects he named were in prison when they supposedly met him on 20 December at Sydney Airport and then saw him at the Flamingo just prior to the fire. He was a credibility termite; he would say something, and then immediately munch through the friable foundations that supported his alibi. Much of his verbiage was patently false.

Rogerson described the story of a takeover as 'bullshit' and 'crap'. He was correct.

Bolton should have known better. For Stuart, the 'southern crims takeover' was an oldie but a goodie. Stuart had been pedalling this nonsense to him since at least 1963.

In one of Bolton's earliest stories on Stuart, the supercrim described a plot to blow up part of Boggo Road Gaol so he could escape. Bolton had written, 'Southern criminals masterminded the plan to free Houdini escapologist John Andrew Stuart ... Two top southern criminals were in Brisbane recently working on details of the escape.' Stuart added that southern criminal 'confederates' had left money hidden on a golf course for him to use. The story is identical to the one he would use prior to the Whiskey slaughter; that southern criminals were behind it all and two top criminals (McPherson and Smith) were in town, ready to cause mayhem.

In the following articles, there were similar anecdotes. In the 'Madmen are about to escape from the Asylum' tale in August 1963, Stuart claimed that prisoners had a contact who carried messages between the escapees and 'the southern underworld'. The Sydney criminals had supplied three hacksaw blades (surely they were more easily sourced from a local store).

Bolton continued these southern fables in 1974, after the fire. Southern gangsters had put a $15,000 price (to be paid into any bank of the hitman's choice) on the head of Stuart—a gaol murder contract. This explained why other prisoners had swallowed wire and other objects to get close to the hospitalised Stuart and kill him.[3] The question of why it needed up to ten prisoners to get close to him was not addressed—was one not enough?

On Stuart's release from his Steele sentence in 1972 and during his first meeting with Bolton, Stuart talked vaguely of southern gangsters. On 2 August 1972, a police inspector at Fortitude Valley told Bolton that he was not interested in Stuart's ramblings on 'southern crims'.

It is not only Stuart's Just So Stories of New South Wales gangsters that are an issue. All of the stories published from 1962 form a fanciful collection, one that would fit comfortably into the fairytale section of any local library. They include flying a plane into the Opera House, explosions to free a supercrim, bloodbaths, attempts to assassinate Stuart in a prison hospital and mass prison breakouts.[4] At best, they reflect poorly on the editors who allowed them to increase circulation—most should never have been published. They are unadulterated drivel, and exploit an obviously disturbed individual.

There is another reason they were nonsense. Stuart never dobbed, which is why the Sandy Gallop Mental Hospital mass escape fantasy, published in August 1963, wherein Stuart supposedly ratted on the inmates and told the authorities of the impending breakout, is bollocks. A story that emerged in 1978 and was repeated in 1988 said that Stuart was recruited as an undercover police agent and given the moniker EMU.[5] He supposedly passed on information from the criminal world to the police. This was impossible; he was a solid crim who hated lagging dogs more than anyone in the entire world, including paedophiles. This is something he repeated ad nauseam to anyone who would listen. In 1966, he wrote, 'The cops fuckin hate me and that can only mean one thing. I don't help them....'

He said two senior officers recruited him to spy on corrupt police. One of the recruiters must have been Hicks. Hicks supposedly had a thick EMU file, which he later destroyed under instructions from Commissioner Whitrod. Hicks makes clear in his notes that he viewed Stuart as mentally ill, erratic, aimless, paranoid and a *useless* source of intelligence. Other members of the CIU and CIB agreed. For eight months, Hicks had valiantly tried to elicit from Stuart some detail on the southern extortion racket and failed.

Solid crims do not talk; therefore they cannot be informants. As an old-school maximum-security prison graduate, this was one of the 'criminal principles' he mentioned to Hicks. Lagging would make him feel like the fucking dog he despised and hated.

It was actually the reverse; Hicks was *Stuart's* informant: Stuart wanted to know how the police viewed him, and absurdly thought his disclosure of a looming Whiskey attack would absolve him of responsibility. It was another of Stuart's tales.

Stuart initially approached Hicks on 28 July 1972, and on 22 September 1972 he introduced the sobriquet EMU, one he would use if *he* wanted to make secret contact. Hicks kept some of the EMU correspondence, which consists of trivia (such as how primitive some of the blacks he saw were) or, most importantly, unbreakable alibis exonerating him from certain crimes e.g., the Maloney murder. This was the point of the code name—to alibi himself from crimes. It was Stuart who obsessively maintained contact with the police on his return to Brisbane in July 1972. Hicks *never* called Stuart. Stuart said he would rather die before he became a dog. His wish came true on 1 January 1979.

Stuart also told Bolton that the police had supplied him with a high-powered late-model car for his drive through Queensland and up to

Darwin in late 1972. This was false; he drove a 1972 Ford Fairlane sedan with Northern Territory number plates, registration no.86-787, owned by Sue; hardly a turbo-charged speed machine.[6]

The talk of a takeover did not start after Stuart's release from gaol following the Richmond theft in December 1972; it was well before that.

The first concrete date we have for Stuart introducing the discussion of southern criminal activity in relation to the Brisbane nightclubs after his release (for the Steele shooting in July 1972) is 16 October 1972, when he told Hicks that McPherson was in town looking them over. Coincidentally or otherwise, by September 1972 the owners of the Whiskey knew they were in financial trouble. The problem with interpreting the threat is that it is a story he used continuously for decades, and with differing motives. It was the joker card in the back pocket, a fiction he pulled out for dramatic effect to intimidate people.

The earliest *specific* link to the Whiskey was on either 30 December 1972 or 6 January 1973, when Stuart spoke to Bolton (who told the police it was a Saturday, but wasn't sure which date). This was soon after Stuart had returned to Brisbane after being released from gaol following the Richmond theft.

Only one club was ever targeted, the Whiskey, with Stuart occasionally mentioning its sister club, Chequers.[7] His reference to the Jet was irrelevant, because he was barred from entering.

The Whiskey was bankrupt. The CIU (Hicks, Becker and Voigt), Commissioner Whitrod and Police Minister Hodges—all good, honest men—knew that extortion was not a credible motive. It would be inexplicable if it was true, but it was not.

The possible explanations for the fire include drugs, revenge, a standover [extortion for protection] (Stuart's talk), competition between clubs, insurance (including eliminating financial difficulties), masking a fraud, 'politically blackening' Commissioner Whitrod and Police Minister Hodges, or a combination of several of these.

There is no evidence for drugs. An article after the fire said the police knew of one former staff member who was a supplier of drugs to young people. The article also said that he was an embezzler and a homosexual. They were referring to John Hannay, but gave no evidence for the assertion that drugs were involved in the abomination.[8]

The Whiskey and Chequers were in dire straits, so competition between clubs is not believable. This is a theory expounded by John

Ryan; specifically, he mentions the National Hotel and the Lands Office Hotel.[9] The incident he uses to back up this claim, the schoolboy spat between Chicka Reeves and Brian Ahern, was unrelated, and is explained later. The same reasoning applies to the theory that it was a police conspiracy to besmirch the two police supremos, Whitrod and Hodges. The Whiskey was a destitute no-frills club—no jewel in the crown for Brisbane's glitterati and an unconvincing target as a means of embarrassment.

In 1972, Stuart said he was going around the clubs, which was a lie. He only ever approached one club's owners, the Littles and Bell, directly, well after Bolton had broken the story to the public. Bolton knew by 6 January *at the latest* that the Whiskey would be bombed, but Stuart only bothered to confront the Littles a month later. He had mentioned the possibility of a general nightclub attack to Farr in mid-January, but this was after Farr had *approached him* about intimidating his wife. Stuart did not specify the Whiskey to Farr.

42

Finances

The most persistent rumour has been that the fire was an insurance scam, or to cover a fraud or mismanagement, or both, with a grievance in relation to a bashing a possible extra incentive. Some say the Littles could also write off the loss and use the money to buy Chequers at auction.[1] At this juncture, there is no evidence to suggest that any of these rumours have any foundation in fact.

The Littles and Hannay blamed each other for the financial crisis.

Chequers Nightclub, in Elizabeth Street, opened in August 1972. It was operated by a company called Cabaret Holdings Pty Ltd, of which Brian Little and Kenneth Little were shareholders and directors. Cabaret Holdings Pty Ltd had no interest in any other club. Little Enterprises Pty Ltd only owned the Whiskey Au Go Go, and had no interest in any other club. Both of these companies were wound up prior to the sale of Chequers, which occurred in May 1973.

In September 1972, it was claimed that due to mismanagement or fraud (or both), both companies were in financial crisis, and on 21 November 1972, they were placed into provisional liquidation, with Mr Lloyd George Rees from the firm Rees & Rees designated provisional liquidator.[2]

A meeting of creditors on 25 January 1973 was told that a small profit was being made. On that date, the Littles were reinstated as managers and the finances continued to improve, with the Whiskey making $1000 a week profit at the time of the fire (according to the Littles), although they were still $2000 in arrears in relation to the rent.[3]

The Littles' debt was well over a million dollars in today's terms. The debt totalled $115,883, consisting of Cabaret Holdings $45,301 and Little Enterprises $70,582.[4]

The Littles pointed the finger at Hannay, who was sacked. They argued that Hannay had caused the debt in two ways. Firstly, he had financed the Chequers venture through the Littles' associate company Cabaret Holdings Pty Ltd, rather than through Little Enterprises Pty Ltd.[5] Cabaret Holdings was undercapitalized, and the debts had mounted up. Secondly, Whiskey staff told them that Hannay had embezzled money.

Hannay denied this, and countered that it was the Littles' fault, and that he had been under the impression that the Littles would have no difficulty in either paying or raising the amount needed to fit out the Chequers premises. Consequently, Hannay used tradesmen that he had worked with for years, and at least fifty per cent of them did the work based on his word that he would pay them.[6]

Hannay quoted amounts of $7000 (electrician), $11,500 (shopfitters), $5000 (painter), $9000 (carpeting), $9000 (tables and chairs) and $5000 (refrigeration) as some of the debts incurred. These alone tally $46,000. It cost $90,000 to make Chequers into a premier nightclub, according to Hannay, although the Littles said that this figure was inflated.[7]

Little Enterprises Pty Ltd was undercapitalised from the outset, and on 23 June 1972, on behalf of the company, the Littles' solicitor John McGrath negotiated a loan of $25,417.40 from United Dominions Corporation Limited. The loan was secured by a Bill of Sale over plant and equipment and a Bill of Mortgage over the lease of the premises. This gave United Dominions a measure of control over the Whiskey in the event of a default, and remains a standard insurance practise today. The Littles provided a security deposit of $4000, lodged with United Dominions.[8] According to the Littles, although Little Enterprises was recapitalised, Hannay financed Chequers through Cabaret Holdings.[9]

Two insurance policies covered the Whiskey's plant, fixtures, fittings and stock. These only applied to Little Enterprises Pty Ltd.[10] The two policies were issued under cover notes, with Little Enterprises Pty Ltd as lessees and United Dominions as lessors. The same company, in the name of Little Enterprises Pty Ltd, also issued another cover note as owners, provisional liquidator appointed. This cover note included $2000 of stock and $3000 in plant and equipment, a total of $5000.

Subsequent to the fire, a claim was made on Mercantile Mutual Insurance (the insurance company for the plant and equipment mortgaged to United Dominions Corporation Limited). They made a payment of $15,090.87 to United Dominions Corporation Limited, the mortgagees endorsed on the policy. Under the personal guarantees given by Brian Little, United Dominions claimed Brian Little was jointly and severally liable for the payment of the balance of $1867.03.[11] This was in addition to the security deposit of $4000, which the Littles forfeited to United Dominions. The Littles said they collectively lost $5867.03 ($4000 + $1867.03) from the lease of the chattels, plus rent of $3630.40 (which had grown from $2000), the sale price of the cold room $450 and the interest on the security deposit of $70.

There were more personal debts. Brian Little was required to pay two arrears he had guaranteed, one to Carlton & United Breweries for liquor to the value of approximately $1800 and another to Claude Neon, an advertising signage firm, for $1100.[12] These were not collected under the liquidation. Because of the non-payment of these debts, a sequestration order was issued by the creditors against Brian Little and he became an undischarged bankrupt. Ken Little avoided the same fate.

Their solicitor John McGrath testified that 'Neither the directors or the shareholders of Little Enterprises Pty Ltd, the proprietors of Whiskey Au Go Go, will receive any monies from the liquidation of that company.'[13] The insurance payout did, however, remove most of the Littles' $115,883 obligation.

Apart from the suggestion that Hannay had been booking costs to an undercapitalised company, there was also the accusation that he had embezzled money. About two months prior to Hannay's sacking, Brian Little was informed by a staff member named Jeni, who worked in the office, that she suspected Hannay was taking large amounts of money out of the company. Brian Little conferred with his accountant, Mr Rees, and he was able to raise enough doubt regarding Hannay to go to the Fraud Squad.[14]

They suggested that he have the books audited, but this proved impossible, as they had been destroyed in the fire at Alice's, which was owned by Hannay. According to a witness statement, Hannay is also said to have admitted to Lin, who was the cashier and receptionist at Chequers, that he was going to destroy the ledgers.

The Littles said that Hannay had stolen anything up to $30,000 over a period of about eight months.[15] Brian Little added, 'I know John Hannay very well, and I believe that he could have something to do with the fire. Hannay is a very good organiser, and he was the original organiser of Whiskey Au Go Go and Chequers. I regard as very suspicious that he has not been in touch with me [since the fire].' Hannay himself said the Littles told their staff he had stolen between $30,000 and $70,000.

Stokes nominated Hannay as a suspect in the fire in his *Port News* articles, saying that Hannay was the 'only man to financially profit from the Whiskey and that he was the man who masterminded the entire plan.' Stokes's thesis was that Hannay had torched the Whiskey and destroyed the books to mask the estimated $50,000 he had stolen.[16] Hannay has consistently denied all the accusations that have been made against him, and they remain uncorroborated.

What cannot be refuted are Hannay's repeated run-ins with the law. One commentator put it that Hannay had 'a career studded with question marks to which answers are not readily forthcoming.'[17]

Born in 1942, the career of the club and hotel manager started early when he left school at 13. Moving to Brisbane at 16, he started work at the Myer Store in the Valley. He would then have a lifetime of involvement in clubs, opening some of Brisbane's most popular venues from the sixties onwards including TCs, Teen City and The Cave.

He quickly gained a reputation as a non-payer, thief and fraudster. A newspaper said that one of the earliest question marks was his supporting evidence that helped to clear a police officer who was 'under a cloud' in the early sixties.[18] They did not elaborate on the circumstances.

The band he was managing for four years in the 1960s, The Planets, had first-hand experience of money vanishing when under Hannay's control.[19] Band member Len Austin recalled that 'John Hannay used to do the banking at the end of the night. It was a considerable sum of money in those days. He came to us and said,

"Someone has got into the boot of my car and all our money is gone." That was our night's takings, and I can't remember the figure, but it was quite a lot of pounds in those days. No one actually believed him. We're all pretty sure that he did it himself because different guys like Brian [Gagen] and so on said that it would be impossible to get through the boot, although he had slashed the back seat to get the money out. But that's John Hannay for you.' John Bell recalled that the amount that had been stolen was 120 pounds. After this theft, The Planets dismissed Hannay as their manager.[20]

There is proof that he stole directly from the Whiskey. On 22 February 1973, Hannay called the pawnshop Monte De Piete in the Valley and requested a loan of $1000 based on office equipment he had available. Hannay offered refrigerators, two typewriters, an electronic calculator and office furniture. Most of the items were too big for the moneylender to handle.

On 1 March 1973, he took an Olivetti electric typewriter and a Canon electronic calculator, both wrapped in a red tablecloth (identical to those used at the Whiskey), to the shop.[21] He also had a six-stone diamond ring, an 18-carat gold white-stone ring and a gent's opal ring, and requested a loan of $400. He accepted an advance of $175 for the property.

Police inquiries showed that the calculator had been sold by Swift & Bleakley to Little Enterprises Pty Ltd on 30 May 1972. The delivery address was the Whiskey Au Go Go nightclub.

Early on 8 March, the day of the Whiskey fire, a private investigator tracked Hannay down at the Park Avenue Hotel Motel in Rockhampton.[22] A $400 cheque he had passed at the Cork-N-Fork Restaurant in Brisbane on 23 February 1973 from his firm John Hannay Promotions Pty Ltd had bounced. The private investigator had been sent to recover the monies. The investigator was told by a band member (who Hannay had employed at this hotel), 'For Christ sake don't upset him. He's worried now. He had a phone call from Brisbane last night [sic] and the Whiskey Au Go Go has been blown up and 15 people have been killed.'

Bounced cheques and non-payment of bills were Hannay trademarks. Before he set foot in the Whiskey, Hannay had left a trail of debt and broken promises, and had been sued a mind-boggling 50-plus times by individuals, companies and the government for debt default between 1968 and 1972. His was a familiar face at the Supreme Court. A sample follows: Harold Vinnicombe and Associates Pty Limited, $147.27; Poster Haste, $193.78; Langlands Park Swimming Centre, $166.10; Deputy Commissioner for

Taxation, $3,635.23; Moreton Bay Trawlers, $176.10; General Motors (Fairlane station wagon), $2147.00; Associated Securities (Fairlane station wagon), $3,887; Commonwealth of Australia, $947.76, and the Deputy Commissioner of Taxation, $2196.00.

According to the Littles, Hannay was known as a confidence trickster. Brian Little stated that 'Hannay, to get acts, would engage people in Sydney, telling them he had booked them at the Whiskey Au Go Go or Chequers and on their arrival in Brisbane, would tell them that these two clubs had cancelled their act, but because he was "honest John Hannay", he would give them a week's work and send them to various places such as Gympie or Rockhampton.[23] In my opinion, this was a complete confidence trick on Hannay's part.' The police had the same intelligence. Hicks would write, '...it is suggested that Hannay owes a lot of money to a lot of artists. The information is that he won't pay anybody.'[24]

Various informants rang the police after the fire. A female advised that a month before the fire, John Hannay had said he would blow up some nightclubs in Brisbane.[25] Another said Hannay had touched the Whiskey for $100,000, mainly by rolling back the till records, and as a result he was sacked.[26]

The cash routine for the Whiskey was as follows. The serving of meals stopped at 1.45am, and then at 2am a balance of the cash register was made against the monies received for cover charges, cigarettes and food. The proceeds from the sale of alcohol were presumably separate. Three separate totals were obtained and checked against the money in the till, which included the float. The takings were then put in a marked envelope on which the totals were shown and the float was handed separately to the manager.[27] From then on, there was no cover charge and no other takings were recorded on the register.[28] The same would have applied to Chequers.

There was sufficient circumstantial evidence to suggest that the former Whiskey manager should have been probed over the Alice's loss. The basis for this opinion is as follows.

The timing was serendipitous; three days after Bolton told the public the Fraud Squad was investigating the disappearance of $50,000, Hannay's business and the Whiskey's books (whatever state they were in) were incinerated.

George Freeleagus, who worked at Chequers as a cleaner and drove artists for Hannay, was seen by Ken Little at 11am, hours after the fire, standing on the footpath opposite Alice's.[29] He was with James Constantine, another employee of Hannay's and a director of Alice's. Both Freeleagus and Constantine worked from Hannay's Prestige Artists Brunswick office.

Ken Little jokingly said to Freeleagus, 'Where were you last night?' Freeleagus replied, 'Don't think I had anything to do with it.' Constantine said much the same thing. Both of them were looking at each other and laughing at the same time.

Two days later, Freeleagus drove Ken Little to Chequers from the Little-owned Kangaroo Hotel[30].

Freeleagus: John Hannay and the landlord are working in together. The landlord offered Hannay a large sum of money if the premises were burnt down. Hannay has offered me $3000 if we do the job. This money will be paid after the insurance company has settled. Jimmy [Constantine] and I discussed it with Hannay on the afternoon that the fire happened in Hannay's office and Hannay said let it go a couple of days more and I said, 'No, I'll do it tonight or never.'

Ken Little: How did you light it?

Freeleagus: Jimmy [Constantine] and me went into the building from the back way and rigged an electrical fault near the stairway going up to the coffee shop. I poured nine gallons of petrol throughout the place. I didn't touch anything in the place.

If I had thought about it I would have taken out those chairs and tables belonging to you and Brian [Little] the day before. After we poured the petrol throughout the building we left and parked the car away from the building for some time, but it never went off.

We had to go back a second time. It was very scary and creepy because we didn't know if it might go off. We rigged it up again and I just got home when I heard the fire brigades.

Ken Little: I don't think you will get your money off Hannay.

Freeleagus: If I don't I'll blow up his Mustang [car].

After this conversation, Little saw Freeleagus a number of times and he continued to brag about how he'd lit the fire: 'I'll give him [Hannay] another to pay [sic] and if he doesn't pay, then I'll blow up his Mustang.' On the Monday before the fire he told Longhurst he was still dirty with Hannay, seemingly for not having received his dues. An eyewitness told Ken Little, "...earlier in the evening before the fire I saw George Freeleagus with a nine-gallon tin...." The insurance for Alice's had not been paid by the time of the October Supreme Court trial.[31]

Ken Little said he believed that Freeleagus would do anything that Hannay asked him to do.[32] He further stated that in 1972, possibly in the middle of the year, Hannay had told him and his brother Brian that he intended to burn Alice's using George Freeleagus and Jimmy Constantine.[33] According to the Littles, Hannay said Constantine was an expert in rigging electrical faults. Constantine warned the Littles not to sack Hannay: 'You had better not, you will find yourself dead.'[34]

Freeleagus later admitted to the police that he had told Ken Little he had ignited the bar, but he was only kidding; it was all a big joke.[35] He told the police he had been doing 'some work' in the upstairs section where the coffee lounge was located and admitted he was the last person to leave the shop at midnight on the 16th, even though it had been closed for 'some weeks'.[36] Alice's went up in flames just after he left. The official police report indicates there was no break in—it looked like an inside job.

Finch's defence counsel pointed out that Hannay had taken out a new insurance note on

Alice's 13 days before the fire. On 4 January, he insured the business for loss of profits of $7,800, machinery, plant, stock and all other contents for $22,500, clothing and personal effects for $3,000, and business and office equipment for the sum of $5,000. The justification—the broker at the insurance company was 'a very, very good friend' of one of Hannay's employees 'and that's the reason that we changed our insurance.' Hannay's action proved portentous, as all the machinery, plant, stock, business and office equipment and other contents were vaporised less than two weeks later.

On 12 September 1973, Hannay was unfit to appear at the Supreme Court trial because of severe head injuries he had suffered as a result of a horse-riding accident at Rockhampton on 19 August. He had 'brain damage', needed surgery on his skull and had 'retrograde amnesia and expressive aphasia'; he could remember nothing, and had problems speaking.[37] He eventually did front the trial, but had a doctor next to him. Hannay was barely coherent: 'It's only about ten days that I not talk at all because I know things up here (indicated forehead) but when I speak them I likely to know what I want to show and say the difference.' He was unsure if he owned Poolside Services Pty Ltd (which owned Alice's) and seemed to deny that he was connected with

John Hannay Promotions Pty Ltd. He also denied that he had made a call to his solicitor from Rockhampton at 'about 2 o'clock' (the time of the Whiskey fire) and denied that he had used a singer as a front to buy Chequers from the Littles for $100,000 after he was sacked.[38]

Hannay said the money that was missing from the Whiskey had been stolen by the bookkeeper (Mr Byers?) and 'another gentleman who worked there but I don't know their name.' There were no follow-up questions. Wasn't Hannay himself the Whiskey bookkeeper?

Eventually, Hannay recovered sufficiently to manage more clubs and hotels, commit more fraud, and ultimately go to gaol.[39]

In 1973, Hannay told the ABC that Stuart had acted separately from Finch.[40] He was adamant that other people, not Finch, were involved, and although he gave police the names of those persons, they were not interested. He mentioned no other names in his police statements. In 1976, after three years of silence, Hannay talked to the *Sunday Sun*. He was on his way to his first million, and maintained that he had had nothing to do with the fire.[41]

After leaving Brisbane, Hannay stayed away until 1986, living first in Rockhampton and then in Mackay, where he initially did well with the Oriental Hotel (as the licensee).[42] He had purchased this shortly after the fire. However, there were setbacks. In 1976, $200,000 in cash and cheques was stolen from the Oriental.[43]

Described as 'a millionaire', he bought the Daydream Island Resort in the Whitsundays in April 1979, announcing ambitious refurbishment plans, but a little over a year later, a receiver and manager had moved in.[44] He became chairman of the Mackay Visitors Bureau, and set his sights on running for mayor, but his political ambition tanked when it was discovered that he had not registered on the electoral roll.

The Mackay businessman planned to spend $5 million creating a tourist resort on Hook Island, south of Hayman Island. The grandiose scheme included an entertainment complex and 100 self-contained accommodation units. He bought Hook Island's observatory and 10.9 hectares on the island for $600,000.[45] This venture fell through soon after.

In 1981, under parliamentary privilege, ALP Member of Parliament Kevin Hooper named Hannay as one of four Queensland mafia godfathers of crime; the others were Geraldo and Antonio Bellino (of Pinocchio's fame) and Luciano Scognamiglio.[46] Kevin Hooper added that Mr Hannay was 'a shadowy businessman who does not pay his debts including, I am told, government charges such as payroll tax ... and, no doubt, licensing fees'.[47] Hooper, an outspoken opposition spokesman for police and prisons, rightly claimed that drug trafficking, prostitution and gambling could not operate without political and police permission at the highest level. He bravely called out Police Commissioner Terence Lewis and Assistant Commissioner Tony Murphy as 'protected criminals'. The Fitzgerald Inquiry vindicated his assertions. Lewis went to gaol and Murphy's name is synonymous with police corruption.

Two years later, in 1983, Hannay earned a one-year gaol sentence for misappropriating the superannuation payout of a deceased employee.[48]

He also faced other fraud-related charges, including stealing money from a member of the Bellino family, although no conviction was recorded. Despite Hooper's description of the Bellinos as mafia godfathers, Hannay described them as some of the most honourable businessmen he had been associated with. Despite Hannay's glowing reference, Geraldo Bellino went to gaol for bribery.

Hannay continued his involvement with nightclubs, owning The Roxy and The Beat from 1980 in Ann Street, Fortitude Valley. The Beat became a 'Megaclub', replete with seven dance rooms, seven bars and three chill-out areas.[49]

It had a reputation for easy availability of amphetamines. These rumours peaked after the 1984 death of a judge's teenage daughter, Deborah Hanger, from an overdose of ecstasy, which she had allegedly obtained from this club. Hannay refuted the accusation, and it was not proven.[50]

On 19 March 1986, the 44-year-old Hannay was convicted of possessing a sawn-off .22 rifle at Mackay. The Mackay Magistrates Court heard that Senior Constable Brian Marlin had found the rifle in the boot of Hannay's car. The result was a $300 fine.[51]

Hannay reappeared in the Mackay Magistrates Court on five charges of false pretences and one charge brought under the Companies Act.[52] He pleaded not guilty to falsely pretending that a loan had been approved, and that he had induced Martin Lingard to lend him $27,000 in cash and spend $13,900 on property, which he then used to build a bottle shop at the Metropolitan Hotel, Mackay, in 1985. Lingard claimed that Hannay had obtained the cash in four lots by telling him a loan had been approved, but was held up by paperwork. Lingard said he had exhausted all civil avenues after Hannay and his mother's company, Central Queensland Liquor Supermarket Pty Ltd, went bankrupt. About $2 million had been lost by companies with which Hannay had been associated since 1982. The charges were dropped in 1987 and then later revived, although ultimately Judge Botting found that Hannay had no case to answer.

Life got surreal for Hannay in 1996. Simeon Pandelis, 41, conspired to murder him on 10 September 1996.[53] Pandelis pleaded guilty to the charge. Prosecutor John Callanan told the court that five men were involved in the plot, which had its origins in the middle of the year. The motive for the 1996 'hit' was the recovery of $58,000 owed to Brian Story for special lighting at one of Hannay's clubs. Hannay believed that the debt was only $3000.

The court heard that Hannay had agreed to pay $15,000, but when the money was not forthcoming, Story approached Pandelis and his boyfriend at the Sportsman Hotel and asked for help in getting the debt paid. Pandelis had originally agreed to terrorise Hannay into paying the money, but became upset when the nightclub owner allegedly tried to seduce his boyfriend. Unbeknownst to Story, Pandelis decided to kill Hannay, and recruited a security officer and a carpenter who worked at Hannay's clubs.

Hannay's employee, Leon Carriage, gave Pandelis a .22 rifle and ammunition for the killing, but then thought better of it and decided to tip off the police, who commenced surveillance.

The police intercepted the three defendants in Newstead. A search of their car's boot revealed a .22 rifle, two concrete blocks, two lengths of chain, pieces of wire cable, clothing and sandshoes. Hannay's body was to be disposed of in a waterway, weighed down by the items found in the vehicle.

Pandelis received a six-year gaol sentence. Three of the other men pleaded guilty to conspiracy to murder and received wholly suspended five-year gaol terms.[54] The judge ordered Story to perform 200 hours of community service with no conviction recorded. The barrister representing Pandelis said that it was all a gay spat: 'This is all played out against the background of Brisbane's homosexual community, it was Alice in Wonderland stuff.' Pandelis had become upset when he had learned that Hannay had tried to seduce his boyfriend. 'Mr Hannay has a reputation for seducing young men; whether it is true or not I don't know.'

In 1999, Hannay had embarked on another venture.[55] The club Heaven opened inside the old Presbyterian church on Warner Street in the Valley. Hannay spent $500,000 fitting the club out in a tongue-in-cheek biblical style. Guests walked through a landscaped area with fountains and life-size figures of Adam and Eve, two angels hung from the ceiling and a life-size figure of St Peter greeted them at the door. On the ceiling, 187 mirror balls sparkled. The church, which was built in 1884, had hosted the wedding of the future premier Sir Joh Bjelke-Petersen and his wife Lady Flo in 1953.

In 2000, the Brisbane Industrial Magistrates Court slapped a $25,500 fine on Hannay for excessive noise levels.[56] The Beat Cabaret and Restaurant was fined $4000 for breaches of the Workplace Health and Safety Act, plus $17,500 in court costs, and Hannay, the club's chief executive officer, was also fined $4000. The Magistrate found that Hannay had placed the bar staff and disc jockey's health at risk after exposing them to noise above the maximum acceptable levels.

Hannay was fined for failing to display the name of the club's liquor licensee.[57] The Beat earned a $225 penalty after *The Courier-Mail* revealed that the Fortitude Valley nightspot did not display the licensee's (Ann St Holdings) details as required under the Liquor Act.

More than 30 years after the Whiskey fire, Hannay's problematic business methods were still in the spotlight. In 2005, the Australian Securities and Investments Commission (ASIC) banned him from managing corporations for five years.[58]

ASIC banned Hannay for the maximum period permissible under the law after an investigation found that he had been a director of eight failed companies including Geecrest Pty Limited, Trexcorp Pty Limited, Nestmere Pty Limited, Permalex Pty Limited (Permalex), Derryford Pty Limited, Mossroy Pty Limited, Widevale Pty Limited and Wildlodge Pty Limited. The failed companies primarily operated nightclubs in and around the Brisbane CBD and the Gold Coast. Mossroy traded as The Beat Nightclub and Permalex traded as Options Nightclub.

ASIC found that Hannay's conduct included breaches of the Corporations Act 2001 relating to directors duties, the requirement to keep proper books and records and the requirement to assist in the orderly and proper winding up of companies, and that these breaches constituted serious misconduct. A spokesman described the records as a 'shemozzle'. He had learnt nothing since losing another company's records (the Whiskey) 30 years earlier.

The liquidators reported that Hannay's companies were unable to pay creditors any more than 50 cents in the dollar. Their debts totalled over $1.2 million, with significant amounts owing to the Australian Taxation Office and WorkCover. Other creditors included Rentokil Initial Pty Ltd, Energex, the Australian Performing

Rights Association Limited and Telstra Corporation Limited.

An investigation by *The Courier-Mail* revealed that the state's liquor watchdog had failed to check possibly false statements provided by Hannay.[59] The Liquor Licensing Division did not pick up on apparent errors about a defunct company in a document signed by Hannay during a licence transfer for the Fortitude Valley dance venue The Beat nightclub. In 2001, Mossroy transferred the Beat's licence to another company that listed Hannay as a director, Ann St Holdings. At this time, Hannay signed a document stating that he had not been involved with any company that had previously been placed into liquidation or receivership. However, a company search listed Mr Hannay as a former director of Oxco Pty Ltd, which had a court order to appoint a liquidator in 1998. Oxco was the licensee of the Valley's Roxy nightclub from 1993 to 1997.

Business failure is not a crime, unless there is criminal intent. However, there had been a pattern of dubious accounting practices, including not protecting a club's ledgers. There were also the repeated accusations and demonstrated accounts of theft, which culminated in a prison sentence. There were many unanswered questions. Why did Hannay drop Stuart off at the Whiskey on 5 March as Longhurst had stated? Why did Stuart lie and say Hannay was working at Kin Kin as a postmaster during this week? John Ryan said that Stuart was seen in remote places with Hannay prior to the fire.[60] Brian Little saw a note from Stuart saying he would do anything for Hannay. Why was he never properly questioned about the missing Whiskey funds? Who was this bookkeeper that he had said had embezzled the funds? Why was he not quizzed about the fire at Alice's, both from the point of view of an alleged insurance scam and the destruction of the Whiskey's financial records when the company was still in the hands of the receiver? What was his relationship with the Clockwork Orange goons, and with McCulkin and O'Dempsey? Why was he never asked about his relationship with Cabaret Holdings Pty Ltd and the alleged misfinancing? Why was he debiting money for the Littles through his own company, Prestige Artists? The police also had intelligence that Hannay had asked Stuart to intimidate Farr, but had never pursued Hannay about this.[61] Why not?

There was nothing dubious about the Littles' insurance practices; they appeared to be appropriate. United Dominions and Mercantile Mutual were reputable financiers and insurers, respectively. After conducting an investigation,

Mercantile Mutual had no qualms about making the insurance payout.

There were rumours that the Littles had torched the Whiskey to wipe out their $115,883 debt with an insurance payout. However, the payout did not extinguish all their debts. Brian Little still had personal debts outstanding, including the $4000 security deposit, which he forfeited to United Dominions (as the licensee of the Whiskey, he had given a personal guarantee). Carlton & United Breweries sued him, as did Claude Neon. Little had put $30,000 of his own money into Little Enterprises Pty Ltd and $15,000 into Chequers.[62] Furthermore, an incident two weeks after the catastrophe demonstrates that these rumours were implausible, as the Littles fought hard to retain the Whiskey, despite the setback.

On 20 March 1973, Brian Little and his solicitor John McGrath visited the building owner Thomas Leighton at his office. Little expounded his theory that the attack on the Whiskey had been carried out by the two persons charged, that Stuart was insane and no criminal would work with him anyway. He was convinced that the fire was an isolated event and would not happen again. Little then asked if Leighton would be prepared to lease him the top floor of the building, previously occupied by the Whiskey, to which Leighton replied that the area was under offer to another person for use as office space, but Leighton would advise him through his solicitor. Leighton said he had 'no intention of acceding to his request whatsoever'.[63]

Two days later, Little returned to Leighton's office, this time alone, and to show him some courtesy, Leighton closed the door. Little again asked about the ex-Whiskey space, to which Leighton replied that he was sorry, but he was semi-committed to a prospective tenant.

Brian Little: Oh no you're not. If you read your lease you will find that you can only terminate it if there is total destruction. I thought I might talk you into leasing the area to me without the creditors knowing, but if you won't cooperate, I intend forcing Rees and Rees to continue the lease, then make them assign the lease to me or one of my companies.

Leighton: Well if that is the way you want it you had better get your solicitor to contact my solicitor.

Brian Little: Well if you want a fight you will get one. I could have traded out of that loss in one year, but I have lost so much now, that even if I have to saddle myself with seventy thousand dollars' worth of creditors I'm going to do it.

His behaviour was completely different from that displayed in previous encounters, indeed it was so aggressive and threatening that Leighton immediately phoned his solicitor, who advised him to phone Buchanan at the CIB.

During the Supreme Court trial, the prosecution homed in on the Littles' post-Whiskey purchase of Chequers and probed the legalities, but to no avail. It was true that they still wanted to retain a stake in Chequers.[64]

Littles Enterprises was liquidated prior to the auction of Chequers, which was held in May 1973. There were three bidders, but it failed to reach the reserve price and was passed in. One of the bidders was John McGrath, the Littles' solicitor. He bid up to $45,000, and later said, 'I was bidding under instructions from Mr Kenneth Little and some other person....' Gramons Pty Ltd, a company incorporated specifically to buy Chequers, obtained the club by private treaty. According to the purchaser, John McGrath, the price of $46,000 was deemed fair market value. The directors of Gramons were John McGrath (on behalf of Ken Little) and John Morris (owner of the De Brazil club), each of whom held two A class management shares.

The contract was subject to a new six-year lease of the premises being granted to Gramons.

The deposit was paid ($19,000 or $16,000, of which Ken Little paid a percentage) and the contract was extended pending the issuing of the new lease. The victuallers licence remained in the name of Cabaret holdings Pty Ltd, with Ken Little as the nominee. There were shares to be distributed to Ken Little, but only after the finalisation of the affairs of Littles Enterprises Pty Ltd. In respect of the dividends (B Class shares), John Morris would hold 33.33% and Ken Little 66.67%. The result of this is not known. The Little brothers, Bell, Chalmers, Longhurst and Spiggy all moved to Chequers. The fact that the Whiskey staff moved en masse to Chequers raised suspicions that the takeover of Chequers was the Littles' aim all along.

It could look odd that the Littles used their solicitor to buy their old club back—it gives the impression of a backdoor way of reacquiring control. It obviously was, purchasing through their solicitor.[65] Finch's defence team questioned whether the transaction was legal. The Littles, no doubt, would have argued that they were making the best of a bad situation, that Hannay had ruined them and they were trying to resurrect as much of their previous business as they could. They did not hide the manoeuvre from the police, and the transaction was deemed legitimate. The Littles had no case to answer.

There were suspicions that the Littles had more money than they had disclosed, and again, the prosecution posed the question. Brian drove a Mercedes Pullman around before the fire, but denied that he owned it.[66] He said that after the fire, he had no financial interest in Chequers, but was employed as the manager with the use of a company car. In October, the Littles were recorded as wage earners at Chequers, with Ken on $120 per week and Brian on $105 per week.

Whiskey staff testified that Brian, especially, could be ruthless. The incident that was described previously involving Peter Morcus having a gun held to his head had started earlier, and would spill out onto the street. Like a scene from *Dirty Harry*, Chicka Reeves had initially pulled the gun on Lands Hotel owner Brian Ahearn.[67] The two petty gangsters had then made their way outside, where they continued to huff and puff like two Siamese fighting fish.

One of the Whiskey staff, Lin, watched them through a window overlooking Amelia Street. She saw Longhurst give Ahern a foot-long wooden baton (the one usually carried by Brian Little). Ahern put the baton in the back of his trousers and pulled his shirt down over it. Ahern put his arms up in the air and Reeves frisked him.[68]

Lin waited for the two hooligans to leave. Thinking it was safe to depart, she then took off, driving her car along Barry Parade. Ken Little, sitting beside her, yelled, 'Look out, you're going to be hit. They've picked the wrong car.' A vehicle with no lights rammed her car as it passed them. Lin had to swerve onto the footpath.[69] The assailants pulled over 25 yards ahead of them.

Ken Little got out of the car and approached the 'dodgem'. He said to the driver, Ahearn, 'What's going on?' There was no response, but the passenger said, 'Meet us back at the Whiskey.' Ken Little turned to Lin and told her, 'They've realised their mistake. They've hit the wrong car.'

Back at the Whiskey, Ahearn mumbled, 'It's a mistake. I thought it was Chicka Reeves, just forget about the whole thing. You never saw anything.' Ken Little replied, 'That's not the thing, Brian, it's not my car, it's Lin's. What about paying for the damage? You can get it from your insurance company.' Ahearn replied, 'Just forget about the whole thing, this is not my car, it is a stolen car.' This was a falsehood; it was Ahearn's private vehicle. Ahearn's companion promised that compensation would be forthcoming.

Bell sent Longhurst down to tell Peter Morcus that he wanted to see him. Morcus went upstairs, and on returning said to Lin, 'I've just had it put to me that I didn't see anything.' Longhurst said to Lin, 'John [Bell] wants to see you.' She went upstairs. She had no conversation with Bell, who ignored her. She went back to her vehicle and, with Ken Little and Morcus in tow, drove to the City Police Station where they reported that Morcus's car had been stolen.

The next day, Brian Little rang Lin's home and Jeni answered the phone. According to her sworn statement, Brian Little told her 'not to report the incident of the previous night to the police. Brian Ahern has no intention of paying for the car', and had said that if Lin did phone the police, she would be found 'floating down the river, and that Jeni would follow her.' Lin was again advised by Ken Little the following day not to report the matter to the police, so she did not. Ken Little later suggested that Lin have a break. She finished at the Whiskey that night and, unsurprisingly, did not go back. Peter Morcus stayed on, but he wanted out. He would end up dead. A day in the life of the Whiskey. Chicka Reeves was shot dead near Wollongong in January 1979, the same month that Stuart died.

43

Guilty

Stuart knew that the fire was planned for some time close to 2.08am on 8 January 1973, but no later than 2.15am. He was no victim, no patsy—he was culpable for the slaughter, and rightly gaoled for life. He held the knowledge that the Torino would be firebombed first, followed by the Whiskey. Stuart even told Bolton on 13 January that the first bombing would occur in about five weeks, which is within a week of when the Torino went up in smoke. He had the knowledge that there was only ever one target; the Whiskey, with Stuart later tossing in the name of Chequers (also bankrupt) to camouflage the fact it was all about a single club. Detective Hicks hit him with a classic touché question: 'How do you know it's true, that it's a conspiracy unless you're part of it?' The man with the unfortunate middle name did not respond. He never took any responsibility for his many crimes.

Stuart had, for many months, been warning of a 'bombing', but did so every couple of weeks. Three days before the fire, he changed his bearing completely. On 5 March, he returned from his mother's and positions Finch ready for a strike. They rent a flat for just one week; there was no point in renting it for any longer. Rose suggested to Stuart that they get a flatette so that he and Finch could cook and look after themselves. Stuart said, 'No, we only want somewhere to sleep for *the next few days.*' Stuart embarks on a whirlwind series of visits and calls.

He called Chalmers at the Whiskey and then Longhurst multiple times. Stuart then visits the club (said to be dropped off by Hannay) and then Freeleagus visits as a follow up. He also called Hicks. Next day he rings the Littles' hotel, sees Bolton at the Crest Hotel (and tells him the crims *were in town ready to strike*), rings Hicks and in the evening turns up at the Whiskey and sees Brian Little.

On the seventh, Stuart sees Bolton, has a long interview with Hicks (where honest cop Hicks has received a tip that Stuart has indicated to someone that something was going to happen the next day), meets Inspector Becker and agrees to meet Bolton at 9pm, supposedly with Col Bennett and Hicks. This is the first time he was going to the clubs with 'independents'.

At 7.30pm, he talked to ex-brother-in-law Lyall, who made the following observation: 'On this night he inferred that he had been told something and I gained the impression from what he said that the attack on the nightclubs *was going to take place soon.*' When Bolton fails to appear, he searches for the Littles, goes to Blinkers and rings Donna Porter at the Whiskey. In addition, he told Hicks he had the radio on all night listening to the bulletins. This made a lie of his disclosure to Bolton that the attack was still two weeks away.

Stuart's camouflage was as transparent as glass: he was a squid with invisible ink. To set up his oft-told alibi, he goes to the Flamingo. He then asks Quick for the time. This involved reassembling the phone to get the voice over, perfect for Stuart, as it makes it memorable. They also chat about the campy nature of the voice to reinforce the occasion. It is 2.15am, and by now he knew that the Whiskey had been attacked. Not content with this alibi, he needs another, so he goes to the manager, Yasse, and asks him *the very same thing, within one minute.* This was pointless, unless there was an ulterior motive. He already had the time from the most accurately known time measure for that era, equivalent to the atomic clock. He regards this as a double alibi. He tried a triple alibi hours before the fire; Bolton, Bennett and Hicks. This was another Stuart lie; he never asked Hicks to meet him (such a request is not seen in Hicks's transcripts) and there is no evidence that he asked Bennett. It was another story for Bolton, another story to alibi him from the fire. Unfortunately, Bolton is a no show, which no doubt spooked his paranoia.

Stuart knew that the attack would be in the early morning, and kept telling Hicks a time of 4am. He was the source of the information regarding the fire; he knew who was behind it, at least those who recruited him and those who lit it. It was not Rodger, Les and Ross.

Finch, the recidivist firebug, had no reason to be in the country. He hid his passport hours before the fire, had an alias, could not account for his time before and after the blaze, and fled into the bush when things went awry. He had not attempted to start work on an oil rig. He was culpable for the slaughter, and rightly gaoled for life.

Ex-brother-in-law Lyall said that Stuart was not bright enough to do it by himself: 'I do not consider that John Stuart would have the intelligence to plan such an extortion racket upon nightclubs in Brisbane and to be able to plan and carry out the fire and deaths of the people in the Whiskey Au Go Go nightclub *as is claimed by you police.*'[1] So did brother Daniel: '...the creation of the first chain of events in the laying of an alibi ... I did not think that [John] Stuart had such cunning to build up this whole business over a long period.'[2] They were both right. And Finch was no smarter.

Stuart captured himself well when he told Hicks that he was just a 'shit pot thief, that's all. I haven't even got away—I've been pinched for more things than I've ever done, than I've got away with.' The same applied to Finch; he was a none-too-bright petty thug, the King of the Cockroaches (see below). They were no patsies and no masterminds. They were bit players, directed by others.

There is the certainty that Stuart and Finch were not alone. So who was behind it?

A car or utility most likely dropped off the drums, which tallies with Finch's confession to Watt in 1988. He said he was not driving. Daniel Stuart said Finch could not drive—so that is consistent. There must have been at least two people delivering the drums on the night, as someone else must have been driving. A black car, as described by Finch, was spotted and reported in the media as leaving the scene.[3] Finch said he was in a stolen black Holden.

Accepting Stuart's intelligence as true, the Torino and Whiskey fires are *inextricably* linked. Stuart told Bolton no later than 6 January 1973, but possibly as early as 30 December 1972, that a group would bomb the empty Torino first and then the Whiskey. That is, the same group or elements of the same group did both. As the two were linked, it is more than likely that Stuart got himself arrested on night of the Torino fire. His reason for going into the Woolloongabba police station was ludicrous, and sounds like a 'please arrest me' moment. His super-paranoia may well have demanded he be alibied on the night.

According to Stuart, there had been too many recent firings of empty clubs (Alice's and the Torino); the Whiskey had to have people in it when it was attacked. Stuart told Hicks that this was the case; the first club, the Torino, would be empty; the next one would be occupied.

So who was in this group? Stuart threw out multiple hints, even if unintentionally. He was a good talker, and although much of it was incoherent waffle, he repeatedly gave clues to their real identity.

We learn that they were (1) young, (2) inexperienced, and (3) hop heads, aka LSD addicts: this was mentioned multiple times, including being drugged at the airport, and (4) two looked similar; they may have been brothers [the Butlers]. By their actions, we infer that they were amateurs. He could have been referring to only one group, one that met all the criteria.

They were the so-called Clockwork Orange goons, as identified by Stokes.

Stuart gave other hints. He also talked of an out-of-work group that was looking for things to do and suggested to ex-brother-in-law Lyall that he be a front man in the disposal of stolen property. It was not his plan, he said, but a couple of his criminal friends had suggested it. They needed a respectable front man to open up a legitimate refrigeration or electrical shop. Stuart would bring in stolen items (passed to him by associates) through the back door, erase the serial numbers and then resell them. Stuart then told Hicks that he would have some information for him in the near future, and that McCulkin had links to three men who had stolen some cameras and wanted to sell them. Breaking and entering, and thieving, was precisely what the Clockwork Orange no-hopers were doing at the time. What's more, he had linked McCulkin to them. The latter reference points strongly to the same gang.

Again, Stuart had inside knowledge that the group that had organised and burnt the Torino had incinerated the Whiskey. The font of all knowledge said so, *before it all happened.* Editor Billy Stokes accurately described the petty crooks of the Clockwork Orange gang as the culprits behind the Torino fire, earning a payday of $500.

Hamilton's sister Caroline Scully told the police in 1988 that the four members of the gang who did the job were her brother Thomas, Peter Hall, Garry Dubois and Keith Meredith. They arrived at her home with bottles of spirits taken from the premises.[4] Stokes and Scully's disclosures proved correct when, in 2016, one of the gang, Peter Hall, told a court that he and the three others had done it. He said Vincent O'Dempsey had recruited them. One name was not mentioned, despite evidence of his involvement. That was McCulkin, who liaised with the group of misfits on behalf of O'Dempsey and the owners of the premises.

The thesis is simple. Stuart said that the same conspirators would bomb an empty joint first (the Torino) and then a 'full' one (the Whiskey). Based on Hall's testimony, we know that a central figure in the Whiskey outrage was a particularly nasty piece of work called Vincent O'Dempsey.

44

Serial Killer?

O'Dempsey used to fight in Selby Moore's tent show in Warwick, south-west of Brisbane. He was well-known in the area, and drew a crowd. People had bad luck around the pugilist, and sometimes even disappeared—permanently. He had the Midas touch in reverse—everything he touched turned to shit, rather than gold. He was a psychopath, an annihilator, a grave digger and an alleged serial killer.

In 1980, the Brisbane Coroner, Mr Bougoure, held a long inquiry into the disappearance of Mrs Barbara McCulkin and her two daughters, Vicki, 13, and Leanne, 11, from their home at Dorchester Street, Highgate Hill, on 16 January 1974. At the end of the three-week investigation, Mr Bougoure found that O'Dempsey and Dubois had abducted the McCulkins and murdered them, and ordered the two men to stand trial.[1]

At 6.00pm on the date of their abduction, young Janet Gayton, who lived opposite the McCulkin's house, saw two men entering it.[2] Gayton was having a party that night. Shortly after, she went over to the McCulkin's home and spoke to her friend Vicki McCulkin. Gayton asked her who the two strangers were. Vicki told her that one was Vince O'Dempsey, and the other was a man her father called Shorty. At this time, Gayton could see Shorty sitting in the kitchen talking to Mrs McCulkin.

The two McCulkin girls then came to her party. The younger one, Leanne, went home at 7.30pm, and Vicki returned home at 10.15pm. Neither girl was seen again. Both girls, when leaving, told the Gayton children that they would see them the following morning. The Gayton siblings went over to the McCulkins' the next day, but there was no response.[3] The McCulkins were murdered by O'Dempsey and Dubois and raped by Dubois.

This was not the first time people had disappeared around O'Dempsey.[4] Vincent Allen vanished while waiting to give evidence against him. Allen was 22 and working as a railway labourer at Karara, outside Warwick, when he vanished on 17 April 1964, leaving all his clothing in his hut. Sixteen years later, the Coroner reported that 'I am unable to find how or where he met his death. The cause of his disappearance would seem to be directly linked with the fact that he was required to give evidence against Vincent O'Dempsey in a criminal proceeding, and there is ample evidence of a motive for his death.'

O'Dempsey and Allen worked together at the Leslie Dam site, and were constant companions in Warwick. Eyewitnesses last saw Allen with O'Dempsey in O'Dempsey's 1957 Holden on a Saturday afternoon in Warwick. The very distinctive individual was hard to miss; a bodgie like Stuart, Allen was flamboyant, wearing vibrant shirts and black-and-yellow leopard-skin pants when he was presumably murdered (he also had fair hair, blue eyes, a bent nose, a scar across the bridge of his nose, and a tattoo of a girl's head in a heart with an arrow on his right arm). As hard to miss as flashing Christmas lights, he simply vanished while being driven by O'Dempsey.

One of the investigators into Allen's disappearance, Detective Sergeant Graham Menary, told how watches, clocks and jewellery were stolen from Piggott's store in Warwick in a break and enter in March 1964. Three safes that were taken from Creighton and Co. in Warwick on the same weekend were later found with paint on them that was 'scientifically' matched to a utility owned by a man named Gunther Janke (who also disappeared at this time). The safes from Creighton's and watches and jewellery from Piggott's were recovered in the general area of the Leslie Dam.

On March 28 that year, O'Dempsey reported to the police that Janke had stolen his car. Police discovered that on 1 April, O'Dempsey and Allen had hitchhiked to Sydney and recovered the vehicle from near a wharf on the Sydney waterfront. O'Dempsey told the police that he found the car at Warwick.

Allen told investigators that when they found the car, there was a watch in it, which O'Dempsey parcelled up and posted from Sydney to his own address in Warwick. Police searched O'Dempsey's house and found the watch, still in its packaging, and identified it as one taken in the Piggott's break-in. O'Dempsey appeared in Warwick Court on 13 June 1964 for committal proceedings on a charge of breaking and entering Piggott's. Although summoned to give evidence for the prosecution, Allen was untraceable. The court found no prima facie case against O'Dempsey, and he was discharged. Billy McCulkin said, 'He [O'Dempsey] made the statement to me that there was a person in Warwick or near Warwick who wouldn't be talking to the police anymore.' O'Dempsey had said, 'Old Vince [Allen] won't be talking to anybody anymore.'[5]

Menary said that he and the other investigators were firmly of the opinion that Allen's body lay buried in the ponded section of the dam before it was flooded. Lending weight to the theory was the fact that the safes and jewellery were recovered from this vicinity. Menary said he believed that the McCulkins' bodies were in the dam at Lake Manchester. Vincent also had property at Warwick—are they entombed there; was he keeping his trophies close to home? There has always been speculation that the McCulkins were buried 'in the bush somewhere'. The police were also told that they may have been dumped at sea.[6]

Margaret Ward also disappeared after last being seen with O'Dempsey. She had grown up on a farm at Gunalda, near Gympie. Her mother had deserted her when she was young, and she lived with her father and his second wife. When she finished school at 16, she became a nurse's aide at Gympie Hospital and lived at the hospital for a year. Then she moved to Redcliffe to reside with her grandmother and landed a job at the Arnott's biscuit factory in Brisbane.

The teenager was 19 when she boarded at the Vogue Private Hotel in Cordelia Street, South Brisbane, in April 1973. It was there that she met Dianne Margaret Pritchard (aka Cheryl Dianne Pritchard, Margaret Dianne Pritchard, Cheryl Dianne Evans, Katrina Weir, Dianne O'Dempsey, Patricia Veschetti, and Sonia Schaffer), who was using the alias Cheryl Dianne

Evans at this time and who subsequently married Vincent O'Dempsey.

Coroner Bougoure found that Ward disappeared from Brisbane on or about 13 November 1973, and was probably dead.[7] Last seen with the O'Dempsey couple, the Coroner said, 'The cause of her disappearance seems to be directly linked with certain court proceedings which were awaiting hearing.'

The court proceedings related to charges of prostitution against Margaret Ward and Vincent O'Dempsey's de facto wife, who ran a 'massage parlour', the Pollonia Health Studio, in Lutwyche Road, Lutwyche. It was a front for a brothel. Ward introduced herself to police as 'Shelly' and told them that Pritchard had instructed her to give customers 'relief massage or intercourse'. They charged her and Pritchard with prostitution.

Detectives told Mr Bougoure that the Vogue had accommodation for 40 or 50 people, and believed that Pritchard, who had a vast number of convictions for prostitution, coerced the normal home-loving girl into a life of sexual exploitation. People with criminal backgrounds mostly inhabited the Vogue. There was evidence that Ward was terrified that her parents would find out about the charge.

Ward left the Vogue with Pritchard and O'Dempsey on 13 November 1973 to consult a solicitor, Mr Patrick Nolan (Stuart's solicitor). After leaving Nolan's office, she disappeared off the face of the earth. This could happen if you were in the presence of O'Dempsey and you posed a problem for him. Ward failed to appear in court on November 16 and copped a fine of $200 in her absence.[8] The court had fined a cadaver.

Cheryl Evans worked part of the 13th at the Polonia Health Studio at Lutwyche.[9] O'Dempsey did not go to the studio on this day. Previously, he had visited the studio daily without fail. That night, O'Dempsey rang Ross Stephens Car Sales at 88 Breakfast Creek Road, Newstead. This company ran an advertisement in the newspaper wanting to buy cars. O'Dempsey offered to sell his car, and a salesman went out that night to inspect it. It was common knowledge that O'Dempsey had had this car from the time it was new, and had looked after it like a baby. It was suggested that if O'Dempsey could possibly love anything, it was this car. He would cover it each night with a sheet of silk and it was a standing joke among everybody who knew him that it was the only thing he really cared for. However, it wasn't a joke, it was the truth—sociopaths have more feelings for objects than people.

O'Dempsey agreed to sell the car for $2,900. Of this figure, he received a cheque for $578.62 and the hire purchase company paid out of the remainder. Evans collected some of her belongings that she had stored at the Vogue and Evans and O'Dempsey were seen carrying property from her flat (No.8) to a car. It was obvious that they were moving all of their chattels out of the apartment.

At the McCulkin coronial inquest, a number of things did not add up: the departure of Dubois and O'Dempsey from Brisbane after the McCulkins were murdered, the disposal by O'Dempsey of an immaculate car and acquisition of a much older one for no obvious reason, the vacation by O'Dempsey of his flat without notice (and forfeiture of the bond), the disposal by O'Dempsey of his interest in land at Warwick that promised to be profitable, a false statement by Dubois that he did not know Mrs McCulkin and the abandonment of a profitable massage parlour/brothel in which O'Dempsey and his de facto had an interest.[10] Later, Evans told undercover police officers that her hubby was 'implicated' in several murders.[11]

Stuart's best mate Billy McCulkin and O'Dempsey had an interesting history. They had first met in Kings Cross in 1966, and were together for two months; O'Dempsey had a prostitute working for him (as he did in Brisbane). They then went to Queensland together and were both arrested in New Farm for breaking, entering and stealing on 4 November 1966. O'Dempsey also copped an explosives and concealable firearm charge, and went to gaol for five years. The pugilist specialised in theft, his first conviction for this being in 1956 at Warwick.

After he was released at Christmas in 1970, McCulkin got O'Dempsey a job in an auction shop, and O'Dempsey lived with McCulkin for six weeks. He would drink with McCulkin at the Lands Office Hotel. He then flatted with call girl Evans. The inquest was told that Billy McCulkin found a job in a massage parlour for O'Dempsey's de facto wife.

McCulkin described his eventual adversary thus: he takes short steps 'like a woman', holds one arm in front when talking with the arm bent at right angles, does not smoke, drinks lightly, is fit and eats healthy foods, was in the Army, is colour blind, is hard to frighten, has false teeth, is pigeon-toed, has a tattoo of St George and the Dragon on his chest, back and both legs, and obtained a high pass in poultry farming. He also had an A+ in criminal activity, and was a certified psychopath.[12] The certification came from Toowoomba Hospital, where, as a teen, he was stamped as a psychopath with 'schizoid tendencies'. One habit included knifing bagged cats to death.[13]

O'Dempsey and McCulkin shared one unusual trait; a tattooed penis. Like brother Billy McCulkin, he also had a mouse etched on his being; fittingly a vermin.[14] Perhaps they had taken advantage of a two-for-one offer from their tattooist mate Billy Phillips.

Dubois's criminal career had begun in 1964, innocuously enough with a $16.40 fine for breaking a traffic regulation. Five months later, he assaulted a female and raped her, and was sentenced to eight years hard labour.[15] While incarcerated, Dubois met O'Dempsey. They would be reacquainted on release.

As a police informant, Billy McCulkin told Detective Hicks that Dubois was known as a 'Sexo' who liked 'knocking off young girls.' [16] O'Dempsey also liked young girls, and was convicted in Warwick in 1959 for the 'aggravated assault of a sexual nature of a female child.'[17] He perpetrated this outrage with two others. The sexual predator would add child murder to his list of contemptible acts, and be sentenced to life imprisonment in 2017.

The Clockwork Orange thugs started in 1966 with six young idiots called The Mongrel Bunch.[18] This obnoxious gang bashed and sexually assaulted a man (referred to as 'unlawful and indecent assault on a person' and 'attempted carnal knowledge of a male person against the order of nature'). Phil Dickie, whose exposé led to the Fitzgerald Inquiry, said that one of the compadres was Brian Toner, aka Jeffrey Bennett or at the time of the Whiskey fire, Peter Hall, who had convictions for theft. Another was Douglas Meredith, who changed his name to Keith.

Dubois hooked up with Hall, Keith Meredith and Hamilton. Their drug of choice was LSD. In October 1973, a police raid at Caboolture caught Meredith, Dubois and Hall growing cannabis on a rented property. Dubois was nabbed again in 1981 for possession of cannabis, and O'Dempsey went to prison for marijuana offences in 1980. In 1985, O'Dempsey was gaoled for 10 years for heroin possession and locked away in Cessnock Gaol.

45

The Interrogators

In his summing up at the Stuart and Finch trial in the Supreme Court in Brisbane, Mr Justice Lucas warned members of the jury that if they were to believe Finch, they had to believe that the police had entered into a conspiracy to defeat the course of justice. 'In fact on Finch's story, it is a conspiracy on the largest scale involving members of the police forces of Queensland, New South Wales and Victoria. Finch's defence is that it [the unsigned record of interview] is a complete fabrication and that a large number of police officers have entered into a conspiracy to defeat the course of justice; thus, the six police officers present at the taking of the record of interview have given perjured evidence. No doubt with policemen, just like jurymen, judges or other sections of the community, there are some good ones and, unfortunately, some bad ones. It has always seemed to me that the larger a conspiracy becomes and the more policemen involved in it, the less likely the story of a conspiracy is to be true.'

As previously stated, there are a number of facts to support the opinion that there are reasonable grounds to suspect that parts of the detectives' evidence conflict with independent testimony. This, *if proven true*, means that the impartiality of all their evidence is obviously questionable.

In the end, the jury unanimously chose to believe the police evidence. They had to.

As time would reveal, the collection of six police officers at Finch's interview had question marks on their character. In 1981, Roger Rogerson shot and killed a criminal, Warren Lanfranchi, on an inner-city Sydney street in suspicious circumstances. A coroner's jury found that he had shot Lanfranchi in the course of making an arrest, but declined to find that he was acting in self-defence. In 1985, a trial jury acquitted him of attempting to bribe another police officer to alter his evidence in a drug trial. In 1986, a police disciplinary tribunal convicted him of departmental offences and dismissed him from the service. In 1990, he was found to have perverted the course of justice.[1] In 2014, he committed the ultimate crime, murder, to obtain three million dollars in an ice deal. At the time of writing, he was serving a life sentence after being convicted in 2016.

Redmond, Atkinson and Hayes were persons of interest in the Fitzgerald Inquiry. Redmond's performance as overseer of the licensing branch from 1982 to 1987 was closely scrutinised, and damned by the commission. Fitzgerald criticised Redmond's administration when he was licensing branch head and recommended that he be encouraged to retire. Redmond's distaste for the branch's work was manifested in an alarming level of disinterest. His perusal of the branch's nightly occurrence sheets should have revealed that the brothel proprietors were not being prosecuted.[2] At best, he simply looked the other way.

At the Fitzgerald Inquiry, Atkinson and Hayes were accused of faking a record of interview. Bruce Wilby, a former licensing branch detective, made the claim during cross-examination by Mr Lindsay Bowden, who appeared for past and present senior police officers. Mr Bowden put it to Wilby, then a farmer and grazier at Clermont, that an unsigned record of an interview with him had been compiled during an investigation of the licensing branch by Hayes and Atkinson in December 1978. 'There was no recorder there when I was interviewed by Hayes and Atkinson and my name isn't even spelt right,' Wilby said after he read the document. 'I deny that this document was ever typed in my presence.' Mr Bowden then put it to Wilby that a shorthand typist, Miss Cotterill, was present and recorded the interview. 'Miss Cotterill wasn't there. Unless Miss Cotterill was disguised as either Mr Hayes or Mr Atkinson, she wasn't there,' came the laconic response. Both men denied the verbal.

The detectives who were present at Finch's interview would rise through the ranks. Redmond became Acting Commissioner, Atkinson, Hayes and Morey rose to Assistant Commissioner, Griffiths retired as superintendent and Rogerson, as an exception, will die in gaol.[3]

46

Stuart

Journalist Mick Barnes provided an insightful and accurate analysis of Stuart soon after his conviction for the Whiskey outrage. The Brisbane killer returned to gaol as a hero after his Whiskey conviction, 'For no matter what the public thinks of him, no matter what his own thoughts are, Stuart last week became a man of stature in the cockeyed world of underworld reasoning.'

From his cell, he now commanded 'absolute respect from the petty thieves, rapists, murderers, forgers, con men, spivs and pimps who inhabit his existence', something he craved. He had reached the pinnacle of his career in crime as a 'new crime legend'.

Barnes rightly said that all his thoughts and actions were coloured by the 'standards and taboos of the underworld', that he was a solid crim to the end. He had strolled into court and spat in the Crown Prosecutor's face: 'You'll never wash that off ... You'll have it on your face until the day you die.' From the dock, he had disparaged his brother Dan: 'May he choke on his caviar which I suppose he will gain from his 30 pieces of silver—the reward.'[1] m

Stuart lived in a fantasy world of cops and robbers. He told Hicks that 'criminals and police are like soldiers at war. They are deadly enemies, and if they can put anything over each other they will.' He said that he 'wouldn't want it to be known that he was associating with police in any way and as far as he was concerned they were all enemies.'[2]

He lived in a poorly scripted 007 novel; a zany world of amateur codes, invisible inks, aliases, secret rendezvous, secret links to the police, guns, macho bravado, violence and retribution. There was also an element of The Riddler, not only in his ciphers, but also in how he would give 'intelligence' to someone like Hicks. There was no straight answer; 'see Alf at the Flamingo, wink wink. He can tell you about these men.'

In his irrational world, fear and anger were the two predominant emotions, something he shared with other maximum-security prisoners.[3] Bashings, rapes and drugs were all part of the mix of prison life. He was a life-long professional criminal, crime his occupation, violence the means to progressing his career. He was more comfortable in prison than out; he described it as having 'prison blood', that it ran in his veins.

Rogerson described him as 'insane', a 'psychopath' and a 'fucking animal; essentially 'fucked in the brain'. John Ryan said, 'no one will ever know the workings of Johnny's mind.'[4] We can make an attempt.

John Stuart was mentally ill, something Hicks suspected. He was diagnosed with paranoia and extreme personality disorder. He was aware that he had mental health issues, and maintained an interest in psychology.[5] Although not allowed access to psychiatry books, he obtained some knowledge. 'Don't worry about the psychiatry books. I have found out what I want to know ... the little knowledge I do have about me and these things isn't dangerous to me as long as I don't overestimate its extent; anyway, I can't have psychiatry books here so I'll just have to wait.'[6]

Just prior to his release from gaol in June 1972, he wrote in defence of Leonard Keith Lawson, a famous comic artist and sadistic rapist and murderer. Lawson had attacked a female entertainer, Sharon Hamilton, with a knife at Parramatta Gaol on 18 June 1972.[7] Traumatised by the vicious assault, she sought psychiatric help and later committed suicide. Being a prisoner within the same confines as Lawson, at Parramatta Gaol, he witnessed the attitude of his fellow inmates, some of whom wanted to kill the assailant.

Stuart said that Lawson was just a 'figurehead, a pawn far removed from a real and larger truth.' He argued that the newspapers were caricaturing Lawson, and that the facts about him were 'deliberately and consciously obliterated ... When a person can be dealt with by our system of so called 'justice' for offences in the realm of moral degeneracy and then sent forever to a cell to stew in that degeneracy, unassisted, without recourse or vent of any description, how can we blame him for resultant [sic] action. He cannot ... obviously, the fact is, he is mentally ill and insanity is a disease, not a crime. He can not be this 'monster' he is depicted as, and sane and responsible....'

Lawson was not to be blamed, but pitied, he said, arguing that Lawson should have been given the extensive psychiatric help he needed. He railed against the Christian dogma that 'governs so-called democracy', that forbade castration or lobotomy or other surgery. How can society condemn him? Stuart saw Lawson in himself, but would never admit his mental illness to his family, especially his mother.[8] He convinced her it was all a con job, a way for him to remain one step ahead of the enemy, the coppers. His deception worked; Mrs Watts intended to pay a psychiatrist to prove that he was not mentally ill.

Stuart wrote endlessly on mental disorders. 'I defy anyone to define in which ways I am insane and by what standards they make the definitions.'[9] He penned to Marge X, 'No matter which way you look at it, I really am nuts.'[10] To another, 'I'm crazy, your [sic] sane.'[11] His brother Daniel was mentally ill and suffered breakdowns, and his father no doubt was—it was a family affair.

Although he was no picture of normalcy, being paranoid and delusional, Stuart was functional. Those he interacted with knew he was different; they viewed him as odd and manic, with rapid speech that jumped from topic to topic in no logical order. When he talked quickly, there was a tendency to repeat his words and stammer. One of his examining doctors noted that he did not blink, but could not surmise the significance of this.[12]

When you are paranoid, you cannot have too many enemies. For Stuart, they were everywhere. There were killer cunts lurking in every shadow and around every corner. He told Bolton that Hicks was untrustworthy, while he told Hicks that Bolton was dishonest. These were his two main confidants. Even Alf, the doorman at the Flamingo, the person who his alibi relied on (for not being at the Whiskey when it was torched), was a lagging cunt.

His behaviour was bizarre. He told Hicks, Bolton, Bell and the Littles that he would have to kill the southern criminal plotters. In addition, he asked the Littles to pay him to liquidate them. Telling the police that you intend to murder someone is never a smart ploy.

Up for murdering 15 people, he told Hicks of the secret untranslated message that would reveal all: 'I want any criminal who can read the code to come forward and tell me what it's about. Someone must think I know it, but I don't.'

Hicks was rarely shocked by Stuart's behaviour, but on this occasion, he was dumbstruck. How could a coded letter *that he had written* exonerate him from the abomination? We know he had composed this fake code because the day before (just prior to Stuart's interview with Bolton on 9 March 1973), Stuart asked his sister-in-law Rose if she would retrieve a coded letter, which he would write and deliver, out of her letterbox. She was to pretend that she did not know how it had arrived, and he would tell Bolton that southern crims had put it there. It would make the story more interesting, and Stuart could get more money. Stuart made a salient point: 'Bolton would do anything to get in on the excitement ... and it would get him back on top again.'[13]

The prime suspect in the firebombing asked Rose, 'Do you think I should go to the funeral?'[14] He also suggested to Bolton that they should visit the clubs so Stuart could tell them he'd had no involvement in the atrocity. Bolton said he would likely get a bullet if he did so.

With an inverted sense of reality, Stuart was deluded in thinking he would have a triple alibi with Hicks, Bennett and Bolton all present when he appeared at the Whiskey on 7 March, even though Hicks was not even asked to be there. Supposedly smart, he made an incredibly stupid assumption that he would not be pegged for the massacre. Supposedly smart, the wild fabricator never demonstrated any criminal intelligence whatsoever during his entire criminal career.

He needed fame. He wanted to be continually in the news, and his mother fed this hunger by passing his letters on to Bolton and sending Bolton's articles back to her son. She could never call him to account for his attention-seeking behaviour. His mother was either unaware or unwilling to admit that her son had a problem. She compounded the issue by telling him that his arch rival was 'after' him. She told the press that his madness was an act, and he was being accused of crimes he had not committed. He was just a rebel, but she loved him.

Mrs Watts believed in his innocence to her death.[15] She was wrong. His mother said that the media had created a monster that did not exist, that he was just 'a little boy who loved other kids and stray dogs.'[16] She was wrong; he raped, bashed, had underage sex, lied and killed 15 innocent people in this diabolical crime. He was an inveterate liar and woman basher. His turbulent childhood contributed to the violence against females, but does not excuse it. She was right in one sense; he never emerged from being a 'little boy', the 15-year-old warrior who believed that full dress kit consisted of a knife and a hat.

He could not stop his behaviour, being a fatalist: '...the insides and what you are will never change.' This was one of the most frustrating aspects of his personality; he knew what would happen after the Whiskey fire—that he would be verballed by six to eight detectives.

Hicks was mistaken when he thought his colleagues would need solid evidence, as some of their testimony is suspect.
Stuart: But look, what good are you going to be Basil against six or eight detectives saying that we questioned Stuart and he said?

Hicks: They've got to get other evidence, now they've got to get other evidence. It's different.

Stuart: Okay, other evidence, what about they're going to come out with little sticks of gelignite and be saying we found this gelignite poking under his lino and er here's a bit of fuse we found out the backyard and er here's all this, see, there's the other bits of evidence.

> Well if they try to get me right for something I didn't do, like they knew I didn't do for Jacky [Steele]. They loaded me up with a shotgun, shotgun shells, they got me verbal, they've got all this little bits of fucking this see? They could have tried and they would have got me life and I didn't do it. Okay what are we going to do about this when there's a heap of citizens blown to the ceiling? Hey? You think they're not going to fall on me because they know that I've been going around there talking about they're, they're at least going to load me up with a bust and try to suck it out of my brain all I know. Aren't they? Course they are.

Hicks: But?

Stuart: Hey? Why don't you think so?

Hicks: I don't think it will happen.

Stuart: Why?

Hicks: I don't think they will do anything like that.

Stuart: I hope you're right, mate. I hope you're right.

His mental descent is revealed in his final Christmas card: 'After 20odd years of prison life, among cockroaches, I know this positive fact: cockroaches hate us. They hate man—sure. Yes, we hate them too, but not in hate from the heart. We actually 'despise' them and we are boss, but they hate us from the heart. I won't try here to tell you how I know, but I know. And they're not supposed to, that's what tumbles me. Like how dare they? They've got uncanny hate instinct in them somewhere. There's something treacherously smart about them somehow. They know something—anyway....'

Days before his death, he was writing incomprehensible messages. He had become a latter day Dr Doolittle, reduced to talking to the insects.[17]

47

Finch

Finch big-noted himself as a fighter in prison. He told Watt that from cell 373 in Boggo Road Gaol, he was a benevolent dictator using king hits, cricket bats and metal jugs to dispense justice. He bashed 30-odd people and gave Watt a blow-by-blow account of some of the epic smash ups. He would not let anyone spit, litter or talk during TV shows, and banned cop shows from the TV viewing room.

Killing a cockroach was the biggest offence someone could commit in gaol, as they had saved Stuart from a walloping in 1976. The story was that officers had massed outside his underground 'Black Peter Cell' where Stuart was being held in complete darkness. They were going to bash the shit out of him, but when they entered the cell, there were cockroaches everywhere, and the officers fled in disgust. The cockroaches had saved Stuart, therefore, like the blessed bovines in India, the sacred cockroaches of Boggo Road Gaol were free to wander around under the reverent eye of the pimps, thieves, murderers, paedophiles and other flotsam within its confines. This farcical decree from the Finch rule book revealed that his period of internment had not increased his intellectual capacity.

In prison, he became a vegetarian, bird lover and fitness fanatic. Rising at 5am, the King of the Cockroaches pummelled a punching bag and ran 12 km around the yard. He swore off meat, fish and eggs, and would not eat anything that had been killed. Finch took over the prison aviary, caring for injured birds found in the gaol grounds. The honorary veterinarian claimed a 60 per cent recovery rate.

The politician Kevin Hooper, who had railed against John Hannay, sent Finch a budgerigar, which Finch named Kevie. Soon the budgie had a partner, Fatty. There was also a white pigeon called Big West, named after Brisbane doctor Weston Allen.[1] But his closest companion for seven years was a one-legged sparrow called Stumpy, which had flown over the gaol walls and 'had to battle with stronger birds for tucker'. Nevertheless, Stumpy returned each day for a feed, but in 1984 the prison cat, Boots, caught the sparrow and then carried it, unharmed, to Finch and placed it at his feet. The bird then took up residence in the Birdman's quarters. Stumpy finally died in February 1986, to Finch's deep sorrow.[2] He'd had Stumpy for seven years, treating it like a child.[3] A loner, Finch ate alone, lying on his back with the plate on his chest to share his food with the birds.[4]

The mass murderer shamelessly used people's sympathy to get out of gaol. He stated his contempt for his support network: 'My claims that I was innocent helped me survive gaol, but it also gave them something to fight for. I didn't ask for their help. People like that need a cause. They'll now go and find something else to crusade for. I might as well have been a rock or a stone. They didn't care about me as a person, only the cause.'[5]

Finch said that the three months he spent living with his new wife Cheryl were worse than the 15 years he spent in prison. She was a 'body slave', on call 24/7. Believing that she had six months to live and would die before Christmas 1986, he had married her as an act of charity.[6] After she returned from her dire trip to the United Kingdom, Cheryl told her friends of his 'mood changes and threats of violence'.

Cheryl Finch eventually saw the light and divorced him in 1991. She banished the wedding photos and other memorabilia from her brief marriage in a cardboard box and sealed it with masking tape. Her carer, Nikki, was blunt in her assessment of the mass killer. She said his contact number could be found in the phonebook by looking up 'A for arseholes'.

He supposedly found an honest job in England as a nightwatchman, and faded into obscurity.[7]

48

The Best Fit

So what is the sequence of events? Despite many of the players being liars, in my opinion, we have a best fit.

There is circumstantial evidence that the same conspirators were behind both the Torino and Whiskey fires. This was known in either the last week of 1972 or the first week of 1973 at the latest. Stuart told Bolton this point-blank, and Bolton passed the information on to Hicks, Whitrod, Hodges and others. This was two years before Stokes argued the same point in the *Port News*.

O'Dempsey, via McCulkin, recruited Hall, Dubois, Hamilton and Keith Meredith to torch the Torino for $500. Human executioner O'Dempsey, via McCulkin, then recruited elements of the Clockwork Orange mob for the crazed Whiskey firebombing. As Stuart intimated, the assailants were young (early 20s), LSD addicts, two could pass for brothers (Hamilton and Hall, aka the Butler brothers), and they were petty pilferers and irresponsible.[1]

In 1988, Finch confirmed to *Sun* reporter Dennis Watt that O'Dempsey and McCulkin had organised *both* assaults. Ex-clan member Peter Hall affirmed both O'Dempsey and the Clockwork Orange gang's involvement in the Torino fire at the McCulkin rape/murder trials of Dubois in 2016 and O'Dempsey in 2017. This admission tallied with Stuart's information, and assuming it is true, links both the Clockwork Orange clan and O'Dempsey to the horror in St Pauls Terrace.

At these trials, a pivotal figure in the Torino fire, Billy McCulkin, remained unmentioned. This is noteworthy, as in 1974 the gang told *Port News* editor Stokes of his guilt. In addition, another witness placed the elephant with the mouse on its dick squarely in the room.

Mrs McCulkin told her neighbour, Peter Nisbet, of her husband's involvement in both fires, that the 'mouse' could have spent time in gaol for the Whiskey homicides, and that Stuart and Finch were 'the easy get for the cops ... collateral damage', that they were just bit players and others were the 'primary movers'.[2] In addition, in an interview during Operation Graveyard, Hamilton's sister Caroline Scully told the police that 'Bill McCulkin received $500 from the owners of [the] Torino nightclub to have her brother, Peter Hall, Gary [sic] Dubois and Keith Meredith burn the building down for insurance purposes.'[3] The puppeteers McCulkin and O'Dempsey jerked the strings of the drug-addled gang and Stuart and Finch.

In plain there is a whole herd of pachyderms origamied into a space no bigger than the closet like watch-house charge room where Stuart and Finch did their confessing. In flailing around trying to rationalise the irrational and blithely ignoring contrary evidence and independent depositions (e.g., Nisbet's), the obvious and most reasonable explanation for the linked happenings in Fortitude Valley in early 1973 was missed. Ignored was evidence that O'Dempsey was so concerned about Finch returning to Australia in 1988 and implicating him in the arson that he told others that Finch would have to be 'knocked', i.e., killed.[4] To connect anyone but Stuart and Finch to the Whiskey would be an admittance of failure or, worse, an unprecedented corruption of the original prosecution.

Finch's disclosure to journalist Watt in 1988 of the names of the two other Whiskey participants, McCulkin and Hamilton, remains the most likely scenario. While it was true that he knew of Stokes's articles blaming the gang, having had the *Port News* supplied to him in gaol, and having corresponded with Stokes at the time, his testimony is very specific. There were three people in the car; McCulkin drove it, and Finch and Hamilton tossed the drums in and lit the fuel.[5]

The day after the fire, Billy McCulkin wandered over to the Treasury Hotel in shock and talked to his then girlfriend. 'He looked terrible, kind of panicky,' she recalled.[6] Something was troubling his limited conscience. Meanwhile, Hamilton had disappeared, first to Adelaide and then to New Zealand.

It was argued in the McCulkin trials that Mrs McCulkin and her children were murdered by O'Dempsey, not because Garry Dubois or Vincent O'Dempsey had any involvement in the Whiskey slaying, but because 'the suspected connection with the Torino fire would provide a motive for Dubois and O'Dempsey to keep Barbara McCulkin quiet. Now, that may not sound a sufficient motive or even a sensible one....' Therefore, O'Dempsey was concerned that he and the gang would be blamed for the Whiskey due to the similarities between the two fires. The similarities are not stated—the Whiskey was bankrupt and was ignited with fuel, while the Torino was viable and the attack was labelled an explosion. Peter Hall told Hamilton's sister that they used gelignite to make it look like a gas blast.[7] Even though they were not responsible, they would be associated by default.

Killing came easy to O'Dempsey, but to suggest that he killed three people to cover what was regarded at the time as a trivial insurance scam is spurious.[8] It is neither a sufficient nor a sensible motive. To fit the established narrative that only two men participated in the massacre, the prosecution had to sledgehammer a square peg into a round hole, which was messy and untenable. A lack of credible motivation to kill the McCulkin 'girls' led to impossible contortions of which Nadia Comaneci would have been proud; a perfect ten in the implausible.

The Torino fire was presumably organised with the agreement of the owners. The site subsequently sold for $85,000.[9] There was no interest in finding the culprits and meting out punishment—it was a win-win for all parties involved. What penalty would O'Dempsey have received anyway if he'd been caught, even with protected informant status? It is hard to imagine that it would have involved anything more than a slap on the wrist.

What's more, there was the suggestion that Mrs McCulkin was blackmailing O'Dempsey for a 'fake crime', blaming him for the Whiskey even though he had no involvement. In the context of Mrs McCulkin's life at that time, it was not only nonsensical but also preposterous and demeaning to her fragile existence. There is zero possibility that Mrs McCulkin was blackmailing O'Dempsey for any reason. When she was around him, she literally feared for her life.

Billy McCulkin 'knew' that O'Dempsey was a killer, as O'Dempsey had told him he had 'disappeared' Vincent Allen. Billy told his wife the same story. We know this because Barbara, in confidence, told her best friend Ellen Gilbert that O'Dempsey had murdered and buried the bodgie in the 1960s.[10]

O'Dempsey had lived at her home for a considerable period, and he often visited. He did so to discuss future criminal jaunts with Billy McCulkin. They discussed the fires, *plural*, not just the Torino fire. Multiple witnesses attested to this, not just McCulkins' neighbour Peter Nisbet but also John Ryan. Ryan maintained that Mrs McCulkin, terrified of her estranged spouse's culpability in both fires, requested the procurement of a safe house for her and the two girls. They disappeared before they could be moved.

The men around her were violent thugs, their intimidation real. Billy McCulkin regularly rained blows on his defenceless wife and knocked his sister's teeth out days after Barbara's disappearance.[11] That a battered, sick wife (she had to wear surgical bras while she recovered from a breast operation) would blackmail someone she believed to be a killer (a correct assumption, as he subsequently murdered her), amateur boxer, thief and pimp called Vince O'Dempsey and someone (Dubois) who had been gaoled for eight years for rape for a crime 'they did not commit' cannot be considered seriously.[12] This is the man that tough dude Billy McCulkin described as someone hard to frighten.

O'Dempsey killed Mrs McCulkin because she knew of her husband and O'Dempsey's central role in the Whiskey outrage and had started to talk to friends of their role in the *fires*, plural. Her conscience got to her; disaffected by her husband's role in the death of innocents, she cathartically confessed to confidants.

In his 1988 confession, Finch told Watt that 'The order to murder Mrs McCulkin was given after she threatened to inform police of her husband's part in the Whiskey firebombing. She had to be murdered, as Finch and Stuart had already been found guilty of the nightclub deaths.'[13] This is far more plausible than the claim that O'Dempsey and Co. were vaguely linked to the Whiskey by their association with the Torino arson, or that it was purely a sex crime. In a previous hearing, Dubois's brother Paul said Garry had said Barbara 'had evidence on O'Dempsey that would have gotten him 20 years [in gaol] and this is how he dealt with it.[14] The 'sufficient and sensible' motive was removing a witness to prevent gaol time, something O'Dempsey had a reputation for—the sex (proven in Dubois's case) was a bonus.

When she was abducted, Mrs McCulkin knew the outcome—that she would die; it was beyond terror.[15]

Dubois and O'Dempsey's victims were cutely dressed, Vicki sporting blue jeans with yellow stars, a tight-fitting red zippered top and a gold zodiac sign on a neck chain. Leanne wore a pink smock top with stripes and flowers and pink stretch shorts. The children's party clothes were ripped off them before they were raped and murdered.

Like all psychopaths, O'Dempsey would have experienced an adrenaline rush, both before and during their deaths. Like a cat playing with a broken-winged bird—tossing it into the air and pawing it along the ground—he toyed with the McCulkins for an extended period before putting them out of their misery.

Billy McCulkin knew why O'Dempsey had killed his wife. For McCulkin, 'preservation knew no limits'. As Stokes observed, McCulkin was fatally compromised; whether he drove the car or not, he was centrally involved. A disclosure to the police of his participation in the massacre would have led to his immediate arrest. He died knowing that the annihilator had murdered his entire family; they paid the ultimate price for *his* crime.

It is a certainty that McCulkin was involved, as was O'Dempsey, in the sickening Whiskey attack. If Hamilton was not involved, the knowledge or involvement of other Clockwork Orange confederates can be considered as plausible. In an interview with police on 8 March 1992, Stokes implicated two of the gang members as being of special interest.[16]

Was Hamilton's disappearance related to the Whiskey?[17] Thomas Hamilton was a talker. He told John Ryan and others of his involvement in the Torino fire, so it is not impossible that the 'Clockwork Orange' himself was vaporised for the same reason Mrs McCulkin had been—he knew too much.

For the ex-gang members, to be associated with an insurance scam was one thing, but an association with 15 deaths was an entirely different matter. The gang's muteness on the Whiskey at the murder/rape trials is understood, and the police had no imperative to ask any awkward questions, as the evidence fitted the decades-old narrative—that Stuart and Finch had done it. This may explain why they also made no mention of Billy McCulkin in relation to the

Torino fire; they simply had no need to. O'Dempsey and one of their own, Dubois, were on trial for the abomination of the McCulkin trio. There was no need to muddy the waters with an extra name. If McCulkin and O'Dempsey were a team, were they responsible for another crime, and was Barbara's death related to this event? It may be, of course, that those witnesses had no knowledge of their colleagues' involvement.

The truth is, it was a chain of events; one begat the next. McCulkin and O'Dempsey organised the successful Torino strike. With confidence they moved on to the Whiskey, but disaster struck. A witness to their mass murder started to waver. She and her daughters were silenced.

McCulkin recruited Stuart; since Stuart's return to Brisbane, the two had been inseparable.[18] Hicks predicted that if they stayed together, they would 'assuredly' commit a crime, and they did; a catastrophic one. Stuart then recruited Finch, his arsonist friend, who was a perfect fit. Burning stuff down was a speciality, in his DNA. Stuart was the perfect candidate for the conspirators—he would never ever reveal the truth, his death a fitting denouement, his honour and legend maintained. He was used by others, and not savvy enough to realize his sacrifice. He was not a scapegoat, but he was disposable. Hicks knew better; crims lack principles.

There were links between many of the players. According to Stokes, the gang knew Hannay and went to his café. He at least knew of them. Stokes maintains that Hannay also knew McCulkin and O'Dempsey. The Littles certainly had contact with McCulkin. As McCulkin and O'Dempsey visited the Whiskey before its destruction, it follows that Brian Little had knowledge of O'Dempsey. Stuart liaised with Hannay, Hamilton and O'Dempsey; his tentacles reached out in multiple directions and latched on to all the personalities in the exceptionally sad narrative.[19]

49

Murphy

There have always been rumours of police involvement. Tony Murphy's name keeps recurring in discussions. A cop is mentioned in the threatening letter to the Littles on 26 June 1973. John Ryan argued that Murphy had his eye on the Torino, while some say that Murphy intended to extort the clubs. Others have argued that Murphy controlled the gang, that the Mongrel Mob, and subsequently the Clockwork Orange gang, were under his wing.[1]

Murphy would never have dealt with Stuart directly, and although sweetly ironical if true, it would be a stupidly clumsy way for a detective to obtain money. Would any top cop have thought it shrewd to allow a loose cannon like Stuart to spend months announcing a pending extortion racket to the world and then target a club that was worthless and owed the equivalent of more than $1,000,000 in today's money?

Criminal extortionists both before and after the Whiskey have never tried this tactic for the obvious reason that they are raising their hands to be instantly clamped in handcuffs—as Stuart found out days after the Whiskey catastrophe.

There were well-trodden and more discreet paths that did not involve unstable and laughably incompetent criminals like Stuart and the Clockwork Orange thugs. Murphy and his cohort had been successfully obtaining graft on the sly through conventional means, to the point where his immediate family still do not believe that it occurred.[2] He and many others were doing very nicely, and had no incentive to compromise their nefarious moonlighting.

There is *no evidence* that any cop instigated the fire. It was a story repeated by Finch in 1988, and he and Stuart may have well have been told by their handlers that this was the case, that Murphy intended to extort 'everything in Brisbane, including restaurants and SP bookies.'[3] What is more credible is that the police protected some of the collaborators. McCulkin and O'Dempsey were known snitches who fed the police crime titbits (there are extant police informant folios from McCulkin). This was something Finch raised as an issue. As he was not alone, why was he the only one who was arrested?

The CIU operatives, the Commissioner and others believed that the spate of fires were insurance/finance related. The extortion threat was solely directed at the Whiskey. The key to the fire has everything to do with the establishment on the corner of St Pauls Terrace and Amelia Street.

Stokes made four claims in the *Port News*.

1) McCulkin through O'Dempsey, conscripted the Clockwork Orange gang to torch the Torino for $500 as an insurance job. Mrs McCulkin had admitted to her husband's role, and O'Dempsey's role was confirmed at the rape/murder trials.
2) Dubois and O'Dempsey abducted, raped and killed the McCulkin females. Both were convicted for murder, and Dubois for rape.
3) McCulkin, through O'Dempsey, conscripted elements of the Clockwork Orange gang to torch the Whiskey. Police records and eyewitness testimony indicate that this is a conclusion that requires consideration.
4) Hannay 'masterminded the entire plan.' Stokes did not provide any direct evidence for this accusation.

50

The Victims

Despite the stupidity of the act, no one should have died. The Whiskey was a death trap, a building ripe for disaster. With no sprinklers, no fire alarm, no staff training, no evacuation procedure, no fire exit sign and inadequate and cluttered fire escape doors (the sliding door was kept permanently closed), the victims stood no chance.[1] Some newspaper reports blamed the avalanche of patrons rushing towards the exit and the ensuing panic for their fate. This shows an ignorance of fire safety research. Studies have shown that if the items listed above, especially sprinklers, are available, mass casualties are impossible.[2]

The fire not only claimed the lives of the 15 who perished early that morning, but also indirectly those of Stuart and Bolton, the latter dying in 1987 aged 51.[3] Bolton experienced much anguish over the Whiskey fire, but whether or not he turned up on the night of 7 March 1973 was irrelevant. It made no difference to the outcome—it would still have occurred. Stuart wanted him to visit the Whiskey because he believed that Bolton's presence constituted a strengthened alibi. He was wrong.

Despite the ridiculous articles Bolton published in the build-up to the tragedy, he genuinely believed that something may happen, and gave it his best shot in attempting to warn the authorities. For that, he should be commended. The problem was that he had burnt too many bridges, and the evidence was not there. His only source, Stuart, had no credibility, so he was ignored. In the end, his alcoholism and depression, at least partly caused by his foreknowledge of actions that he believed could have prevented the fire, led to his suicide. He was mistaken in his influence; he had served his purpose, most probably for Stuart alone, as he believed that Bolton was assisting his alibi. The fire was locked in, whether Bolton turned up or not. Stuart and Bolton used each other well before the Whiskey tragedy unfolded, and they danced a co-dependant tango until their separate deaths.

The police received a torrent of abuse from 8 March 1973 onwards stating that through their inaction, they were responsible. Yes, both the state and federal forces had received prior notification. Hicks spent dozens of hours with Stuart trying to validate the threat, but Stuart told him *nothing*, as he succinctly stated on 10

March: 'I haven't told you anything have I?' Here was a mentally ill criminal who continually lied to him with a nonsense story about trying to stand over a club that was on the verge of bankruptcy. The police read the unbelievable stories that Bolton wrote, as told by Stuart, these by a reporter who had offered to have Stuart knocked off. There was no corroborating evidence, before and after the conflagration, for Stuart's sophistry. They are free from blame for the horrible fire; blameless before the fire, but culpable for later events if it is eventually found that there was manipulation.

For the firemen, medical staff and club staff who had witnessed the heinous scenes in the Whiskey, their only counselling came from a chat around the mess-room table.

The families and friends of the deceased suffered a permanent 'living death', with the billion-to-one shot impacting them with the force of an atomic bomb. Like all the victims' parents, Clyde and Sheila Palethorpe were devastated. Mrs Palethorpe lamented, 'To have a son killed is heart-breaking enough but to have him murdered in a crime that obviously could have been prevented is really soul tearing.'[4] Leslie Palethorpe's sister, Helen, said her mother 'never got over it; ever, ever, ever. Until she died a year ago. Never.'[5]

Helen herself was 14 when her brother was burned to death. She described Leslie as her hero, as he had literally saved her life: 'He saved me once when I was drowning. All I can remember is this arm coming down in the water and he dragged me out of the water.' The psychological scarring was exasperated by her birthday falling on March 9, the day after the inferno. Her 'beautiful big brother' never saw his sons grow up and become the confident adults they now are. Indeed, he never met his second son, Craig, who was born in August 1973. Partly inspired by his father's career choice, Craig followed Leslie into the Army, serving with peacekeepers in Cambodia and Rwanda. He now works as a policeman in remote Queensland.

At Colin Folster's funeral, the family remembered mum's favourite; the apprentice printer and talented musician who had learnt the piano at school and then moved on to the drums.[6] They recalled his first band, Flipside, formed with a couple of mates and a couple of go-go girls who tagged along with the group. Like his mum Dorothy, he loved to sing, especially *Que Sera, Sera*, so much that some people called him 'Happy'.

His brother Max heard the tragic news from his wife Maureen, who had caught it on the news. 'Your brother has been killed,' she told him. Working for the army, he stoically replied, 'I have got to go to work.' After finishing his night shift the next morning, he identified his brother's body and brought his seared clothes home.

The grief at his death was exacerbated by the repossession of Colin's beloved Holden. The family searched high and low, eventually locating it at the financiers. Despite having only two repayments due, the Folsters did not get it back. The response was, 'Madam, he's dead and it's our car now.'

After the funeral, the family retreated to sister Carol's house. Parents Dorothy and Marx disappeared into a bedroom and did not reappear. They 'never ever got over it'. Colin's drums were donated to a church.

There are stories like these for each of the 15 families who lost their loved ones, with parents, sons, daughters, brothers, sisters and others all being impacted.[7]

51
Future

One author describes the Whiskey as the 'horrific epicentre of all the crime and filth, the corruption and deaths that came before and followed that tragic night in March 1973, when 15 innocent people lost their lives' to which many still seek the answers.[1]

As early as 18 March 1973, the *Sunday Sun* demanded a Royal Commission, and soon after, Leslie Palethorpe's wife Nancy demanded justice for her two sons: 'I want to be able to tell him (the then unborn Craig) and his older brother—Shane Gordon Palethorpe, aged two—why their father was allowed to die in such a horrible way. And the only way I can find out is through an open inquiry. I am bitter because it is quite obvious from the evidence that he died needlessly.'[2] More than four decades later, the calls remain relevant.[3]

The smoke shrouding the truth behind the Whiskey Au Go Go massacre has never lifted. It smells like a cold case, rather than a closed case. The masterminds have never been called to account. Yet there remains time to unmask them.

There are enough survivors still alive to warrant an inquiry, enough time to finally excise the primary tumour from which the cancer spread and metastasized beyond Fortitude Valley; if more years pass, the chance will be lost forever.

As this book goes to press, the Coroner has been asked by the Queensland Attorney General to reopen the inquest. Like this author, the Attorney General must feel that there is more to the Whiskey Au Go Go story.

Principal Primary Source

Queensland State Archives
Series: 5023 Murder files [Investigative]
Items: Murder File: Whiskey Au Go Go [Boxes 33 to 40]
Item IDs: 814606 to 814613

Other Primary Source

Queensland State Archives
Supreme Court Trial: R v John Andrew STUART and James Richard FINCH
TR1908/1/664
Series ID: 4508
Item ID: 790416
Box 664
Despite a five-year search, only days 8 to 16 have been found transcribed.
Available but not used is; Appeal: TR 1696, Item ID 784214, Box 114.

Acknowledgements

I sincerely thank the Queensland police in allowing access to the original Whisky murder investigative files. This book was impossible without this privilege.

Thank you to publisher Denny Neave for accepting the manuscript so quickly and Geoff Whyte for the meticulous editing.

Thanks also to David and Michael for their specialist assistance.

Endnotes

Preface

[1] Little Fish Are Sweet, Matthew Condon, St Lucia, Queensland; University of Queensland Press, 2016.
[2] This last question asked by Condon.

Chapter 1

[1] Statement, Vicki Lucas, 8 March 1973. *The Courier-Mail*, 9 March 1973. Coroner's Inquest, Vicki Lucas, 9 March 1973.
[2] Development Through Life: A Psychosocial Approach, 12th Edition, Barbara M Newman, Philip R Newman Cengage Learning, 2015.
[3] *The Courier-Mail*, 9 March 1973.

Chapter 2

[1] It was closed by October 1971. Hannay knew the owner, Walter Bright. Statement, John Hannay, 10 March 1973.
[2] Statement, John Hannay, 10 March 1973.
[3] Ironically, the Birdland was previously called the Cocoanut Grove; used by the

Americans in World War Two, it was named after the club in their homeland where 492 revellers were incinerated in a fire.

[4] Statement, John Hannay, 10 March 1973. The fixtures belonged to Thomas Leighton. Statement, Thomas Leighton, 22 March 1973. The equipment was leased through United Dominion Corporation.

[5] On 16 March 1972. Fire Loss – Thomas James Leighton as Owner and Commonwealth Trading Bank of Australia as Mortgagee, 8 March 1973. Coroner's Inquest, Leo McQuillan, 8 March 1973. Hannay says it opened on 11 March. The company was formed in late 1970, Statement, Brian Little, 9 March 1973.

[6] Although no go-go girls were active around the time of the fire.

[7] Hannay was paid $100 per week, plus he was making $200 a week on the bookings. Statement, John Hannay, 10 March 1973.

[8] Statement, Thomas Leighton, 22 March 1973. Re: Fire at Whiskey Au Go Go. Cnr of Amelia Street and St Pauls Terrace, Fortitude Valley, Undated.

Statement, Ernest Miller, 5 April 1973. Alternate spelling 'Luckies'.

[9] Plan of the Whiskey Au Go Go in police records. Also well described by the Littles in their statements.

[10] Statement, Kenneth Little, 8 March 1973.

[11] Addendum Statement, John Bell, 15 May 1973, 'About mid-June, 1972, I can recall that Brian Ahern came into the Whiskey Au Go Go and introduced me to two men, one named Len McPherson from Sydney and the other Paddles Anderson, a more frailer type of man. They were very respectable at all stages.'

[12] Addendum Statement, James Chalmers, 10 March 1973.

[13] Addendum Statement, James Chalmers, 10 March 1973.

[14] Statement, Thomas Leighton, 22 March 1973. Statement, Brian Little, 9 March 1973. Statement, John Hannay, 10 March 1973.

[15] According to Hannay. His figure was disputed. Brian Little said the amount was $40,000 (testimony at the Supreme Court trial). $120,000

according to the *Sunday Sun*, 14 January 1973.
[16]   12th or 14th, Statement, John Hannay, 10 March 1973.
[17]   On Hannay's departure Jack Farr was the operations manager of both clubs.

Chapter 3

[1]   Coroner's Inquest, Leo McQuillan, 8 March 1973. The hydraulic hose reels were strategically located and conformed to the standards. There were recommendations for minor requirements in regard to provision of the fire extinguisher and certain signs.
[2]   Fire Loss – Thomas James Leighton as Owner and Commonwealth Trading Bank of Australia as Mortgagee, 8 March 1973. Coroner's Inquest, Leo McQuillan, 8 March 1973. This decree was issued to both the Little's as the Licensees and the owner Leighton.
[3]   On 5 February 1973. They were issued with a 'Show Cause Notice'. Fire Loss – Thomas James Leighton as Owner and Commonwealth Trading Bank of Australia as Mortgagee, 8 March 1973.

[4] Ryan was also a private investigator, Esgaurds Security Service and International Investigations Agency. Record of Interview Conducted between John Wayne Ryan and Inspector M A Hopwood. Present also Mr T Mellipont and Detective Senior Sergeant R B Hayes. Miss C I Cotterell – Typist, 15 March 1973. In his autobiography, he said he was fired on the weekend of 3/4 March 1973, I Survived: The Story of John Wayne Ryan, Private Detective: An Australian (Brisbane) Underbelly Survivor, John Ryan, Book Pal, 2012. Statement, Dennis Fritz, 10 March 1973. Statement, Daniel Clift, 11 March 1973.
[5] Statement, John Bell, 8 March 1973.

Chapter 4

[1] Statement, Lola Roy, 15 May 1973. Lola Roy, Supreme Court Testimony. Statement, Sandra Kinnane, 17 June 1973.
[2] 12.15am.
[3] Statement, James Chalmers, 8 March 1973 who had been a cleaner at Chequers. Addendum Statement, James

Chalmers, 10 March 1973. James Chalmers, Supreme Court Testimony.

[4] Fire Loss – Thomas James Leighton as Owner and Commonwealth Trading Bank of Australia as Mortgagee, 8 March 1973.

[5] Statement, Francis Longhurst, 8 March 1973. Statement, Francis Longhurst, 10 March 1973. Francis Longhurst, Supreme Court Testimony.

[6] *Sunday Mail,* 18 February 1996. Come a Little Bit Closer: Harmony, Disorder and the Delltones, Ian 'Peewee' Wilson, Vic Affirm Press, 2013.

[7] *The Courier-Mail,* 9 March 1973.

[8] Statement, Francis Longhurst, 10 March 1973.

[9] *The Courier-Mail,* 9 March 1973.

[10] Addendum Statement, James Chalmers, 10 March 1973.

[11] Statement, Lin, 8 March 1973. Statement, Charels [sic Charles] Reeves, 8 March 1973. Statement, Darryl Schlecht, 8 March 1973. *The Courier-Mail,* 9 March 1973.

[12] Statement, Francis Longhurst, 10 March 1973.

[13] Addendum Statement, James Chalmers, 10 March 1973.

[14] Statement, Clarence Bingham, 8 March 1973. Clarence Bingham, Supreme Court Testimony.
[15] Statement, John Bell, 8 March 1973.
[16] Statement, John Bell, 8 March 1973. Longhurst said there could be 500 to 600 on a Friday (Supreme Court Testimony) while Brian Little said 400 for a Friday, Saturday, Sunday night with 150 Monday to Thursday (Supreme Court Testimony). Seating was said to be for 400.
[17] Statement, Donna Porter, 7 September 1973. Married name, Phillips, *Brisbane Times*, 7 March 2015.
[18] Statement, Jeannette Zidich, 10 March 1973.
[19] 1.45am.
[20] He said he went to see John Morris at the De Brazil nightclub for 10 minutes, arriving at their Kangaroo Motel at 2am. Addendum Statement, Brian Little, 10 March 1973.
[21] Statement, Michael Dee, 8 March 1973. Michael Dee, Supreme Court Testimony.
[22] At 10.30pm.
[23] Statement, Patrick Mahony, 8 March 1973. This is the spelling on his signed

statement, spelled Mahoney in news articles.
[24] Addendum Statement, John Bell, 15 May 1973.
[25] *The Courier-Mail*, 9 March 1973.
[26] Statement, John Bell, 8 March 1973.

Chapter 5

[1] Statement, Christine Corney, 10 March 1973. An accounts clerk. Statement, John Koch, 8 March 1973. The Coroner's Inquest has two variants of Drew's middle name, Leonne or Leanne.
[2] At 8.30pm.
[3] Statement, Leonard Salmon, 24 July 1973. He said at 11pm, Corney said at 10.30pm.
[4] Statement, Jack Carew, 8 March 1973. Statement, Leonard Salmon, 24 July 1973.
[5] At 12.30am.
[6] At 1.25am.
[7] The Coroner's Inquest has two variants of Green's middle name, Ann or Anne.
[8] *The Courier*-Mail, 9 March 1973.

Chapter 6

[1] Statement, Hunter Nicol, 8 March 1973. 8pm.

[2]   Different from the previously mentioned Allan.
[3]   Statement, Daniel Will, 8 March 1973.
[4]   Statement, Daniel Will, 8 March 1973. *The Courier-Mail*, 9 March 1973.
[5]   *The Courier-Mail*, 9 March 1973.
[6]   Statement, Flora Simpson, 10 March 1973.
[7]   Around 2.00am.
[8]   Statement, Graham Rennex, 8 March 1973. Statement, Kenneth Little, 8 March 1973. He calls her Julie Abes. Ken Little is the only person who mentions her presence on this night.
[9]   Statement, Laurence Kuhlmann, Undated.
[10]   Statement, Raymond Roberts, Undated.
[11]   Statement, David Neden, 8 March 1973. Statement, Graham Rennex, 8 March 1973.
[12]   Running Sheet, Whiskey Au Go Go Fire and Fatality, 8 March 1973.
[13]   *The Courier-Mail*, 9 March 1973. *The Sun*, 31 October 1988. Statement, Bevan Childs, 8 March 1973. *Sydney Morning Herald*, 9 March 1972. The drummer was Foyle. The saxophones were found on the stage.

Chapter 7

[1] Statement, David McSherry, Undated. Statement, David McSherry, 8 March 1973. Statement, Daniel McGrath, 15 May 1973. Statement, Kaye Suhr, Undated.
[2] Statement, Gregory Clark, Undated.
[3] Statement, David McSherry, Undated.
[4] Statement, Vincent Murphy, Undated. Addendum Statement, Vincent Murphy, 2 October 1973. At the time he did not know who she was but later recognised her from a photo as Carol Green. The time does not match that of Christine Corney's testimony.
[5] Statement, Michael Dee, 8 March 1973. Statement, David McSherry, Undated.

Chapter 8

[1] Statement, Neil Raward, Undated. The lids were never found. No fingerprints were found on any evidence, including the drums. Statement, Patrick O'Brien, 27 July 1973. Super-grade petrol, probably AMOCO. Running Sheet, Whiskey Au Go Go Fire and Fatality, 8

March 1973. The three-quarters figure comes from Finch.

[2] Thomas Atkinson Diary, 9 March 1973 (mislabelled as Robert Hayes Diary in one police record). The five-gallon drum had been manufactured by SC Johnson & Son and had previously contained a cleaner called 'Traffic Grade'. Six hundred and ninety-six drums were distributed throughout Queensland between 1 July 1972 and 31 December 1972. All were non-returnable and were sent to motels, hotels, hospitals, clubs, contract cleaners etc. Statement, Keith Linnane, 1 May 1973. Statement, Leslie Bardwell, Undated. Statement, Neil Raward, Undated.

[3] Statement, Leslie Bardwell, Undated. The five-gallon drum had 550 millilitres remaining.

[4] Statement, James Stewart, 8 March 1973. Coroner's Inquest, James Stewart, 9 March 1973. James Stewart, Supreme Court Testimony.

Chapter 9

[1] Now Amelia House.

[2] Statement, Mavis Kann, Undated. Mavis Kann, Supreme Court Testimony.
[3] Statement, Arthur Parkinson, 22 March 1973.

Chapter 10

[1] Statement, Francis Longhurst, 10 March 1973.
[2] Statement, Clarence Bingham, 8 March 1973. Statement, James Chalmers, 8 March 1973.
[3] Statement, Francis Longhurst, 8 March 1973.
[4] Statement, Neil Raward, Undated.
[5] Statement, John Bell, 8 March 1973.
[6] Statement, Leslie Bardwell, Undated.
[7] Statement, Clarence Bingham, 8 March 1973.
[8] Statement, Lola Roy, 15 May 1973.
[9] Bag content description, undated police note.
[10] Statement, Donald Davidson, 12 May 1973. Statement, Roger Lund, 11 May 1973. Statement, Daniel McGrath, 15 May 1973.
[11] Statement, David McSherry, 8 March 1973.

[12] Statement, James Stewart, 8 March 1973.
[13] Statement, David McSherry, Undated.
[14] Statement, Daniel McGrath, 15 May 1973.
[15] Statement, John Bell, 8 March 1973.
[16] Statement, Kaye Suhr, Undated.
[17] Fire Loss – Thomas James Leighton as Owner and Commonwealth Trading Bank of Australia as Mortgagee, 8 March 1973.
[18] Statement, David MacIntosh, 4 April 1973. Statement, Edward Kropp, 4 April 1973.
[19] Statement, James Chalmers, 8 March 1973.
[20] Statement, Patrick Mahony, 8 March 1973. *Telegraph*, 9 March 1973.
[21] Addendum Statement, Alex Lueck, 10 September 1973. Oddly, in a previous statement he said he went through the back door. Statement, Axel Lueck, 10 March 1973.

Chapter 11

[1] Statement, Christine Corney, 10 March 1973.
[2] Statement, Jack Carew, 8 March 1973.

[3] Statement, Christine Corney, 10 March 1973.
[4] Viewable in a police photo.
[5] John Bell commented that there was no visibility until he reached the laneway. Statement, John Bell, 8 March 1973.

Chapter 12

[1] Statement, Davis Neden, 8 March 1973.
[2] Statement, George Power, 8 March 1973. Coroner's Inquest, George Power, 9 March 1973. *Telegraph,* 9 March 1973.
[3] Statement, Graham Rennex, 8 March 1973.
[4] Statement, Bevan Childs, 8 March 1973.
[5] Day did not exit and then re-enter the club to retrieve his sax as newspaper reports at the time indicated.
[6] Statement, Raymond Roberts, Undated.
[7] Statement, Neil Raward, Undated.
[8] Statement, Donna O'Brien, Undated.
[9] Statement, Hunter Nicol, 8 March 1973.
[10] Statement, Ernest Miller, 5 April 1973. Hunter Nicol has told the author he may have exited through the kitchen window. If so, he would have been the only person who reported having done so. In addition, the unbroken

	kitchen windows appear to be in front of the gate he said he climbed over.
[11]	Statement, Edward Kropp, 4 April 1973.
[12]	Statement, Neil Raward, Undated.
[13]	Statement, Francis Longhurst, 8 March 1973.
[14]	*Brisbane Times,* 7 March 2015. Statement, Donna Porter, 7 September 1973.
[15]	Police Note, Undated.
[16]	*Sydney Morning Herald,* 9 March 1973.
[17]	Statement, Vincent Murphy, Undated.

Chapter 13

[1]	Statement, Neil Raward, Undated.
[2]	They captured a shot of the Whiskey (top floor) on fire. This was later attached to a photo of the ground-floor shops to produce a 'fake' composite.
[3]	Statement, Hunter Nicol, 8 March 1973.
[4]	Departed 2.10am. Information Sought by Crown Prosecutor from Fire Chief, Undated.
[5]	Statement, Edward Kropp, 4 April 1973.
[6]	Fire timings, Information Sought by Crown Prosecutor from Fire Chief, Undated.

[7]	Statement, Clarence Bingham, 8 March 1973.
[8]	Statement, Jack Carew, 8 March 1973.
[9]	Statement, David MacIntosh, 4 April 1973.
[10]	Statement, Francis Longhurst, 8 March 1973.
[11]	Statement, Kaye Suhr, Undated.
[12]	Statement, Kenneth Little, 8 March 1973. Statement, Darryl Schlecht, 8 March 1973.
[13]	Statement, Kenneth Little, 8 March 1973.
[14]	Statement, David MacIntosh, 4 April 1973.
[15]	Body No 5. Statement, Vincent Murphy, Undated.
[16]	Statement, Edward Kropp, 4 April 1973.
[17]	Described as a 'nasty' scene by the fire chief. Statement, Vivian Dowling, 17 May 1973.
[18]	Statement, Kenneth Browning, Undated. *The Courier-Mail*, 7 July 1989. In this newspaper article, the retiring David Macintosh said death was the hardest part of job. He named the Whiskey Au Go Go blaze as the most tragic.

[19]	Statement, Vivian Dowling, 17 May 1973. Statement, Edward Kropp, 4 April 1973. Information Sought by Crown Prosecutor from Fire Chief, Undated.

Chapter 14

[1]	Statement, David McSherry, Undated. Statement, David McSherry, 8 March 1973.
[2]	Statement, Kenneth Little, 8 March 1973.
[3]	Statement, Darryl Schlecht, 8 March 1973.
[4]	Statement, Jack Carew, 8 March 1973.
[5]	Police note, untitled and undated. *The Courier-Mail*, 9 March 1973.
[6]	Statement, Hunter Nicol, 8 March 1973.
[7]	Statement, Christine Corney, 10 March 1973.
[8]	Statement, G Hildebrand, 9 March 1973. Statement, Daniel McGrath, 15 May 1973.
[9]	Statement, Vincent Murphy, Undated. Statement, Vincent Purcell, Undated. Transported to the Institute of Forensic Pathology.
[10]	Statement, Kaye Suhr, Undated.

[11]   Statement, Alfred Green, Undated. At 4.55am.
[12]   Statement, Murray Rowley, 24 May 1973.

Chapter 15

[1]   Running Sheet, Whiskey Au Go Go Fire and Fatality, 8 March 1973.
[2]   Undated, unsigned:
Just lately we had a most terrible fright
Brisbane night was bombed in the night
Fifteen dead in an awful fire
Just to satisfy some fiend's hellish desire....
[3]   Running Sheet, Whiskey Au Go Go Fire and Fatality, 9 March 1973. On 23 October 1973, a mental patient sent a telegram to Stuart.
[4]   Basil Hicks Notes 14 February 1972. Information had been passed from the Sydney armed hold-up squad that O'Driscoll had been associating with Stuart. On 28 February 1973, Hicks asks Stuart directly if he has seen O'Driscoll.
[5]   http://adb.anu.edu.au/biography/stuart-john-andrew-11795. Statement, Edna Watts, 28 March 1973.
[6]   Letter John Stuart to Carmel, 28 May (circa) 1968.

[7] Charge sheet, 27 September 1963. Later, he went to Brisbane Boys College. Regina vs John Andrew Stuart and Raymond Patrick O'Connor, 8 June 1966, Transcript State Archives NSW.

[8] Letter Edna Watts to John Stuart, 25 April 1965. See also letter Edna Watts to John Stuart, 28 April 1965. In Letter Edna Watts to John Stuart 16 February 1964 she mentions that Uncle Jack and Charlie also had TB.

[9] Torch Man, Frank Robson, *Playboy*, October 1982.

[10] Letter Edna Watts to John Stuart, 23 November 1964.

[11] Letter Edna Watts to John Stuart, 25 April 1965.

[12] Charge sheet, 27 September 1963.

[13] Torch Man, Frank Robson, *Playboy*, October 1982.

[14] Letter Edna Watts to John Stuart, 23 November 1964.

[15] Torch Man, Frank Robson, *Playboy*, October 1982.

[16] Letter Edna Watts to John Stuart, 2 September 1972.

[17] Statement, Edna Watts, 28 March 1973.

[18] He had just turned 13 years old.

[19] Bundaberg Petty Sessions.
[20] Petty Sessions. On 31 March 1955. Police criminal record.
[21] 12 December. Police criminal record.

Chapter 16

[1] *The Courier-Mail*, 21 March 1956.
[2] Letter John Stuart to Daniel Stuart, 16 April 1973.
[3] 20 March 1956 in the Brisbane Supreme Court.
[4] Police criminal record.
[5] Police criminal record.
[6] 24 April 1956, Brisbane Children's Court. Disorderly conduct, failed to appear, 'Bond of £1 entering into mother.' At the time he was hanging around the Railway Institute Dances, 9 May 1956.
[7] Torch Man, Frank Robson, *Playboy* October 1982 and Verbal: Mass Murder, Mother's Love, Faith, Loss, Hope, Betrayal, Tim Roy, Book Pal, 2011. Roy admits his book is a work of fiction: 'This biography/supposition ... is not absolutely correct.'
[8] Report. Westbrook Farm Home for Boys Inquiry, 27 September 1961. http:/

/www.parliament.qld.gov.au/documents/tableOffice/TabledPapers/1961/3661T299.pdf

[9] Westbrook, William Stokes, Pan Macmillan Australia, 2010. Brutal, Surviving Westbrook Boys Home: A Horrifying but Sadly True Story, Alfred Fletcher, Rev. edn, New Holland Publishers (Australia), 2006.

[10] Letter Daniel Stuart to John Stuart, 13 February 1970, when Daniel talked of 'our generation of angry young men.' See also Torch Man, Frank Robson, *Playboy*, October 1982.

[11] 19 August 1958, Police criminal record.

[12] It's Only Rock 'n' Roll but I Like It: A History of the Early Days of Rock 'n' Roll in Brisbane as Told by Some of the People Who Were There. Geoffrey Walden, Queensland University of Technology, January 2003.

[13] 11 years of age. John Bell, Supreme Court Testimony.

[14] John Stuart, Record of Interview, 8 March 1973. In his early career, Bell was associated with De Brazil club (Brisbane) and various Sydney teenage sound lounges and dancehalls in Bankstown and Liverpool. Fire Loss –

Thomas James Leighton as Owner and Commonwealth Trading Bank of Australia as Mortgagee, 8 March 1973.
[15] Police criminal record. Also seen at Busteeds Dance Hall, 21 April 1956.
[16] Statement, John Hannay, 21 May 1973.
[17] According to John Hannay.
[18] Fire Trail, Susan Johnson, Unidentified magazine and date, http://Johnwryan.net
[19] Letter John Stuart to Edna Watts from NSW State Penitentiary, 14 October 1959. She wrote a statutory declaration for him.
[20] Torch Man, Frank Robson, *Playboy*, October 1982.
[21] Letter Wally to John Stuart, Undated.
[22] Charge sheet, 27 September 1963. Two uncles worked on the Brisbane Waterfront, Charlie and Lennie Lockery (alternate spelling), Statement, Robert Glover, 24 March 1973.
[23] Charge sheet, 4 August 1961.

Chapter 17

[1] He had first gone to Sydney at least as early as 1959, being incarcerated in the

	State Penitentiary NSW, October 1959 (Long Bay).
[2]	*The Daily Advertiser*, 1 and 4 October 1960.
[3]	Letter Lorrie to John Stuart,? October 1960.
[4]	Letter John Stuart to Lorrie, 21 October 1960.
[5]	'On charge of assault occasioning actual bodily harm of 1/10/61 the Attorney General has decided not to proceed further.' John Stuart, Police criminal record.
[6]	Postcard John Stuart to Lorry, 7 November 1972. He sent this from Townsville during his trip north despite being with girlfriend Sue at the time. A Lorry is mentioned in a letter John Stuart to Edna Watts, 25 February 1968.
[7]	Police criminal record.
[8]	Charge sheet, 4 August 1961.
[9]	On the 15th. Police criminal record.
[10]	From 19 January 1961, Police criminal record. Another police record indicates he was admitted to the Ipswich Mental Hospital on 30 March 1961.
[11]	Police criminal record.
[12]	Police criminal record. Stealing and assault, 2 October 1961.

[13] On the 25th, Police criminal record. *Sunday Truth*, 28 January 1962.

Chapter 18

[1] *Sunday Truth*, 28 January 1962.
[2] On 4 February 1962, Stuart received his second mention in the *Sunday Truth*. A paragraph noted the Australia-wide search for Stuart after his escape from Callan Park and speculated that he might not be in Brisbane.
[3] Danny's story: The stink of the Whiskey case won't go away, Frank Robson, *Griffith Review* 45, 2014.
[4] *The Courier-Mail*, 5 March 1987.
[5] Letter John Stuart to Doctor, Her Majesty's Prison, 9 March 1962.
[6] The actions on ward 2, while being treated, were those of a completely sane person, which happened to be his 'natural disposition.'
[7] Letter Marge X to John Stuart, 6 May 1964.
[8] John Stuart note, undated (perhaps circa 1963).
[9] Charge sheet, 27 September 1963. This claim was repeated in a court trial. Also see *Sunday Truth*, 28 January 1962,

	where he is referred to as a drug addict.
[10]	Letter Marge X to Stuart, 6 May 1964. Regina vs John Andrew Stuart and Raymond Patrick O'Connor, June 1966. In Stuart's hand (undated) he writes AMPHETAMINE.
[11]	Police criminal record. On 29 June 1962.
[12]	*Sunday Truth*, 1 July 1962.
[13]	Hawke and Hovey from undated and unknown newspaper article, police records.
[14]	Reproduced in *Port News*, December 1976. Arrested 30 June 1962.
[15]	*Sunday Truth*, 8 July 1962. Police criminal record.
[16]	Undated and unknown newspaper article, police records.
[17]	*Sunday Truth*, 15 July 1962.
[18]	Letter Con Lianos to John Stuart, 2 November 1962.
[19]	Callan Park Mental Hospital (twice), Wagga Wagga (twice) and the General Hospital Mental Ward 16. On 13 January 1963, *Sunday Truth*.
[20]	*Sunday Truth*, 13 January 1963.
[21]	*Sunday Truth*, 11 August 1963.
[22]	*Sunday Truth*, 18 August 1963.

[23]　From 7 March 1964 for break enter steal, Police criminal record.
[24]　On 27 April 1964, Police criminal record. A special suicide circular was issued for him on 1 March 1970, Police criminal record.
[25]　Letter Chief Probation Officer to John Stuart, 14 December 1964.
[26]　Letter John Stuart to Edna Watts, 17 April 1965.
[27]　Consorting cards in 1965 show him hanging around with Billy McCulkin and Billy Phillips.

Chapter 19

[1]　100 Wallace Street.
[2]　*Daily Mirror*, 27 November 1965.
[3]　Interview between Detective Sergeant Noel Morey and John Andrew Stuart at Criminal Investigation Branch on 1 December 1965.
[4]　For Steele shooting see *Daily Mirror*, 29 November 1965; *Daily Mirror*, 30 November 1965; *Daily Mirror*, 14 December 1965.
[5]　Typed letter, Undated.

[6] Regina vs John Andrew Stuart and Raymond Patrick O'Connor, 28 June 1966.
[7] Or 'Wharton'. See also *Daily Telegraph*, 29 June 1966.
[8] Based on a police statement, name and date withheld by the author.
[9] On 29 December 1965 at 8pm.
[10] Basil Hicks Notes, 15 September 1972. *Daily Telegraph*, 29 June 1966.
[11] *Daily Telegraph*, 29 June 1966.
[12] Regina vs John Andrew Stuart and Raymond Patrick O'Connor, 22 August 1966.
[13] Letter John Stuart to Herb, 17 August 1966.
[14] Letter John Stuart to Anthony Bellanto, Maitland Gaol, Undated.
[15] *Daily Mirror*, 30 November 1965.
[16] *Daily Mirror*, 16 March 1967.
[17] Regina vs John Andrew Stuart and Raymond Patrick O'Connor, 26 August 1966.
[18] Basil Hicks Notes, 15 September 1972.
[19] As soon as he arrived back in Brisbane in mid-1972 he told his sister June that he had been 'involved' with nightclubs in Sydney. Statement, June Beckman, 8 March 1973. He would tell his

brother-in-law Lyall Beckman that he was standing over gambling dens and prostitutes. Lyall Beckman, 29 March 1973.

[20] McPherson denied it. Statement, Leonard McPherson, 17 September 1973.

[21] Letter John Stuart to Anthony Bellanto, Maitland Gaol, Undated.

[22] *Daily Mirror*, 16 March 1967 and Roger Rogerson quoted in Three Crooked Kings, Matthew Condon, University of Queensland Press, 2013.

Chapter 20

[1] The article is not authored. Although Bolton wrote for the *Daily Mirror*, he never referred to Stuart as 'the Tornado' in the Queensland newspapers.

[2] *Daily Mirror*, 16 March 1967.

[3] Statement, Graham Miller, 10 March 1973. Letter John Stuart to Edna Watts, Grafton Gaol, 2 July 1967.

[4] Letter John Stuart to Edna Watts, Grafton Gaol, 7 May 1967.

[5] Nagle Report. 1976–77–78. Parliament Of New South Wales Report Of The

Royal Commission Into New South Wales Prisons.

[6] Two weeks later, 21 May 1967. Letter John Stuart to Edna Watts, Grafton Gaol, 21 May 1967.

[7] Letter John Stuart to Edna Watts, Grafton Gaol, 28 May 1967.

[8] Daniel Stuart, Supreme Court Testimony.

[9] On the 27th.

[10] Letter John Stuart to Edna Watts, Grafton Gaol, 27 August 1967.

[11] His mother sent him a list of everyone's birthday. Letter John Stuart to Edna Watts, 13 July 1972. *Brisbane Times*, 22 December 2010.

[12] Family Secrets, Frank Robson, *Sydney Morning Herald Magazine*, 18 December 2010.

[13] Stuart's writing, Undated.

[14] Letter John Stuart to Edna Watts, 17 April 1965.

[15] Letter John Stuart to Edna Watts, 17 April 1965.

[16] Died aged 90, 2003. Family Secrets, Frank Robson, *Sydney Morning Herald Magazine*, 18 December 2010.

[17] Letter John Stuart to Edna Watts, Grafton Gaol, 25 June 1967.

[18] Letter John Stuart to Edna Watts, 17 April 1965.

[19] For example, in the Parramatta Gaol Magazine *Contact*. Statement, Leslie Newcombe, 11 April 1973. Letter Edna Watts to John Stuart, 8 April 1971. Torch Man, Frank Robson, *Playboy*, October 1982.

[20] For example, on the back of letter Edna Watts to John Stuart, Undated. The example is in Stuart's writing.

[21] Letter Edna Watts to John Stuart, 23 November 1964.

[22] Letter Edna Watts to John Stuart, 25 April 1965.

[23] Although the family claimed he found Christ just prior to his death.

[24] Letter Edna Watts to John Stuart, 16 September 1971, 'I'm still going to church each week, but sometimes I wonder if that makes me a hypocrite, instead of a Christian. Principles in this matter are somewhat of a curse, because by going to church I have to abide at all times by God. If I didn't, I'd keep asking myself which is the lie. Perhaps it's been this that has kept me a criminal for so long.' Letter John

	Stuart to Edna Watts, Grafton Gaol, 24 September 1967.
[25]	Letter John Stuart to Edna Watts, Grafton Gaol, 25 June 1967.
[26]	Jeff Blick sent him a book called Zen Buddhism, Letter Jeff Blick to John Stuart, 14 June 1962?. 'I found Zen', John Stuart's writing.
[27]	Letter Edna Watts to John Stuart, 27 January 1972.
[28]	Letter John Stuart to Edna Watts, Grafton Gaol, 24 September 1967. Was he bipolar?
[29]	Letter John Stuart to Jeff, Undated. In the Letter Daniel Stuart to John Stuart, 13 February 1970, John wrote about hitting his head on the wall.
[30]	John Stuart's writing, Undated.
[31]	Letter Elvena[i?] to John Stuart, 7 January 1965?
[32]	Letter John Stuart to Edna Watts, 9 July 1967.
[33]	Letter Daniel Stuart to John Stuart, 13 February 1970.
[34]	Letter Daniel Stuart to John Stuart, 18 April 1971.
[35]	Letter Edna Watts to John Stuart, 25 March 1970.

[36] Letter Daniel Stuart to John Stuart, 10 March 1971.
[37] Letter Daniel Stuart to John Stuart, 7 April 1971. Also Letter Daniel Stuart to John Stuart, 18 April 1971, where he wrote 'Fellow sufferer of the dementia Preacox [psychotic disorder] club ... Received your light-weight clay tablet, read it and then took it for my headache....'
[38] Letter Daniel Stuart to John Stuart, circa 1965 (date erased). John Stuart replied on the back of the same letter.
[39] Stuart's writing, Undated. The Underdogs (Spanish: Los de abajo) is a novelistic treatment of the Mexican Revolution by Mariano Azuela.
[40] Letter John Stuart to Con, after 2 November 1962.
[41] Letter John Stuart to Daniel Stuart, circa 1965 (date erased).
[42] Daniel Stuart, Supreme Court Testimony.
[43] Letter Daniel Stuart to John Stuart, 10 March 1971. He said he was diagnosed with kidney problems in the Islands (Papua New Guinea) and may need a transplant. His brother offered his.

[44] Letter John Stuart to Daniel Stuart, Undated, 'spread the dynamite of your emotions around a bit, then when that explosion comes....'
[45] Family Secrets, Frank Robson, *Sydney Morning Herald Magazine*, 18 December 2010.
[46] Family Secrets, Frank Robson, *Sydney Morning Herald Magazine*, 18 December 2010.
[47] Family Secrets, Frank Robson, *Sydney Morning Herald Magazine*, 18 December 2010. Statement, name withheld, 'Daniel was always cruel to his first wife Del and punched her and knocked her about something terrible.' Between 1960 and 1962, Dan brought his first wife out to a relative's place and hid himself and the children there after doing crimes. 'Dan Stuart lived for some time with Rose, his present wife, before marrying her and he has punched and knocked her about too. He said that on one occasion he assaulted Rose and had blackened her eye. John went to her assistance and Dan became insanely jealous of John and in fact any man who paid attention

[48] or went to the assistance of either Del[erie] or Rose.'
[48] Family Secrets, Frank Robson, *Sydney Morning Herald Magazine*, 18 December 2010.
[49] Letter Edna Watts to John Stuart, 11 May 1965.
[50] Letter John Stuart to Anthony Bellanto, Maitland Gaol, Undated.
[51] 3 October 1971, *Sunday Sun?* Reproduced in Letter Edna Watts to John Stuart, 14 October 1971.
[52] For example, Stuart Plans Mass Prison Suicide, *Sunday Sun*, 28 April 1974.
[53] Letter John Stuart to Superintendent, Parramatta Gaol, 23 January 1972.

Chapter 21

[1] *Sunday Sun*, 4 June 1972.
[2] Basil Hicks Notes, 15 September 1972.
[3] Letter Judges' Chambers, Supreme Court, Sydney, 30 June 1972.
[4] Combined Police Special Operations Group, From Sydney to Brisbane, 9 June 1972.
[5] Queensland Police sent a Crime Circular on 14 June 1972.

[6]   Letter John Stuart to Edna Watts, Grafton Gaol, 25 June 1967.
[7]   Police note, 25 July 1973.
[8]   Letter Edna Watts to John Stuart, 13 July 1972.
[9]   There were two police officers there. Letter Davey Heming to John Stuart, 19 August 1972.
[10]   Police note, 25 July 1972. Statement, Rosealie Stuart, 8 August 1973. Statement, Daniel Stuart, 11 March 1973. Daniel moved to Jindalee in September 1972, Daniel Stuart, Supreme Court Testimony.
[11]   Addendum Statement, Lyall Beckman, 29 March 1973. Addendum Statement, June Beckman, 8 March 1973.
[12]   For example, Sue.
[13]   Addendum Statement, Lyall Beckman, 29 March 1973.
[14]   Addendum Statement, Lyall Beckman, 29 March 1973. Statement, June Beckman, 8 March 1973.
[15]   Letter Edna Watts to John Stuart, 2 September 1972.
[16]   Basil Hicks Notes, 28 July 1972.
[17]   In June. Statement, Basil Hicks, Undated.
[18]   Statement, Basil Hicks, Undated.

[19] Statement, Basil Hicks, Undated.
[20] Police note.
[21] Before I Sleep: Memoirs of a Modern Police Commissioner, Ray Whitrod, University of Queensland Press, 2014. John Ryan Agrees, I Survived: The Story of John Wayne Ryan, Private Detective: An Australian (Brisbane) Underbelly Survivor, John Ryan, Book Pal, 2012.
[22] Before I Sleep: Memoirs of a Modern Police Commissioner, Ray Whitrod, University of Queensland Press, 2014. *The Courier-Mail*, 5 September 1988, Phil Dickie, 'Hicks and Saunders visited Brisbane Gaol in 1978 to see a prisoner now known as Katherine James. She had allegedly given a statement to police about photographs of her and Hicks in a compromising position which put an end to a plan by Sir Joh Bjelke-Petersen to have Hicks replace Murphy as head of the CIB. Katherine James allegedly told Saunders that no photographs existed but Tony Murphy and detectives Graham Leadbetter and Barry O'Brien had told her to say that they did.

Murphy and O'Brien have denied any wrongdoing before the inquiry.'

[23] Letter Fortitude Valley Area Office, 3 August 1972.

[24] I Survived: The Story of John Wayne Ryan, Private Detective: An Australian (Brisbane) Underbelly Survivor. John Ryan, Book Pal, 2012.

[25] Statement, Brian Bolton, 18 May 1973.

[26] Letter Edna Watts to John Stuart, 27 August 1972.

[27] Letter Edna Watts to John Stuart, 2 September 1972.

[28] Basil Hicks Notes, 18 September 1973.

[29] Statement, Robert McCulkin, 3 July 1973.

[30] He did so on 22 September, Basil Hicks Notes.

[31] *Sunday Truth*, 28 January 1962.

[32] The Tangled Web, Des Sturgess, Beside Books, 2001.

[33] Statement, Rosealie Stuart, 8 August 1973. Statement, Daniel Stuart, 11 March 1973.

[34] Basil Hicks Notes where he describes the code, 22 September 1973. A police note also has a description of the code.

[35] Daniel Stuart, Supreme Court Testimony.

[36] He told this to many people, for example, Statement, Abraham Yasse, 8 March 1973.

[37] Addendum Statement, Lyall Beckman, 29 March 1973.

[38] Statement, Stuart Hannay, 10 March 1973. I Survived: The Story of John Wayne Ryan, Private Detective: An Australian (Brisbane) Underbelly Survivor, John Ryan, Book Pal, 2012.

[39] Statement, Stuart Hannay, 10 March 1973. See also Addendum Statement James Chalmers, 10 March 1973. Alternate spellings Zibnew, Staniszewski and Staniziski.

[40] State Government Insurance Office (Form 4), 6 October 1972, signed by J Trauts. Statement, Stuart Bray, 21 May 1973. The claim was forwarded to the State Government Insurance Office (Queensland). Statement, Francis Ready, 24 May 1973.

[41] Statement, Robert McCulkin, 3 July 1973. Basil Hicks Notes, 23 November 1972, 'He lifted his shirt and held up his arm and I saw his shoulder blade tighten up. He said I can't lift my arm

any higher than this and then laughed. I'd doubt that he has any real injury. He says that he is going to make the compensation last as long as he can.' The compensation amounted to $120 a fortnight. See also State Government Insurance Office statement, 2 October 1973. Memo James Campbell, 9 October 1973.

Statement, Rosealie Stuart, 8 August 1973, 'He asked Daniel to hit him across the back where he has scars and then say he had fallen down, Dan refused so he said Billy McCulkin did it.'

Statement, Sue, 11 March 1973, 'A few days after he came to live with me he started to receive compensation for an alleged injury to his back. I believe that McCulkin deliberately injured Stuart's back, at Stuart's request. I can remember McCulkin and he was laughing about it and Stuart saying you did a good job of that, because I got so many dollars out of it.'

[42] Addendum Statement, Lyall Beckman, 10 August 1973.

[43] Statement, Antonio Bellino, 22 March 1973. Time for Truth: Tony Bellino Tells It As It Is: Crimes, Courts and

Corruption. Antonio Bellino, self-published, 2009.
[44] Basil Hicks Notes, 9 October 1973.
[45] She possibly had a background in prostitution.
[46] Circa 3rd October.
[47] Basil Hicks Notes, 10 and 12 October 1973.
[48] Statement, Trevor Coulter, 18 July 1973 and 27 August 1973. Addendum Statement, Kenneth Little, 11 March 1973.
[49] A 'Stewart' produced a flick knife at the Lands Office Hotel.
[50] Addendum Statement, Brian Little, 10 March 1973.
[51] He told Bell, 'Hannay's lucky. I have been paid to knock him off if he doesn't pay money that is outstanding to Parkinson.' Addendum Statement, John Bell, 15 May 1973.
[52] Brian and Bell went together on a number of occasions. Addendum Statement, Brian Little, 10 March 1973. A local criminal at the Lands Office Hotel told him that Stuart had said that the best way to stand over Hannay was to cause trouble in the

clubs. Addendum Statement, John Bell, 15 May 1973.

[53] Statement, John Hannay, 21 May 1973. Hannay said it occurred on Friday afternoon, 6th or 13th. Brian Little said the next night (Saturday) that Hannay did not work and shot down to the Gold Coast because of Stuart. Statement, Brian Little, 9 March 1973.

[54] See also Statement, George Freeleagus, 17 August 1973.

[55] Statement, John Hannay, 21 May 1973. The Littles concur with this statement.

[56] Statement, John Hannay, 21 May 1973.

[57] Addendum Statement, Brian Little, 10 March 1973. Addendum Statement, Kenneth Little, 14 May 1973.

[58] Addendum Statement, John Bell, 15 May 1973. Addendum Statement, Brian Little, 10 March 1973. Addendum Statement, Kenneth Little, 11 March 1973. Stuart kept a shanghai in his car and Detective Atkinson asked if he used it to create the holes, John Stuart's Record of Interview, 8 March 1973, reproduced in Robert Hayes Testimony, Supreme Court Testimony.

Chapter 22

[1] Basil Hicks Notes, 18 October 1973.
[2] On 17 October. McPherson was in Brisbane from 14 to 15 September in transit to Bali, Memorandum Re Movements and whereabouts of Leonard Arthur McPherson during October 1972, 30 July 1973.
[3] Statement, John Hannay, 21 May 1973. In Stuart's Record of Interview, 8 March 1973, he said they shook hands.
[4] Basil Hicks Notes, 18 October 1973.
[5] There would be no immigrant in the narrative.
[6] Statement, Sue, 11 March 1973.
[7] Postcard John Stuart to Basil Hicks, 7 November 1972. Sent from Townsville.
[8] 21st. Three days after the call to Hicks. Basil Hicks Notes, 21 October 1973.
[9] He carried siphoning hoses. Addendum Statement, Lyall Beckman, 29 March 1973. Statement, Daniel Stuart, 11 March 1973.
[10] Postcard John Stuart to Basil Hicks, 29 October 1972.
[11] Last Monday in October. Statement, John Hannay, 10 March 1973.

[12]	Statement, John Hannay, 10 March 1973.
[13]	They swapped Sue's Cortina for a Kelly Green Ford Fairlane. A police note records it as 14 November 1972, but this was impossible as he was already back in Brisbane. Stuart mentions it in a postcard dated 4 November 1972 from Cloncurry.
[14]	Basil Hicks Record, Telegram.
[15]	29 October, Daly Waters: 4 November Cloncurry (stamped Julia Creek) and 7 November Townsville.
[16]	He was in Townsville 7 November 1972. One postcard was sent to an old 'girlfriend' Lorrie and the other to Baz.

Chapter 23

[1]	Basil Hicks Notes, 9 November 1972. Statement, Basil Hicks, Undated.
[2]	10 November 1972.
[3]	Statement, George Doolan, Undated. Statement Alan Freeman, Undated.
[4]	This was the second meeting there. 12 November, Sunday.
[5]	Basil Hicks Notes, 13 November 1972.
[6]	Of November.

[7] The only record is from the Treasury Tavern Hotel, where they say they were threatened by Stuart in April 1972 but the date is impossible, because he was in gaol at the time. Statement, Estelle Long, 25 April 1973.
[8] Statement, John Hannay, 21 May 1973. Addendum Statement, Brian Little, 10 March 1973.
[9] Statement, Thomas Leighton, 22 March 1973.
[10] Statement, John McGrath, Undated.
[11] According to Hannay. Statement, John Hannay, 10 March 1973, about 2pm.
[12] Ralph is unidentified.
[13] Statement, John Hannay, 10 March 1973.
[14] Addendum Statement, Brian Little, 10 March 1973.
[15] 21 November. Statement, John McGrath, Undated.
[16] Where he saw Detectives King and Richeion.
[17] He forewarned Lin, the Chequers cashier and receptionist, that he was going to do it.
[18] According to Hannay. Statement, John Hannay, 10 March 1973.

[19] Statement, Jack Farr, 8 March 1973. Fire Loss – Thomas James Leighton as Owner and Commonwealth Trading Bank of Australia as Mortgagee, 8 March 1973. Statement, Darryl Schlecht, 8 March 1973. With Hannay gone, Bell, Longhurst, and Spiggy were all employed at the Whiskey.
[20] 23 November 72. Basil Hicks Notes, 23 November 1972.
[21] Statement, Sue, 11 March 1973. Stuart stayed at her house at Banyo for two weeks before leaving for Sydney.
[22] Message, 23 November 1972.
[23] Statement, Sue, 11 March 1973.
[24] Police Circular, 29 November 1972.
[25] Postcard John Stuart to Basil Hicks, 29 November 1972. 1 December, Hicks gets postcard from North Richmond.
[26] Basil Hicks Records, copied (photostat) photo.
[27] Police Circular, 29 November 1972.
[28] Statement, Leslie Brown, 19 July 1973.
[29] It reached Hicks on 8 December. Statement, Basil Hicks, Undated.
[30] Decoded version. Police note, Undated.

Chapter 24

[1] Statement, James Cox, Undated. Police note, 20 December 1972.

[2] At 7pm, Statement, Norman Koazeaha, 23 March 1973. The police attempted to contact Des Anderson, Barrister, Sydney on 30 July 1973 to see whether he had arranged bail with Lou Miller. Memorandum re: Des Anderson 30 July 1973. Miller used to frequent the Surrey Hills Lebanese Club and knew Koazeaha from there. It was Miller's own money. There was a one-dollar filing fee.

[3] Statement, Graham Miller, 10 March 1973. Statement, Graham Miller, 18 March 1973. Memorandum, 30 July 1973. Assault and grenade.

[4] He made no mention of seeing any other men at the airport.

[5] Police message, 20 December 1972.

[6] Statement, Rosealie Stuart, 8 August 1973.

[7] Daniel Stuart, Supreme Court Testimony.

[8] Basil Hicks Notes, 22 December 1972.

[9] She had separated from Lyall.

[10] Statement, Graham Miller, 18 March 1973.

[11]   Checks by police showed no evidence of this.
[12]   Addendum Statement, June Beckman, 5 May 1973, 'After his release from prison and before returning home in August, 1972, he told me that he was approached by three men he had known from that previous stage in his life, and asked to look over the nightclub situation in Brisbane. He told me that they had approached him at the airport after he had been bailed out and that he was. Said they were drug addicts and were pretty far gone. John was evasive in his answers to them because he did not want to involve himself.' She meant after he returned on 20 December 1972.
[13]   One Saturday afternoon either late in December 1972 or early in January 1973. Statement, Brian Bolton, 18 May 1973.

Chapter 25

[1]   Basil Hicks Notes, 3 January 1972.
[2]   Statement, Jeffray Skene, Undated.
[3]   Basil Hicks Notes, 15 January 1972. He rang at 6pm on Friday night.

[4]   Statement, Robert Glover, 24 March 1973.
[5]   Statement, Brian Bolton, 18 May 1973.
[6]   Basil Hicks Notes, 14 January 1972.
[7]   The ban was confirmed by Skene and Glover. Statement Jeffray Skene, Undated. Statement, Robert Glover, 24 March 1973.
[8]   Statement, Terence Ferguson, 3 July 1973.
[9]   Statement, Mervyn, 24 May 1973.

Chapter 26

[1]   *Sunday Sun*, 14 January 1973.
[2]   Statement, Darryl Schlecht, 8 March 1973. Running Sheet, Whiskey Au Go Go Fire and Fatality.
[3]   Running Sheet, Whiskey Au Go Go Fire and Fatality. At the liquidator meeting, Bell was reinstated after McAlary's departure. When Farr left, Ken Little took over Chequers.
[4]   From 20 December. Brian Little said he 'drank heavily', Brian Little, Supreme Court Testimony.
[5]   Statement, Terence Channells, 14 August 1973. John Ryan said Longhurst and Spiggy did it. Record of Interview

Commenced on 6th September 1973 at the Public Defender's Office. Bell had been replaced by McAlary and was not happy about it. Running Sheet, Whiskey Au Go Go Fire and Fatality.

[6] I Survived: The Story of John Wayne Ryan, Private Detective: An Australian (Brisbane) Underbelly Survivor, John Ryan, Book Pal, 2012. Statement, Dennis Fritz, 10 March 1973. Statement, Daniel Clift, 11 March 1973.

[7] Running Sheet, Whiskey Au Go Go Fire and Fatality.

[8] In the 8 March 1973 Record of Interview, Detective Atkinson asks John Stuart whether John Hannay got him to heavy Jack Farr.

[9] Statement, Jack Farr, 8 March 1973.

[10] *The Courier-Mail*, 9 March 1973.

[11] I Survived: The Story of John Wayne Ryan, Private Detective: An Australian (Brisbane) Underbelly Survivor, John Ryan, Book Pal, 2012.

[12] At least in their post-Whiskey statements.

[13] 17 January 1973.

[14] Statement, John Hannay, 21 May 1973. Considine alternate spelling. Hannay, who employed him, uses Constantine,

so this is used in this book. The building was brick with an iron roof: the ground floor housed two shops (pet supplies and food bar) opening onto Brunswick Street.

[15] Statement, name withheld, Undated.
[16] *Sunday Mail*, 15 September 1996.
[17] Statement, Brian Bolton, 18 May 1973.
[18] Basil Hicks Notes, 24 January 1972.
[19] Statement, Jo, 31 August 1973.
[20] Bazzare? Bazzar?
[21] Statement, Rosealie Stuart, 8 August 1973.

Chapter 27

[1] Statement, Thomas Leighton, 22 March 1973.
[2] On 3 February, Stuart and tattooist Phillips caused a riot at the Wickham Hotel, using chairs as weapons. The bouncer had refused them admission, as Phillips was wearing a singlet. Stuart punched the bouncer in the mouth, ran across the road and picked up a long piece of four-by-four timber, ran back to the lounge and smashed all its windows. The damage totalled $130, of which the reprobates paid $90.

Addendum Statement, William Phillips, 21 March 1973. Running Sheet, Whiskey Au Go Go Fire and Fatality.

[3] About six weeks prior to the fire. Statement, John Bell, 8 March 1973. In Addendum Statement, John Bell, 15 May 1973 he said three months but he mentions the Butler brothers. This story came after 20 December 1972.

[4] Brian Little said he met Stuart for the first time in February, Addendum Statement, Brian Little, 14 May 1973. It was early in the week at 9pm. It was two weeks before 20/21 January where Ken Little and John Stuart sat on the Chequers steps (as stated by Brian Little in Addendum Statement, Brian Little, 14 May 1973). Statement Kenneth Little 14 May 1973. He was in the company of a girl, possibly girlfriend Jo, as she mentions going there with him.

[5] Basil Hicks Notes, 14 February 1972.

[6] Statement, Brian Bolton, 18 May 1973.

[7] Addendum Statement, Brian Little, 14 May 1973. Addendum Statement, Kenneth Little, 11 March 1973.

[8] Saturday, February 24. Statement, Brian Bolton, 18 May 1973.

[9] Statement, Edward White, Undated. *The Courier-Mail*, 26 February 1973.
[10] Criminal Offence Report, 6 March 1973?
[11] Statement, Brian Bolton, 18 May 1973.
[12] Interview between Det Sgts I/C J.H. Kay and E.W. White and *Sunday Sun* reporter Brian Bolton at the *Sunday Sun* Office on Thursday 8th March, 1973. This was a repeat of the one on 26 February 1973.
[13] Statement, Brian Bolton, 18 May 1973.
[14] Statement, Brian Bolton, 18 May 1973. Statement, William Humphris, 12 March 1973.
[15] Statement, William Humphris, 12 March 1973.
[16] The Brisbane detective did not seem aware Mt Big was McPherson.
[17] Statement, Rosealie Stuart, 8 August 1973.
[18] On 27 February. Running Sheet, Whiskey Au Go Go Fire and Fatality. Charge Sheet.
[19] Running Sheet, Whiskey Au Go Go Fire and Fatality. He probably meant David Baker.
[20] Basil Hicks Notes, 27 February 1972.
[21] Basil Hicks Notes, 28 February 1972.

[22]	Statement, Rosealie Stuart, 8 August 1973. Rose says there was something in the car.
[23]	Abridged. Basil Hicks Notes, 28 February 1973.

Chapter 28

[1]	Running Sheet, Whiskey Au Go Go Fire and Fatality. Mrs Watts sent a telegram to Daniel saying John Stuart had arrived safely on the 2nd. John Stuart sent his mother a telegram from North Quay saying he had arrived safely on the 5th. See also Statement, Clyde Watts, Undated. Clyde Watts was introduced to Doug on 28 February 1973.
[2]	Thomas Atkinson diary, 6 February 1973.
[3]	Statement, Brian Bolton, 18 May 1973. *Sunday Sun*, 4 March 1973.
[4]	Statement, Helena Kostellar, Undated, 'He was in company with a shorter man, about 5' 8" to 5' 9", medium build, he had lighter coloured and shorter hair than Stuart. He did not speak. Stuart said "Sometimes my friend may sleep here".' See also Statement, William McAvoy, Undated.

[5] Statement, Dorothy Jones, 29 March 1973.
[6] Addendum Statement, James Chalmers, 10 March 1973.
[7] Statement, Francis Longhurst, 8 March 1973.
[8] Statement, Francis Longhurst, 8 March 1973.
[9] Bell said Longhurst told him Stuart arrived in Hannay's car. Statement, John Bell, 8 March 1973. Chalmers says he saw Freeleagus and Hannay talking to Brian Little in the middle of February.
[10] Statement, Francis Longhurst, 8 March 1973. Statement, Brian Little, 9 March 1973.
[11] Statement, George Freeleagus, 17 August 1973.
[12] Statement, Francis Longhurst, 8 March 1973.
[13] Basil Hicks Notes, 6 March 1973.
[14] For court appearance see Thomas Atkinson diary, 6 March 1973.
[15] Around the same time Longhurst did? Addendum Statement, Brian Little, 10 March 1973. Addendum Statement, James Chalmers, 10 March 1973. In Stuart's Record of Interview, 8 March

1973, he denied even knowing Freeleagus.

[16] Statement, Brian Little, 9 March 1973. Statement, Mervyn Little, 14 May 1973.
[17] Statement, Brian Bolton, 18 May 1973.
[18] Interview between Det Sgts I/C J.H. Kay and E.W. White and *Sunday Sun* reporter Brian Bolton at the *Sunday Sun* Office on Thursday 8th March, 1973, which was a repeat of the one on 26 February 1973.
[19] Statement, Basil Hicks, Undated. He was looking for McCulkin when he saw the TV crew.
[20] Statement, Brian Bolton, 18 May 1973. See also Statement, J Kay, Undated. Interview between Det Sgts I/C J.H. Kay and E.W. White and *Sunday Sun* reporter Brian Bolton at the *Sunday Sun* Office on Thursday 8th March, 1973, which was a repeat of the one on 26 February 1973.
[21] Basil Hicks Notes, 6 March 1972.
[22] Memo, Edmund Muller, 2 October 1973.
[23] Statement, Helen Kostellar, Undated.
[24] Addendum Statement, Lyall Beckman, 10 August 1973. Memorandum, 2 October 1973.

[25] Statement, John Bell, 8 March 1973. Statement, Francis Longhurst, 8 March 1973.
[26] Statement, Brian Little, 9 March 1973.
[27] Statement, Brian Little, 9 March 1973.
[28] Statement, William Phillips, 8 March 1973. Addendum Statement, William Phillips, 21 March 1973.

Chapter 29

[1] Running Sheet, Whiskey Au Go Go Fire and Fatality.
[2] Statement, Brian Bolton, 18 May 1973.
[3] Stuart had already arranged to meet Hicks.
[4] Basil Hicks Notes, 7 March 1972. Abridged version shown.
[5] Statement, Brian Bolton, 18 May 1973.
[6] Glover and Stuart attempted to enter the Jet and Stuart was told he was barred. Statement, Robert Glover, 24 March 1973. Statement, Jeffray Skene, Undated.
[7] 'I saw Brian Bolton again at approximately 4pm on 7.3.73 in front of the *Sunday Sun* Office, Brunswick Street, Fortitude Valley.' Statement, William Humphris, 12 March 1973.

[8] Statement, Daniel Stuart, 8 March 1973.
Statement, Daniel Stuart, 11 March 1973.
[9] Addendum Statement, Lyall Beckman, 10 August 1973.
[10] Statement, Rosealie Stuart, 8 August 1973.
[11] Addendum Statement, Lyall Beckman, 29 March 1973.
[12] Record of Interview, John Stuart, 8 March 1973.
[13] Statement, Daniel Stuart, 8 March 1973. At 9.30pm.
[14] *Sunday Sun*, 11 March 1973.
[15] Statement, Brian Bolton, 18 May 1973.
[16] Danny's story: The stink of the Whiskey case won't go away, Frank Robson, *Griffith Review* 45, 2014.
[17] Statement, Geoffrey Kopittke, 8 March 1973. Furniture assembler.
[18] Statement, John Bell, 8 March 1973.
[19] Statement, Brian Little, 9 March 1973.
[20] Statement, Rosealie Stuart, 8 August 1973. Statement, Daniel Stuart, 11 March 1973.

Chapter 30

[1] Statement, Alf Quick, 11 March 1973.

[2] Statement, Halina Mikulak, 10 August 1973.
[3] Statement, Abraham Yasse, 8 March 1973. See also Addendum Statement, Abraham Yasse 29 May 1973. Statement, Abraham Yasse 25 July 1973. Statement, Alfred Quick, 11 March 1973. Addendum Statement, Alfred Quick, 9 May 1973. Addendum Statement, Alfred Quick 25 July 1973. Quick knew Stuart from the Railway Institute dances, and initially Stuart refused to pay the entry when entering the Flamingo.
[4] Quick was not wearing his watch at the time as it was on a shelf in the office (he did not check his watch to get the time for him).
[5] Statement, Patricia Flynn, 11 May 1973. Statement, Andrew Warner, Undated. *Sunday Sun*, 11 March 1973.
[6] Statement, June Beckman, 8 March 1973.
[7] Statement, Robert Hayes, 17 May 1973. Statement, Ronald Redmond, Undated. *The Courier-Mail*, 9 March 1973. *The Courier-Mail*, 5 July 1989 has some biography on Redmond. Robert Hayes, Supreme Court Testimony.
[8] Statement, Brian Bolton, 18 May 1973.

[9] Interview between Det Sgts I/C J.H. Kay and E.W. White and *Sunday Sun* reporter Brian Bolton at the *Sunday Sun* Office on Thursday 8th March, 1973. This was a repeat of the one on 26 February 1973.
[10] Special Circular, 8 March 1973.
[11] Statement, William Humphris, 12 March 1973.
[12] At about 9am.
[13] Statement, William Humphris, 12 March 1973.
[14] Statement, David Rooney, 16 March 1973.
[15] Statement, Rosealie Stuart, 8 August 1973. At 8am Lyall had run Rose and said if Stuart rang, Rose should say he should go to the police.
[16] Basil Hicks Notes, 8 March 1972.
[17] Statement, Brian Bolton, 18 May 1973. Interview between Det Sgts I/C J.H. Kay and E.W. White and *Sunday Sun* reporter Brian Bolton at the *Sunday Sun* Office on Thursday 8th March, 1973 This was a repeat of the one on 26 February 1973.
[18] About 11am.
[19] Basil Hicks Notes, 8 March 1972.
[20] Basil Hicks Notes, 8 March 1972.

[21] John Stuart, Record of Interview, 8 March 1973. Reproduced in Robert Hayes, Supreme Court Testimony. Statement, Robert Hayes, 17 May 1973. Statement, Robert Hayes, 13 October 1973. Statement, Ronald Redmond, Undated. Statement, Thomas Atkinson, 15 May 1973. Weir was acting in Patrick Nolan's absence.

[22] Thomas Atkinson under cross examination, Supreme Court Testimony.

[23] For 45 minutes, Robert Hayes, Supreme Court Testimony. Thomas Atkinson, Supreme Court Testimony.

[24] To say he would give a handbag back to a girl.

[25] Extracts.

[26] Police note. Information Received from Det/Sgt Noel Morey of the CIB Sydney on the morning of 30th March 1973. This identifies the three.

[27] Running Sheet, Whiskey Au Go Go Fire and Fatality, 9 March 1973.

[28] Special Circular, 9 March 1973.

[29] At 11.15pm. Addendum Statement, Lyall Beckman, 29 March 1973.

[30] Running Sheet, Whiskey Au Go Go Fire and Fatality, 9 March 1973.

[31]   Statement, Daniel Stuart, 11 March 1973. Statement, Rosealie Stuart, 8 August 1973.
[32]   Statement, Geoffrey Kopittke, 8 March 1973. Statement, James Chalmers, 8 March 1973. Addendum Statement, James Chalmers 10 March 1973.

Chapter 31

[1]   Statement, Rosealie Stuart, 8 August 1973.
[2]   Additional [sic] Statement, Neil Raward, Undated. Addendum Statement, Brian Little, 14 May 1973. Undated Note.
[3]   Statement, Brian Bolton, 18 May 1973.
[4]   *Sunday Sun*, 11 March 1973.
[5]   Statement, Rosealie Stuart, 8 August 1973. Rose said, 'On the night of the 10th March, 1973, Stuart said to me "*Sunday Sun* has given me $200.00 to pay my Solicitor, Mr. Weir, and I'm going on television next Wednesday night to tell of police brutality and I'll get $800.00 for that."'
[6]   Coroner's Inquest papers. Criminal Investigation Branch, Robert Hayes, 22 November 1973.

[7]   *Sunday Sun,* 11 March 1973. *Telegraph,* 10 March 1973. *Daily Mirror,* 14 March 1973.

[8]   *Sunday Sun,* 11 March 1973. *The Courier-Mail,* 9 March 1973. *The Courier-Mail,* 10 March 1973. At a special press conference, he would confirm that the Commonwealth Police had officially warned the Queensland police two weeks prior that the Whiskey was a target. He said he had not received the warning until after the bombing, which was a falsehood.

Hodges later got into a feud with Bolton saying he was a drunk, and they drank together a lot, *Sunday Sun* 4 November 1973.

[9]   Abridged, Basil Hicks Notes, 10 March 1972.

[10]   Addendum Statement, Lyall Beckman, 29 March 1973.

[11]   At 5.30pm. Basil Hicks Notes, 10 March 1972.

[12]   Statement, Attililio Bianchetti, 10 May 1973. Statement, Daniel Stuart, 11 March 1973. Statement, Daniel Stuart, 7 August 1973.

[13]   At 4.30pm. Statement, Nanette Bianchetti, 14 August 1973.

[14] 3.30pm. Daniel Stuart, Supreme Court Testimony.
[15] About dark, 7pm.
[16] Attilio says 7.30pm. He had rung before he arrived. Daniel Stuart, Supreme Court Testimony.
[17] Statement, Rosealie Stuart, 8 August 1973.
[18] The call was made between 8.30 and 9pm.
[19] Daniel Stuart, Supreme Court Testimony.
[20] Statement, Ronald Redmond, Undated. Statement, Patrick Glancy, Undated. Statement, Evan Griffiths, Undated.
[21] Daniel Stuart, Supreme Court Testimony.
[22] At 9.15pm. Statement, Evan Griffiths, Undated. Statement, Statement, Ronald Redmond, Undated. Summary of Facts (Thomas Atkinson), 10 March 1973. Statement, Patrick Glancy, Undated. Thomas Atkinson, Committal Testimony, 14 June 1973. For overnight bag, see Statement, Colin Sullivan, Undated. Property taken, dangerous weapon.
[23] Thomas Atkinson Diary, 10 March 1973. Also Court Brief.

[24] Addendum Statement, Lyall Beckman, 10 August 1973.

[25] Thomas Atkinson Diary, 10 March 1973. Daniel Stuart did not deny under cross examination in court that he had told the police on the phone he would put on a show. Daniel Stuart, Full Court Testimony. Hayes and Atkinson also admitted this in court.

[26] Statement, Thomas Atkinson, 15 May 1973 (also 13 October 1973). Statement, Robert Hayes, 17 May 1973. Statement, Samuel Sheehan, 20 August 1973. Statement, Ian Timms, Undated. Statement, Bruce Anderson, Undated. Statement, Patrick Glancy, Undated. Statement, Leslie McDonnell, Undated. Statement, Leonard Mallow, Undated. The money order is covered in Statement, Edward Harvey, 23 May 1973 and Statement, William Stewart, 23 May 1973.

[27] Statement, Thomas Atkinson, 15 May 1973. Put in cell 19.

[28] Statement, Attilio Bianchetti, 10 May 1973.

[29] Statement, Daniel Stuart, 11 March 1973.

Chapter 32

[1] *Sunday Sun*, 11 March 1973.
[2] Rose rang at 8.30am, and Daniel told her Doug was there. Daniel Stuart, Full Court Testimony.
[3] Statement, Noel Morey, Undated. Statement, Robert Hayes, 17 May 1973. Statement, Thomas Atkinson, 15 May 1973. Statement Paul Delanus, Undated (from Melbourne). Running Sheet, Whiskey Au Go Go Fire and Fatality, List of those involved on the day.
[4] Statement, Paul Delanus, Undated.
[5] Thomas Atkinson, Supreme Court Testimony.
[6] Statement, Trevor Cooper 3 May 1973.
[7] Statement, Daniel Stuart, Undated. Statement, Daniel Stuart, 8 March 1973.
[8] Statement, Thomas Atkinson, 15 May 1973.
[9] Daniel was also taken in to make a statement. Daniel Stuart, Supreme Court Testimony.

Chapter 33

[1] *Sunday Sun*, 2 November 1988.

[2] Central Office New Scotland Yard, 17 October 1973. *Sunday Sun*, 2 November 1988. Letter Tony Finch to Jim Finch, 18 March 1970, in which he said he was working on top of a shop soldering stereo speakers and he liked the job. Johnny's wife had a baby. Johnny was labouring. David had a girlfriend, 'We all heard that you might stand a chance of being home with us by Christmas and we hope you will be. We all miss you very much here. And we are all looking forward to the day that we will see you again. Wonder if you still stick up for Tottenham.'

[3] *The Sun*, 8 November 1988.

[4] *The Sun*, 2 November 1988.

[5] Statement Daniel Stuart 11 March 1973. *The Sun*, 8 November 1988.

[6] Neddy: The Life and Crimes of Arthur Stanley Smith: An Autobiography with Tom Noble. Balmain, NSW, Kerr Publishing, 2003.

[7] Police criminal Record, James Finch. Also from a police profile, 'On 5/6/63 at the court of pretty sessions, Brisbane, was sentenced to 3 years imprisonment, after serving 9 months, the remainder of the sentence suspended on entering of 50

to be of good behaviour for balance of sentence and to appear for judgement if called upon during that period on three charges of breaking and entering a dwelling with intent and one charge of entering a dwelling with intent.' Released 21 April 1964.

[8] Regina v James Richard Finch. 1966 Criminal E-F, 3/7688, NSW State Archives.

[9] John told Rosealie, 'He has done 14 years for me.' Statement, Rosealie Stuart, 8 August 1973. See List of charges against James Richard Finch.

[10] *Daily Mirror*, 30 November 1965.

[11] Newspaper article, unknown date. Statement, Leslie Bates, Undated. Statement, Leslie Bates, 4 May 1973.

[12] *The Sun*, 3 November 1988.

[13] Card, John Stuart to Jim Finch, 24 June 1969.

[14] Addendum Statement, William Phillips, 21 March 1973. He talked about writing to him in February 1968, John Stuart to Edna Watts, 11 February 1968. He may be referring to his brother Jim.

[15] Letter Manager Dr Barnardo's in Australia to John Stuart, 20 July 1970.

[16]   Letter Edna Watts to John Stuart, 4 August 1972. Letter Edna Watts to John Stuart, Undated.

[17]   Statement, Edna Watt, 28 March 1973. Danny's story: The stink of the Whiskey case won't go away, Frank Robson, *Griffith Review* 45, 2014.

[18]   *Sunday Sun*, 21 October 1973. He told Lyall Beckman he had 'one really good mate that he could trust and that each one was prepared to die for the other one. All that Stuart told me about 'Terry' was that he had bailed him out in relation to the charge against Stuart of possession of the firearm.' Addendum Statement, Lyall Beckman, 10 August 1973.

[19]   The Tangled Web, Des Sturgess, Beside Books, 2001.

[20]   Letter Tony Finch (brother) to Jim Finch, 18 March 1970.

[21]   Statement, Roger Paul Brennan, 12 April 1973.

[22]   Statement, David Rutter, 27 July 1973. Outgoing Passenger Card. David met brother James at London Airport, September 1972.

[23]   Central Office, New Scotland Yard, 17 October 1973.

[24] Addendum Statement, Lyall Beckman, 10 August 1973. Statement, Rosealie Stuart, 8 August 1973, 'He was a cell mate of mine. He has done 14 years for me ... he would do anything for him and he was the only man he would die for and John called him his other self or other half. He also said that this other person had no friends in England and hated his family and that was the reason he was bringing him out to Australia.'

Chapter 34

[1] Statement, Noel Morey, Undated. Noel Morey, Supreme Court Testimony.
[2] Statement, Thomas Atkinson, 15 May 1973.
[3] Statement, Robert Hayes, 17 May 1973.
[4] Morey said he heard this. Statement, Noel Morey, Undated. Statement, Roger Rogerson, Undated.
[5] Statement, Donald Buchanan, Undated.
[6] *Sunday Sun*, 30 September 1973. Delanus was brought up from Victoria for the same reason.
[7] See also Statement, Peter Slatter, Undated.

[8] Three floors, the police had the two lower floors and the Harbours and Marine department occupied the top floor.

[9] Present; Det Sergt I/C T S C Atkinson, Det Sergt I/C E G Griffiths, Det Sergt 2/C N C Morey, Det Sen Const R C Rogerson. Statement, Evan Griffiths, Undated.

[10] Record of Interview between Det Senior Sergt R B Hayes and James Richard Finch, 11 March 1973. Statement, Noel Morey, Undated. Statement, Ronald Redmond, Undated. Statement, Roger Rogerson, Undated. Break at 7.10pm for tea. Record resumes at 7.16pm.

[11] The attempts to link the two drums in the station wagon to the fire failed.

[12] Removed from typewriter 7.53pm. Replaced in typewriter at 8.7pm [sic] after being read aloud.

[13] Statement, Thomas Atkinson, 15 May 1973.

[14] 8.25pm. Statement, Leslie McDonnell, Undated. Statement, Robert Hayes, 17 May 1973.

[15] Statement, Samuel Sheehan, 20 August 1973. Statement, Leslie McDonnell, Undated.
[16] Statement, Evan Griffiths, Undated. Statement, Noel Morey, Undated.
[17] In his mini-interrogation just before Stuart said he did not want to read it.
[18] At 8.35pm.
[19] Statement, Leslie McDonnell, Undated.

Chapter 35

[1] Statement, Helen Kostellar, Undated.
[2] *The Age*, 13 March 1973.
[3] Statement, Ross Beer, 9 October 1973. *The Courier-Mail*, 13 March 1973. *The Age*, 13 March 1973.
[4] *The Courier-Mail*, 13 March 1973.
[5] Some marks were later found on Stuart's body. Statement, Robert Green, Assistant Government Medical Officer, 3 October 1973.
[6] Summary of Facts, 10 March 1973, T.S.C. Atkinson.
[7] On 14 March 1973 and 19 March 1973. One addressed to Rose and Daniel, the other to Pete from Darryl Pacey. Daniel Stuart, Supreme Court Testimony. It was

undoubtedly written in urine, easily available cf: *Sunday Mail*, 2 March 2008, where lemon is suggested. Robert Hayes, Supreme Court Testimony.

[8] Daniel Stuart, Supreme Court Testimony. *Sunday Sun*, 17 June 1973.

[9] Statement, Robert Hayes, 17 May 1973. Statement, Thomas Atkinson, 15 May 1973. Memo undated.

[10] On 4 May 1973. On 11 April Hayes and Atkinson were given another envelope by Daniel. Statement, Thomas Atkinson, 15 May 1973.

[11] Letter John Stuart to June Beckman, 25 March 1973.

[12] Statement, Ronald Redmond, Undated. Memo undated.

[13] BEGIN HERE. BOTH JIM AND ME ARE INNOCENT. INNOCENT. YOU KNOW THE ANIMALS AR LYING, WHENN WE LEFT YOR PLACE SAT NITE WE WERE ON WAY TO GET LAWYER AND GIVE COPS STATEMENT OF ALL JIMS MOVEMENTS BUT WE WENT BACK TO YOUR PLACE INVESTIGATING ROW THAT BUGGERED US, THATS FACT DAN NOT LIES. NOW TO TRY TO AROUSE YOU IN OUR

FAVOUR. WHEN WE LEFT YOUR PLACE THAT WED NITE EYE TOOK JIM BAK TO FLAT AND WENT ON QUICK CRUISE SEEKING BOLTON THEN GOT STUK AT FLAMINGOO (LUKILLY) JIM WAS AT FLAT IN BED EVENTUALY WHEN COPS GOT JIM ALONE THEY VERBAL HIM INTO SAYING ME AND HIM DID FIRE THEREFORE IF THEY PROVE THAT WETH LIES EYE MUST GET LIFE ALSO. IN TRUTH WE WERE BOTH GETING JOBS ON OILRIGS MUM CAN TELL YOU WE WERE GOING TO SLAVE OUR GUTS OUT FOR MAX TO GET OUR FARES AND LEAVE BEFORE M NEXXT COURT APERRANCE YOU MUST HELP US DAN YYOU MUST, YOU ROSY AND DANNY MUST MAKE STATUATORY DECLARATNS TOO WEIR-NOW NOW-THAT JIM DIDNT LEEVE WITH ME WED NITE BUT SLEPT ALL THAT NITE ON YOUR COUCH THEN LEFT FOR FLAT AFTER LYAL PHONEDD HE WAS ON COUCH ASLEEP WHEN YOU GOT UP AT DAWN AND DANNY SAW HIM THERE WHEN HE GOT UP LATER

JIM WAS STILL ON WAY TO FLAT WHEN EYE RANG ROSE OVER JOBS WITH MAX DANNY MUST COME INTO IT IT WILL CARRY HUGE WEIGHT WITH JURY MENTION IT TO HIM FIRST AS THO IT DID HAPPEN THAT WAY IF YOUVE MADE OTHER TO OOPS ITS BECOS EYE TOLD YOU TO AVOID INVOLVEMENT AS WE HAD NOTHING TO HIDE BUT NOW YOUVE ALL MADE STAT DECS BECOS ITS TOO BIG AND YOU CANT STAY SILENT BECOS YOU KNOW WE MUST BE INNOCENT. EYE AM IN CAGE HERE NOW HANDCUFFED IF YOU DONT HELP ME EYE GET LIFE AND WILL KILL MYSELF EYE MEAN IT ALL. YOR KIDNEY.

[14] *Sunday Mail*, 7 February 1988.
[15] *Sunday Sun*, 8 April 1973.
[16] Letter John Stuart to June Beckman, 16 April 1973.
[17] Letter John Stuart to Daniel Stuart, 16 April 1973.
[18] Statement, Brian Little, 14 May 1973.
[19] Typed Medical Note, 28 May 1973. The North Brisbane Hospitals Board

to certify James Richard Finch will not be medically fit to appear in court on 4 June 1973. 1 June 1973.

[20] *The Courier-Mail*, 13 August 1992, 'James Finch wants his finger back. Recently, while clearing out the room after the closure of the 109-year-old prison late last month, staff found the finger.' *The Courier-Mail*, 29 April 1997, 'Gaol warders kept prisoners' body parts as trophies, including the severed finger of infamous Whiskey Au Go Go firebomb killer James Finch, *The Courier-Mail* has learned. A remorseful warder, who wanted to remain anonymous, yesterday handed the macabre souvenir to *The Courier-Mail* saying he wanted it returned to its owner. The "pinkie" finger is in a specimen jar labelled J Finch 28/5/73. The warder said he had obtained the jar from a medical room when the Boggo Road Gaol was being closed down in 1992.

[21] The stabiliser was bound between two shoes with a belt. Stuart supposedly hacked it off. The *Sun*, 31 October 1988.

[22] *Sunday Sun*, 16 September 1973.

[23]   Statement, Denis Heffernan, 30 August 1973. Statement, Stuart Henderson, Undated.
[24]   *Sunday Sun*, 17 June 1973.
[25]   *Sunday Sun*, 24 June 1973. On 21 June, after they were committed to trial, they were taken downstairs to the cells and Stuart said to Finch, 'We've got to make sure, Jimmy, that they don't try us together.' Statement Denis Heffernan, 30 August 1973. According to the Coroner's Report, it was 22 June, which is wrong.
[26]   Memorandum, Robert Hayes, 25 June 1973.

Chapter 36

[1]   *Sunday Sun*, 16 September 1973.
[2]   Supreme Court Argument, Day Eight. He was said to have swallowed 27 safety pins before he was sent to Grafton, *Sunday Sun*, 27 November 1977.
[3]   CIB message, 20 December 1972.
[4]   *Sunday Sun*, 16 September 1973.
[5]   *Sunday Sun*, 16 September 1973.
[6]   *Sunday Sun*, 30 September 1972.
[7]   Statement, Leonard McPherson, 17 September 1973.

[8] Supreme Court Argument, Day Eight. *Sunday Sun*, 14 October 1973.
[9] At 10.12am. Statement, Gregory Early, 18 September 1973.
[10] Supreme Court Argument, Day Eight.
[11] *Sydney Morning Herald*, 20 September 1973.
[12] Gangland Queensland, James Morton, Susanna Lobez, Melbourne University Press, 2012.
[13] *The Courier-Mail*, 17 June 1988, 'Murdock's cage resembles a dog pound. The outside area is about 3 m square, concrete-floored, with an open shower in the northern corner. His outdoor furniture comprises two plastic basins, a bucket, two old-fashioned scrubbing brushes, the mirror, some stick lather and several safety razors. At the back of the cage is Murdock's small, steel-doored cell built of concrete. It houses an open lavatory pedestal, a single bed, a bench for books and private possessions and a box for clothing. See also *The Courier-Mail*, 4 March 1988.
[14] Police criminal record, Arthur Murdock.

[15]   Statement, Arthur Murdock, 6 September 1973. *Sunday Sun*, 27 November 1977.
[16]   Boggo Road Prison: Riots to Ruin: 1976–2008, Stephen M. Gage, Sid Harta Publishers, 2009. *Sunday Mail*, 21 January 2001.
[17]   *Sunday Mail*, 21 January 2001.
[18]   *Sunday Mail*, 31 March 1985.
[19]   *Sunday Mail*, 9 March 1986.
[20]   Police criminal record, Arthur Murdock.
[21]   *The Courier-Mail*, 18 June 1977.
[22]   *The Courier-Mail*, 26 September 1973.
[23]   Graham Miller, Supreme Court Testimony. *Sunday Sun*, 30 September 1972.
[24]   Statement, Graham Miller, 10 March 1973. Statement, Graham Miller, 18 March 1973.
[25]   Running Sheet, Whiskey Au Go Go Fire and Fatality. Memorandum Re Interview with Stuart John Regan, Criminal, 30 July 1973. Three Crooked Kings, Matthew Condon, University of Queensland Press, 2013.
[26]   Statement, Ceciley Lodge, Undated.
[27]   Statement, Rosealie Stuart, 8 August 1973. She saw the money.

[28]	Statement, Barry Short, Undated. Statement, Trevor Cooper, 3 May 1973. Statement, Patrick Banks, 15 June 1973. Statement, Peter Freeleagus, Undated. Stuart had made out a money order, under the pseudonym A Mason for 26.07 to Cubitt Town, London. On 23 February Stuart rang Qantas reservations, 'My name is Mr Mason. I paid for a fare for a Mr Finch to travel from London.' He was eager for Finch's travel plans. A cable came the next day with the proposed flight details. On page 6 of his passport C159691, the immigration officer stamped 'immigration Permanent Entry Stamp No.55'.
[29]	Statement, Brian Bolton, 18 May 1973.
[30]	Statement, Roger Paul Brennan, 12 April 1973.
[31]	Statement, Leslie Newcombe, 11 April 1973.
[32]	Statement, Ross Gardner, 12 April 1973. He was at the State Penitentiary on 20 December 1972. Stuart said he gave them his phone numbers at the airport and the Dodger called him. The men matched the age Stuart described and where Stuart was incarcerated.

[33] Statement, Reginald Hannam, 20 June 1973. Statement, Richard Harris, 26 July 1973. Statement, Richard Harris, Undated. Statement, Peter O'Connor, 26 July 1973. Statement, Suzanne Cook, 28 September 1973. Statement, Kenneth McKinnon, 2 August 1973. See also photo Misc 1915/73 and description in photo.
[34] Statement, Peter O'Connor, 26 July 1973. Statement, Bruce Hall, 2 August 1973.
[35] Statement, Daniel Stuart, 11 March 1973.
[36] *Sunday Sun*, 14 October 1973.

Chapter 37

[1] *Sydney Morning Herald*, 5 February 1988.
[2] Result of Committal to Supreme, Circuit or District Court, 23 October 1973 with hard labour, under Section 302 of the criminal code.
[3] Daniel Stuart, Supreme Court Testimony. *The Courier-Mail*, 29 February 1988, 'The brother of convicted Whiskey Au Go Go murderer John Andrew Stuart emerged from 15 years of seclusion yesterday to claim that Stuart and James

Finch were guilty of the 1973 nightclub firebombing which killed 15 people.'
[4] Operation Graveyard – Investigations into all aspects surrounding the Whiskey Au Go Go Night Club firebombing deaths and other involved murders between 1973 and 1977.
[5] *Sunday Sun*, 4 November 1973.
[6] 1 March 1970, Police criminal record.
[7] *Sunday Sun*, 6 January 1974. *Sunday Sun*, 13 January 1974. He used cellulose tape and rubber bands.
[8] Operated on January 12, 1974. *Sunday Sun*, 13 January 1974. *Sunday Sun*, 17 February 1974.
[9] *Sunday Sun*, 13 January 1974.
[10] *Sunday Sun*, 20 January 1974.
[11] Lived with the McCulkins for three months.
[12] *Sunday Sun*, 28 April 1974.
[13] Boggo Road Prison: Riots to Ruin: 1976–2008, Stephen M. Gage, Sid Harta Publishers, 2009.
[14] *Sydney Morning Herald*, 9 May 1974.
[15] Appeal: TR 1696 Item ID 784214 Box 114, Queensland State Archives.
[16] *Sunday Mail*, 31 March 1985. *Sydney Morning Herald*, 4 June 1988.
[17] *Sunday Sun*, 31 March 1973.

Chapter 38

[1] Stuart knew Stokes, see Letter John Stuart to Carmel (and vice versa), 24 May 1968.

[2] The name came from Stokes, they did not use the name itself.

[3] Police note, 28 October 1977. Stokes had rented a car from Brisbane Letz-Rent-A-Car and had repairs made to the interior the day after the abduction. It was slashed and smelt of excreta and urine. Stokes said it was vandalised by persons unknown unhappy with his *Port News* articles.

[4] Crime Intelligence Squad, 17 September 1977. He had reason.

[5] *Gold Coast Bulletin*, 30 August 1977. *Sunday Sun*, 21 August 1977.

[6] On 30 August 1977. Crime Intelligence Squad, 6 September 1977.

[7] *Sunday Sun*, 30 October 1977.

[8] 1977 *Port News* edition not available in Australia's library network.

[9] *Sunday Mail*, 12 January 1992, 'Stokes has been allowed out of prison on a work-to-release scheme. Billy Stokes, who has served 13 years of a life sentence for the 1975 abduction and

murder of Queensland boxing champion Thomas Ian Hamilton, is expected to work in the community during the day. He will return each day to a half-way house operated by the Queensland Corrective Services Commission at Kennigo Street, Fortitude Valley.'

[10] Letter Edna Watts to John Stuart, 26 June 1977.

[11] 26th. *Sunday Sun*, 27 November 1977. *The Sunday Mail*, 27 November 1977. *The Courier-Mail*, 28 November 1977. *The Courier-Mail*, 29 November 1977.

[12] *The Courier-Mail*, 2 January 1973. *The Sunday Mail*, 7 January 1979.

[13] Self-mutilation, which he would practise regularly, including inflicting a wound to his leg while in custody at Central cells on 27 April 1964 (with a piece of a razor blade). He had multiple scars on his stomach from multiple suicide attempts, Police Message, 20 December 1972.

[14] *The Courier-Mail*, 15 March 1999.

Chapter 39

[1] Despite his time in Australia he maintained an accent.

[2] This quote from his record of interview.
[3] *Sydney Morning Herald*, 4 June 1985.
[4] *The Sun*, 25 February 1988. *The Courier-Mail*, 9 July 1985. *Sydney Morning Herald*, 4 June 1985. *The Courier-Mail*, 17 July 1986.
[5] Letter Homicide Squad, 10 November 1986.
[6] *The Courier-Mail*, 27 June 1986.
[7] Statement, Dennis Watt, 10 March 1992.
[8] *The Courier-Mail*, 11 July 1986. *The Courier-Mail*, 13 June 1988.
[9] *The Courier-Mail*, 18 April 1986. *Sunday Mail*, 11 May 1986.
[10] Finch would write to Watt at least a couple of times a week, and his family and friends eventually got caught up in the whole drama.
[11] *The Courier-Mail*, 20 February 1986.
[12] Mr Russell Cooper. *The Courier-Mail*, 2 February 1988.
[13] Under its existing framework any evidence before January 1977 could not be considered. *Sydney Morning Herald*, 25 February 1988.
[14] *The Courier-Mail*, 19 February 1988, 'Conservative MP Mr Teddy Taylor, said, "It is quite irresponsible of the authorities in Australia to let him out

and order his deportation somewhere where he will not be supervised. I have spoken to the Home Secretary who is concerned and will look into it.'"

[15] *Sydney Morning Herald*, 25 February 1988.

The Courier-Mail, 24 February 1988, 'A third police officer claimed Finch was framed by police for the Whiskey Au Go Go bombing which killed 15 people. The identity of the former policeman, who appeared on Channel 7's Carroll at Seven program last night, was not revealed.' The former policeman interviewed last night said he was at the Brisbane watch-house on the night Finch and Stuart were brought there after being questioned about the nightclub fire. He said watch-house staff were jubilant over the capture of the two men and had said words to the effect "we've really fixed those bastards".

The Courier-Mail, 23 February 1988, 'One of the serving police officers said last night, "He (Atkinson) used the words, wrapping a brief around. That means fabricating evidence, knocking up a confession. He went on and elaborated. He drew attention to his own conduct and indicated all the police had to do was stick together and it was one word against the other. He went on to tell me that they'd done the same with Whiskey Au Go Go.'

See also *The Courier-Mail*, 3 March 1988.

[16] 11am show. *Sydney Morning Herald*, 25 February 1988.

[17] *The Sun*, 31 October 1988 (Monday).

[18] As it turned out, the whole affair cost far more than the $40,000 they were able to sell the video for.

[19] To the TV networks by the Editor in Chief, Michael Quirk.

[20] *The Chronicle* (Toowoomba), 2 November 1988. *The Courier-Mail*, 2 November 1988.

[21] Watt wrote an article in the paper in response to an article in the *Sunday Mail*. Finch had told the *Sunday Mail* that Watt offered him $50,000, which was a falsehood.

[22] Soon after Watt's articles, the Bulletin ran a three-issue story on 15 and 22 November and 6 December 1988.

[23] Operation Graveyard – Investigations into all aspects surrounding the Whiskey Au Go Go Night Club firebombing deaths and other involved murders between 1973 and 1977.

[24] Operation Graveyard – Investigations into all aspects surrounding the Whiskey Au Go Go Night Club firebombing deaths and other involved murders between 1973 and 1977.

[25] Covered in Operation Graveyard. *The Courier-Mail*, 13 December 1989, 'A former police informant who claimed to have information about the unsolved murder of Barbara McCulkin and her two daughters, was yesterday found guilty of making a false complaint to police. Robert John Griffiths, 42, of Beenleigh, was fined $200 in the Southport Magistrates' Court and ordered to pay restitution of $5580.70, the cost of the police investigation into the allegations, as well as $40.75 court costs. Consultant psychiatrist Dr Ormonde Orford said he first treated Griffiths in February and last saw him about a week ago. Griffiths had been psychotic when he first started treating him. Griffiths had difficulty differentiating between reality and fantasy and suffered delusions.'

Chapter 40

[1] Defence Supreme Court Testimony.
[2] Defence Supreme Court Testimony.
[3] Peter Slatter and Thomas Atkinson Supreme Court Testimony.
[4] Police Notice.
[5] Robert Hayes, Committal Testimony, 12 June 1973.
[6] Thomas Atkinson Diary.
[7] Robert Hayes, Supreme Court Testimony.
[8] Statement, Michael Dee, 8 March 1973.
[9] Statement, Jennifer Armstrong, Undated. Statement, Gregory Clark, Undated. Statement, Maree German, Undated. Statement, Anthony Coates, 10 March 1973. Statement, Geoffrey Kopittke, 8 March 1973.
[10] Statement, John Bell, 8 March 1973. Addendum Statement, James Chalmers, 10 March 1973.
[11] *The Sun*, 31 October 1973.
[12] Statement, Wayne Jarred, Undated. Statement, Leslie McDonnell, Undated. Statement, Samuel Sheehan, 20 August 1973. Statement, Bruce Anderson, Undated.
[13] Statement, Wayne Jarred, Undated.

[14]	Statement, Noel Morey, Undated. Statement, Robert Hayes, 17 May 1973. Statement, Roger Rogerson, Undated. Statement, Ronald Redmond. Statement, Thomas Atkinson, 15 May 1973. Statement, Evan Griffiths, Undated. Statement, Peter Slatter, Undated. Slatter was the only detective who nuanced his statement and included banal interactions with Finch, chat about his family etc.
[15]	Sheehan and two detectives took Stuart to an upstairs cell. Sheehan returned. Constable Jarred then took Finch to the fingerprinting room.
[16]	Later in the night several attempts were made to print Finch. Timms and Sergeant Mallon recorded conversations similar to the ones that occurred in the charge room.

Finch: They are going to take my fingerprints. [Timms, Mallon]

Stuart: Don't let them take them. [Timms, Mallon]

[17]	None of the watch-house staff heard Stuart admitting to Finch that he had been loose-mouthed about it. No one could have missed him saying he needn't have talked about the matches.

All the staff in the room agreed that Finch was seated and the others were standing.

[18] *The Courier-Mail*, 24 February 1988.
[19] Property Sheet, James Richard Finch.
[20] Statement, Colin McDonald, 11 October 1973.
[21] Letter John Stuart to Det. Hayes, 12 March 1973.
[22] Letter John Stuart to Det. Morey, 12 March 1973.
[23] Letter John Stuart to Atkinson, 12 March 1973, 'This morning, for the first time, I heard you say to me that the night before in the City Watchhouse cells I had admitted to you that I was guilty of a part of the crime committed against the 'Whiskey Au Go Go' and its patrons. You know that is not true and that all along I have denied all involvement in the disaster. I say again to you here that I am innocent of any part of that disaster at the 'Whiskey' and beg you to please tell the truth regardless of, as you said to me earlier, the fact that the Police Commissioner is "screaming for an arrest". Wrongfully charging me

with this crime does not stop the guilty ones, or whoever is responsible.'

[24] Letter John Stuart to Det. Hayes, 12 March 1973.

[25] Letter John Stuart to Det. Atkinson, 12 March 1973.

[26] Operation Graveyard – investigations into all aspects surrounding the Whiskey Au Go Go Night Club firebombing deaths and other involved murders between 1973 and 1977.

[27] *The Bulletin*, 22 November 1988.

[28] Supreme Court Cross Examination. *The Courier-Mail*, 23 September 1973. *Sunday Sun*, 30 September 1972.

[29] Daniel Stuart, Supreme Court Testimony.

[30] Robert Hayes, Supreme Court Testimony.

[31] Daniel Stuart, Supreme Court Testimony.

[32] Thomas Atkinson, Supreme Court Testimony.

[33] Handwritten on Record of Interview, 28 May 1973.

[34] Record of Interview between Det/Senr/Sgt R B Hayes and John Andrew Stuart and James Richard Finch in the Presence of Det/Sgt I/C T S C

	Atkinson, conducted in the cells at the Holland Park Magistrate Court, Brisbane, on Monday morning, 28th May 1973.
[35]	28 May 1973. 10.14am.
[36]	*Sunday Sun*, 30 September 1972. At the Supreme Court trial Atkinson agreed that at the end of the Record of Interview, 8 March 1973, Stuart had said if he was ever interviewed by police again he wanted a solicitor.
[37]	*Sunday Sun*, 30 September 1972.

Chapter 41

[1]	Statement, Basil Hicks, Undated.
[2]	Statement, Basil Hicks, Undated.
[3]	*Sunday Sun*, 21 July 1974.
[4]	*The Sun*, 4 November 1988. Another nonsense story Stuart told was of a code book that had detailed all the names of those who did the Whiskey and how. It was stolen by a Boggo Road prison officer and led to the 1977 rooftop protest.
[5]	22 October 1978, *Sunday Sun*.
[6]	Addendum Statement, Lyall Beckman, 29 March 1973.

[7]   The nominee of the Treasury Tavern Hotel stated she had been warned by Stuart of takeovers. The problem was she said this occurred on 25 April 1972 when Stuart was in Parramatta Gaol. Statement, Estelle Long, 25 April 1973. A resident manager at the Leichardt Hotel said Stuart rang around September 1972 and said the big boys were coming for a takeover. Statement, Leigh Paten, 20 April 1973.

[8]   *The Courier-Mail*, 10 March 1973.

[9]   Record of Interview commenced on 6 September 1973 at the Public Defender's Office, Brisbane.

Chapter 42

[1]   Auctioned by Alex Ocerett & Co.
[2]   Statement, John McGrath, Undated.
[3]   Statement, Brian Little, 9 March 1973.
[4]   Record of Interview commenced on 6 September 1973 at the Public Defender's Office, Brisbane.
[5]   Statement, Brian Little, 9 March 1973.
[6]   Statement, Stuart Hannay, 10 March 1973.
[7]   This figure was from Hannay. Little said $40,000.

[8] Statement, Brian Little, Undated.

[9] Fire Loss — Thomas James Leighton as Owner and Commonwealth Trading Bank of Australia as Mortgagee, 8 March 1973. United Dominion hold a lease dated 23 June 1972 in respect of most of the plant and equipment in the nightclub involving a sum of $18,150, while there is a bill of sale associated with a further $5000 of property (This totals $23,150, which does not match $25,417.50, and so it may not include McGrath's fee).

[10] Statement, John McGrath, Undated. After the date of the provisional liquidation order, under the management of Mr Rees the clubs functioned at a profit, in particular Whiskey Au Go Go, which was returning in the vicinity of $1000.00 per week net ($7000 gross). John McGrath, solicitor, states, 'Certain articles and fixtures in the Whiskey premises were owned by Thomas James Leighton, the owner of the building, who insured them himself through the State Government Insurance Office (an all-risk policy for $157,000, a separate policy for the

glass and $6000 cover for the airconditioning through Independent Insurance Brokers).'

[11] Statement, Brian Little, Undated.
[12] Statement, Brian Little, Undated.
[13] Statement, John McGrath, Undated.
[14] Saw Detectives King and Richeion.
[15] $20,000 is quoted in court.
[16] Port News, April 1975.
[17] *Sunday Mail*, 15 September 1996.
[18] *Sunday Mail*, 17 March 1996.
[19] Possibly earlier at Myers. See I Survived: The Story of John Wayne Ryan, Private Detective: An Australian (Brisbane) Underbelly Survivor. John Ryan, Book Pal, 2012.
[20] It's Only Rock 'n' Roll But I Like It: A History of the Early Days of Rock 'n' Roll in Brisbane as Told by Some of the People Who Were There. Geoffrey Walden, Queensland University of Technology, January 2003.
[21] Running Sheet, Whiskey Au Go Go Fire and Fatality.
[22] At 10pm, Statement, Daniel Cliff, 11 March 1973.
[23] Statement, Brian Little, 9 March 1973.
[24] Basil Hicks Notes, 18 October 1972.

[25]   Running Sheet, Whiskey Au Go Go Fire and Fatality.
[26]   Running Sheet, Whiskey Au Go Go Fire and Fatality.
[27]   Statement, Sandra Martin, 10 March 1973.
[28]   Running Sheet, Whiskey Au Go Go Fire and Fatality.
[29]   Addendum Statement, Kenneth Little, 11 March 1973.
[30]   Addendum Statement, Kenneth Little, 11 March 1973.
[31]   Supreme Court Testimony.
[32]   John Bell also heard that George Freeleagus and Jim Constantine were responsible. Statement, John Bell, 8 March 1973. See also Running Sheet, Whiskey Au Go Go Fire and Fatality. A tip from an ex-Whiskey and Chequers employee, Marcel.
[33]   Addendum Statement, Kenneth Little, 11 March 1973.
[34]   Addendum Statement, Brian Little, 10 March 1973.
[35]   Statement, Stuart Roche, Undated.
[36]   Statement, George Freeleagus, 17 August 1973.
[37]   Hospital Board Note, 12 September 1973.

[38] John Hannay, Supreme Court Testimony.
[39] In spite of his 1973 injuries, Hannay later managed and owned a number of hotels and businesses.
[40] *Sydney Morning Herald*, 5 February 1988.
[41] *Sunday Sun*, 18 January 1976.
[42] *Sunday Mail*, 15 September 1996. *Sunday* Mail, 17 March 1996.
[43] *Canberra Times*, 3 January 1976.
[44] *Sunday* Mail, 17 March 1996.
[45] *Canberra Times*, 15 December 1980, 'He said he would develop the island in three stages, the first beginning immediately. Stage two would begin early next year and would include construction of a restaurant and entertainment area. He expected that stage of development to be completed by June, after which the final stage involving plans for self-contained units would be carried out.' See also https://www.whitsunday.qld.gov.au/DocumentCenter/View/1177
[46] *Sunday* Mail, 17 March 1996.
[47] *Sunday Mail*, 15 September 1996.
[48] *Sunday Mail*, 15 September 1996.

[49] Megaclub, *The Courier-Mail*, 28 March 2002.
[50] *Sunday Mail*, 15 September 1996.
[51] *Sunday Mail*, 11 June 1989. An officer now suspended after being named adversely at the Fitzgerald Inquiry.
[52] *Sunday Mail*, 7 February 1988. *The Courier-Mail* 26 August 1989. *The Courier-Mail*, 25 August 1989. *The Courier-Mail*, 25 April 2001. *The Courier-Mail* 2 July 1997. *The Courier-Mail*, 25 April 2001.
[53] *The Courier-Mail*, 12 September 1996. *The Courier-Mail*, 27 March 1998. *The Courier-Mail*, 15 September 1996. *The Courier-Mail*, 25 April 2001.
[54] Judge Margaret McMurdo said that for someone planning a murder, Pandelis had 'very loose lips'. It was nevertheless a very serious offence, which appeared to be premeditated and elaborate.
[55] *The Courier-Mail*, 12 November 1999. *The Courier-Mail*, 14 February 2003. *The Courier-Mail*, 4 May 2002.
[56] *The Courier-Mail*, 26 September 2000.
[57] *The Courier-Mail*, 15 May 2002.
[58] http://asic.gov.au/about-asic/media-centre/find-a-media-release/2005-releases/05-

	90nightclub-operator-faces-the-music/ *The Courier-Mail*, 20 April 2005. *The Courier-Mail*, 13 April 2005.
[59]	*The Courier-Mail*, 20 April 2005.
[60]	Billy McCulkin as an informant linked Stuart and Hannay: 'he vaguely suggests that John Andrew Stuart and John Hannay know something about the matter. He suggests this because Hannay's café – Alice's Coffee Shop – was burnt out about 3 months ago.' Informant Robert McCulkin, Crime Intelligence Report.
[61]	Record of Interview and Supreme Court Testimony.
[62]	Brian Little, Supreme Court Testimony.
[63]	Memo, Thomas Leighton, 22 March 1973.
[64]	Statement Kenneth Little RE: Gramons Pty Ltd. Supreme Court Testimony. *The Courier-Mail*, 27 September 1973.
[65]	Robert Hayes, Supreme Court Testimony.
[66]	Brian Little, Supreme Court Testimony. *The Courier-Mail*, 28 September 1973.
[67]	Addendum Statement, Charles Reeves, 15 March 1973. Chicka had a fight with Stuart in gaol six years previously.

[68]   Statement, Lin, 8 March 1973. Addendum Statement, Kenneth Little, 11 March 1973.
[69]   A two-tone Fairlane sedan, white and a dark-coloured hood.

Chapter 43

[1]   Addendum Statement, Lyall Beckman, 10 August 1973.
[2]   Addendum Statement, Lyall Beckman, 29 March 1973.
[3]   *Telegraph,* 10 March 1973.
[4]   Operation Graveyard – Investigations into all aspects surrounding the Whiskey Au Go Go Night Club firebombing deaths and other involved murders between 1973 and 1977.

Chapter 44

[1]   *Sunday Mail,* 11 December 1988. *Sunday Mail,* 2 April 1989.
[2]   Untitled Police Crime Intelligence Report, 22 January 1974.
[3]   At about 6.00pm, Billy McCulkin went to 6 Dorchester Street to see his wife. He found the house locked. He broke in through the front door and found the kitchen light on with the bulb blown,

and the light on in the back sitting room. There was no sign of his wife or children. Everything was in order in the house. He found the following unusual things, which made him believe that his wife and daughters had not gone away voluntarily. (1) His wife's change purse with £8 and private papers in it were left on the fridge. This would be the only money she had (2) None of her clothes or personal effects were taken other than the dress he saw her in on the bus on the 16/1/74. This was blue with white and yellow spots and a white collar. (3) None of the children's clothing or personal effects was missing other than the clothes they were dressed in on the 16/1/74. (4) None of the beds had been slept in. (5) Two pet cats were locked in the house without food. (6) There was fresh food in the fridge, which his wife had bought on the 16/1/74 for the following few days. (7) A dress his wife was making was still in the sewing machine where she had been sewing it. (8) None of his wife's cosmetics or sunglasses, which she always wore, were missing from the house. (9) She had had an operation on her breasts and had to wear a special surgical bra-She had two of these. One was missing and the other was hanging in the bathroom. (10) A cheque for two hundred dollars, which she had been waiting for, was still in the letter box. (11) Both children had money and other personal effects in their room, including their transistors. None of these had been taken by them. McCulkin spoke to the Gayton girls, and they then told him that O'Dempsey and Dubois had been at the house on the Wednesday night and that they had not seen Mrs McCulkin or the two girls since that night. Untitled police Crime Intelligence Report.

[4] *Sunday Mail*, 11 December 1988.

[5] *Sunday Mail*, 11 December 1988.

[6] Operation Graveyard — investigations into all aspects surrounding the Whiskey Au Go Go Night Club firebombing deaths and other involved murders between 1973 and 1977.

[7] As stated in the *Sunday Mail*, 11 December 1988. Untitled Police Crime Intelligence Report, 22 January 1974, says Ward saw Nolan on 15 November and disappeared that day.

[8] Untitled Police Crime Intelligence Report, 22 January 1974. *Sunday Mail*, 11 December 1988, 'Mrs O'Dempsey allegedly told the detectives she had worked for Simone Vogel, a massage parlour madam who also disappeared from Brisbane without explanation. Menary said he had told Vincent O'Dempsey in the presence of a solicitor that he believed O'Dempsey had murdered Margaret Ward to prevent her from giving evidence against his de facto wife on the prostitution charge. He said O'Dempsey had replied "no comment" to all his questions. After Mr Bougoure ruled that O'Dempsey could not claim privilege to avoid answering questions, O'Dempsey adopted the same tactic in the Coroner's Court. His examination was abandoned after he replied "no comment" to a long series of questions put to him.'

[9] On the afternoon of this date, Ernest Latima Watkins, Manager of 'Vogue Private Hotel' was speaking to Cheryl Evans in a hotel at Lutwyche. This was after the races. Evans had had a fair amount to drink. She told Watkins that a friend of hers and her children were

missing and she was very concerned about them. She also said that the missing woman and her husband were separated. (At this time she was no doubt referring to Mrs McCulkin and her two daughters). Evans told Watkins also she was concerned because O'Dempsey had been in trouble with the police and she was frightened that the police might contact him about the missing woman and children. Watkins felt that Evans was very concerned about the whole affair.

[10] *Sunday Mail,* 2 April 1989.
[11] Operation Graveyard — investigations into all aspects surrounding the Whiskey Au Go Go Night Club firebombing deaths and other involved murders between 1973 and 1977.
[12] Informant Robert McCulkin, 7 February 1974, Crime Intelligence Report.
[13] *The Courier-Mail,* 27 May 2017.
[14] *The Courier-Mail,* 29 May 2017.
[15] 23 November 1964, Garry Dubois, Police criminal record.
[16] Informant Robert McCulkin, 22 January 1974, Crime Intelligence Report.
[17] 13 May. Vincent O'Dempsey, Police criminal record.

[18] *The Courier-Mail*, 27 April 1988.

Chapter 45

[1] *The Tangled Web*, Des Sturgess, Beside Books 2001.
[2] *Sydney Morning Herald*, 23 February 1988.
[3] From Operation Graveyard. *The Courier-Mail*, 1 April 2005, 'During his 40 years in the force, in which he worked at posts all around Queensland, the former deputy commissioner [Atkinson]. In 1980, not only was he honoured with the Queen's Police Medal, he was also named Gold Coast Father of the Year.'

Chapter 46

[1] *Sunday Sun*, 28 October 1973.
[2] Basil Hicks Notes, 18 September 1972.
[3] For example, Grafton and Long Bay.
[4] *I Survived: The Story of John Wayne Ryan, Private Detective: An Australian (Brisbane) Underbelly Survivor*, John Ryan, Book Pal, 2012.
[5] He told Daniel he studied psychology a lot, Daniel Stuart, 11 March 1973.
[6] Letter John Stuart to Con just after 2 November 1962. Con told him not to learn about the human mind.

[7] The Canberra Times, 16 December 1972.
[8] Stuart's writing, Undated.
[9] Stuart's writing, circa 17 April 1963.
[10] Quoted in letter Marge X to John Stuart, 6 May 1964.
[11] Letter Stuart to Carmel, 24 May 1968.
[12] Statement, Dr A.V., 16 May 1973.
[13] Statement, Handwritten, Rosealie Stuart, Undated.
[14] Statement, Rosealie Stuart, 8 August 1973.
[15] Letter Edna Watts to John Stuart, 1 May 1973.
[16] Sunday Sun, 7 January 1979.
[17] Sunday Sun, 7 January 1979.

Chapter 47

[1] Sunday Mail, 13 July 1986.
[2] The Courier-Mail, 24 February 1988. Sunday Mail, 7 October 1990.
[3] The Sun, 1 November 1988.
[4] The Sun, 31 October 1988.
[5] The Sun, 1 November 1988.
[6] The Sun, 1 November 1988. Sunday Mail, 30 June 1985. Sunday Mail, 18 November 1990, 'The wife of convicted Whiskey Au Go Go firebomber James Finch has given the killer the boot after falling in

love with a new man. Cheryl Finch confirmed yesterday she has begun divorce proceedings against the mass murderer, who cruelly tricked her into marriage to help obtain his release from gaol.' *The Courier-Mail*, 24 May 2001, 'The former wife of Whiskey Au Go Go killer James Finch has died in Brisbane after a long battle with a debilitating muscular disease. The couple divorced in 1991 and Mrs Finch claimed to have last had contact with her husband in 1996.'

[7]   *Sunday Mail*, 1 September 1991.

Chapter 48

[1]   Statement, June Beckman, 8 March 1973.

[2]   *Brisbane Times*, 4 May 2017, *The Courier*-Mail, 8 November 2016, Sunshine Coast Daily, 5 May 2017. 'I got the impression the convicted men were not the only ones (men) involved.'

[3]   Operation Graveyard – investigations into all aspects surrounding the Whiskey Au Go Go Night Club firebombing deaths and other involved murders between 1973 and 1977.

[4]   *The Australian*, 1 June 2017.

[5] Reports that Billy McCulkin did not drive are untrue. Matthew Condon, pers. comm., who has interviewed members of Barbara's family (the Ogdens).
[6] *The Courier-Mail*, 27 May 2017.
[7] Operation Graveyard – investigations into all aspects surrounding the Whiskey Au Go Go Night Club firebombing deaths and other involved murders between 1973 and 1977. Although more recently Hall said the explosion was due to petrol vapour pressure, Interview with *60 Minutes*, 28 May 2017.
[8] The Defence's argument that Billy killed his wife is also spurious. He had no motive and was frantic in his attempts to find his ex. Killers do not behave the way he did.
[9] *Sunday Sun*, 19 August 1973.
[10] Interview with *60 Minutes*, 28 May 2017.
[11] *The Northern Star*, 5 May 2017.
[12] To remove stretch marks around her breasts and stomach, *The Courier-Mail*, 27 May 2017.
[13] *The Sun*, 2 November 1988.
[14] *The Courier-Mail*, 27 January 2016.
[15] Whether Barbara was coerced to get in the car is unknown. While evidence

at the O'Dempsey trial indicated that 'Vince O'Dempsey used to take Barbara for drives', it was after 10.30pm and a strange time to take two young, tired girls for a cruise. In the February 1975 edition of the Port News, Stokes said it was convivial, 'When "The Loner" and "Shorty" suggested a drive to break the monotony indoors, she [Barbara] accepted, and suspecting nothing, took her children with her.' Regardless, she soon knew this was a terror drive.

[16] Operation Graveyard – investigations into all aspects surrounding the Whiskey Au Go Go Night Club firebombing deaths and other involved murders between 1973 and 1977.

[17] He was unstable, a problem and his body not found. Dubois, possibly driven by O'Dempsey, was looking for Hamilton hours before he disappeared. Dubois had visited Hamilton's sister asking whether Hamilton could do some work for him the next day (Operation Graveyard – investigations into all aspects surrounding the Whiskey Au Go Go Night Club

firebombing deaths and other involved murders between 1973 and 1977).

[18] Finch said there was direct contact between Stuart and O'Dempsey, that O'Dempsey offered a sum of money to Stuart to recruit Finch. *The Sun*, 2 November 1988.

[19] According to John Ryan.

Chapter 49

[1] Gangland Queensland, James Morton & Susanna Lobez; Melbourne University Publishing, 2012.

[2] Tony Murphy, An Honest Cop, Murphy, Maureen Joy, Robina, Qld, M J Murphy, 2015.

[3] Operation Graveyard – Investigations into all aspects surrounding the Whiskey Au Go Go Night Club firebombing deaths and other involved murders between 1973 and 1977.

Chapter 50

[1] Francis Longhurst, Supreme Court Testimony.

[2] Let the Bums Burn: Australia's Deadliest Building Fire and the Salvation Army

	Tragedies. Geoff Plunkett, 2015, Leech Cup Books.
[3]	*The Courier-Mail*, 5 March 1987.
[4]	*Sunday Sun*, 25 November 1973.
[5]	*Brisbane Times*, 6 and 9 March 2013.
[6]	Carol 'Bobby' Maltby (sister), Interview 15 October 2017. Maureen Folster, Interview 13 October 2017.
[7]	After the fire, Darcy Day's mother hugged her dead son's shoes. *The Gympie Times*, 11 March 2013.

Chapter 51

[1]	Little Fish Are Sweet, Matthew Condon, St Lucia, Queensland; University of Queensland Press, 2016.
[2]	*Sunday Sun*, 25 November 1973.
[3]	*Sunday Sun*, 18 March 1973.

Available now online or at all good bookstores

View sample pages, reviews and more information on this and other titles at www.bigskypublishing.com.au

Available now online or at all good bookstores

View sample pages, reviews and more information on this and other titles at www.bigskypublishing.com.au

Available now online or at all good bookstores

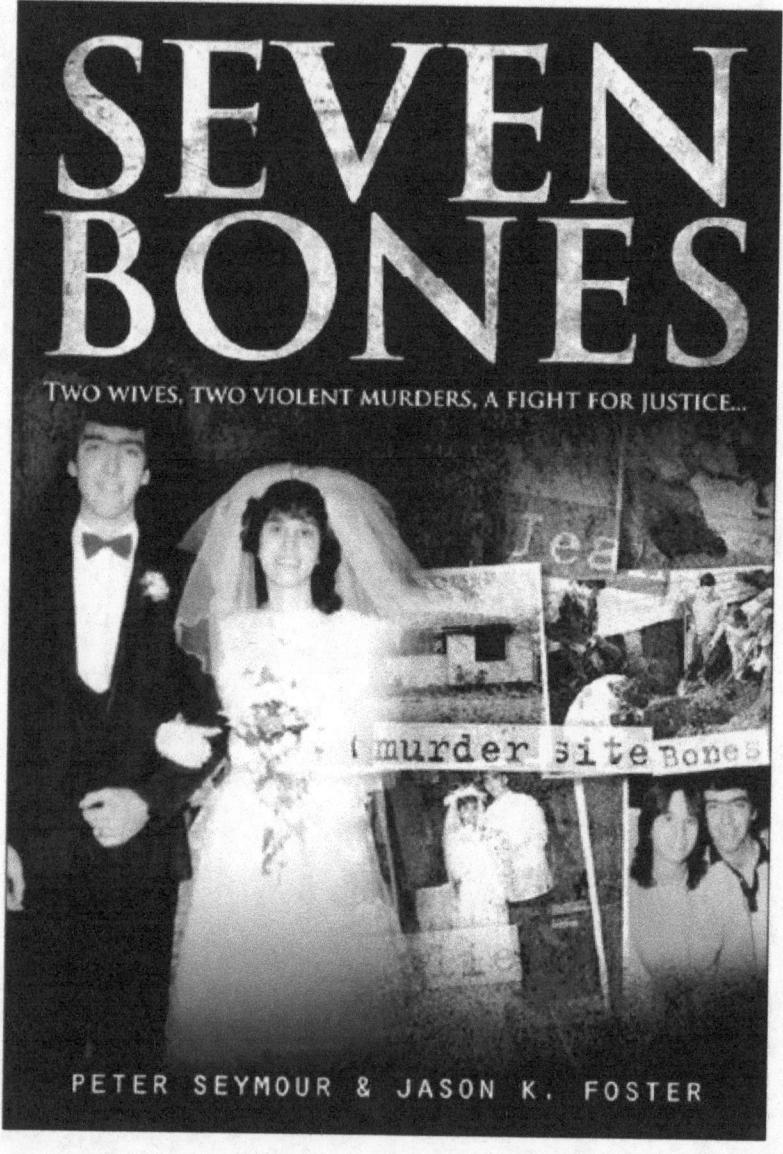

View sample pages, reviews and more information on this and other titles at www.bigskypublishing.au

Back Cover Material

On the hacker scale of terror is rated a 10.

The Whiskey Au Go Go nightclub massacre was a defining moment in 1970s Australia, the horrific epicentre of all the crime and filth, the corruption and deaths that came before and followed that tragic night in March 1973, when 15 innocent people lost their lives.

Despite the quick arrest and subsequent conviction of John Stuart and his sidekick James Finch, the affair have never stopped smouldering. Rumours have swirled around that horror-filled night for decades. Were Stuart and Finch framed? Were others involved? Were a further atrocities committed to hide the truth behind the outrage? For decades, it was impossible to uncover the truth behind the tragedy. That changed in 2013, when the author had the privilege of being the first person to view the files created by the original lead detectives. Those files reveal what occurred prior to, during, and after that conflagration. They reveal startling facts. They

Back Cover Material

One the hichter scale of terror it rated a 10...

***

The Whiskey Au Go Go nightclub massacre was a defining moment in 1970s Australia: the 'horrific epicentre of all the crime and filth, the corruption and deaths that came before and followed that tragic night in March 1973, when 15 innocent people lost their lives'.

Despite the quick arrest and subsequent conviction of John Stuart and his sidekick, James Finch, the ashes have never stopped smouldering. Rumours have swirled around that horror-filled night for decades: were Stuart and Finch framed? Were others involved? Were futher attocities committed to hide the truth behind the outrage?

For decades it was impossible to uncover the truth behind the tragedy. That changed in 2012, when the author had the privilege of being the first person to view the files created by the original lead detectives. These files reveal what occurred prior to, during, and after the conflagration. They reveal unsettling facts. They reveal that the full story of that night has never been told – until now.